LONELY PLANET PUBLICATIONS

D0970664

MATTHEW LEE
JOHN A VLAHIDES

DUBAI

CITY GUIDE

INTRODUCING DUBAI

Reaching for the sky – the city skyline reflects the mix of traditional Arabian and modern architecture (p39)

The world has never seen a larger construction site. Dubai stretches upwards and outwards – even underwater – paving the desert, colonising the ocean and piercing the clouds.

Aboard approaching airliners, passengers wrestle against fastened seatbelts for an aerial view: traditional wind-towers yield to space-age skyscrapers mushrooming across the desert beside a coastline dominated by bizarre palm-shaped archipelagos that look like something from another planet.

For Dubai's rulers, whose remarkable vision has turned a small town into a major metropolis within a mere half century, there's little concern for earthly matters – no elections, no opinion polls, no accountability – just billions of dollars to spend on making Project Dubai like nowhere else on earth. It's a game of *SimCity* that never ends, a hybrid of *1001 Arabian Nights* and *Futurama*, an anything-goes boomtown where even the sky is no longer the limit.

This unflinching ambition and can-do spirit certainly has its disciples. But Dubai's numerous successes are undermined by protests on building sites, where workers toil in the sun for Dh25 a day – the cost of a pint of beer. The men putting the roof on the Burj Dubai, the tallest manmade structure in history, are being trampled by the gold rush.

But Dubai is not all about manmade islands, multimillionaires and mega projects. Its culture is rooted in Islam and generations of Bedouin heritage, and it's this juxtaposition of the traditional past and the hi-tech present that makes it such an intriguing and compelling place to visit.

CITY LIFE

Dubai's success has been shaped by forward-thinking governments, but the achievements wouldn't have been possible without the foreign workforce that has helped carry out their vision. While everyone in Dubai in some way shares in the city's accomplishments, expatriate workers – some of whom were born and raised in the emirate but haven't qualified for UAE citizenship – find it hard to escape the

'It's…an anything-goes boomtown where even the sky is no longer the limit'

feeling that they're the 'hired help' in this grand experiment. While buying property in Dubai now allows expats to have an open-ended residency visa, it's still not citizenship – and effectively they have no political voice. Then again the disparity of wealth in Dubai is colossal and only a minority of expats can even dream of owning a property here.

To local Emiratis, who make up around 5% of the city's population, Dubai's sudden acquisition of wealth has been a double-edged *khanjar*. The vast majority have a lot of faith in their leaders and appreciate the perks they receive: free health care, education, land, zero-interest loans and marriage funds. However, Emiratis are facing challenges in the employment market. How can they compete when a foreigner will do the same job for a tenth of the price? Plus the segregated society means many expat managers don't even know any Emiratis, let alone employ any.

There is also debate about whether the Emiratis' heritage and traditions are endangered as the city becomes increasingly multicultural, or if being a minority helps reinforce Emiratis' sense of identity; many display their roots, wearing national dress such as *hijabs* and *abayas* with pride.

Dubai today is friends with the West; for progressive Arabs it's a shining example of a modern Arab city. But conservative branches of Islam are less than impressed by its tolerance of alcohol and pork and failure to curb prostitution. How Dubai manages to balance all these factors is just as important as keeping up its spectacular growth. Given the track record of Dubai's leaders over the past few decades, it would be unwise to bet against them.

Family and friends gather at Creekside Park in the late afternoon (p67)

❶ Burj Al Arab
The landmark hotel, known throughout the world, floats on its own man-made island (p75).

❷ National Bank of Dubai
The awe-inspiring architecture makes the bank building a special feature of any journey along the Creek (p40).

❸ Emirates Towers
Traditional dancers performing in front of the iconic Emirates Towers (p158).

FANTASTIC LANDMARKS

The world's tallest skyscraper, a giant indoor ski-slope and the earth mapped out on water – experiencing Dubai's fantastical next-gen architecture up close is a guaranteed highlight of every trip.

TRADITIONAL DUBAI

Walk alongside the Creek and it's easy to imagine life in Dubai half a century ago. The wooden dhows, whirring abras, bustling souqs, stately wind-towers and graceful mosques have barely changed over the decades.

1 *Abras* **at an** *abra* **station**
Waiting to ferry passengers at dusk (p68).

2 **Jumeirah Mosque**
Breathtaking in its intricate beauty (p75).

3 **Al-Ahmadiya School**
Dubai's oldest school dates back to 1912 (p58).

4 **A wind-tower in Bastakia**
Wind-towers cooled traditional buildings (p61).

5 **Dhow Wharfage**
The dhows transport goods across the Arabian
Sea for importing and re-exporting (p58).

BACK STREETS

Dubai's otherworldly megaprojects have you craving a dose of reality? Wander the bustling back streets to find the true heart of a city that's become home to hundreds of thousands of people from across the globe.

❶ Hindi Lane
An Indian lady shops for offerings before taking them to the local Hindi temple (p66).

❷ Satwa Rd
Indian and Pakistani workers sample the snacks on a Friday night, the only time off for many workers (p79).

❸ Bur Dubai
Baking bread at a traditional back-street bakery (p66).

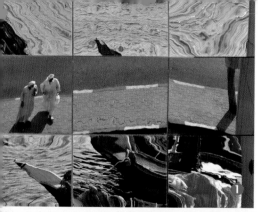

❶ Dubai Creek
Creekside windows form exotic reflections of the traffic along the Creek (p187).

❷ Wild Wadi Waterpark
You won't notice the view as you hurtle down at speeds up to 80km/h (p78).

❸ The lake at Dubai Wildlife & Waterbird Sanctuary
Flocks of people come to this nature reserve at Ras al-Khor to watch the pink flamingos and enjoy the serene surroundings (p71).

WATERWAYS

The Palm Islands are nothing new – Dubai was built on water. Pearlers, fishermen, oilmen and dhow captains worked the Gulf and the Creek in the city's formative years, and today tourists flock to see the canals, marinas, water parks and beaches.

PARTY PEOPLE

The phrase 'work hard, play hard' could have been coined for Dubai. Whether it's at the nightclub, the sheesha café, the wine bar or the restaurant, the city lets its collective hair down on Thursday and Friday nights.

❶ Global Village
Traditional dancing by street performers at the annual Dubai Shopping Festival (p88).

❷ iBO
A visiting international DJ sets the mood for a big night at the popular iBO nightclub. Sure hope it reopens soon (p131).

❸ Zinc
Zinc's bands and DJs stick to crowd-pleasing popular tunes, so it's always a great choice of nightclub, especially if you're out to dance and drink, not to show off (p132).

SHOPPING

The mall-makers' game of one-upmanship – from City Centre to Mall of the Emirates to Mall of Arabia – has turned this town into one big spree for shopaholics. Dubai isn't only the name of the city – it's an instruction.

❶ Gold Souq
Surround yourself with gold jewellery (p93).

❷ Mall of the Emirates
A sparkle of light and colour to put you in the mood to shop (p101).

❸ S*uce
One of the first independant boutiques, S*uce is famous for its idiosyncratic fashions (p100).

DESERT-SCAPES

If you're feeling fearless, you can ski, snowboard or drive across the desert dunes in a 4x4. If you don't want to do the hard work yourself, travel the old-fashioned way and take a ride on the back of a camel.

❶ Camel riding in the desert
So far so good – tourists look uncomfortable about their sunset camel ride (p169).

❷ Sandboarding
A local enjoying a slippery scratchy board ride down the dunes (p169).

❸ Camel road-crossing sign
There are camel-crossing-sign fridge magnets at the souqs, but this sign is for real (p100).

CONTENTS

THE AUTHORS

Matthew Lee

When Matthew Lee stepped out of the arrivals hall to start a new life in Dubai in 2004, the soaring July heat almost had him booking a seat on the next flight home. But after getting through his first summer without spending more than three minutes at a time outside, he grew fond of this strange city. Being *Time Out*'s food critic helped – he gleefully piled on the pounds at hundreds of Dubai restaurants before becoming the editor of *Time Out*'s guidebooks to the city and the rest of the Gulf. In addition to writing for Lonely Planet, he edits the in-flight magazine of Jazeera Airways. He enjoys riverside walks in his hometown of London, wilfully obscure folk music, aquariums and picnics, and has plans to write the perfect sitcom. Matthew wrote the Introducing Dubai, Highlights, Getting Started, Background, Neighbourhoods, Desert Safaris & Day Trips, Transport and Directory chapters.

MATTHEW'S TOP DUBAI DAY

I love Fridays in Dubai, when construction workers and CEOs alike head to the Creek for a spot of fresh air. After a wake-up coffee at XVA Café (p113), I'd go there too, and ensure my waterside walk incorporates as many Dh1 *abra* rides as possible – by far my favourite activity in the entire city. Once I've admired the beautiful *dhows* that cling to the Deira side of the water, I'd stroll to Creekside Park (p67) for a picnic lunch, ideally a plateful of Lebanese mezze from Wafi Gourmet (p98). Following a lazy afternoon in the sun, I'd make sure I'm at Russian Beach (p78) before it gets dark, so I can perch on the wall at the end of the breakwater and watch the sun plunge behind the Burj Al Arab (p159) while the call to prayer rings out from the floodlit Jumeirah Mosque (p75). After an indulgent dinner at the dazzling Verre By Gordon Ramsay (p107), I'd pop by Troyka (p127) for a nightcap – and some hilarious Russian cabaret – on the way home.

John A Vlahides

High-end travel specialist John A Vlahides is a former luxury-hotel concierge and a member of the prestigious Les Clefs d'Or, the international union of the world's elite concierges. He studied cooking in Paris, where he earned a degree from La Varenne, Ecole de Cuisine. In addition to writing about luxury travel for such publishers as Conde Nast, he is the cofounder of the tell-it-like-it-is travel site 71miles.com. He appears regularly on TV and radio; watch some of his travel videos on lonelyplanet.com. When not exploring the Middle East, John lives in California, singing with the San Francisco Symphony, downhill-skiing the Sierra Nevada and touring the American West on his motorcycle. John wrote the Sleeping, Eating, Shopping, Entertainment, and Sports & Activities chapters.

GETTING STARTED

Having invested vast amounts of money into the development of its tourism sector, Dubai is becoming increasingly easy for visitors to negotiate. Crime is rare, almost everyone speaks English and tourists are unlikely to be hassled or ripped off.

While Dubai is a highly developed destination, it's important to realise that the United Arab Emirates is an Islamic country and behaviour that's tolerated in Western countries – such as kissing in public, drunkenness or swearing – may cause offence, or worse, get you into trouble with the law. While it boasts countless settings tailor-made for romance and plenty of good bars and pubs, Dubai might not be the perfect destination if you're planning a honeymoon or a stag weekend.

Glitzy big-name hotels open in the emirate every few months, and such intense competition in the five-star sector can result in very attractive room rates, especially in summer. Midrange and budget travellers, however, will struggle to find comfortable accommodation for under Dh400 per night. It's always advisable to book beds before you travel, particularly if you are visiting during a major festival or exhibition.

This may sound obvious, but don't enter Dubai carrying any illegal substances. Dubai's drug laws are extremely strict and even a microscopic speck of a controlled substance could see you arrested (see p186).

WHEN TO GO

The eye-catching room rates advertised for July and August come with a catch: the scorching heat (up to 48°C) and high humidity makes being outside for longer than 10 minutes extremely uncomfortable. The best time to visit Dubai is between November and April, when the weather is pleasant and there's lots going on. The month of Ramadan is a fascinating time to visit if you're interested in Islam, but those planning to indulge themselves in Dubai's restaurants and bars might find the conservative laws imposed for the month too restrictive.

FESTIVALS

As part of its effort to lure tourists to the city, the Dubai authorities have encouraged the development of several major sporting and cultural events. All of these, with the exception of Dubai Summer Surprises, take place between October and March.

January

DUBAI MARATHON

www.dubaimarathon.org

Equipped with a prize fund of a million dollars, the Dubai Marathon attracts the biggest names in long-distance running. For the opportunity to compete with them over 26 miles, you have to register by the end of the previous year. Less energetic types can enter a 10km run or a 4km 'fun run'.

DUBAI SHOPPING FESTIVAL

www.mydsf.com

Reports of Russian millionaires chartering passenger jets so they can return from the Dubai Shopping Festival with planeloads of purchases are probably exaggerated, but the annual instalment of DSF certainly attracts millions of tourists each year. Don't expect to find stupendous bargains in the malls; the sale prices are rarely spectacular. Do expect to find plenty of live music, kids' events, sporting activities, nightly fireworks over the Creek, and the hugely popular Global Village, which runs for three months from mid-December.

February

DUBAI INTERNATIONAL JAZZ FESTIVAL

www.dubaijazzfest.com

Held in the week following the Shopping Festival, this increasingly popular event is staged at Dubai Media City over three nights. While the mainstream is well catered for, jazz purists may sneer at the choice of performers, with recent headliners including Toto, ELO, Robin Gibb of the Bee Gees, and Roger Hodgson of Supertramp.

DUBAI DESERT CLASSIC
www.dubaidesertclassic.com

Until November 2009, when the biggest names on the greens will compete for a US$10-million prize purse at the first Dubai World Championship, the Dubai Desert Classic remains the emirate's leading golf event. It takes place on the first weekend of February at the immaculate Emirates Golf Club, and has earned a reputation for delivering high drama on the last day of competition.

DUBAI TENNIS CHAMPIONSHIPS
www.dubaitennischampionships.com

Held over two weeks in February and March, the championships consist of a Women's Tennis Association (WTA) event followed by an Association of Tennis Professionals (ATP) event. It's a great opportunity to see some of the best players in the world in a relatively small stadium. Ticket prices – especially for the earlier rounds – offer great value for money.

March

DUBAI DESERT ROCK
www.desertrockfestival.com

Dubai's surprisingly large contingent of Goths can be spotted nervously adjusting to sunlight in the mosh-pits of this annual live rock music event. In recent years, headliners of the two-day festival have included Iron Maiden, Robert Plant, Megadeth and Muse.

ART DUBAI
www.artdubai.ae

The arrival of this ambitious international art fair in 2007 confirmed that art is big business in the Gulf, despite a lack of major galleries. The Madinat Jumeirah provides a suitably glamorous setting for the artists, dealers and gallery owners to mingle in and show off their stuff.

DUBAI WORLD CUP
www.dubaiworldcup.com

The Dubai International Racing Carnival, running from February through to the end of March, culminates in the Dubai World Cup, the world's richest horse race and the city's biggest social event. While there's no betting, many of Dubai's society women take a punt in wearing some of the silliest hats this side of the Melbourne Cup. Godolphin, the

stable owned by Dubai's royal family, tends to dominate proceedings on the racetrack.

June, July & August

DUBAI SUMMER SURPRISES
www.mydsf.com

Perhaps the most surprising thing about DSS is that it manages to attract any visitors at all. It takes place, after all, at the sweaty height of the sweltering summer. But a combination of free kids' entertainment, sales in shopping malls, and Modhesh, a springy yellow mascot, draws in plenty of tourists from other Gulf nations.

October

UAE DESERT CHALLENGE
www.uaedesertchallenge.com

This desert rally, the final race of the FIA Cross-Country Rally World Cup, starts in Abu Dhabi and finishes in Dubai. It's held over five days, takes in some challenging terrain, and attracts car, truck and motorbike riders.

DESERT RHYTHM FESTIVAL
www.desertrhythmfestival.com

Following the success of the second instalment of Desert Rhythm in 2007, at which Kanye West, Mika, Joss Stone and Madness made their UAE debuts, it seems likely that this two-day music festival will go from strength to strength in the coming years.

November

DUBAI RUGBY SEVENS
www.dubairugby7s.com

Part of the IRB World Sevens Series, the Dubai Rugby Sevens features 16 international squads, a huge number of amateur teams and live entertainment over three days. While England and Australia receive plenty of support from the mainly expatriate crowd, the Arabian Gulf team, consisting of players from Bahrain, Kuwait, Qatar, Saudi, Oman and the UAE, get the biggest cheers of the day.

December

DUBAI INTERNATIONAL FILM FESTIVAL
www.dubaifilmfest.com

Independent and art-house cinema is thin on the ground in Dubai, making this excellent non-competitive film festival the cultural highlight of the year for the city's cinephiles. There's a focus on cinema from Arab countries and the Indian sub-continent, while visits from the likes of George Clooney, Sharon Stone and Morgan Freeman help get the public excited.

COSTS & MONEY

The rising cost of living almost rivals traffic as Dubai's most moaned about subject. Rapid economic growth and a booming property market coupled with a falling dollar, which the dirham is pegged to, has resulted in annual inflation of around 10%. While the cost of living in Dubai continues to increase, the emirate's expatriates are finding that their dirhams are worth increasingly less in their home countries. Despite this, Dubai remains reasonably good value for tourists from Western countries.

Accommodation is likely to be your greatest expense. In the peak season, between October and April, Dubai boasts one of the world's highest hotel-occupancy rates (around 85%), so despite plenty of competition, rates remain sky-high. If you can cope with the stifling heat, summer hotel rates are a bargain – book in advance and you can get a night in a five-star beach resort for under Dh800. Before booking, check room rates on both hotel websites and online agencies such as Expedia (www.expedia.com), Lastminute (www.lastminute.com) and Opodo (www.opodo.com).

Visitors on a low budget might struggle. Dubai isn't built for backpackers and there's a chronic shortage of respectable budget hotels. By staying in a dormitory at the youth hostel, taking buses rather than taxis, sunbathing at public beaches and eating at budget restaurants, it's possible to see Dubai for under Dh200 a day. If the youth hostel is full, there are numerous hotels in Deira charging between Dh200 and Dh300 a night (ask to see the room before checking in and don't take rooms directly above nightclubs), while the Ibis (p159), EasyHotel Karama (slated to open in late 2008) and Fusion (p161) charge around Dh500 a night.

Dubai is more accessible to midrange travellers. For around Dh1000 you can get a room at a moderate hotel such as the Radisson SAS Deira Creek (p152). If you don't have the budget for a beach resort, it's worth considering buying day passes for a beach club (see boxed text, p78). If you're prepared to splash out, rooms at Jumeirah's luxury hotels start at Dh2000 a night during the peak season. A meal for two with a bottle of wine at a top restaurant will cost around Dh700.

To save money when going out, it's worth picking up *The Entertainer,* a book containing hundreds of two-for-one meal vouchers. By asking for local water rather than expensive imported bottles, you'll also save a few dirhams. Women can also take advantage of ladies' nights (usually on Tuesdays), when they get several free drinks or free-flowing champagne just for turning up.

INTERNET RESOURCES

www.timeoutdubai.com Up-to-date event listings, reviews of new restaurants and bars, and excellent coverage of the city's art scene.

www.dubai-eating.com A pale imitation of its London and New York sister sites (many major restaurants are missing), but useful for up-to-date user reviews of Dubai's restaurants.

www.dubizzle.com Spot short-term lets at this handy online marketplace.

www.dubaidonkey.com A busy listings website. Also useful for finding short-term lets.

ADVANCE PLANNING

Unless you're visiting during the summer, it is essential you book accommodation at least a few weeks in advance. Demand continues to outstrip supply and occupancy rates are nearly always high.

Considering how hard it can be to get a hotel room, it's surprisingly easy to book tables at popular restaurants a couple of hours before turning up, although a handful of restaurants always require advance booking. These include Zheng He's (p118), Verre (p107), Rhodes Mezzanine (p119), JW's Steakhouse (p107), Pierchic (p118) and all the restaurants at the Burj Al Arab.

If you're hoping to catch a major sporting event such as the final of the Dubai Tennis Championships, Desert Classic or Rugby Sevens, it's necessary to book tickets several weeks in advance as these sell out every year. Time Out Tickets (www.itp.net/tickets) and Box Office Middle East (www.boxofficeme.com) sell tickets for major events.

SUSTAINABLE DUBAI

Conserving the environment during a period of rapid growth is one of the greatest challenges facing Dubai (see p33). Unless you're travelling overland from Oman or Saudi Arabia, you'll be adding another shoe size to your annual carbon footprint just getting to and from Dubai. But there are a few things you can do while in the city to make your visit more sustainable.

The Dubai Metro is scheduled to open in September 2009. Until then public transport in Dubai remains an unappealing alternative to taking taxis. The buses are cheap (between Dh1 and Dh4), safe and well-lit, but infrequent, unreliable and slow. However, it's not all bad news. The arrival of air-con bus shelters means taking public transport during the summer is no longer a life-threatening option.

Dubai's recycling centres are badly publicised and often poorly maintained. The skips for newspaper and plastic-bag recycling are often overflowing and the machines that handle plastic-bottle recycling are all too often broken. Some of the better centres can be found at the Ramada, Trade Centre Rd and Umm Suqeim branches of Spinneys, and at Emarat service stations.

HOW MUCH?

1L petrol Dh1.50

1L bottled water Dh1.50

Pint of draught beer Dh22

Espresso coffee in a café Dh10

Taxi from Gold Souq to Burj Al Arab Dh50

Entry to Wild Wadi Waterpark Dh180

Evening desert safari Dh200

Set meal at a budget Indian restaurant Dh10

Main course in a top restaurant Dh120

Two hours of indoor skiing Dh150

The Emirates Environmental Group (www.eeg-uae .org) runs several campaigns every year to try to increase environmental awareness. These include desert and city clean-ups and tree-planting campaigns. If you can't spare a day to pick up litter – you're on holiday after all – you'll help by doing the simple things: turning off the air-con when you go out, switching off lights during the day and resisting the temptation to spend all morning in the shower.

BACKGROUND

HISTORY
EARLY SETTLEMENT

Little is known about the early history of the area that now forms the United Arab Emirates. However, archaeological remains found in Al-Qusais, on the northeastern outskirts of present-day Dubai, show evidence of humans here as far back as 8000 BC, after the end of the last Ice Age.

Up until 3000 BC the area supported nomadic herders of sheep, goats and cattle; these early inhabitants camped on the coast and fished during winter, then moved inland with their herds during summer (not so very different to what the Bedu did here just a short time ago). The first signs of trade emerged with the discovery of pottery from Ubaid (in present-day Iraq) dating back to 5000 BC. Agriculture developed with the cultivation of the date palm around 2500 BC, which not only provided food and a range of materials for building and weaving, but also shelter for smaller plants grown for food.

Archaeological evidence also suggests that this area, together with present-day Oman, was closely associated with the Magan civilisation during the Bronze Age. The Magans apparently dominated the ancient world's copper trade, exploiting the rich veins of copper in the hills throughout the Hajar Mountains, and near Sohar, in Oman. It's also likely that they traded pearls with people in Mesopotamia (now Iraq), and with the Indus Valley civilisation in present-day Pakistan. However, all records of the Magan civilisation cease after the 2nd millennium BC, with some historians speculating that the desertification of the area hastened its demise.

There's little archaeological evidence of occupation of Dubai during the Iron Age, with the next major habitation of the area appearing to have been by the Sassanid empire. Archaeological excavations at Jumeirah reveal a caravan station dating from the 6th century AD, which is thought to have had links with the Sassanids. A dynasty that ruled in Persia from AD 224 to 651, the Sassanids wielded amazing power over the region during this time, until the Umayyads, an Islamic tribe, uprooted them. Archaeologists seem to think that the buildings at Jumeirah were restored and extended by the Umayyad dynasty, making it the only site in the UAE to span the pre-Islamic and Islamic periods.

With the Umayyads came the Arabic language and unification with the Islamic world. Christianity made a brief appearance in the form of the Nestorian sect, members of which had a monastery on Sir Bani Yas Island, west of Abu Dhabi, in the 5th century. However, it was the arrival of Islam that shaped the future of the region. Unfortunately the early Islamic period from the 7th to the 14th century hasn't been well documented in the UAE. All that's known is that during this period the area was loosely under the control of the Umayyads and their successors, the Abbasids. After the Baghdad-based Abbasid dynasty went into decline around AD 1000, the centre of power in the Islamic world shifted to Cairo, leaving the UAE on the periphery. In the absence of centralised control, the tribes of the Arabian Peninsula asserted themselves in the hinterlands, while the coastal regions were dominated by trading ports such as Julfar, near present-day Ras al-Khaimah, and Hormuz, an island in the Strait of Hormuz.

TIMELINE

c 3000 BC	AD 700	1580
The Dubai area is populated by nomadic herders of sheep, cattle and goats. The Magan civilisation dominates the world's copper trade and mines for metal near the Hajar Mountains.	From their capital in Damascus, the Umayyads introduce Arabic and Islam to the region. The Umayyad Caliphate was the first dynasty of Islam, and lasted from AD 650 to AD 750.	Gasparo Balbi, a Venetian jeweller, tours Dubai to investigate its potential for the pearling trade. He notes in his records that he visits a town in the Persian Gulf called 'Dibei'.

It wasn't until the early Islamic period that the Gulf experienced its first boom in maritime trade, due to its location on the major trading routes between the Mediterranean Sea and Indian Ocean. However, trade soon became the backbone of the local economy as ships travelled as far as China, returning laden with silk and porcelain.

EUROPEAN PRESENCE

Portugal became the first European power to take an interest in this part of the Gulf, attracted by lucrative trade routes to India and the Far East. The arrival of the well-armed Portuguese was a disaster for Muslim traders. The Portuguese wanted a monopoly on trade routes between Europe and India and tolerated no rivals. Local trade dried up to the extent that many coastal settlements were just about abandoned, with tribes taking refuge in oases far from the coast such as Liwa and Al-Ain. While Portugal's occupation lasted until the 1630s, eventually extending as far north as Bahrain, the only evidence of their presence are the two cannons on display at the Dubai Museum (p61).

Next to arrive were the French and Dutch, who infiltrated the area in the 17th and 18th centuries and aspired to control the trading routes to the east. The Brits were equally intent on ruling the seas to protect the sea route to India, and in 1766 the Dutch finally gave way to Britain's East India Company, which had established trading links with the Gulf as early as 1616.

Throughout this time Dubai remained a small fishing and pearling hamlet, perched on a disputed border between two local powers – the seafaring Qawasim of present-day Ras al-Khaimah and Sharjah to the north, and the Bani Yas tribal confederation of what is now Abu Dhabi to the south. The region was also affected by the rivalries between bigger regional powers – the Wahhabi tribes (of what is now Saudi Arabia), the Ottoman Empire, the Persians and the British.

THE TRUCIAL COAST

At the beginning of the 19th century, Dubai was governed by Mohammed bin Hazza, who remained ruler of Dubai until the Al Bu Fasalah, a branch of the Bani Yas tribe from Abu Dhabi, came to dominate the town in 1833, severing it from Abu Dhabi. The Bani Yas were the main power among the Bedouin tribes of the interior. Originally based in Liwa, an oasis on the edge of the desert known as the Empty Quarter (Rub al-Khali) in the south of the UAE, the Bani Yas engaged in traditional Bedouin activities of camel herding, small-scale agriculture, tribal raiding and extracting protection money from merchant caravans passing through their territory. At the end of the 18th century, the leader of the Bani Yas moved from Liwa to the island of Abu Dhabi on the coast.

About 800 people from the Bani Yas tribe settled on the Bur Dubai Creek under the leadership of Maktoum bin Butti, who established the Maktoum dynasty of Dubai, which still rules the emirate today. For Maktoum bin Butti, good relations with the British authorities in the Gulf were essential to safeguard his new and small sheikhdom against attack from the larger and more powerful sheikhdoms of Sharjah to the north and Abu Dhabi to the south.

In 1841 the Bur Dubai settlement extended to Deira on the northern side of the Creek, though throughout the 19th century it largely remained a tiny enclave of fishermen, pearl divers, Bedouin, and Indian and Persian merchants. Interestingly, the Indians and Persians (now Iranians) still give much of the Creek its character today.

1833	1892	1930
Approximately 800 members of the Al-Maktoum family leave Abu Dhabi for Bur Dubai and establish power in the emirate under Maktoum bin Butti. When smallpox breaks out in 1841 people relocate to Deira which soon becomes larger than Bur Dubai.	The sheikhdoms sign a treaty with Britain; they'd have no dealings with other foreign powers and receive protection from British armed forces in return. Sheikh Maktoum lures foreign traders to Dubai by declaring they would be exempt from paying taxes.	The worldwide depression precipitated by the Wall Street Crash of 1929, paired with the arrival of a new method of creating pearls artificially, prompts Sheikh Rashid to conclude that the pearling industry is finished.

HISTORY BOOKS

There's lots of terrific stuff out there on Dubai history. While not all of these books are specifically about Dubai, there's some great reading here about the region's history.

- *Telling Tales: An Oral History of Dubai* by Julia Wheeler – A beautiful book of black-and-white photography and interviews with a cross-section of Emiratis reveals what life in Dubai was like before it started resembling a set from a science-fiction movie.
- *Father of Dubai: Sheikh Rashid bin Saeed al-Maktoum* by Graeme Wilson – A photographic and narrative tribute to Sheikh Mohammed's father.
- *From Trucial States to United Arab Emirates* by Frauke Heard-Bey – An insight into a society in transition, including the development of Dubai, by a leading scholar and long-term UAE expat.
- *Seafarers of the Emirates* by Ronald Codrai – This remarkable record recreates the lives of pearl divers, merchants, shipbuilders and seafarers, with photos taken in Dubai in the middle of the 20th century.
- *Arabian Destiny* by Edward Henderson – This wry memoir by a British colonial official includes perceptive observations of the society he lived in: Dubai hasn't simply changed since the 1950s, it's become a different place altogether.
- *Sheikhdoms of Eastern Arabia* by Peter Lienhardt and Ahmed al-Shahi – An insight into how oil wealth altered Arabia, tribal structure, gender relations, and the complex relationship between the ruling sheikhs and their subjects.
- *The Merchants: the Big Business Families of Saudi Arabia and the Gulf States* by Michael Field – A brief sketch of the rise of Dubai as a trading centre, and the role played by its powerful tribal relationships.

Things really began to change around the end of the 19th century. In 1892 the British, keen to impose their authority on the region and protect their Indian empire, extended their power through a series of so-called exclusive agreements, under which the sheikhs accepted formal British protection and, in exchange, promised to have no dealings with other foreign powers without British permission. As a result of these treaties, or truces, Europeans called the area 'the Trucial Coast', a name retained until the 1971 federation.

At the end of the 19th century, Sharjah, the area's main trading centre, began losing its trade to Dubai. In 1894 Dubai's visionary ruler at the time, Sheikh Maktoum bin Hasher al-Maktoum, decided to give foreign traders tax exemptions, and the free port of Dubai was born. Around the same time, Lingah (now Bandar-e Langeh), across the Strait of Hormuz in Iran, lost its status as a duty-free port. The Maktoums lured Lingah's disillusioned traders to Dubai at the same time as it managed to convince some of Sharjah's merchants to relocate.

At first the Persians who came to Dubai believed that it would just be a temporary move, but by the 1920s, when it became evident that the trade restrictions in southern Iran were there to stay, they took up permanent residence in Bastakia (p61).

More good news for Dubai came in the early 20th century when the Maktoums, probably with the assistance of the Persian merchants, prevailed on a British steamship line to switch its main port of call in the lower Gulf from Lingah to Dubai. This gave Dubai regular links with British India and the ports of the central and northern Gulf – Bahrain, Kuwait, Bushire and Basra. Dubai's importance to Britain as a port of call would remain in place for half a century, marking the beginning of Dubai's growth as a trading power and fuelling the prosperity that would follow.

1940	1946	1951
There is a brief conflict between Dubai and Sharjah following a dispute in the Maktoum family. Hostilities ceased after the British cut off the supply lines and both sides ran out of gunpowder.	Sheikh Zayed bin Sultan al-Nahyan makes his political debut at the age of 38 when he is appointed ruler's representative in his hometown of Al-Ain.	The British government establishes the Trucial States Council, which brings together the leaders of the sheikhdoms that would later form the UAE. It was the first time the leaders had regularly gathered to communicate.

BOOKS: ARABS & THE ARAB WORLD

Dubai may get only the briefest of mentions in these books, but they'll give you a solid understanding of the region in which Dubai is now a central focus.

- *The Arabs* by Peter Mansfield – This must-read book discusses Arabs, their characteristics, aspirations and future, from the pre-Islamic Arabian nomads, through the life of Prophet Mohammed, to the modern Arab renaissance.
- *Arabia and the Arabs: From the Bronze Age to the Coming of Islam* by Robert G Hoyland – From inscriptions, poetry, histories and archaeological evidence, you learn about Arabia, from ancient Sheba to the deserts and oases of the north.
- *A History of the Arab Peoples* by Albert Hourani – A bestseller when first published in 1991 (updated 2003), this superb book covers politics, culture, society, economy and thought.
- *Travellers in Arabia* by Robin Bidwell – Arabia as experienced by its earliest tourists: Burckhardt, Burton, Palgrave, Philby, Stark, Cox and Thesiger.
- *Arabian Sands* by Wilfred Thesiger – Fascinating accounts of five years spent with the Bedu of the Arabian peninsula in the Empty Quarter in the 1940s.

THE EXPANDING CITY

Dubai was well established as an independent town, with a population of about 10,000, by the beginning of the 20th century. Deira was the most populous area at this time, with about 1600 houses, inhabited mainly by Arabs, but also by Persians and Baluchis, who came from parts of what are now Iran, Pakistan and Afghanistan. By 1908 there were about 350 shops in Deira and another 50 in Bur Dubai, where the Indian community was concentrated. To this day the Bur Dubai Souq (p66) shows a strong Indian influence, and Bur Dubai is home to the only Hindu temple in the city.

The development of Dubai as a major trading centre was, ironically, spurred on by the collapse of the pearling trade, which had been the mainstay of its economy for centuries. The pearling trade had fallen victim both to the worldwide depression of 1929 and to the Japanese discovery (in 1930) of a method by which pearls could be cultured artificially. Sheikh Rashid concluded that the pearling industry was finished, and started to look for alternative forms of revenue. This chain of events heralded a new era in Dubai's trade – re-exporting. Dubai's enterprising merchants began importing goods to sell them on to other ports. In practice, this involved the smuggling of goods, particularly of gold, to India. The goods entered and exited Dubai legally; it was the countries at the other end of the trade that saw it as smuggling.

The Second World War also played a role in the growth of the re-export trade. The war brought much of Dubai's trade to a standstill and this was compounded by a shortage of basic food supplies. The British government supplied the Trucial sheikhdoms with plenty of rice and sugar. Dubai merchants bought these goods cheaply and, finding themselves oversupplied, shipped them off to the black market in Iran.

In 1939 Sheikh Rashid bin Saeed al-Maktoum took over as regent from his father, Sheikh Saeed, but he only formally succeeded to the leadership when his father died in 1958. He quickly moved to bolster the emirate's position as the main trading hub in the lower Gulf, at the same time as the rulers of Sharjah made the costly mistake of allowing their harbour to silt up. Sheikh Rashid quickly improved facilities along the Creek, until January 1940, when war broke out briefly between Dubai and Sharjah.

1958	1959	1966
After almost 20 years of de facto leadership, Sheikh Rashid officially becomes ruler of Dubai. He had been regent since 1939 but could only assume the position of leader after his father's death.	Sheikh Rashid borrows millions of dollars from the Emir of Kuwait to dredge the Creek so it can handle large ships, enhancing Dubai's reputation as a Persian Gulf trade hub. Dubai airport opens a year later, with plenty of room for expansion.	Eight years after oil is discovered offshore in Abu Dhabi, Dubai makes its own discovery. The arrival of oil persuades traders from across the region to settle in Dubai, spurring a period of rapid economic growth.

The origins of the brief conflict stem from a complicated struggle within the Al-Maktoum family. Sheikh Saeed al-Maktoum, the ruler of Dubai, was challenged in the 1930s by his cousin, Mani bin Rashid, who at one point controlled Deira while Sheikh Saeed held onto Bur Dubai across the Creek. Sheikh Saeed gained the upper hand and sent his cousin into exile in 1939. Mani bin Rashid and his followers then settled in Sharjah, too close to Dubai for Sheikh Saeed's comfort. Sheikh Saeed asked Sheikh Sultan of Sharjah to exile Mani bin Rashid, but Sheikh Sultan refused on the grounds that it compromised the traditions of Arab hospitality. After much fruitless diplomacy, a desultory war broke out in January 1940 between Dubai and Sharjah, all of 23km apart. The British tried to quell the war by restricting the import of firearms and ammunition. The rival forces then resorted to using ancient muzzle-loading cannons. The soldiers were sometimes able to recover the cannonballs fired at them and to fire them back. When the ammunition and gunpowder had nearly run out, the rival sheikhs began negotiating again. Mani bin Rashid died peacefully soon after, and the matter was put to rest with him.

In 1951 the Trucial States Council was founded, bringing the leaders of what would become the UAE together. The council comprised the rulers of the sheikhdoms and was the direct predecessor of the UAE Supreme Council. Then it met only twice a year, under the aegis of the British political agent in Dubai. It was around this time that modern Dubai began to take shape. Sheikh Rashid became one of the earliest beneficiaries of Kuwait's Fund for Arab Economic Development, which loaned him money to dredge the Creek (it had become badly silted up, reducing the volume of Creek traffic) and to build a new breakwater near its mouth. The project was completed in 1963, and gold smuggling took off like a rocket, using the trade networks built up through the pearling business. India had banned gold imports after 1947 to stabilise its currency, which sent the price of gold in India soaring. In 1967 the price of gold in Dubai was US$35 an ounce, while in India it sold for US$68 an ounce.

PEARLING

The heyday of pearling is laced with romanticism. But unfortunately for those who dove in the depths to collect pearls, it was a life of hardship and the rewards were no match for the dangers involved. Most of the divers were slaves from East Africa and the profits of the industry went straight to their master, the boat owner.

The only equipment the divers used was a rope tied around their waist, a turtle-shell peg on their nose and leather finger gloves to protect their hands from the sharp coral and shells. At certain times of the year they'd wear a muslin bodysuit to protect them from jellyfish stings. The best pearls were found at depths of up to 36m and divers would be underwater for around three minutes. To reach this depth, they held a rope weighted with a stone and tied to the boat, and then were thrown overboard.

The pearl-diving season lasted from May until September. On the ship there would be divers, men responsible for hauling up the divers after each job, a cook, and boys employed to serve food and water, and open the oyster shells. Each boat also had a singer, called the *naham*, whose job was to lead the crew in songs or lighten their mood by singing to them. Many of the songs were about lucky men who had become rich through diving, and the joys of returning home after the diving season.

Back on shore, pearl merchants would grade the pearls according to size by using a number of copper sieves, each with different-sized holes. The greatest market for pearls was originally India, but in the early 20th century the UK and US also became keen buyers. The discovery of the means to make artificial pearls in the early 20th century triggered the demise of the industry. The Dubai Museum (p61) and the Diving Village (p67) feature informative displays on pearling.

1968	1971	1973
The British announce that they will be ending their relationship with the Trucial States by 1971 and local leaders discuss the possibility of a future nation. Dubai starts exporting crude oil and petrodollars flood in, reaching a peak in 1991.	The Trucial States is re-established as the United Arab Emirates. Qatar and Bahrain opt out of the union and declare independence. Sheikh Zayed of Abu Dhabi is named the new nation's first president.	The dirham replaces the riyal as the official unit of currency in Dubai. Until 1966, all the sheikhdoms had used the Gulf rupee. The dirham has been pegged to the US dollar since 1997.

THE ARCHITECTS OF MODERN DUBAI

Sheikh Rashid bin Saeed al-Maktoum

Remembered fondly as the 'Father of Dubai', Sheikh Rashid laid the foundations of the modern city. When he became ruler in 1958, Dubai was a small town with a very limited infrastructure. Within a few years of coming to power, he had dramatically improved the police force and school system, built a modern hospital and a network of roads, and established a steady supply of electricity and water. His decisions to dredge the Creek and construct an international airport provided a huge logistical boost to Dubai's trade-focused economy. The discovery of oil in 1966 enticed people from across the region to migrate to Dubai and tap into the petrodollar boom, doubling the emirate's population between 1967 and 1973. In the last two decades of his life, Sheikh Rashid oversaw the construction of the ports at Mina Rashid and Jebel Ali; the World Trade Centre; the Maktoum Bridge and the Shindagha Tunnel; and the city's first free zone, in Jebel Ali. In 1985 he helped establish Emirates airline, which has been instrumental in fashioning Dubai as a tourist destination.

Sheikh Maktoum bin Rashid al-Maktoum

When Sheikh Rashid passed away in 1990 after a prolonged illness, Sheikh Maktoum officially succeeded his father, although in reality he'd already been working hard to ensure that Dubai's next generation reaped the benefits of the burgeoning economy. Spreading the wealth through education, housing and greater job opportunities, and all the while diversifying Dubai's economic portfolio, his work set a solid platform for the phenomenal growth of Dubai today. In the later years of his reign, his younger brother Sheikh Mohammed began working on a more active (and economically aggressive) expansion of Dubai.

The end of World War II, India's independence and the decline of the British Empire saw the end of Britain's presence in the region and prompted the creation of the UAE. But before withdrawing from the region, the British set in motion the means by which the UAE borders were drawn. The British withdrawal and the discovery of oil accelerated the modernisation of the region. Incredibly, drawing the UAE's borders involved a British diplomat spending months riding a camel around the mountains and desert, asking village heads, tribal leaders and Bedouin which sheikh they swore allegiance to.

THE RECENT PAST

When Britain announced its departure from the region in 1968, an attempt was made to create a nation that included the Trucial States (today's United Arab Emirates), Bahrain and Qatar. While the talks collapsed with Bahrain and Qatar (who both moved on to their own independence), the leader of Abu Dhabi, Sheikh Zayed bin Sultan al-Nahyan (see the boxed text, opposite), and of Dubai, Sheikh Rashid bin Saeed al-Maktoum, strengthened their commitment to creating a single state.

After persistent persuasion by Sheikh Zayed, the federation of the United Arab Emirates (UAE) was born on 2 December 1971, consisting of the emirates of Dubai, Abu Dhabi, Ajman, Fujairah, Sharjah and Umm al-Quwain, with Ras al-Khaimah joining in 1972. Impressively, the UAE remains to this day the only federation of Arab states in the Middle East.

Under that agreement, the emirs had approved a formula whereby Abu Dhabi and Dubai (in that order) would carry the most weight in the federation, but would leave each emir largely

1979	1985	1990
Sheikh Rashid is declared prime minister of the UAE. The post had been held by his son, Sheikh Maktoum, who stepped aside to give his father more power.	The Emirates airline is established in Dubai. It initially only flew to Karachi and Mumbai. Today it is one of the 10 biggest airlines in the world in terms of passengers carried.	Sheikh Rashid dies during the first Gulf War and his son, Sheikh Maktoum, takes over as ruler of Dubai. Five years later, Sheikh Mohammed is made Crown Prince of Dubai, assumes de facto rule and is soon seen as the major figure in local politics.

autonomous. Sheikh Zayed became the supreme ruler (or president) of the UAE, and Sheikh Rashid of Dubai assumed the role of vice-president.

Since federation, Dubai has been one of the most politically stable city-states in the Arab world; however, the fledgling nation has still had its teething problems. Border disputes between the emirates continued throughout the 1970s and '80s, and the level of independence that each emirate assumes has always been the subject of long discussions.

While Dubai and Abu Dhabi had an agreement to cooperate long before the nation was born, the relationship has not been without its difficulties. Achieving an equitable balance of power between the two emirates, as well as refining a unified vision for the country, was much debated until 1979 when Sheikh Zayed and Sheikh Rashid sealed a formal compromise under which each gave a little ground on his vision of the country. The result was a much stronger federation in which Dubai remained a bastion of free trade while Abu Dhabi imposed a tighter federal structure on the other emirates. Rashid also agreed to take the title of Prime Minister as a symbol of his commitment to the federation.

Sheikh Rashid, the driving force behind Dubai's phenomenal growth and 'father of (modern) Dubai', died in 1990 after a long illness, and was succeeded as emir by the eldest of his four sons, Sheikh Maktoum bin Rashid al-Maktoum. Maktoum had been regent for his sick father for several years already, so he continued to follow in his father's footsteps with the expansion of Dubai.

Overseeing Dubai's transformation into a 21st-century metropolis is the third son of the dynasty, Sheikh Mohammed bin Rashid al-Maktoum, who was the face of modern Dubai even before he succeeded his older brother as ruler in 2006. Having ruled Dubai as a de facto leader

FATHER OF THE NATION

Visitors to Dubai will no doubt see enormous posters of a smiling sheikh in a pair of Ray Ban–style sunglasses – this is Sheikh Zayed bin Sultan al-Nahyan, the first, and up until his death in 2004, the only President of the UAE. Revered by his people, and often called 'father' by Emiratis, he commanded huge respect across the Middle East.

Sheikh Zayed was born in Abu Dhabi in 1918, and his father was ruler of the emirate from 1922 to 1926. After his father's death in 1927, Sheikh Zayed relocated to Al-ain and spent his time studying the Quran and learning from local Bedouin tribesmen; the knowledge he gained here was crucial to his ability to pull a nation together decades later.

His first taste of politics came in 1946, when he was appointed ruler's representative in Al-ain, where he honed his famed negotiating skills. When the oil began flowing in Abu Dhabi in 1962, it soon became apparent that Sheikh Zayed had the right skills to handle the massive changes that were to come, and the sheikh soon took over from his older brother in managing Abu Dhabi's affairs. Seizing the opportunity, Sheikh Zayed built schools, hospitals and housing for his people, and when the British decided to withdraw from the Trucial States in 1968, he set out to federate the states and create a nation.

The act of pulling together these often-squabbling, sometimes-fighting seven states is key to Sheikh Zayed's legacy. Few thought it could be done, and fewer thought it would last, but for three years Sheikh Zayed negotiated, cajoled and convinced the other states that a United Arab Emirates was the only way forward.

After he became President in 1971 (and was continually re-elected to the post up until his death), the distribution of wealth to the poorer emirates, as well as his handling of an ambitious Dubai, were key in keeping the fledgling nation together.

Sheikh Zayed had an almost obsessive ambition to 'green' the Emirates and to keep tradition alive. Even though in the Middle East it's almost obligatory to praise leaders, both past and present, in the UAE even the most cynical students of Arab politics note that the affection the people have for this leader runs far deeper than that.

1996	2003	2006
Two major annual events, the Dubai Shopping Festival and the Dubai World Cup, are launched. American racehorse Cigar is the first winner of the Cup. The tallest hotel in the world the Burj Al Arab opens, enhancing Dubai's reputation as a tourist mecca.	The International Monetary Fund and the World Bank recognise Dubai as a financial hub. Sheikh Zayed, the UAE's first president, dies and is replaced by his son Sheikh Khalifa who announces plans for the country's first ever elections to take place in 2006.	Sheikh Mohammed becomes ruler of Dubai after Sheikh Maktoum's passing, and is also confirmed as Prime Minister and Vice-President of the United Arab Emirates. Two years later, US president George W Bush visits Dubai as part of his Middle East tour.

since the mid '90s, Sheikh Mohammed has brought consistency and continuity to Dubai in a period of tremendous social, cultural and economic change. In February 2008 he named his son Hamdan bin Mohammed bin Rashid al-Maktoum, also known as 'Fazza 3', as the emirate's crown prince and his likely successor. The young prince is already tremendously popular – check out his fan videos on YouTube.

ECONOMY

Dubai is the second richest emirate in the UAE, after the capital Abu Dhabi. While most visitors think Dubai became rich through oil, what it's actually done is use its modest oil resources to create the infrastructure for trade, manufacturing and tourism. About 70% of the UAE's non-oil GDP is generated in Dubai, and about 95% of Dubai's GDP is not oil-based. Dubai's reserves of oil and gas were never huge and by 2010 it is estimated that oil will account for less than one percent of Dubai's GDP. In the same year, tourism is expected to create at least 20% of the GDP.

While many analysts believe that Dubai has expanded too far, too fast, and that its economy is heading for trouble, others believe the city has a sufficiently sturdy economic base to survive any bumps in the road – such as the current inflation level (10%) or further strikes by workers on construction sites.

Dubai's main exports are oil, natural gas, dates and dried fish; top export destinations are Japan, Taiwan, the UK, the US and India. Imports are primarily minerals and chemicals, base metals (including gold), vehicles and machinery, electronics, textiles and foodstuffs; the main importers into Dubai are the US, China, Japan, the UK, South Korea and India. Dubai's re-export trade (where items such as whitegoods come into Dubai from the manufacturers and are then sent onwards) makes up about 80% of the UAE's total re-export business. Dubai's re-exports go mainly to Iran, India, Saudi Arabia, Kuwait, China and Afghanistan.

Dubai is also home to a huge dry-dock complex, the Middle East's busiest airport and duty-free operations, the region's biggest airline, and large free-trade zones at Jebel Ali, 30 minutes from the city centre, and at Dubai airport. Dubai airport is so busy now that a new airport (mainly catering for cargo) is being built at Jebel Ali. Attracting foreign business to its free-trade zones has been one of Dubai's greatest economic achievements in the last 20 years, with companies enticed here by the promise of full foreign ownership, full repatriation of capital

SHEIKH MOHAMMED – MR DUBAI

Having spent several years as a de facto ruler while he was crown prince, Sheikh Mohammed was the only candidate for the top job when Sheikh Maktoum died in early 2006. He has spoken about managing Dubai as if it were a business, and like the most successful CEOs he has a knack for making the right decision at the right time.

Although he is surrounded by some of the greatest minds in the Gulf, as well as political and economic expertise imported from all over the world, there's no uncertainty about where executive power lies. He has a flair for generating publicity for the city and was deeply involved in the planning and construction of landmark projects such as the Burj Al Arab, the Palm Jumeirah and the Burj Dubai. For the Burj Al Arab project, it's said that the sheikh wanted a design that would be as resonant as the Eiffel Tower and the Sydney Opera House. And it's perhaps from this that we can get an idea of the breadth of what he wants to achieve. His enterprising and frequently audacious efforts to put the city on the map have given Dubai several iconic buildings to choose from.

Aside from handling the day-to-day running of the emirate, in his capacity as Prime Minister and Vice-President of the UAE he strengthens the bond between Dubai and the other six emirates, while his ownership of Dubai Holding gives him control of numerous businesses such as the Jumeirah Group (properties including the Burj Al Arab), Tatweer (Dubailand) and TECOM (Internet City). He's also a keen fan of falconry and equestrianism and runs the Godolphin stable. He is believed to be worth at least US$10 billion.

Visitors from Western countries may feel uncomfortable with the large-scale portraits of the ruler on billboards and buildings around town. Yet these are not simply the propaganda tools of an autocratic regime; many people in Dubai revere their ruler. Few world leaders are able to drive themselves around town without a bodyguard and without any fear of being attacked. Although dissenting voices aren't tolerated and the local media is uncritical, most people admire the Emirates' leaders for creating a haven of peace and prosperity in a troubled part of the world.

TOURISM & DEVELOPMENT

Sheikh Maktoum realised that oil wealth wouldn't last forever, and so diversified Dubai's economy. In the early 1990s, there were only a handful of five-star hotels in Dubai and the area that is now Dubai Marina was virtually untouched. The announcement of the Burj Al Arab project in 1994 represented a new phase of Dubai's long-term strategy, a bid to become one of the world's major tourist destinations. In 1996 the city launched its two leading annual events, the Dubai Shopping Festival and the Dubai World Cup, and the start of 1997 saw the creation of the Department of Tourism and Commerce Marketing, a body tasked with developing the city's tourism infrastructure at home and its profile abroad.

Over the past decade, a succession of press conferences announcing audacious 'megaprojects' has kept Dubai in the headlines. The curiosity factor has helped tourist numbers skyrocket from just over half a million visitors in 1990 to over six million in 2006. The city hopes to welcome 15 million visitors in 2015.

Dubai's forthcoming attractions, many of which blur the line between the sublime and ridiculous, will ensure the city continues to command column inches. Falconcity of Wonders, a bird-shaped mini-city, will be home to replicas of the Eiffel Tower, the Taj Mahal and the Hanging Gardens of Babylon. The complex will compete for tourist dirhams with an underwater hotel, a park with roaming dinosaurs, a ski slope with a revolving mountain, and perhaps most unusually a large-scale reconstruction of the French city of Lyon.

Unsurprisingly, questions are being asked about whether Dubai's indefatigable ambition and taste for the bizarre will result in a circus sideshow, a Vegas-like theme park that will be shunned by business travellers and a luxury travel sector looking for more sophistication. There is also a concern that short supplies of oil will lead to heavily taxed long-haul air travel, and holidaymakers in some of Dubai's biggest markets, such as the UK and Germany, will choose to holiday closer to home. For the time being, however, tourist numbers keep going up and up.

and profits, no corporate tax for 15 years, no currency restrictions, and no personal income tax for staff.

The Dubai Internet City and neighbouring Dubai Media City have been equally successful in adding a new hi-tech information and communication stratum to the city's economy, as well as gaining credibility by leading the big media players, such as CNN, to base their Middle East operations in Dubai.

Dubai's tourism industry has also exploded (see the boxed text, above). The city's tolerance of Western habits, profusion of quality hotels, long stretches of beach, warm winter weather, shopping incentives and desert activities have helped it become the leading tourist destination in the Gulf, and local tourism authorities expect to attract 10 million visitors per annum by 2010.

For Emirati citizens all this prosperity translates into benefits of which the rest of the world only dreams: free health care, free education, heavily subsidised utilities and, in some cases, free housing. Dubai's per capita income is around Dh80,000 per annum, while the monthly salary of an unskilled expat labourer is anywhere between Dh500 to Dh1000 per month.

But while the globalisation of the international labour market (read: cheap foreign labour) has made the phenomenal growth of Dubai so attainable, there is one hurdle in the economy that Dubai is seeking to overcome. Dubai is highly dependent upon this expat labour and, at the same time, its citizens are having trouble finding meaningful employment. While the government in the past had made some attempt to 'Emiratise' the economy by placing nationals in the public workforce and imposing local employee quotas on private companies, this hasn't been particularly successful. Rightly seeing this as a major concern, Dubai's new ruler, Sheikh Mohammed, has taken over responsibility for this – and given his track record, meaningful results are expected.

One of the problems he faces with this issue is that private companies are reluctant to hire nationals, often due to the misguided notion that they are lazy. However, one of the key problems is that nationals expect to start on a salary that's far above what the equivalent expat would receive. There is no doubt that Dubai will be dependent on foreign labour and expertise for a long time to come.

GOVERNMENT & POLITICS

Dubai is the second most powerful of the seven emirates that make up the UAE, with Abu Dhabi being both the capital and home to most of the country's oil wealth. In each emirate, power rests with a ruling tribe, which in Dubai's case is the Maktoums. The term emirate is derived from the term 'emir', which means ruler, although the rulers of the emirates are known as sheikhs. As yet, there are no political parties or general elections in Dubai, and even if there were, it would be hard to imagine the Maktoums being deposed, having resided over such extraordinary growth.

Despite Dubai becoming so strong over the last few years, it has had to fight long and hard to preserve as much of its independence as possible and to minimise the power of the country's federal institutions. Along with Ras al-Khaimah, it maintains a legal system that is separate from the federal judiciary.

Politically, the relative interests of the seven emirates are fairly clear. Abu Dhabi is the largest and wealthiest emirate and has the biggest population. It is, therefore, the dominant member of the federation and is likely to remain so for some time. Dubai is the second largest emirate by population, with both an interest in upholding its free-trade policies and a pronounced independent streak. The other emirates are dependent on subsidies from Abu Dhabi, though the extent of this dependence varies widely.

The forum where these issues are discussed is the Supreme Council, the highest legislative body in the country. The council, which tends to meet informally, comprises the seven emirs. New federal laws can be passed with the consent of five of the seven rulers. The Supreme Council also elects one of the emirs to a five-year term as the country's president. After the death of the founder of the country and its first president, Sheikh Zayed, in late 2004, power passed peacefully to his son Sheikh Khalifa bin Zayed al-Nahyan.

There is also a cabinet, and the posts within it are distributed among the emirates. Most of the federal government's money comes from Abu Dhabi and Dubai, so members of these governments hold most of the important cabinet posts.

The cabinet and the Supreme Council are advised, but cannot be overruled, by the Federation National Council, a consultative body with 40 members, half of whom are voted in by a tiny electorate (see the boxed text, opposite).

The Dubai Municipality is effectively the local government for the emirate, handling everything from economic planning to rubbish collection. Above the municipality is Sheikh Mohammed's private office, the Executive Office, along with the official administrative body called the Diwan or the Ruler's Office.

HAWALA: THE BUSINESS OF TRUST

Imagine a money transfer system with quick delivery and minimal or no fees, which is available to people in the poorest countries in the world. This is *hawala,* and Dubai is one of the key centres of this controversial practice.

Hawala is an Arabic term for a written order of payment. It works like this. You hand over your dirhams and the contact details of the recipient to your neighbourhood *hawala* trader. In return you get a code – say, a letter and four numbers. Then you ring up the recipient and give them the code. The trader contacts the people in his network. The next day, maybe two days later, the *hawala* trader's partner hands over the money, sometimes delivering it to the door of the recipient. The commission taken by the *hawala* traders might be as little as 1% or 2%, even zero if they can make a little profit on exchange-rate differences.

Some newspaper reports say as much as 90% of wages remitted to developing countries from the UAE were sent via this system until recently. Sending Dh100 to India via a bank would yield Rs 1050, while via a *hawala* trader it yields Rs 1130; while this is only US$2 difference, this amount still goes a long way in India's poorer regions and is a huge benefit to workers who can only afford to send home small amounts.

The *hawala* system has existed among Arab and Muslim traders for centuries as a defence against theft. It's a uniquely Islamic system, completely dependent on trust and honour. If a *hawala* trader breaks this trust, he'll be out of work, as his reputation is crucial to his business.

The *hawala* system in Dubai grew through gold smuggling in the 1960s. Once the gold was sold in India or Pakistan, the traders couldn't get the money back to Dubai. They found their solution in the growing number of expatriate workers. The workers gave their wages to the gold traders in Dubai, and the gold traders in India paid their relatives.

Since the attacks of 9/11, the system is under increased pressure, as the USA – and its media outlets – has claimed that *hawala* is being used to transfer money to terrorists. *Hawala* operators in Dubai have been subject to further regulations yet there's no sign that this long-standing alternative to Western Union and the other money transfer giants is under threat anytime soon.

IDENTITY & LIFESTYLE
IDENTITY

The best recent estimates put Dubai's population at 1.5 million, a giant leap from 183,200 in 1975. Three quarters of the population is male. These statistics apply to the whole of the Dubai emirate, though the UAE is overwhelmingly urban with more than 90% of the population living in cities. The emirate's population has been growing by as much as 7% a year, and the authorities are planning for a population of two million by 2010. Fewer than 10% of the total population of Dubai are Emiratis; the expatriate community makes up the rest of the population – one of the most multicultural in the world.

In stark contrast to neighbouring Saudi Arabia and nearby Iran, Dubai is a tolerant and easygoing society, with its cultural and social life firmly rooted in Islam. Most religions – Judaism is a noteworthy exception – are tolerated and places of worship have been built for Christians, Hindus and Sikhs. Day-to-day activities, relationships, diet and dress are very much dictated by religion (see the boxed text, p41). Gender roles are changing, with more and more women wanting to establish careers before marriage. With successful Emirati women such as Sheikha Lubna al-Qasimi (the first female Minister of Economy and Planning) and Dr Amina Rostamani (Executive Director of Dubai's Media City) serving as role models, women's contribution to the workforce has grown considerably in the past decade.

There may only be limited 'bricks and mortar' representation of traditional Arabic and Bedouin life in Dubai, but the cultural and national identity of Emiratis is strong. The physical representations of the past still exist in the form of the traditional architecture (see p39) on the Shindagha waterfront in Bur Dubai and Al-Ahmadiya School (p58) and Heritage House (p58) in Deira, but to gain a good insight into traditional culture, visit Dubai Museum (p61) or venture out of the city to the East Coast villages (p172) or Al-Ain (p170), where life appears little changed from the way it was before federation.

Take comments you may hear about Dubai being fake and a 'shopping culture' with a pinch of salt – shopping is merely a pastime, albeit an extremely popular one. Emirati cultural identity is expressed through poetry, traditional song and dance, a love of the desert and nature, and of camels, horses and falconry, all of which remain popular activities. If you're lucky enough to be invited to a wedding (and you should take up the offer), it's a great way to see some of these cultural traditions in action.

Dubai has been very active in preserving and publicly displaying many local traditions. The Dubai Museum (p61), Bastakia (p61), Al-Ahmadiya School (p58), Heritage House (p58) and the Heritage Village (p67) in Shindagha all give insights into traditional and cultural life, and the aim of such work is not just to attract and entertain tourists, but to educate young Emiratis about the value of their culture and heritage. Families also make an effort to maintain their heritage by taking their kids out to the desert frequently and teaching them how to continue traditional practices such as falconry.

One matter of great concern to the authorities is the ongoing trend for Emirati men to marry foreign women. One reason for the trend is the prohibitive cost of a traditional wedding, plus the dowry the groom must provide – essentially, it's cheaper and easier to marry a foreign woman. Another factor is that as Emirati women are becoming better educated, they're less willing to settle down in the traditional role of an Emirati wife. The issue comes up frequently in the Arabic press – in a culture where women who are still unmarried at the age of 26 are referred to as spinsters, or even as slighting the family's honour, the growing numbers of single women is a hot topic indeed. The UAE Marriage Fund, set up by the federal government in

THE ROAD TO DEMOCRACY

The United Arab Emirates has recently taken the most tentative of steps towards democracy. Half the country's Federal National Council (FNC), a 40-person body established to review and debate legislation, is now elected. But the FNC has no real power; it can only advise the government, and only 6689 people have been hand-picked to vote – under 1% of Emiratis and a tiny fraction of the UAE's total population of over four million – for candidates on a list approved by the government.

While full democracy in the UAE may be decades away, there are plans to grant the FNC some legislative powers and to eventually give the vote to all UAE citizens. In the inaugural elections in December 2006, 382 women were able to vote and one woman was elected onto the council.

HOT PROPERTY

If you bought a house in Dubai in 2002, when foreigners were first allowed to purchase property, there's a good chance your ear-to-ear grin still hasn't faded. This landmark ruling kick-started Dubai's property boom, and prices doubled and sometimes trebled in value over the next few years. However, confusion regarding the ownership of the properties (buyers only received a guarantee of ownership from the developers but no legal freehold rights) persisted until 2006, when a new law was introduced giving owners full freehold rights including title deeds in certain parts of town. Freehold owners are also now entitled to a renewable three-year residency visa.

Unfortunately it's no longer possible to exchange a grotty, cramped apartment in London or Sydney for a sparkling four-bedroom villa in Jumeirah, but prices remain attractive to buyers from Western countries. Bargain hunters may want to look outside Dubai, with freehold property prices in Ajman, Ras al-Khaimah and Sharjah undercutting those in the big city.

1994 to facilitate marriages between UAE nationals, provides grants to pay for the exorbitant costs of the wedding and dowry and promotes mass weddings to enable nationals to save for a down payment on a house. These initiatives have reduced the rate of intermarriages between Emirati men and foreign women to a degree, but not sufficiently to ensure that every Emirati woman has a husband.

LIFESTYLE

Don't be surprised if you hear expats make crude generalisations about Emiratis. You may be told they're all millionaires and live in mansions, or that they refuse to work in ordinary jobs, or that all the men have four wives. Such stereotypes simply reinforce prejudices and demonstrate the lack of understanding between cultures in Dubai.

Not all Emiratis are wealthy. While the traditional tribal leaders, or sheikhs, are often the wealthiest UAE nationals, many have made their fortune through good investments, often dating back to the 1970s. As befits a small oil-producing nation, all Emiratis have access to free healthcare and education as well as a marriage fund (although the budgets don't often meet the expenses of elaborate Emirati weddings). These types of social benefits, and charities operated by generous sheikhs, such as Sheikh Mohammed, are essential to the survival of poorer Emiratis in modern Dubai.

The upper and middle classes of Emirati society generally have expansive villas in which men and women still live apart, and male family members entertain guests in the *majlis* (meeting room). In all classes of Emirati society, extended families living together is the norm, with the woman moving in with the husband's family after marriage, although some young couples are now choosing to buy their own apartments for a little more privacy than the traditional arrangement allows.

Most Emiratis work in the public sector, as the short hours, good pay, benefits and early pensions are hard for young people (whose parents and grandparents still recall hard times) to refuse. The UAE government is actively pursuing a policy of 'emiratisation', which involves encouraging Emiratis to work in the private sector, and encouraging employers to reject negative stereotypes and hire them. In the long term the government hopes to be much less dependent on an imported labour force.

Living with such a large proportion of expats, and an increasing amount of Western 'culture', has seen an increasing conservatism as well as liberalisation in Dubai. This is especially

THE MAJLIS

Majlis translates as 'meeting place' or 'reception area'. The *majlis* was a forum or council where citizens could come and speak to their leaders and make requests and complaints or raise issues. In Dubai the *majlis* system was preserved until the 1960s. In its domestic sense, a *majlis* is a reception area found in all older buildings in Dubai (such as Al-Fahidi Fort, the Dubai Museum and the Heritage House in Al-Ahmadiya). Its Western cousin is probably the lounge room. The *majlis* is still an important room in an Arab household and is usually the domain of the male members of the family. It's a place where they can get together and talk without disturbing the women of the house, as most traditional houses still have a separate *majlis* for women.

RACISM IN DUBAI

Notice something weird about the job ads in the classified section of the newspaper? In the UAE, it's quite normal for employers to specify the preferred nationality or gender of applicants in advertisements. Ads often include phrases such as 'Arabs only', 'UK/US/AUS only', or even 'males preferred'. Some employers expect female candidates to send photographs with their application. The open discrimination you'll see in job ads is often reflected in pay. A European can expect to earn more than a Filipino or Indian doing the same job. In 2007 *Xpress* newspaper sent four men, two from India and two from Britain, to nightclubs across Dubai. At several of the clubs the Indian men were turned away by the bouncers while British men got in without any problems.

It's a similar situation when it comes to finding accommodation. Moments after I signed a lease to rent an apartment in Satwa, the (European) estate agent revealed she had good news for me. 'There are no Indians or Pakistanis in your building,' she announced. I asked why she considered this such good news. 'Because you don't get the smell of curry all day,' she replied. Dubai may be one of the most multicultural cities in the world, but it has a very long way to go before it can be considered a true melting pot.

noticeable among young women: some are beginning to dress in Western fashion (usually ones with foreign mothers), others are sticking with traditional dress yet individualising it, while yet others are 'covering up'. One aspect that's not going away is the importance of traditional dance, song and customs. All Emiratis know their traditional songs and dances, and activities such as falconry are being passed from father to son. So is the love of the desert – Emiratis are as comfortable in the sands as they are in Switzerland, where many of them take a summer break away from the heat.

As far as the foreign community goes, there are as many different lifestyles being played out in Dubai as there are grains of sand on Jumeirah Beach. Disposable income plays a big part in how people live. At the top end of the pay scale is the professional and wealthy management class. They can enjoy a good salary package, a nice car, a large villa with a maid and nanny, and a lifestyle that allows them to travel overseas for two months a year to escape the summer heat. Housewives left with little to do at home spend much of their time with other women in similar circumstances. These 'Jumeirah Janes', as other expats call them with a hint of derision, keep the cosmetics and spa industries alive and the coffee shops ticking over during the day. These residents are generally Western, but there are plenty of Indians, Iranians and Lebanese (mainly in business) that fall into this category too.

There is another category of professional expat – the academics, health professionals, media and IT people – who earn much the same as they would back home in gross terms, but with no tax, free or subsidised housing, great holidays and other benefits like schooling and healthcare, they come out ahead in financial terms. These expats are also generally Western, but there are a large number of Indians working in the IT field and Arabs working in the media, health and education sectors. Depending on how many children they have, some families have a full-time or part-time maid or nanny. But not all Western expats are on big salaries. Many aren't paid enough to save money in Dubai, especially since the cost of renting an apartment is now almost the same as in Paris or London.

Dubai has a huge service sector and traditionally workers come from India, Pakistan and the Philippines, but now there are employees coming from other parts of Asia and increasingly Africa too. Working as line cooks and waiters and in supermarkets, these expats stand to make more money in Dubai than at home, usually working six days a week and sharing rooms in cheap accommodation. With rent for a single bedroom around Dh4000 a month – more than most workers in the service sector earn in a month – it's necessary to share living spaces.

There are a huge number of maids employed in Dubai – check the classifieds of *Gulf News*. Indian, Pakistani, Indonesian and Sri Lankan maids are generally paid between Dh500 and Dh800 a month and live in a tiny room in their employer's villa or share an apartment with friends. While the money earned is a fraction of a Western professional's starting salary, it's still more than unskilled work pays at home. Depending on the family, some of these maids become an integral part of their employer's family structure, forming close bonds with the children. Unfortunately, UAE labour law doesn't yet fully cover domestic workers, and a small but significant number of maids are exploited and subjected to violence and abuse.

WASTA

When visiting Dubai, you might hear expats talking about *wasta*. The term translates loosely as 'influence high up' and having *wasta* can grease the wheels in just about every transaction in Dubai. Most Westerners get a little outraged at the thought of a select few receiving favours and special treatment because of powerful contacts – until, of course, they want some help themselves. Then being friends with a local who has *wasta* becomes a very desirable thing. But the funny thing is that those who claim to have *wasta* usually don't and those that do generally don't mention it.

Indians, Pakistanis and workers from other countries in the region go about the hazardous business of construction in Dubai. These men usually work six or six-and-a-half days a week on 12-hour shifts and live in what are known locally as 'labour camps' (compounds) provided by the construction companies. Conditions in the labour camps vary enormously; while some are spacious and comfortable, others cram ten to 15 people into small and filthy rooms.

Estimates vary wildly, but there are as many as 250,000 construction workers living in an area near the Sharjah border known, perhaps ironically, as Sonapur. Its name, meaning 'city of gold' in Hindi, can't be found on any road signs or maps. The better camps in Sonapur aren't that bad, but much of it is a slum. Workers are sometimes forced to sleep on the floor without mattresses and the usually reticent *Gulf News* has carried reports about people living among flies and pools of sewage. The difference in quality of life between the people who book rooms in Dubai's luxury hotels and those who toil to build them could hardly be greater.

Over the past few years, a number of riots have broken out on construction sites, including the Burj Dubai and Dubai Mall sites, with workers protesting against low pay and bad conditions. Typical pay for construction workers is Dh25 to Dh28 for a 12-hour day and most workers have to pay off large debts to the agents who initially arranged their employment.

The summer heat is extremely oppressive, in some cases reaching 45°C. A Human Rights Watch report from 2006 entitled 'Building Towers, Cheating Workers' claims that as many as 5000 construction workers per month were sent to the accident and emergency department of Rashid Hospital in July and August of 2004 with heatstroke. The government has banned outdoor work in July and August between 12.30pm and 3pm, although some construction firms continue to ignore the ruling. Another serious concern is that the rate of suicides among expatriates from this sector is on the increase.

The response of the expatriate community to the hardships suffered by construction workers has been apprehensive and slow. One nonpolitical organisation trying to make a difference is Helping Hands UAE (www.helpinghandsuae.com). If you'd like to donate clothes, food, toiletries, books or CDs to construction workers, see Helping Hands' website for information on collection points.

FASHION

Emirati women have been showing a growing pride and renewed confidence in their own national dress, the *abaya* (black cloak) and *shayla* (black veil), despite the ever-increasing Western influences in Dubai and recent reports in the media from doctors attacking *abayas* for causing osteoporosis and recruiters saying companies won't hire women who cover their faces. The latest trend is for young women to wear *abayas* and *shaylas* playfully embellished with jewels, beads, sequins, embroidery, feathers, lace, tassels and tiny plastic toys. And while Emirati men are occasionally seen in Western dress (women very rarely are, unless travelling outside the country), they're increasingly wearing their *dishdashas* (man's shirt-dress) in smart new colours, such as slate, teal and chocolate.

Hand-in-hand with this development of national fashion is the exciting emergence of several young Emirati and Dubai-born expat or Dubai-based designers, whose designs experiment in a tongue-in-cheek fashion with their own cultural symbols. At the same time, expats living in Dubai seem to be increasingly incorporating exotic Arabic (and Indian) dress into their own style and are wearing giant Bedouin earrings, pendants and bangles, long flowing colourful kaftans, and floaty smocks featuring embroidery, beads, jewels and gem stones.

The older men and women still seem set in their ways, and it's common to see men wearing the white *dishdasha* and a white or red-and-white checked *gutra* (headcloth) with *agal* (a black headrope used to hold the *gutra* in place), while older women still wear a black or gold burqa on their face, whether they're on the street or in the shopping mall.

THE MULTICULTURAL CITY

The majority of Dubai's expatriate population (comprising 90% of the emirate's population) is from India (about 60%), supplying the city with cheap labour as well as filling management and professional positions. Most of Dubai's construction workers and men in low-prestige positions (taxi drivers, hotel cleaners etc) come from Kerala, a southern Indian state, while there are also a lot of workers from the Indian states of Tamil Nadu and Goa. In contrast, most of the Indians in office jobs or managerial positions are recruited by agencies based in Mumbai, while IT guys come from Bangalore. All of the leading Indian mercantile communities – Jains, Sindhis, Sikhs and Marwaris – are also represented here.

About 12% of expats are from other Arab countries (mainly Lebanon, Syria, Jordan and Egypt) while there's also a substantial Iranian community. The first wave of Iranians built the Bastakia neighbourhood in the 1930s. They were mostly religiously conservative Sunnis and Shiites from southern Iran. After the 1979 Islamic revolution, a more affluent and often Western-educated group of Iranians settled in Dubai. There is also a growing community of Filipino expatriates, many of whom work in the hospitality sector, as well as some Chinese, Indonesian, Malaysian and Vietnamese residents. Western expats make up about 5% of the population, with at least 100,000 British citizens and increasing numbers of workers from Australia, Canada, South Africa, Ireland, Germany and France.

SPORT

The traditional Emirati sports of horse, camel and boat racing have been supplemented by the wide variety of sports that the expat community enjoy. Even during the fiercest heat of summer you'll see people playing golf or partaking in a social game of cricket in an empty car park. Just about any sport you can think of has a small group of dedicated enthusiasts finding a way to indulge in their favourite pastime, despite the heat and often relative lack of facilities.

Given the fierce summer heat, obviously the best time to play or watch sport in Dubai is during the winter months when all of Dubai's sports lovers make the most of the marvellous weather. Tennis and golf are extremely popular as are all varieties of football, but water sports are more suitable as a year-round activity. Scuba diving, sailing and kite surfing are all popular as are skateboarding and surfing (when there are waves, that is). For more on these activities, see p138.

ENVIRONMENT & PLANNING
THE LANDSCAPE

Dubai sits on the Gulf, in the northwest region of the UAE. This city is the capital of the emirate of the same name, which is the second largest of the seven emirates that compose the UAE. The emirate of Dubai is 3885 sq km and the city is roughly 35 sq km but will swell to over double this size with the addition of the three Palms, the Waterfront, the World and the Universe, along with Dubailand and the construction in the desert.

Prior to settlement, this area was flat *sabkha* (salt-crusted coastal plain). The sand mostly consists of crushed shell and coral and is fine, clean and white. The *sabkha* was broken only by clumps of desert grasses and a small area of hardy mangroves at the inland end of the Creek. Photographs of the area from the early 20th century show how strikingly barren the landscape was.

East of the city, the *sabkha* gives way to north–south lines of dunes. The farming areas of Al-Khawaneej and Al-Awir, now on the edge of Dubai's suburbia, are fed by wells. Further east the dunes grow larger and are tinged red with iron oxide. The dunes stop abruptly at the gravel fans at the base of the rugged Hajar Mountains, where there are gorges and waterholes. A vast sea of sand dunes covers the area south of the city, becoming more and more imposing as it stretches into the desert known as the Empty Quarter, which makes up the southern region of the UAE and the western region of Saudi Arabia (you can see the Empty Quarter from Al-Ain, p170). North of Dubai, along the coast, the land is tough desert scrub broken by inlets similar to Dubai Creek, until you reach the mountainous northern emirates.

PLANTS & ANIMALS

In Dubai's parks you will see indigenous tree species such as the date palm and the neem (a botanical cousin of mahogany), and a large number of imported species, including lovely-smelling

THE GULF – ARABIAN OR PERSIAN?

To avoid causing offence, you must not refer to the body of water off the coast of Dubai as the 'Persian Gulf'. This is an exceptionally sensitive issue in Arab Gulf countries, where the water is definitely, emphatically and categorically called the 'Arabian Gulf', even if the rest of world, including the UN, disagrees.

The term 'Persian Gulf' is banned in Dubai. It is ripped out of school textbooks and crossed out on maps (as is the word 'Israel'), and any newspaper or magazine using these words by mistake can expect to be severely reprimanded. Even historical maps in the city's museums have been altered so the original inscription of 'Persian Gulf' isn't legible.

It's an equally sensitive issue in Iran, which banned the *National Geographic* for using the term 'Arabian Gulf' on a map, although it was in parenthesis below a much larger 'Persian Gulf'. They even banned *The Economist* for using the neutral term 'The Gulf'. Tech-savvy Iranians have also taken their battle to the internet. Do a Google search for 'Arabian Gulf', click on the first result, and you'll see what we mean.

eucalypts. The sandy desert surrounding the city supports wild grasses and the occasional date-palm oasis. In the salty scrublands further down the coast you might spot the desert hyacinth emerging in all its glory after the rains. It has bright yellow and deep-red dappled flowers.

Decorating the flat plains that stretch away from the foothills of the Hajar Mountains, near Hatta, are different species of flat-topped acacia trees. The *ghaf* also grows in this area; this big tree looks a little like a weeping willow and is incredibly hardy, as its roots stretch down for about 30m, allowing it to tap into deep water reserves. The tree is highly respected in the Arab world, as it provides great shade and food for goats and camels; it's also a good indicator that there's water in the surrounding vicinity.

As in any major city, you don't see much wildlife. Urbanisation, combined with zealous hunting, has brought about the virtual extinction of some species. These include the houbara bustard, the striped hyena and the caracal (a cat that resembles a lynx). The Arabian oryx (also called the white oryx), however, is one success story. As part of a programme of the Dubai Desert Conservation Reserve (see the boxed text, p166), it has been successfully reintroduced.

On the fringes of the city, where the urban sprawl gives way to the desert, you may see a desert fox, sand cat or falcon if you are very lucky. Otherwise, the only animals you are likely to encounter are camels and goats. The desert is also home to various reptile species, including the desert monitor lizard (up to a metre long), the sand skink, the spiny-tailed agama and several species of gecko. The only poisonous snakes are vipers, such as the sawscaled viper, which can be recognised by its distinctive triangular head. There are even two remarkably adapted species of toad, which hibernate for years between floods burrowed deep in wadis.

The city is a hot spot for bird-watchers; because of the spread of irrigation and greenery, the number and variety of birds is growing. Dubai is on the migration path between Europe, Asia and Africa, and more than 320 migratory species pass through in the spring and autumn, or spend the winter here. The city's parks, gardens and golf courses sustain quite large populations, and on any day up to 80 different species can be spotted. Species native to Arabia include the crab plover, the Socotra cormorant, the black-crowned finch lark and the purple sunbird.

Artificial nests have been built to encourage flamingos to breed at the Dubai Wildlife & Waterbird Sanctuary (p71) at the inland end of Dubai Creek. In addition to flamingos, ducks, marsh harriers, spotted eagles, broad-billed sandpipers and ospreys all call the sanctuary home – for bird-watchers, this place is a must-visit.

The waters off Dubai teem with around 300 different types of fish. Diners will be most familiar with the hammour, a species of groper, but the Gulf is also home to an extraordinary range of tropical fish and several species of small sharks. Green turtles and hawksbill turtles used to nest in numbers on Dubai's beaches, but today their nesting sites are restricted to islands. Although you won't see them around Dubai, the coastal waters around Abu Dhabi are home to the Gulf's biggest remaining population of dugongs, where they feed off sea grasses in the shallow channels between islands.

PROGRESS & SUSTAINABILITY

There's no shortage of sand in Dubai, so converting it into islands that cost several million dollars each is a very profitable venture. But environmentalists have argued that Dubai's offshore projects such as the Palm Islands and The World may be causing considerable long-term damage. To create The World, around 33 million cubic metres of sand and shell from the seabed of the Gulf has been dredged and redistributed. Critics claim that this work has damaged the marine environment, with dredging destroying the seabed and plumes of sediment from the construction wrecking fragile coral reefs.

The developers, Nakheel, claim to take environmental matters seriously and employ marine biologists to monitor the reefs. They insist the artificial reefs they're creating, which will include sunken wrecks to entertain divers, will provide a calm environment that sea life can thrive in. The shelter created by the 11km-long breakwater at the Palm Jumeirah, they assert, has resulted in many species of fish returning to the area.

Structures such as the Burj Dubai and Ski Dubai have been criticised for the amount of energy they require to operate, but happily there seem to be more environmentally conscious constructions appearing on the horizon. The world's first rotating tower, 55° Time Dubai, will be powered by solar panels and use recycled water. The Iris Bay tower, meanwhile, will draw in air at night, cool it with water and distribute it as an alternative to energy-sapping air-conditioning systems. A third project, the Burj Al-Taqa (Energy Tower) will use wind turbines and solar panels to produce all its own energy. Dubai could do worse than look to Abu Dhabi for inspiration, because Masdar City will be the world's first carbon-neutral city. Solar panels will provide power for the community of 15,000 people.

Dubai consumes resources at a much faster rate than it can replace them, which is why its ecological footprint is so high (see the boxed text, p37). It won't be easy to reverse the trend and achieve environmental sustainability because the UAE relies so heavily on imported goods. Nearly everything on the supermarket shelves is expensively flown in, and most of what you'll eat in restaurants has been transported from overseas too. There are a few farms in the UAE (including a couple of organic pioneers), but in a country where the economy – and the local mentality – is so urbanised, it will take some effort to entice UAE nationals or expatriates to work in the agricultural sector to lessen the nation's dependency on imported goods. The labour force is also imported, as are the millions of tourists who drive the economy. With the world's biggest airport opening soon in Jebel Ali, Dubai's dependency on aviation, the single greatest cause of climate change, is unlikely to wane.

There will always be a huge demand for air conditioning in such a hot climate. (For information on Dubai's climate, see p182.) Future residential buildings are likely to be more energy efficient, but people have to become less wasteful too, and switch off the air conditioning when they're not at home. At 133 gallons per day, the UAE has the highest per capita rate of water consumption in the world, and rainfall is infrequent. The government has vowed to cut the water consumption rate in half by 2012. Most of the UAE's tap water is desalinated, an expensive and energy-intensive process, but necessary to convert seawater into water clean enough to drink.

THE CREATION OF A METROPOLIS

It may have taken Dubai a little longer than other major cities to get its own metro system, but let's keep a sense of perspective: until the 1960s donkeys and camels provided the only transport around town. As is the case today, *abras* (water taxis) were used to transport people across the Creek. The first roads were only built in the 1960s.

The development of a modern infrastructure started long before the discovery of oil in 1966, although this was the principal catalyst for rapid growth. The first bank, the British Bank of the Middle East, was established in 1946, and when Al-Maktoum Hospital was built in 1949 it was the only centre for modern medical care on the Trucial Coast until well into the 1950s. When Sheikh Rashid officially came to power in 1958, he set up the first Municipal Council and established a police force and basic infrastructure, such as electricity and water supply.

Construction of the airport began in 1958 and the British Overseas Airways Corporation (BOAC) and Middle East Airlines (MEA) launched regular flights to Dubai soon after. Even after oil revenues began coming in, trade remained the foundation of the city's wealth, though oil has contributed to trade profits and encouraged modernisation since its discovery. Work on the Port Rashid complex began in 1967, after it became obvious that the growing maritime traffic could no longer be managed by the existing facilities, and was completed in 1972. The mid-1970s saw the start of a massive programme of industrialisation, resulting in the construction of Jebel Ali Port, the largest artificial port in the world, and the adjacent industrial centre, which was to become a free-trade zone.

It remains to be seen whether the Dubai Metro persuades a large number of people to ditch their private vehicles in favour of public transport. The government is also looking into opening more bus routes and introducing solar-powered *abras* in the future.

ENVIRONMENTAL AWARENESS

There is a disturbing lack of environmental awareness in Dubai. You will often see rubbish left on beaches, in parks or thrown out of car windows. As a result, an enormous number of workers are employed to make sure the rubbish on the streets doesn't stay around to sully the city's image, and the municipality has slapped a Dh500 fine on littering. But people are also throwing rubbish out of car windows in the nearby desert. A trail of plastic bags, soft drink cans and water bottles are scattered along the edge of the sands.

Recycling continues to be a fringe activity. The Emirates Environmental Group (www.eeg-uae.org) has opened a number of recycling centres around the city (see p18), but these are not always in convenient locations or in the best condition. With the emirate's landfill sites struggling to cope with demand, the government is building an integrated waste-management facility, Dubai Recycling Park, due to open in 2009.

It's estimated that a third of the cars on Dubai's roads are sports utility vehicles (SUVs), which are famed for their capacity to guzzle gas. But petrol is very cheap and many expatriates like to have a big car for reassurance on Dubai's volatile roads. Many drivers, of course, require four-wheel drive vehicles for their off-road leisure pursuits.

While some Dubai residents come from countries where the environment isn't a pressing concern, far too many others are well-informed on the topic of global warming but stop recycling after moving to the emirate. This may be because the facilities are inconveniently located, or perhaps because they're not concerned about the long-term health of a city they're only living in temporarily.

BUILDING THE BRAND

When the Burj Al Arab project was announced, it was a clear message that Dubai meant business; that it would face the challenge of dwindling oil supplies with ambition, innovation and courage. Opening the world's tallest hotel was a marketing masterstroke. Another was publicising a journalist's hyperbole that the Burj was the world's first 'seven star hotel'. The hotel's management never claimed they'd magically exceeded the five-star limit, but they were happy to let the misconception spread and Dubai suddenly became *the* luxury tourism destination. The Burj Al Arab hosted Dubai's greatest publicity stunt to date, when in 2005 tennis stars Roger Federer and Andre Agassi were invited to exchange a few rallies on the tower's helipad. The following day images from the resulting photo shoot appeared on the front pages of newspapers around the world.

Dubai has been very successful at building its brand identity, although the nature of this identity depends on where you're viewing it from. In the Indian subcontinent the city wants to be seen as a land of opportunity, a place where people can make money and pursue their ambitions. In Europe, Dubai's a brave new world, a sun-soaked paradise free of the scourges of bureaucracy, rain clouds and income tax. And in the Middle East, Dubai projects itself as an all too rare Arab success story: a model Muslim state that proves Islam and modernity are fully compatible.

Yet Dubai's proud Islamic identity may be an obstacle when it comes to establishing a strong business relationship with the US. The news that DP World (owned by the Dubai government), through their purchase of P&O, would take control of the management of six American ports triggered a national debate in the States. Opponents of the deal said it created a security risk, implying that Dubai has links with terrorists. A period of intense, and arguably Islamophobic, debate followed. Articles appeared in the US press about the two Emirati 9/11 hijackers and about how Dubai banks transferred funds to the terrorists in Florida, all suggesting that DP World couldn't be trusted. The US Senate threatened to block the takeover and DP World retreated.

The UAE-USA relationship has been further tested by a class-action lawsuit filed by American lawyers against the Dubai royal family. A case alleging that Sheikh Mohammed is partly responsible for the abduction and trafficking of thousands of children to be used as camel jockeys was dismissed by a Miami court, but the case was later refiled in Kentucky – where the Maktoums own stables – against Dubai's deputy ruler, Sheikh Hamdan.

Despite the occasional setback, the Dubai marketing machine shows no sign of slowing down. Tiger Woods has followed in the footsteps of Roger and Andre and hit golf balls off the helipad at the Burj Al Arab; Arsenal play their Premier League football at the Emirates Stadium in London, and 'Dubai Towers' will soon open in Doha, Qatar and Istanbul, Turkey.

DUBAI'S ECOLOGICAL FOOTPRINT

Dubai's transformation from a small town into a major metropolis in the space of a few decades has been remarkable. But such rapid expansion has inevitably had a negative impact on the environment.

According to the World Wildlife Fund (WWF), the United Arab Emirates is the least environmentally friendly country in the world. The WWF measures the ecological footprint of countries by calculating how many global hectares – an area of biologically productive land or sea – is required to sustain the average person. According to their 2006 'Living Planet' report, the average person in the UAE requires the equivalent of 11.9 global hectares, compared to 9.6 in the United States and a global average of 2.2.

The good news is that something is being done about a problem that threatens to embarrass the city. Soon after the WWF's report was released, the government launched an initiative called *Al Basma Al Beeiya* (ecological footprint), which set out a plan for both the public and private sector to make a greater effort to work towards sustainable development.

Being environmentally responsible in Dubai can be a challenge. Many offices don't have recycling bins for waste paper, newspapers routinely come wrapped in plastic for no apparent reason, it's impossible to live without air conditioning for half the year, and efforts to re-use plastic bags in supermarkets are nearly always greeted by bemused stares.

Local Environmental Organisations

The Federal Environmental Agency legislates on environmental issues and encourages communication on these issues between the emirates. There are also a number of NGOs concerned with the environment.

Emirates Diving Association (☎ 393 9390; www.emiratesdiving.com) This association is an active participant in local environmental campaigns, with an emphasis on the marine environment.

Emirates Environmental Group (☎ 344 8622; www.eeg-uae.org) This group organises educational programmes in schools and businesses as well as community programmes, such as clean-up drives.

MEDIA
NEWSPAPERS

A few years ago the front pages of the local newspapers were reassuringly familiar. A sheikh said something wise, had a successful meeting or received a message of congratulations and hardly a day went by without a call for Arab unity in the op-ed columns. As an ever-increasing number of journalists leave countries with a free press to work in Dubai, this situation is slowly improving, although critical coverage of the government remains off-limits.

The most reliable local English-language broadsheet is the *Gulf News* (www.gulfnews.com), which despite being toothless in its domestic reporting, features solid coverage of the Middle East and the Indian subcontinent. Its publisher, Al Nisr, also produces *Xpress* (www.xpress4me.com). In spite of its chatty, informal style and irritatingly spelt name, the weekly paper occasionally publishes stories other newspapers won't touch, such as investigating racist door policies at nightclubs (see boxed text, p31).

The other major English-language broadsheet is the *Khaleej Times* (www.khaleejtimes.com), which until recently had been a relatively independent voice in Dubai media, although its credibility was constantly undermined by dismal writing, spelling mistakes and factual errors. It's now partly government-owned and avoids contentious issues. Its strapline, 'The Truth Must Be Told', is a regular source of amusement for resident cynics.

The government also owns the Arab Media Group, which publishes *Emirates Business 24/7* (www.business24-7.ae), the UAE's first business newspaper. The paper used to be known as *Emirates Today,* which after a lively start changed management, lost dozens of journalists and rapidly gained a reputation for being a government mouthpiece. The best free newspaper is still *7 Days* (www.7days.ae), although after some high-profile scraps with rival publications and a major distributor it seems to have lost its edge. Amusingly published six days a week,

7 Days is still worth a read for its frequently entertaining letters page.

If you're after something more internationally minded, both the *Times* and the *Financial Times* publish Middle East editions. Todaily (www.todaily.com) print same-day editions of many international newspapers including the *Guardian*, *Daily Telegraph*, *Le Monde* and *Sydney Morning Herald* – these are usually available in branches of Carrefour.

MAGAZINES

You'll find dozens of English-language magazines that have been locally produced on the shelves of Dubai's shops. In a city so flush with cash, the magazines with famous names rarely struggle to find advertisers willing to splash out on expensive spreads. The most popular magazines are the titles imported from Europe. ITP, the region's biggest publisher, makes Dubai editions of *Grazia*, *Time Out*, *L'Officiel* and *Harper's Bazaar*, while Motivate puts out an ultra-gossipy local version of *Hello!* and an electronics mag *Stuff*.

top picks

LOCAL MAGS

- *Ahlan!* Dubai's even gossipier version of *Hello!*
- *Bidoun* Cutting-edge art and culture from the Arab diaspora.
- *Time Out Dubai* Local news, event previews and punchy food reviews.
- *Identity* A stylish interior design and property magazine.
- *Soura* A showcase for work by young Arab photographers.

ONLINE

While all the major newspapers and magazines have an online presence, bloggers are making the biggest impact. Websites such as Secret Dubai (www.secretdubai.blogspot.com), An Emirati's Thoughts (www.aethoughts.blogspot.com) and The Emirates Economist (www.emirateseconomist.blogspot.com) often cover topics the mainstream press steer clear of. While *Secret Dubai* has a large following, and its comments pages host some of the bitterest debates in the city, it also has its detractors with many arguing that it isn't respectful enough to the local culture. Secret Dubai was briefly blocked in 2005 by the state internet proxy, a decision overturned after a public outcry. More recently, the entertaining *Sex and Dubai* blog was banned, owing to its frequently risqué content.

THE CENSORSHIP QUESTION

The mechanics of censorship in Dubai are complex and ill-defined. All journalists working in Dubai know that some topics, such as criticism of the UAE's rulers or anything that could be perceived as negative treatment of Islam, are completely off-limits. It's also perilous to write about sex, drugs, alcohol, homosexuality or Israel. At other times the line isn't so clear. Can journalists write about prostitution, domestic violence, human trafficking or drug addiction in the emirate? Possibly, but very few, if any, Dubai editors are prepared to take the risk. Most follow the golden rule – don't write anything negative about Dubai if you want to keep your job.

It's usually self-censorship, rather than direct government interference, that hinders press freedom in Dubai, although the fear of reprisals is very real. Journalists should no longer be sent to prison, though. Hours after two *Khaleej Times* reporters were sentenced to prison for libel in 2007, Sheikh Mohammed issued a pardon and declared that journalists should not be jailed for reasons relating to their work.

Sometimes the authorities order publishers to withdraw offending publications from circulation, but such direct interference is uncommon. In most cases, journalists and editors (many of whom work for government-owned publications) self-censor because their publishers' profit margins are threatened. A publication that upsets the wrong people can soon expect its revenue to dwindle, as so many major advertisers are wholly or partly government-owned, while private companies may fear the repercussions of associating with the wrong people. In other cases, a publisher may find its distributors suddenly pull the plug, or that their license to print a certain title is revoked.

In a democracy, journalists are expected to scrutinise the activities of government and hold it to account. But the UAE is not a democracy, and the vast majority of journalists are guests in Dubai. While the media tries to get its collective head around the emirate's nebulous press-freedom laws, a wider debate about whether Western journalists have the right to impose their values on a culture unused to transparency and openness rages on.

TELEVISION

Dubai isn't a city accustomed to playing catch-up, but when it comes to TV news in the Gulf, Qatar has stolen a march on the opposition. Al Jazeera is the most popular news network in the Arab World and its English-language service has helped put this small country on the map.

While Dubai's rulers, unlike their Qatari counterparts, haven't bankrolled a home-grown media superpower, they have attracted many of the big names in the broadcasting world to set up Middle East headquarters at Dubai Media City. CNN, Reuters, CNBC, BBC World and Showtime Arabia are all residents. Media City is meant to be free of government intervention, hence its motto 'Freedom to Create'. But this isn't always the case. In November 2007, two private Media City–based Pakistani news channels, Geo News and Ary One World, were temporarily shut down by Dubai authorities, presumably at the request of the Pakistani government

There are a few English-language TV channels in Dubai, although only a couple – the amateurish City 7 (www.city7tv.com) and Dubai One (www.dubaione.ae) – produce their own shows.

ARCHITECTURE

Surprisingly, for a city with few buildings older than 100 years, the economic boom of the last 30 years has left it an architectural mishmash. But the incongruous blend of traditional Arabian architecture with modern constructions straight out of science fiction make the city a remarkable sight. A boat ride along the Creek takes you from the wind-tower houses in the Bastakia Quarter of Bur Dubai to the pointed dhowlike roof of the Dubai Creek Golf & Yacht Club, via the sail-like National Bank of Dubai. As you'll notice, these modern structures sit comfortably with the traditional architecture of the cosmopolitan city, its contrast representative of other juxtapositions in Dubai – East and West, old and new. Interestingly, much of the city's recent architecture, such as Madinat Jumeirah (but also private residences), sees a return to traditional Arabian forms, although projects such as Burj Dubai show that the cloud-busting skyscraper isn't going anywhere in Dubai but up.

TRADITIONAL ARCHITECTURE

On your wanderings around the city, you'll notice that Dubai's traditional architecture consists of essentially four types of buildings – domestic (residential homes), religious (mosques), defensive (forts and watchtowers) and commercial (souqs). Readily available materials, such as gypsum and coral from offshore reefs and from the banks of the Creek, were put to use. The Sheikh Saeed Al-Maktoum House (p66) in Shindagha is a fine example of this kind of construction. Limestone building blocks were also used and mud cemented the stones together. However, mud constructions suffered badly in the heat and had a limited lifespan, sometimes only a few years. Interestingly, the dimensions of buildings were often governed by the length of timber, mainly from India or East Africa, that could be loaded onto a *dhow*. There were two types of traditional house – the *masayf*, a summer house incorporating a wind-tower, and the *mashait*, a winter house with a courtyard. You'll see both of these in the Bastakia Quarter (p61).

When you explore the lanes surrounding Bur Dubai Souq (p66) and behind Al-Ahmadiya School (p58) in Deira, you'll see that the alleyways are narrow and the buildings close together. The lanes are narrow to increase the velocity of wind, keeping the neighbourhood cooler, while houses, souqs and mosques were built close together to provide maximum shade so that inhabitants could move around town in comfort, protected from the harsh sun.

Wind-towers

Wind-towers, or *barjeel* in Arabic, are the Gulf's unique form of nonmechanical air-conditioning, and scores of original wind-

> ### HOT CONVERSATION TOPICS
>
> When will the bubble burst?
> Where have all the taxis gone?
> Is the ban on outdoor music destroying Dubai's nightlife?
> Why didn't I buy a house five years ago?
> Could local radio get any worse?
> Will we ever be allowed to use Skype in the UAE?
> Who's the better chef: Gordon Ramsay or Gary Rhodes?
> Will the government abandon the dollar peg?

DUBAI'S NOTABLE BUILDINGS

Burj Al Arab (p75) The Burj was completed in 1999, and is set on an artificial island 300m from the shore. The 60-floor, sail-shaped structure is 321m high. A translucent fibreglass wall serves as a shield from the desert sun during the day and a screen for an impressive light show each night. Until the Burj Dubai arrived on the scene to steal its thunder, it was *the* iconic symbol of Dubai.

Burj Dubai (Map pp72–3) To retain an edge over rival skyscrapers, developers Emaar chose to keep the final height of the Burj Dubai under wraps for as long as possible. Upon completion, it will be at least 700m tall, easily surpassing the 555m CN Tower in Toronto, and it could even rise above the 800m mark. Adrian Smith, the American architect responsible for the Burj's cloud-tickling design, claims that the tower's geometric shapes and spirals are directly influenced by traditional Islamic architecture.

Dubai Creek Golf & Yacht Club (p144) When you cross the bridges over the Creek, you'll notice the pointed white roof of the clubhouse set amid artificial, undulating hillocks. The idea behind this 1993 design was to incorporate a traditional element – the white sails of a *dhow* – into the form and style of the building, and while this motif is becoming overused now, it's ageing well.

Dusit Dubai (p158) Sheikh Zayed Rd features many modern skyscrapers, but few are as eye-catching as this one. The 153m-high building has an inverted 'Y' shape – two pillars that join to form a tapering tower. It's supposed to evoke the Thai joined-hands gesture of greeting, appropriate for this Thai hotel chain, but looks more like a giant tuning fork.

Emirates Towers (p158) Designed in an ultramodern internationalist style, the twin, triangular, gunmetal-grey towers on Sheikh Zayed Rd soar from an oval base and are among the world's tallest. The taller of the two (355m) houses offices, while the other (305m) is a hotel. Balanced by the curvilinear base structure, the curved motif is also repeated in the upper storeys of the buildings. Perhaps the best-loved building in the city.

Jumeirah Beach Hotel (p160) This long S-shaped construction represents a wave, with the Gulf as its backdrop. The glimmering façades of the hotel and its close neighbour, the Burj Al Arab, are achieved by the use of reflective glass and aluminium. The two structures combined – a huge sail hovering over a breaking wave – symbolise Dubai's maritime heritage.

National Bank of Dubai (Map pp54–5) This shimmering building off Baniyas Rd in Deira, overlooking the Creek, has become another quintessential symbol of Dubai. Designed by Carlos Ott and completed in 1997, it combines simple shapes to represent a *dhow* with a sail billowing. The bronze windows reflect the activity on the Creek and at sunset, when the light is just right, it's a beautiful sight.

World Trade Centre (Map pp72–3) As soon as rumours started to spread that they might pull down Dubai's beloved first skyscraper, built in 1979, everyone started to reappraise the city's first icon. The kind of structure *Wallpaper** likes to do photo spreads on – its beehive-like exterior is a form of sun-shading. But who knows how much time it has left?

---

towers still exist in Bastakia (p61). Traditional wind-towers, rising 5m or 6m above a house, are open on all four sides to catch the breezes, which are channelled down around a central shaft and into the room below. In the process, the air speeds up and is cooled. The cooler air already in the tower shaft pulls in, and subsequently cools the hotter air outside through simple convection. It works amazingly well. Sitting beneath a wind-tower when it's a humid 40°C, you'll notice a distinct drop in temperature and a consistent breeze even when the air outside feels heavy and still. Test out the one at Dubai Museum (p61).

The wealthy Persian merchants who settled in Dubai around the beginning of the 20th century were the first to build a large number of wind-towers in Bastakia. In some houses the tallest wind-tower was above the master bedroom, while smaller wind-towers cooled the living rooms. The merchants brought red clay from Iran, which they mixed with manure to make *saruj*. This was baked in a kiln and used to build the foundations of the wind-tower house. Other materials included coral rock and limestone for the walls and plaster for decorative work. The walls were built as thick as 60cm, so the house could be extended upwards if the family expanded. Chandel wood from East Africa, palm-frond matting, mud and straw were used to build the roofs.

Courtyard Houses

Houses in Dubai were traditionally built around a central courtyard. The courtyard, known as *al-housh* in Arabic, was the heart and lungs of a house. All the rooms of the traditional house surrounded the courtyard and all doors and windows opened onto it, except those of the guest rooms, which opened to the outside of the house. A veranda provided shade, kept sun out of rooms at certain times of the day, and was usually the place where the women did weaving and sewing. For great examples of courtyard houses, visit the Heritage House (p58) in Deira or XVA (p68) in Bastakia.

Barasti

Barasti describes both the traditional Arabian method of building a palm-leaf house and the completed house itself. *Barasti* houses are made from a skeleton of wooden poles (date-palm trunks) onto which *areesh* (palm leaves) are woven to form a strong structure through which air can still circulate. They were extremely common throughout the Gulf in the centuries before the oil boom, though few examples of this type of house survive today. They were relatively easy to build and maintain since, unlike the mud-brick houses you find in the oases around Al-Ain and Buraimi, their construction didn't require water. The circulation of air through the palms also made *barasti* houses much cooler than mud-brick ones during the summer. The courtyard in the Dubai Museum (p61) and the Heritage Village (p67) in Shindagha both contain examples of *barasti* houses.

Mosques

Fundamentally simple structures, mosques are made up of a few basic elements which are easy to identify. The most visible of these is the minaret, the tower from which the call to prayer is broadcast five times a day. Virtually every mosque in the world has a minaret; many have several. The first minarets were not built until the early 8th century, some 70 years after the Prophet's death. The idea may have originated from the bell towers that Muslim armies found attached to some of the churches they converted into mosques during the early years of Islam. The more minarets on a mosque, the more important it is. No mosque has more than seven minarets, the number on the Grand Mosque in Mecca.

A mosque must also have a *mihrab*, a niche in the wall facing Mecca, indicating the *qibla*, the direction believers must face while praying. *Mihrabs* were thought to have been introduced

BACKGROUND ARCHITECTURE

THE FIVE PILLARS OF ISLAM

Islam is the official religion of Dubai and the majority of Emiratis are Sunni Muslims. Many of Dubai's expatriates also practice Islam, and in some parts of town, mosques have largely Pakistani congregations. The diversity of Dubai's large expatriate population means most other religions are also represented.

Shahadah The profession of faith: 'There is no god but God, and Mohammed is the messenger of God.'

Salat Muslims are required to pray five times every day: at dawn (*fajr*), noon (*dhuhr*), mid-afternoon (*asr*), sunset (*maghrib*) and twilight (*isha'a*). Loudspeakers on the minarets of mosques transmit the call to prayer (*adhan*) at these times, and you can expect to be woken up at dawn if your hotel is situated in the cluttered streets of Deira or Bur Dubai. During prayers a Muslim must perform a series of prostrations while facing the Kaaba, the ancient shrine at the centre of the Grand Mosque in Mecca. Before a Muslim can pray, however, he or she must perform a series of ritual ablutions, and if water isn't available for this, sand or soil can be substituted.

Zakat Muslims must give a portion of their income to help the poor. How this has operated in practice has varied over the centuries: either it was seen as an individual duty (as is the case in Dubai) or the state collected it as a form of income tax to be redistributed through mosques or religious charities.

Sawm It was during the month of Ramadan that Mohammed received his first revelation in AD 610. Muslims mark this event by fasting from sunrise until sunset throughout Ramadan. During the fast a Muslim may not take anything into his or her body. Food, drink, smoking and sex are forbidden. Young children, travellers and those whose health will not allow it are exempt from the fast, though those who are able to do so are supposed to make up the days they missed at a later time.

Haj All able Muslims are required to make the pilgrimage to Mecca at least once, if possible during a specific few days in the first and second weeks of the Muslim month of Dhul Hijja, although visiting Mecca and performing the prescribed rituals at any other time of the year is also considered spiritually desirable. Such visits are referred to as *umrah*, or 'little pilgrimages'.

into Islamic architecture around the beginning of the 8th century, and like minarets they can be simple or elaborate. The *minbar,* a pulpit chair traditionally reached by three steps, dates from the Prophet's lifetime.

Mosques need to have a water supply so that worshippers can perform the *wudu* or ablutions required before they begin praying. Neighbourhood mosques in Dubai are visited five times a day for prayers, with worshippers travelling further afield to larger mosques for Friday prayers.

The Jumeirah Mosque (p75) is based on the Anatolian style, identified by a massive central dome, while other mosques in Dubai are based on Iranian and Central Asian models, which have more domes covering different areas of the mosque. Shiite mosques are identifiable by their exquisite green and blue faience tile work covering the façades and main dome. One stunning example is the Iranian Mosque (p79) on Al-Wasl Rd, while the multidomed Grand Mosque (p67) in Bur Dubai is a variation on the Anatolian style.

MODERN ARCHITECTURE

In contrast to the traditional architecture that was all about function over form, and was built for the environment, modern architecture in Dubai (until recently) has embraced an 'anything goes' ethos with complete disregard to the climate. About 90% of Dubai's architecture can be described as cosmopolitan or international and is built using concrete, steel and glass. However, many architects have recently started to question the thinking behind building glass towers in a country with extreme heat. The huge cooling costs alone are reason to go for designs that better respond to and integrate with the weather and surroundings. Because these cosmopolitan materials absorb heat and transfer it to other parts of the construction, they also cause damage over time. As a result, hi-tech, state-of-the-art materials with greater heat resistance are now starting to be used. Certainly some of the newer housing developments are doing so. Other developments, such as the Jumeirah Beach Residence, consist of dozens of high-rise towers.

Designs that are ageing well – and plenty aren't – are usually the ones produced by established architects, such as Carlos Ott (National Bank of Dubai building). While most of Dubai's new buildings have been designed by international firms, the most significant local architect-designers happen to be members of the Sharjah royal family. Sisters Sheikha Mai and Sheikha Wafa al-Qasimini set up their own company, Ibtikari (Arabic for 'my innovation') in 2001 in association with a British architect. Their commissions include both interior design (check out Amzaan boutique, p96) and architecture.

ARTS

British satirist Rory Bremner once said that going to Dubai for its culture was like going 'to Tibet in search of nightlife'. It's really not quite that bad. It will be many years before Dubai can compete with the major European cities when it comes to music, theatre, art, literature and film, but progress is being made.

VISUAL ARTS

At the turn of the millennium there were only a handful of galleries in Dubai, most of which offered little more than clichéd watercolours of Arabian horses, camels and the like. Within the space of a few years, the city has become a focal point for contemporary Arabic and Persian art. With customary foresight, Dubai's decision-makers have recognised the potential of the art market in the region and gone all out to make sure it doesn't miss a trick.

top picks

DUBAI ARTS EXPERIENCES

- B21 Progressive Art Gallery (p71) As close to the cutting-edge as you'll find in Dubai. Controversial exhibitions by the likes of Iranian photographer Shadi Ghadirian have caused quite a stir.
- Meem Gallery (p71) Mishal Kanoo's smart Al-Quoz space focusing on contemporary Islamic art.
- 1x1 Art Space (p80) The only gallery in Dubai dedicated to showing Indian art.
- The Third Line (p71) Exhibits adventurous, provocative and playful work with an emphasis on female Arab photographers and mixed-media artists.
- XVA (p68) A wonderful art gallery, laid-back café, boutique hotel and film club nestled in the wind-towers of Bastakia.

The inaugural Gulf Art Fair in 2007, retitled Art Dubai the following year, brought gallerists, artists and dealers from around the world to the plush setting of Madinat Jumeirah to talk business. Dubai's location at the crossroads of the Middle East, the Indian subcontinent and Africa, has helped it become an art industry hub. But it's also Dubai's relative openness that makes it such an attractive location for artists hoping to show their work. All the usual taboos, including anything that could be construed as criticism of Dubai, remain off limits. Nudity is a no-no, but Dubai is still more open than cities such as Tehran and Damascus, where some of the artists come from. Major exhibitions at venues such as the British Museum have fuelled a keen interest in Middle Eastern contemporary art, and Dubai is a lot more accessible to Western dealers than other cities in the region.

Although Dubai's art boom is being propelled mainly by commerce, rather than creativity, there are signs that ordinary residents of the city are becoming more interested in the art world. Much of the credit for the invigoration of the art scene goes to Sheikha Hoor al-Qasimi, Director of the Sharjah International Biennial, who excited art lovers once again with a vibrant 8th Biennial in 2007. On the theme of 'Art, Ecology and the Politics of Change', 80 artists from around the world put on an engaging and challenging show. Another biennial is scheduled to take place in April 2009.

Perhaps the most surprising thing about Dubai's sudden enthusiasm for art is the development of an art district, tucked away in the otherwise uninviting Al-Quoz area. This featureless congregation of industrial estates along the edge of Sheikh Zayed Rd is home to several cutting-edge galleries including B21 (p71), The Third Line (p71) and Meem Gallery (p71). Art isn't part of the school curriculum in the Emirates and is rarely written about in the Arabic-language press, but it is hoped that these galleries, along with events such as Art Dubai, will inspire a new generation of home-grown artists.

For its second outing in 2008, Art Dubai doubled in size, hosting close to 70 galleries from around the world. Although it's certainly put Dubai on the art map, it's been criticised for being too industry-focused and not doing enough to stimulate a grassroots art movement in the region. Several Dubai galleries (including some that don't participate in the main fair) take part in an annual fringe event, the Creek Contemporary Art Fair. Organised by the evergreen XVA (p68), the Creek Fair pools together the city's independent galleries to give visitors a more representative taste of the city's art scene.

Dubai isn't the only place in the Gulf experiencing an upsurge in art interest. The Qatari government has funded a Museum of Islamic Art in Doha, while Abu Dhabi is opening branches of the Guggenheim and the Louvre on Saadiyat Island. This ambitious and hugely expensive endeavour (the emirate is rumoured to have paid US$1 billion for the Louvre's name, expertise and paintings) leaves Abu Dhabi open to a charge you could also direct at Dubai: that it's spending millions of dollars on importing culture while home-grown artists receive no help at all. Only a tiny percentage of the artists who exhibit in Dubai were raised in the Emirates and there are no government-funded galleries in the country.

CINEMA

The history of Emirati feature films, for the time being, starts and ends with a single movie. Hani al-Shabani's *Al Hilm* (The Dream) was a light-hearted drama about a young writer's struggle to produce a script and a film, and reflected the challenges many aspiring Emirati filmmakers face. It took until 2005 to produce this single feature-length film. Now there is a small but committed group of Emirati filmmakers planning to follow it up with bigger and better features.

While the Dubai International Film Festival (www.dubaifilmfest.com) is arguably the city's cultural highlight of the year, it has been criticised in the past for being preoccupied with Hollywood stars and for not doing enough to cultivate local talent. This is beginning to change. The 2007 festival featured a new segment, Emirati Voices, which featured nine short films by local directors.

Emirati filmmaking talents have had other opportunities to have their work screened. The Emirates Film Competition (www.efilmc.com) has taken place annually since 2001 and offers cash awards and places at the Abu Dhabi Film Academy to Emiratis who make short films that successfully represent the culture and heritage of the country. The Mini Film Festival (named for its car-making sponsors and not for the length of its films) accepts shorts from across the region and is held every December,

DUBAI INTERNATIONAL FILM FESTIVAL

Every December, the Dubai International Film Festival delivers a much-needed dose of culture to the city's blockbuster-weary cinemagoers. Launched in 2004, the festival has two main aims: to create cultural bridges and promote understanding, tolerance and peace; and to develop Dubai as a regional film hub. While some residents have complained that the organisers have an unhealthy obsession with luring star names onto their red carpets (Morgan Freeman, Oliver Stone, Orlando Bloom and Sharon Stone have all visited), there's no questioning the quality of the programming. The 2007 festival saw critically acclaimed movies such as *The Diving Bell and the Butterfly* and *No Country for Old Men* screened several months before their release dates in Europe, while the categories established to promote the region's filmmaking talents – Arabian Nights and Emirati Voices – increase in size and scope every year and give upcoming Dubai directors an opportunity to show their talents off to a wider audience.

and the inaugural Middle East International Film Festival (www.meiff.com), which took place in Abu Dhabi in 2007, incorporated Hayah (www.hayahfilm.com), a short film competition for Emirati filmmakers.

By launching its own film festival, Abu Dhabi hopes to lure Hollywood studios to shoot more movies in the region. Dubai has already hosted George Clooney and *Syriana,* while Abu Dhabi provided the backdrop to Jamie Foxx in *The Kingdom.* Dubai Studio City offers world-class production facilities and it seems likely that more American crews will shoot in Dubai, especially since so many films about the recent Iraq war are in the pipeline. If Studio City does lure the megabucks of the big studios – and there's already word of a Paramount theme park in Dubai – the hope is that some of the foreign expertise will trickle down to local filmmakers. Film schools in the Emirates have already been established: the Hollywood Film Institute (www.hollywoodindubai.com) in Dubai and the New York Film Academy (www.nyfa.com) in Abu Dhabi.

The main challenge facing filmmakers is lack of funding. Although there's plenty of cash swilling around the Emirates at the moment, funding an independent Emirati film is seen as a huge financial risk when an indigenous film culture barely exists. What the industry needs is a film commission, a script fund, and grants for local talent. Until that happens, your only chance of seeing Emirati films is to visit the country during one of the film festivals.

Aspiring filmmakers also have to contend with the country's unpredictable censorship policies. Scenes involving nudity, drug taking, homosexuality and references to Israel are likely to be chopped. Even though it was filmed in Dubai, *Syriana* was cut so scenes depicting south Asian workers being mistreated didn't make it to emirate screens. Most movies make it through with minor cuts, although some films, such as *Brokeback Mountain,* are handed full bans. Scenes of violence, on the other hand, are very rarely cut.

One way Dubai residents sidestep censorship is by purchasing illegal DVDs, usually imported from Malaysia or China. Piles of counterfeit DVDs can easily be found in the alleyways and basements of Karama, although most people living in Dubai have a 'DVD woman' turn up to their front door twice a week with a bag of pirated goods. Although these discs only work half the time, many people are prepared to spend Dh10 and take the risk. Fighting on behalf of the film industry is the Arabian Anti-Piracy Alliance (www.aaa.co.ae), who work with the Dubai authorities to tackle the problem. They're becoming increasingly successful at seizing the discs, and have trained sniffer dogs to help snuff out the problem. Sellers of pirated discs can expect a prison sentence and deportation if caught, with harsher punishments if they're also caught selling pornography.

DANCE

Dubai's contact with East and North African cultures through trade, both seafaring and by camel caravan, has brought many musical and dance influences to the UAE shores. Thus, traditional songs and dances are inspired by the environment – the sea, desert and mountains.

One of the most popular dances is the *liwa,* performed to a rapid tempo and loud drumbeat. Most likely brought to the Gulf by East African slaves, it is traditionally sung in Swahili. Another dance, the *ayyalah,* is a typical Bedouin dance, celebrating the courage, strength and unity of the tribe. The *ayyalah* is performed throughout the Gulf, but the UAE has its own variation, performed to a simple drumbeat. Anywhere between 25 and 200 men stand with their arms linked in two rows facing each other. They wave walking-sticks or swords in front of themselves and sway back and forth, the two rows taking it in turn to sing. It's a war dance and the words expound the virtues of courage and bravery in battle. You can see the dance on video at Dubai Museum (p61).

The instruments used at traditional musical celebrations in Dubai are the same as those used in the rest of the Gulf. The *tamboura*, a harplike instrument, has five strings made of horse gut, which are stretched between a wooden base and a bow-shaped neck. The base is covered with camel skin and the strings are plucked with sheep horns. It has a deep and resonant sound, a little like a bass violin.

A much less sophisticated instrument is the *manior*, a percussion instrument that's played with the body. It's comprised of a belt made of cotton, decorated with dried goats' hooves, which is wrapped around the player who keeps time with the beat of the *tamboura* while dancing. The *mimzar* is a wooden instrument a little like a small oboe, but it delivers a higher-pitched sound, which is haunting and undeniably Middle Eastern.

An unusual instrument and one that you'll often see at song and dance performances is the *habban*, the Arabian bagpipes. Made from a goatskin sack, it has two pipes attached. The sack retains its goat shape and the pipes resemble its front legs. One pipe is used to blow air into the sack and the other produces the sound. The *habban* sounds much the same as the Scottish bagpipes, but is shriller in tone.

The *tabla* is a drum, and has a number of different shapes. It can resemble a bongo drum that is placed on the floor, or it can be a *jasr*, a drum with goatskin at both ends, which is slung around the neck and hit with sticks.

Traditional music and dance is performed spontaneously at weddings, social occasions and family gatherings. You may be lucky to see a performance if you're exploring an Emirati neighbourhood and come across a wedding tent; otherwise you'll have to visit the Heritage Village (p67) or catch a performance during the Dubai Shopping Festival or Summer Surprises.

CONTEMPORARY MUSIC

You won't find much original music in Dubai. You will, however, find plenty of bored-looking cover bands playing 'Hotel California' for the millionth time.

The good news is that a local rock scene is taking shape, albeit at a cripplingly slow pace. Loosely formed around Phride (www.phride.com), a website that connects the Middle East's rock and metal fans, this budding scene has produced a few Dubai bands worth taking notice of. The political ska-punk of Gandhi's Cookbook won't be used in adverts by the Dubai tourist

ARAB POETRY

Just as programmes such as *American Idol* and *The X Factor* dominate TV schedules in Western countries, talent shows get huge viewing figures in the Middle East. But *Millions' Poet*, a widely watched programme made by Abu Dhabi TV, doesn't feature skimpy skirts, temper tantrums or boorish judges. Instead it sees *nabati* poets from across the Arab World compete for a Dh1 million prize.

Nabati, or vernacular poetry, is especially popular in the Gulf. The late Sheikh Zayed, former President of the UAE, and Sheikh Mohammed bin Rashid al-Maktoum, Dubai's ruler, are noted writers in this tradition. The Jebel Ali Palm Island project features small islands shaped out of Sheikh Mohammed's poetry. Many Arabic-language newspapers and magazines publish pages of *nabati* poetry.

In Bedouin culture a facility with poetry and language is greatly prized (even now). A poet who could eloquently praise his own people while pointing out the failures of other tribes was considered a great asset. Modern poets of note from the UAE include Sultan al-Owais, some of whose poems have been translated into English, and Dr Ahmed al-Madani, who wrote in the romantic *baiti* style. Palestinian resistance poets such as Mahmood Darwish and Samih al-Qasim are popular, though traditionalists complain that they have broken with the 16 classical metres of poetry developed by the 8th-century Gulf Arab scholar Al-Khalil bin Ahmed. There are currently over 50 well-known male poets in the UAE who still use the forms of classical Arabic poetry, though they often experiment by combining it with other styles. There are also some well-known female poets, most of who write in *tafila*, or prose.

Emiratis spontaneously recite poetry with their friends, during social occasions, public events and even in shopping centres. Young people publish their own poetry, particularly romantic poems, on websites and in student magazines, and produce documentaries about the Emirati passion for poetic works.

board anytime soon (their EP *In the Cesspool of Culture* wasn't very complimentary about their hometown), while Indiephone produce hyperactive rock. The only Dubai band to break into the mainstream is Abri, a soulful funk outfit fronted by Dubai-born Hamdan Al-Abri. Since releasing their debut album, *Sunchild,* they've shared a stage at the Desert Rhythm festival with Kanye West and Joss Stone, and appeared on the cover of *Time Out Dubai*.

Dance music is a different story, and there are plenty of home-grown (although rarely Emirati) house and techno DJs. The Arabic music you're most likely to hear on the radio is *khaleeji,* the traditional Gulf style, recognisable to those familiar with Arabic pop music. Popular singers include Mohammed Nasser, who had a major hit with 'Ya Bint', and Dubai-born Yaseer Habeeb, the first UAE national to have a hit in Europe and the Middle East.

For information on live music, see p132.

NEIGHBOURHOODS

top picks

- **Dubai Museum** (p61) This low-key museum tells the Dubai story with minimal fuss and plenty of charm.
- **Deira Gold Souq** (p53) All that glitters is gold (and occasionally silver) at this colourful market.
- **Deira Spice Souq** (p53) Just follow your nose to the best buys at this atmospheric souq.
- **Bastakia Quarter** (p61) Get lost in the narrow lanes of Dubai's old town.
- **Jumeirah Mosque** (p75) The only mosque non-Muslims can visit – don't miss the regular guided tours.
- **Burj Al Arab** (p75) The world's most extravagant hotel – you'll either love it or hate it.
- **Al-Ahmadiya School** (p58) This splendid old school building offers a peaceful retreat from the bustle of Deira.
- **Madinat Jumeirah** (p75) A city within a city, the Madinat Jumeirah is a Dubai must-see.
- **Dubai Wildlife & Waterbird Sanctuary** (p71) Head to the flamingo park for a unique skyline view.

What's your recommendation? www.lonelyplanet.com/dubai

NEIGHBOURHOODS

Let's make this absolutely clear. There is no excuse for spending your entire holiday lazing by the pool. It's essential you explore Dubai's sights and no, a trip to the Mall of the Emirates does not count as sightseeing.

Long before it began conquering the desert and the ocean, Dubai centred around the Creek, a 15km inlet that runs through the centre of town. Deira and Bur Dubai hug either side of the Creek and remain the heart and soul of the city. They offer something the megaresorts and gleaming skyscrapers of the new city simply can't provide – real life. For all the billions of dollars spent on making Dubai the greatest show on earth, a five-minute, Dh1 *abra* (water taxi) ride between Deira and Bur Dubai is still the single greatest thrill in the city.

Deira covers Al-Sabkha, the souqs area; Rigga and Al-Mateena, in Deira's centre; and Al-Garhoud, the area between Al-Garhoud Bridge and the airport. Moving from east to west, there are five ways to cross the Creek other than using public transport. There's Al-Shindagha Tunnel, close to the open sea; Al-Maktoum Bridge; the very new Floating Bridge (open 6am to 10pm) near Creekside Park; Al-Garhoud Bridge; and the Business Bay Bridge near Festival City. Despite the widening of Al-Garhoud Bridge, the introduction of two new bridges and a road toll, traffic across the Creek is still terrible, especially from 5pm to 8pm on weekdays.

Bur Dubai takes in the area immediately south of the Creek as far as Al-Dhiyafah Rd, from the sea in the east to Al-Garhoud Bridge in the southwest, including the Shindagha waterfront area; the Bastakia heritage district; busy Karama; and Oud Metha, the area between Al-Maktoum Bridge, Wafi City mall and the Grand Hyatt hotel.

Sheikh Zayed Rd begins at the 2nd Za'abeel Rd, by the edge of Karama and Bur Dubai, and heads southwest towards Jebel Ali as far as Interchange No 4. A throng of iconic skyscrapers including the Emirates Towers, the Shangri-La and the Dusit opened on Sheikh Zayed Rd during Dubai's growth spurt in the late '90s. Also included here is Al-Quoz, an industrial area just off Sheikh Zayed Rd that's home to a growing number of art galleries.

Jumeirah is not to be confused with the hotel group of the same name. It's home to several public beaches, a couple of historical sites and hundreds of luxury villas. The spine of this sprawling area is Jumeirah Rd, which begins by the flagpole at the end of Al-Dhiyafha Rd and runs parallel to the coast for about 16km as far as Al-Sufouh Rd, near Madinat Jumeirah. The road stretches inland a couple of blocks from the sea and takes in a number of areas, including the three Jumeirah areas (logically named 1, 2, 3), Umm Suqeim (1 and 2), Safa, and so on.

We've called the rest of the city New Dubai. This area encompasses everything between the Mall of the Emirates and Jebel Ali, including the Palm Jumeirah and Dubai Marina. With the exception of a few hotels, everything in this area has been built in the last five years and most future developments are happening on this side of town. While Deira and Bur Dubai are best explored by foot, Jumeirah, Sheikh Zayed Rd and New Dubai aren't pedestrian-friendly. If you don't have your own transport and don't want to waste time waiting for taxis, you can go on an organised city tour. For information on the options available, see p187.

> 'Deira and Bur Dubai hug either side of the Creek and remain the heart and soul of the city…a five-minute, Dh1 *abra* (water taxi) ride between Deira and Bur Dubai is still the single greatest thrill'

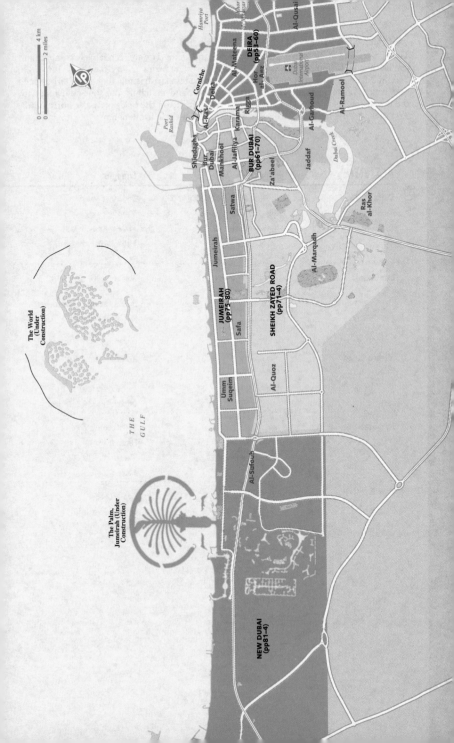

ITINERARY BUILDER

Two days is enough time to explore Bur Dubai and Deira. The area is relatively compact and can be covered by foot, with *abras* (water taxis) or water buses to cross the Creek. Jumeirah, Sheikh Zayed Road and New Dubai are not so pedestrian-friendly and you'll either need to drive or take taxis. While it's fascinating to mix-and-match the old souqs of Deira with the beach resorts of New Dubai, the rush-hour traffic on the bridges can be horrendous, so it makes sense to stick to one side of the Creek at these times of day.

AREA	ACTIVITIES	Sights	Shopping
	Deira	Al-Ahmadiya School (p58)	Deira Gold Souq (p53)
		Dhow Wharfage (p58)	Deira Spice Souq (p53)
		Heritage House (p58)	Pride of Kashmir (p94)
			Virgin Megastore (p94)
	Bur Dubai	Bastakia Quarter (p61)	Amzaan (p96)
		Bur Dubai Souq (p66)	Five Green (p97)
		Dubai Museum (p61)	Karama Shopping Centre (p97)
			Wafi Gourmet (p98)
	Sheikh Zayed Road	B21 Gallery (p71)	Azza Fahmy Jewellery (p98)
		Meem Gallery (p71)	Boutique 1 (p99)
		Third Line (p71)	Emilio Pucci (p99)
			Organic Foods & Café (p99)
	Jumeirah	Burj Al Arab (p75)	Blue Cactus (p99)
		Jumeirah Mosque (p75)	Fleurt (p100)
		Madinat Jumeirah (p75)	Mercato Mall (p100)
			S*uce (p100)
	New Dubai	Ski Dubai (p142)	Aizone (p101)
			Ginger & Lace (p101)
			Mumbai Se (p102)

HOW TO USE THIS TABLE

The table below allows you to plan a day's worth of activities in any area of the city. Simply select which area you wish to explore, and then mix and match from the corresponding listings to build your day. The first item in each cell represents a well-known highlight of the area, while the other items are more off-the-beaten-track gems.

Eating	Drinking	Sports, Spas & Outdoor Activities
Aroos Damascus (p109)	Issimo (p126)	Al-Mamzar Park (p58)
Kiku (p108)	Ku-Bu (p126)	Amara (p140)
Thai Kitchen (p114)	Terrace (p126)	Dubai Creek Golf Club (p144)
Verre by Gordon Ramsay (p107)	Velvet Lounge (p126)	
Bastakiah Nights (p111)	Chi@The Lodge (p131)	Creekside Park (p67)
Fire & Ice (p110)	Ginseng (p126)	Pharaohs Club (p139)
Gazebo (p113)	New Asia Bar (p127)	Za'abeel Park (p68)
Karachi Darbar (p113)	Troyka (p127)	
Al-Nafoorah (p116)	Agency (p127)	Dubai Wildlife & Waterbird Sanctuary (p71)
Amwaj (p114)	Cin-Cin Wine Bar (p128)	1847 (p141)
Exchange Grill (p115)	Lotus One (p128)	
Zaatar W Zeit (p117)	Vu's Bar (p128)	
Lime Tree Café (p119)	Al-Qasr (p117)	Jumeirah Beach Park (p78)
Pisces (p118)	Bahri Bar (p128)	Talise Spa (p141)
Ravi (p119)	Sho Cho (p129)	Wild Wadi Waterpark (p143)
Zheng He's (p118)	Skyview Bar (p129)	
Almaz by Momo (p121)	Barasti Bar (p130)	Emirates Golf Club (p144)
Nina (p121)	Maya (p130)	Oriental Hammam (p139)
Rhodes Mezzanine (p119)	Rooftop Bar (p130)	Softtouch Spa (p141)

GREATER DUBAI

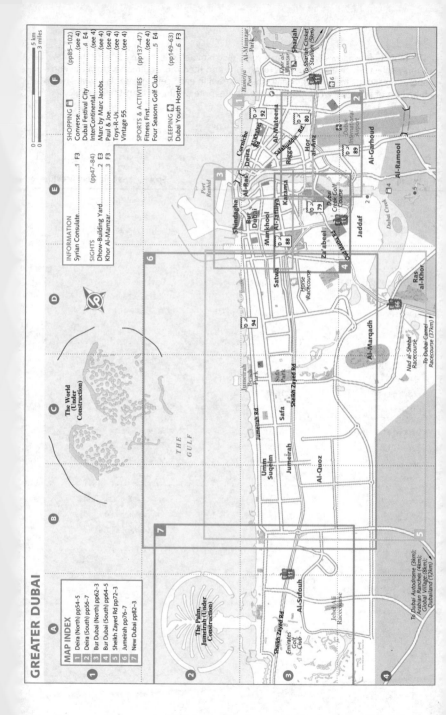

0 _____ 5 km
0 _____ 3 miles

DEIRA

Eating p106; Entertainment p125; Shopping p91; Sleeping p151

Dubai isn't meant to look like this anymore. Old, dirty, crowded and chaotic, Deira is a world away from the slick and sanitised city piercing the clouds at the other end of town. Yet at the same time, Deira says more about Dubai than any hotel or shopping mall ever could.

It's been a trading centre for centuries. At the Dhow Wharfage, colourful wooden boats that have spent decades plying the waters between Dubai and Iran arrive with boxes of cuddly toys, televisions and batteries to be sold at the souqs down the road. At these atmospheric ancestors to today's colossal shopping malls, you can sip sugary tea and haggle for bargains with traders who have often worked in the same shop for decades.

Deira is fascinatingly multicultural. The language of the signs on shop windows changes every 50m, from Tamil to Sinhalese, Malayalam, Urdu, Pashto, Tagalog and Amharic. (Don't worry, everybody speaks a little English.) Adventurous foodies can lap up authentic fare in the Syrian, Ethiopian, Iraqi and Afghan parts of Deira, and if you're there at night, prepare for a wild ride. You'll find Russian, Filipino, Lebanese, Indian and Pakistani nightclubs, often all on the same floor and typically featuring ear-rupturingly loud house bands, overpriced beers and plenty of illicitly seedy goings-on. Sound appealing? Honestly, these dives are not without their charms; some of the best live music in the city is there for the taking if you keep your ears, eyes and mind open.

While New Dubai feels like a blend of Singapore and Las Vegas, Deira feels more like a cross between Cairo and Karachi. The authorities, quite understandably, are keen to revitalise the area, to clean it up and gentrify the poorer districts. While no right-minded person would want to sustain poverty for the sake of aesthetic gratification, you can't help but fear the area will lose its unique character. The contrast between Deira and New Dubai is one of the city's most fascinating features; the striking juxtaposition of the old and the new, the haves and the have-nots, and the east and the west.

top picks
DEIRA

- **The Souqs** Wander through the souqs, with spicy aromas at the Spice Souq (right), glittering gold at the Gold Souq (above), and a glimpse of expat life at the Deira Covered Souq & Naif Souq (p58).
- **Al-Ahmadiya School** (p58) and **Heritage House** (p58) Step back in time to discover the simpler life of old Dubai.
- **Dhow Wharfage** (p58) Marvel at how the dhows manage to stay afloat when there are several cars, a truck, and a warehouse's worth of electrical goods on deck.

DEIRA GOLD SOUQ Map pp54–5
On & around Sikkat al-Khail St, btwn Souq Deira & Old Baladiya Sts

Even to people not interested in buying gold or jewellery, the Gold Souq is impressive for both its size – there are hundreds of shops here – and variety. Every kind of jewellery imaginable is available, from gold, diamonds and pearls to elaborate Arabian and Indian wedding necklaces, bangles and headdresses, to more contemporary styles. Some of it is beautiful, lots of it is incredibly tacky. It's the largest gold market in the region, and one of the largest in the world (with ambitions to rival Antwerp in diamonds). The passing people parade is almost as fascinating as the sheer amount of jewellery. Once you're done with gawking at the bling-tastic jewellery displays, take a seat on one of the wooden benches on the main thoroughfare and note how many different types of people circulate among the atmospheric wooden-latticed arcades: sun-bothered Europeans shopping for gold, blokes from the Indian subcontinent selling copy watches and fake DVDs, sweaty Afghan guys dragging heavy carts of goods here and there, East African women in colourful caftans trading something… It's all rather extraordinary.

DEIRA SPICE SOUQ Map pp54–5
Btwn Baniyas Rd, Al-Sabkha Rd & Al-Abra St

The small but atmospheric covered Spice Souq, once known as the Old Souq, was the largest in the region at the beginning of the 20th century, with over 300

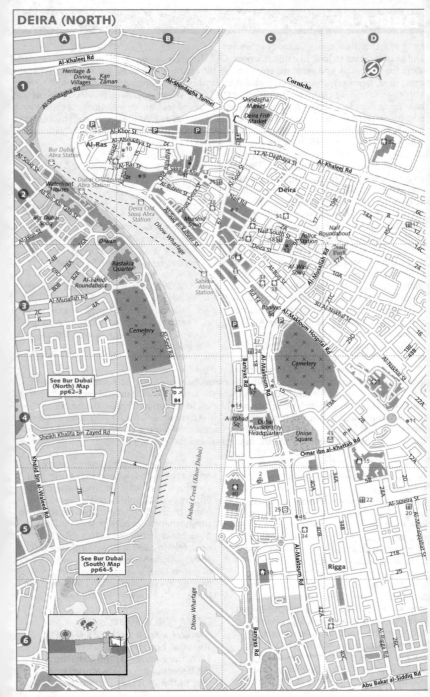

DEIRA (NORTH)

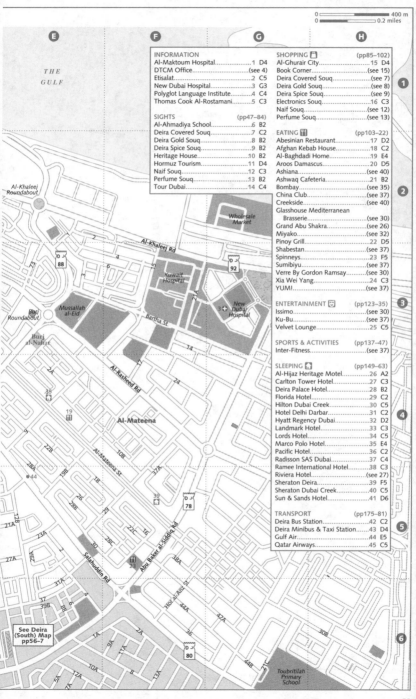

INFORMATION	
Al-Maktoum Hospital	1 D4
DTCM Office	(see 4)
Etisalat	2 C5
New Dubai Hospital	3 G3
Polyglot Language Institute	4 C4
Thomas Cook Al-Rostamani	5 C3

SIGHTS	(pp47–84)
Al-Ahmadiya School	6 B2
Deira Covered Souq	7 C2
Deira Gold Souq	8 B2
Deira Spice Souq	9 B2
Heritage House	10 B2
Hormuz Tourism	11 D4
Naif Souq	12 C3
Perfume Souq	13 B2
Tour Dubai	14 C4

SHOPPING	(pp85–102)
Al-Ghurair City	15 D4
Book Corner	(see 15)
Deira Covered Souq	(see 7)
Deira Gold Souq	(see 8)
Deira Spice Souq	(see 9)
Electronics Souq	16 C3
Naif Souq	(see 12)
Perfume Souq	(see 13)

EATING	(pp103–22)
Abesinian Restaurant	17 D2
Afghan Kebab House	18 C2
Al-Baghdadi Home	19 E4
Aroos Damascus	20 D5
Ashiana	(see 40)
Ashwaq Cafeteria	21 B2
Bombay	(see 35)
China Club	(see 37)
Creekside	(see 40)
Glasshouse Mediterranean Brasserie	(see 30)
Grand Abu Shakra	(see 26)
Miyako	(see 32)
Pinoy Grill	22 D5
Shabestan	(see 37)
Spinneys	23 F5
Sumibiyu	(see 37)
Verre By Gordon Ramsay	(see 30)
Xia Wei Yang	24 C3
YUMI	(see 37)

ENTERTAINMENT	(pp123–35)
Issimo	(see 30)
Ku-Bu	(see 37)
Velvet Lounge	25 C5

SPORTS & ACTIVITIES	(pp137–47)
Inter-Fitness	(see 37)

SLEEPING	(pp149–63)
Al-Hijaz Heritage Motel	26 A2
Carlton Tower Hotel	27 C3
Deira Palace Hotel	28 B2
Florida Hotel	29 C2
Hilton Dubai Creek	30 C5
Hotel Delhi Darbar	31 C2
Hyatt Regency Dubai	32 D2
Landmark Hotel	33 C3
Lords Hotel	34 C5
Marco Polo Hotel	35 E4
Pacific Hotel	36 C2
Radisson SAS Dubai	37 C4
Ramee International Hotel	38 C3
Riviera Hotel	(see 27)
Sheraton Deira	39 F5
Sheraton Dubai Creek	40 C5
Sun & Sands Hotel	41 D6

TRANSPORT	(pp175–81)
Deira Bus Station	42 C2
Deira Minibus & Taxi Station	43 D4
Gulf Air	44 E5
Qatar Airways	45 C5

55

DEIRA (SOUTH)

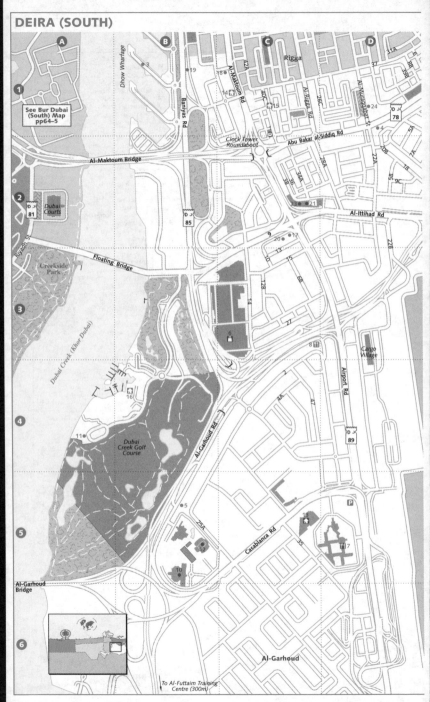

See Bur Dubai (South) Map pp64–5

Dhow Wharfage

Rigga

Baniyas Rd

Al-Maktoum Rd

Al-Rigga Rd

Al-Muraqqabat St

Clock Tower Roundabout

Abu Bakar al-Siddiq Rd

Al-Maktoum Bridge

Dubai Courts

Al-Ittihad Rd

Riyadh St

Floating Bridge

Creekside Park

Dubai Creek (Khor Dubai)

Cargo Village

Airport Rd

Dubai Creek Golf Course

Al-Garhoud Rd

Casablanca Rd

Al-Garhoud Bridge

Al-Garhoud

To Al-Futtaim Training Centre (300m)

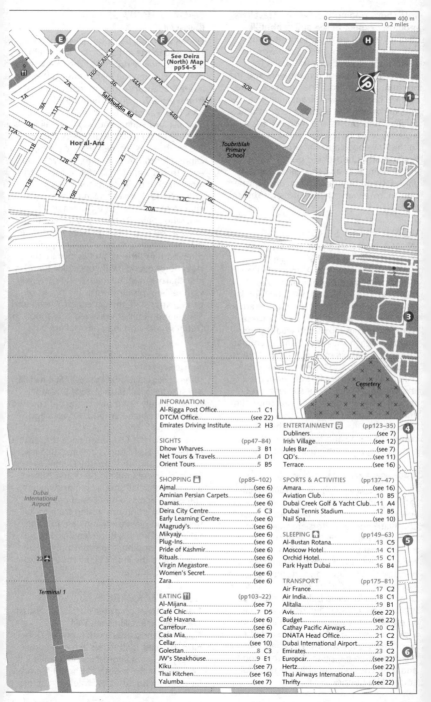

See Deira (North) Map pp54–5

0 — 400 m
0 — 0.2 miles

Salahuddin Rd

Hor al-Anz

Toubritilah Primary School

Cemetery

Dubai International Airport

Terminal 1

INFORMATION
Al-Rigga Post Office..................1 C1
DTCM Office.........................(see 22)
Emirates Driving Institute........2 H3

SIGHTS (pp47–84)
Dhow Wharves........................3 B1
Net Tours & Travels.................4 D1
Orient Tours..........................5 B5

SHOPPING (pp85–102)
Ajmal.................................(see 6)
Aminian Persian Carpets..........(see 6)
Damas...............................(see 6)
Deira City Centre....................6 C3
Early Learning Centre..............(see 6)
Magrudy's...........................(see 6)
Mikyajy..............................(see 6)
Plug-Ins.............................(see 6)
Pride of Kashmir...................(see 6)
Rituals..............................(see 6)
Virgin Megastore...................(see 6)
Women's Secret....................(see 6)
Zara.................................(see 6)

EATING (pp103–22)
Al-Mijana...........................(see 7)
Café Chic............................7 D5
Café Havana........................(see 6)
Carrefour...........................(see 6)
Casa Mia...........................(see 7)
Cellar..............................(see 10)
Golestan.............................8 C3
JW's Steakhouse.....................9 E1
Kiku.................................(see 7)
Thai Kitchen.......................(see 16)
Yalumba............................(see 7)

ENTERTAINMENT (pp123–35)
Dubliners...........................(see 7)
Irish Village.......................(see 12)
Jules Bar...........................(see 7)
QD's................................(see 11)
Terrace.............................(see 16)

SPORTS & ACTIVITIES (pp137–47)
Amara..............................(see 16)
Aviation Club.......................10 B5
Dubai Creek Golf & Yacht Club....11 A4
Dubai Tennis Stadium..............12 B5
Nail Spa............................(see 10)

SLEEPING (pp149–63)
Al-Bustan Rotana....................13 C5
Moscow Hotel........................14 C1
Orchid Hotel.........................15 C1
Park Hyatt Dubai....................16 B4

TRANSPORT (pp175–81)
Air France...........................17 C2
Air India............................18 C1
Alitalia.............................19 B1
Avis................................(see 22)
Budget.............................(see 22)
Cathay Pacific Airways..............20 C2
DNATA Head Office.................21 C2
Dubai International Airport.........22 E5
Emirates.............................23 C2
Europcar...........................(see 22)
Hertz..............................(see 22)
Thai Airways International..........24 D1
Thrifty.............................(see 22)

57

little shops trading their wares. Travellers shouldn't expect to see an Istanbul-like bazaar – they'll be disappointed – but this tiny aromatic market is still worth a half-hour of your time to take in the wonderfully restored wind-towers and the pungent aromas from the jute sacks. The place is brimming with frankincense and *oud*, herbs and spices, dried lemons and chillies, nuts, pulses and more. This is a working souq, not just a tourist attraction, so the tiny shops also sell groceries, plastics and other household goods for people living in the area and the sailors from the *dhows*. Good buys include incense burners, saffron, rose water, henna kits and *sheesha* pipes.

AL-AHMADIYA SCHOOL Map pp54–5
☎ 226 0286; Al-Ahmadiya St, near Gold Souq; ☻ 8am-7.30pm Sat-Thu, 2.30-7.30pm Fri
Sheikh Mohammed bin Ahmed bin Dalmouk established Al-Ahmadiya, Dubai's first school, in 1912, and his father Sheikh Ahmed owned the traditional house adjoining it. Semiformal schools such as these were set up by sheikhs and wealthy merchants to teach the Holy Quran, grammar, Arabic calligraphy, mathematics, literature and astronomy, and while most students paid a couple of rupees to attend, the sheikhs paid for the poor students. Very special is the simplicity of the architecture and the exquisite detail – check out the intricate carving within the arches of the courtyard inside and the decorative gypsum panels near the entrance outside.

HERITAGE HOUSE Map pp54–5
☎ 226 0286; Al-Ahmadiya St; ☻ 8am-7.30pm Sat-Thu, 2.30-7.30pm Fri
Feeling peckish? At this renovated 1890 courtyard house, visitors are treated to cups of tea and little bowls of chick peas, a traditional Emirati snack. Don't race off the moment you've finished your free food, because this is a rare opportunity to see inside a wealthy pearl merchant's residence. Like the old Bastakia buildings, the house is built from coral and gypsum, and has a central courtyard onto which all rooms look, plus verandas to prevent sunlight from heating the rooms. The charming staff are more than happy to show you around and refill your bowl of chick peas, should you still be hungry.

DHOW WHARFAGE Map pp56–7
Baniyas Rd
Dhows are long, flat, wooden sailing vessels used in the Indian Ocean and Arabian Sea, and they've docked at the Creek since the 1830s when the Maktoums established a free-trade port, luring merchants away from Persia. The *dhows* here now trade with Iran, Iraq, Pakistan, Oman, India, Yemen, Somalia and Sudan, and you'll see all kinds of crazy cargo – air-conditioners, flat-screen TVs, mattresses, kitchen sinks, clothes, canned food, chewing gum, car tyres, cars, even trucks – almost all of it re-exported after arriving by air from countries like China, South Korea and Singapore. Try to chat to the sailors if you can – if you find one who speaks English, you'll learn that it takes a day to get to Iran by sea and seven days to Somalia, and the *dhow* captains often earn as little as $100 a month, the stevedores even less. If your sailor friend is in a chatty mood, he may even regale you with real-life pirate stories. The gangs of thieves that stalk the waters off Yemen and Somalia sometimes make life very tough for Dubai's hard-working *dhow* sailors.

DEIRA COVERED SOUQ & NAIF SOUQ Map pp54–5
Covered Souq btwn Al-Sabkha Rd, 67 St & Naif Rd; Naif Souq btwn Naif South St, 9a St & Deira St
Unfortunately not much of the old covered souqs that existed around 30 years ago remain now – the Deira Spice Souq (p53) is all that's left of the Old Souq, once the largest in the Gulf. Naif Souq is covered, like traditional bazaars, while nearby Deira Covered Souq is covered only in parts and is more a warren of small shops on narrow lanes spreading across a number of old Deira blocks. You'll find everything from tacky textiles and plastic kitchenware to Iranian saffron and henna, but even if you're not keen on shopping, the souqs provide an insight into the lives of Emiratis and expat workers in Dubai.

AL-MAMZAR PARK Map p52
Al-Mamzar Creek; per person/car Dh5/30; ☻ 8am-11pm, women & children only Wed
This lush landscaped park is one of Dubai's hidden gems. It stretches across a couple of very pleasant kilometres on a small headland at the mouth of Khor al-Mamzar. Situated on an attractive inlet, just across

from Sharjah, there are lovely white sandy beaches, a swimming pool, barbecues, and kiosks. For kids there are also plenty of open spaces and play areas and a wooden castle. Lifeguards are on duty between 8am and 6pm on at least one of the small beaches. Friday is busy, but during the week you can have the place to yourself.

DEIRA SOUQ STROLL
Walking Tour

1 Spice Souq As soon as you step off the *abra* at Deira Old Souq Abra Station, the heady scents of sumac, cinnamon, cloves and other spices will lure you across to the Spice Souq (p53). Take some time to explore. Chat to the shop-keepers. If you can't guess what's in those sacks, ask. Buy something (see p93): saffron is excellent value; frankincense, *oud* and an incense burner make a memorable souvenir; and *sheesha* kits are much cheaper here than they are in the malls. When you exit the souq on Al-Abra St, turn right. At the end of the street, turn left onto Al-Ras St, continue to Al-Hadd St and turn right. The intriguing stores on these streets, selling sacks of nuts,

pulses and rice, belong to wholesalers trading mainly with Iran and using the *dhows* to ply their goods.

2 Heritage House At the end of the street turn right and walk along Al-Ahmadiya St until you arrive at the beautifully restored Heritage House (opposite). It's worth a brief diversion for an insight into Dubai's history and culture, and you'll enjoy the simple but splendid archi-tecture, exquisite detail and, if you're lucky, a free cup of tea and a bite to eat.

3 Al-Ahmadiya School Situated directly behind Heritage House, Al-Ahmadiya School (opposite) is another example of simple but elegant early-20th-century architecture. After a brief look round, continue your journey along

WALK FACTS

Start **Spice Souq**
End **Afghan Kebab House**
Distance **2km**
Duration **Three hours (including souq shopping)**
Fuel Stop **Afghan Kebab House**

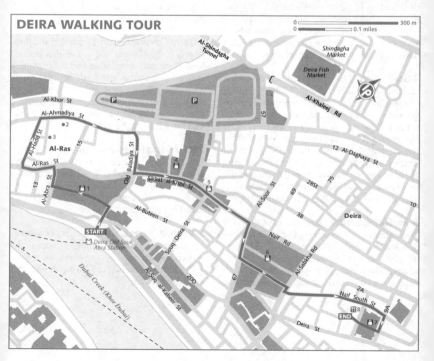

DEIRA WALKING TOUR

Sometimes it pays to rip up the script and improvise. Some of the most fascinating parts of town aren't home to a single tourist attraction worth recommending, but are brimming with the soul the city is so frequently accused of lacking. Dubai's soul can be found in its people, particularly its migrant workers, and the stories of the hundreds of thousands of individuals who have moved here – some from Saddam's Iraq, others from Afghanistan under the Taliban – in search of a better life.

Dubai is a very safe city – there aren't any no-go areas and even the scariest-looking alleyways will be quite harmless. Be adventurous and spontaneous. Put away the maps and follow your instinct. But before you hurl this guidebook into the Creek, read our suggestions of the best places in Deira in which to get hopelessly, joyously lost.

Naif (Map pp54–5) The area between Naif Rd and Al-Khaleej Rd is a labyrinthine muddle of slim, cluttered streets, and one of the best places in town for urban photography. It's not always pretty, but here you'll find old men smoking *sheesha* and playing backgammon on the pavements; pockets of Ethiopia and Somalia (the potent coffee poured in the African cafés will rouse the sleepiest of sleepyheads); hilariously awful fake watches (Rolex, Longynes etc); games consoles (including the PolyStation and the notorious Gold Leopard King); perfumes (one's called 'Our Man on the Titanic'); blindingly bright neon shop façades (what's with all the photos of babies?); and the occasional goat, walking nonchalantly down the centre of the street. You just don't get this on the Palm Jumeirah…

Mateena (Map pp54–5) Despite its out-of-the-way location, Al-Mateena St is one of the most walkable roads in town, with wide pavements, palm trees, and a long, narrow park running right through its centre. There are lots of Iraqi restaurants and cafés on this strip, which means you can see *masgouf* – a whole fish sliced in half, spicily seasoned and barbecued over an open flame – being prepared in some of the windows. And with rock gardens, dangling fronds and artificial lakes, the *sheesha* cafés on this road have to be seen to be believed. If you're interested in Arabic food, check out nearby Al-Muraqqabat Rd, where there are excellent Syrian and Palestinian eateries.

Al-Ahmadiya St, turning right into Old Baladiya St, where you'll find more wholesalers, this time trading in *gutras* (white headcloths) and *agals* (headrobes used to hold *gutras* in place), sandals, cheap shoes and Chinese products. If you're considering buying an Emirati national dress as a souvenir, here's the place to shop.

4 Gold Souq Ahead, to the left, is the wooden latticed archway entrance to Dubai's famous Gold Souq (p53). Take time to drop into shops to get a closer look at the jaw-dropping (sometimes for the wrong reasons) jewellery. The elaborate gold pieces created for brides' dowries are particularly over the top – find them by the camera flashes going off. Wander along the atmospheric narrow lanes that lead off the main arcade: you'll discover tiny teashops, simple cafeterias, busy tailors and barber shops.

5 Perfume Souq Exiting the souq (usually poorer than when you entered), continue along Sikkat al-Khail St to the Perfume Souq. This is really just a string of shops selling heady Arabian *attars* and *oud,* fake 'European' colognes with ridiculous labels, and pretty tinted perfume

bottles. Hang a right into 107 St, where it can be bedlam some nights with hawkers competing to sell off their cut-price clothes, Chinese-made shoes and kitschy souvenirs.

6 Deira Covered Souq Tucked behind these streets is Deira Covered Souq (p58) which doesn't look like a traditional souq and isn't covered. Instead you'll find hundreds of little shops on alleys selling everything from textiles to luggage, groceries and *sheesha* pipes. Arriving near Al-Sabkha Rd bus station, cross the road and head into Naif South St.

7 Naif Souq Follow Naif South St, turn right into 9A St and wander down until you arrive at Naif Souq (p58), a small covered market popular with Emirati women buying copy Dior *shaylas* and *abayas,* children's clothes and toys – it can get crazy here at night.

8 Afghan Kebab House If you've worked up an appetite rambling though Deira's souqs, a carnivorous meal at the Afghan Kebab House (p109), hidden behind Naif Mosque, will keep you sated for ages.

BUR DUBAI

Eating p110; Entertainment p125; Shopping p95; Sleeping p155

Bur Dubai is the oldest part of the city and presents visitors with a slice of life from the emirate's early days. There are several distinct districts within Bur Dubai. Shindagha, the area near the entrance to the tunnel, is quiet and relatively undeveloped. It's a great place for a stroll and a light meal by the Creek. The souq district is every bit as vibrant as its Deira counterpart and exploring 'Little India' in the surrounding streets can easily absorb a couple of hours of your time. A little further east along the Creek is Dubai's administrative district; an area dominated by government buildings and overseas consulates.

Moving inland from Bastakia and the souqs, there are three main districts, each with their own distinctive character. Mankhool compensates for its lack of sights with quirky nightlife and scores of great restaurants. Unfortunately, much of the district is consumed by a bland concrete jungle known rather optimistically as Golden Sands. On the other side of the BurJuman Mall is Karama, home to rundown apartment blocks housing mainly Filipino and Indian expat workers. It's well worth a wander – it has a real community feel to it, and there's great shopping (watch out for the fakes) and dozens of Indian, Pakistani and Filipino restaurants where you can eat like a king for under Dh20. Further south is the rather nondescript Oud Metha, although in among its malls, hotels and theme parks are a few well-hidden gems, such as the restaurant at the Iranian Club (p108) and the cutting-edge clothing store Five Green (p97).

top picks

BUR DUBAI

- Dubai Museum (above) Visit the museum for a speedy and entertaining introduction to the city.
- Sheikh Saeed al-Maktoum House (p66) Stroll through the elegantly restored house where there's a rare collection of amazing black-and-white photographs of early Dubai.
- Bastakia Quarter (right) Walk through Dubai's 'old town' and pop into XVA (p68) for a salad, a fruit juice and a peek at their latest exhibition.

DUBAI MUSEUM Map pp54–5

☎ 353 1862; Al-Fahidi St, opp Grand Mosque & Diwan; adult/child Dh3/1; ⏰ 8.30am-8.30pm Sat-Thu, 3-9pm Fri

Some tourists mock the very notion of Dubai having a museum: 'Historical Dubai? What, they have exhibits about the year 1995?' But Dubai does have an interesting history, and this is a surprisingly nifty little museum. Rather than bewilder guests with unnecessary detail, this is an accessible and entertaining introduction to Dubai and its history, culture and traditions. The museum occupies the early-19th-century Al-Fahidi Fort, possibly the oldest building in Dubai, and once the seat of government and the residence of Dubai's rulers. Apart from a small fishing boat, a traditional weapons display and a *barasti* house with wind-tower (step under it and feel the difference it makes in summer), much of the air-conditioned museum is thankfully underground. There's an excellent (albeit somewhat dated) multimedia presentation covering the city's history and growth that gives a real understanding of how rapidly Dubai has developed. Then there are a series of cutesy dioramas of old Dubai life, supported by video, sound effects and disturbingly lifelike mannequins. A highlight for many is the complete grave from the Al-Qusais archaeological site and finds from digs at Al-Qusais (dating back to 2500 to 500 BC) and Jumeirah (6th century AD). All displays in the museum have explanations in Arabic and English. Photography is not officially permitted, although many visitors find it impossible to resist posing with the mannequins for a sneaky snap or two...

BASTAKIA QUARTER Map pp54–5

With its arty feel and narrow breezy lanes, the atmospheric old Bastakia Quarter on the waterfront east of the Bur Dubai Souq is a pleasant place to explore. Here you'll find the highest concentration of traditional old wind-tower houses in Dubai. Built at the beginning of the 20th century, these buildings were once the homes of wealthy pearl and textile merchants who came from Bastak in southern Iran, enticed to Dubai by its free trade. The elegant

BUR DUBAI (NORTH)

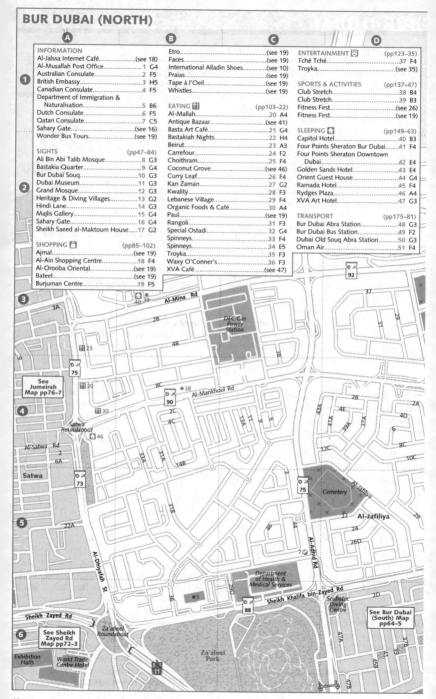

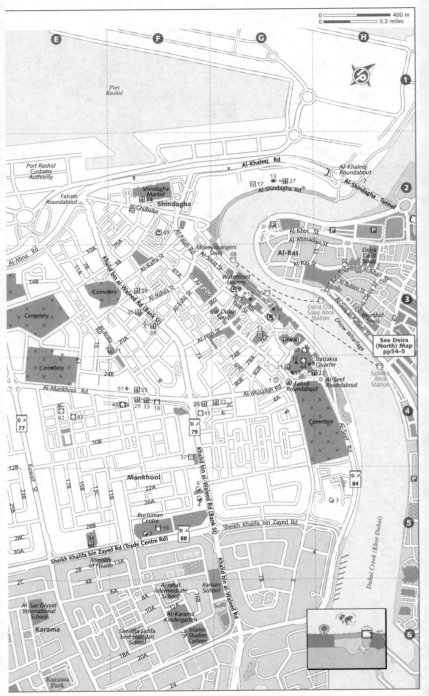

0 _____ 400 m
0 _____ 0.2 miles

E · F · G · H

1

Port
Rashid

Port Rashid
Customs
Authority

Al-Khaleej Rd

Al-Khaleej
Roundabout

Al-Shindagha Rd

Al-Shindagha Tunnel

2

Falcon
Roundabout

Shindagha
Market

Al-Ghubaiba
Rd

Shindagha

13 ▤17 ▤27

Al-Khor St

Al-Ahmadiya St

P   P   P

▤49

Al-Faheidi Rd

Al-Souq St

Moneychangers
Souq

48

Al-Ras

Al-Ras St

Deira
Gold
Souq

Sikkat al-Khail St

Al-Mina Rd

10A

75A

Al-Raffa St

38

6TA

39

Al-Fahidi St

Waterfront
Houses

Old Baladiya St

Al-Buteen St

Deira St

3

Cemetery

▤28

Al-Nahda St

Al-Sabkha St

35 Al-Fahidi St

▤

3

▤9 ·10 ·50▤

Al-Hisn St

Bur Dubai
Souq

Ali bin Abi Talib St

·14

▲ ·2

Deira Old
Souq Abra
Station

Dhow Wharfage

Al-Sabkha Rd

Al-Seef Rd

Murshid
Souq

Khalid bin al-Waleed Rd (Bank St)

7C 36

Al-Rolla Rd

Diwan

See Deira
(North) Map
pp54–5

Cemetery

24B

Al-Mankhool Rd

51● ▤25

29 33 18

4C

▤42 ▲43

45▤

26▤ ▤32 2C
▤41   6

Bastakia
Quarter

16 ▲ 44
·15 ▤22

1· Al-Fahidi
Roundabout Al-Seef
Roundabout

21▤

Sabkha
Abra
Station

4

24B

9

Kuwait St

12B   23B

25B

15B   3C

17B   11B

Mankhool

10B

37▤

6

26A

Khalid bin al-Waleed Rd (Bank St)

Cemetery

Al-Seef Rd

D 77

D 79

D 84

P

5

28B

28C

34▤

BurJuman
Centre

▤19

D 88

Sheikh Khalifa bin Zayed Rd

6

Sheikh Khalifa bin Zayed Rd (Trade Centre Rd)

Ministry
of Health

13A

A'ishat
Intermediate
School

Iranian
School

Dubai Creek (Khor Dubai)

2B

30A

2C

4B

6A

8A

10A

Al-Sae Diyyat
International
School

Karama

Sheikha Latifa
bint Hamdan
School

Al-Karama
Kindergarten

Islamic
Studies
College

Karama
Park

63

BUR DUBAI (SOUTH)

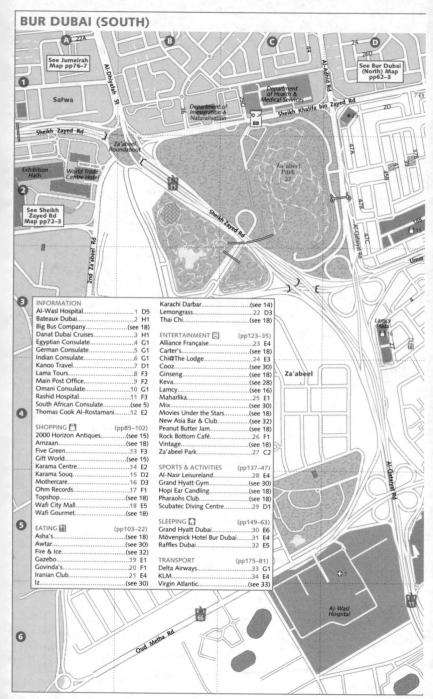

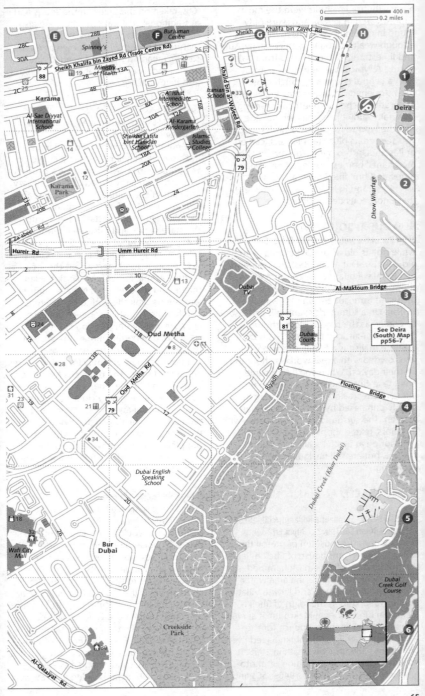

homes the traders built were the most sophisticated in Dubai, and were only found in coastal towns where there was enough wealth to build with coral, gypsum and limestone – a big step up from palm fronds. A typical house was two-storeys with a central courtyard, which most rooms opened onto, and which boasted decorative arches with intricate carvings. Generally fairly plain from the outside, they had the wonderful carved wooden doors you see today, plus crenulations, carved grilles and stucco panels on the wealthier merchants' homes – many of Bastakia's renovated buildings, such as XVA (p68), Majlis Gallery (p68) and Basta Art Café (p113), have these gorgeous decorations.

BUR DUBAI SOUQ Map pp54–5
Btwn Bur Dubai waterfront & Al-Fahidi St
While not as old as the Deira souqs – in the old days Bur Dubai and Bastakia residents had to take a boat across to Deira to go shopping – this breezy renovated souq can be just as atmospheric and lively a place to visit. On a summer's evening it can also be cooler, as the breeze blows through the wooden-latticed arcades. The buzziest time to visit is a Friday evening when it's crowded with expat workers shopping on their day off. While you'll find some great take-home items, what's primarily on offer are cheap clothes, shoes and textiles, mainly purchased by Emirati and Indian women. The surrounding backstreets – with its tailors, textile shops and sari shops – may not be as aesthetically pleasing to the eye, but are still intriguing and worth exploring.

SHEIKH SAEED AL-MAKTOUM HOUSE Map pp62–3
☎ 393 7139; Al-Shindagha Rd; adult/child Dh2/1; ☻ 8am-8.30pm Sat-Thu, 3-9.30pm Fri
Now a wonderful museum of pre-oil times, the grand courtyard house of Sheikh Saeed, the grandfather of Sheikh Mohammed, sits splendidly on the Shindagha area waterfront, near the Heritage and Diving Villages. Built in 1896, during the reign of Sheikh Maktoum bin Hasher al-Maktoum, it served for many years as the residence for the Al-Maktoum family, and Sheikh Saeed lived here from 1888 until his death in 1958. It houses an engaging exhibition of photographs, primarily from the 1940s, '50s and

'60s, taken on the Creek, in the souqs and at traditional celebrations. There are also displays of postage stamps and coins (one featuring Edward VII was known as *umm salaah,* meaning the 'bald headed one') and a model of Bur Dubai from the 1950s also helps tell the story.

SAHARY GATE Map pp62–3
☎ 353 5660; www.saharygate.com; Bastakia House no 14; ☻ 9am-6pm
The number of expats living and working in Dubai who have never had a single conversation with a UAE national is a cause for concern. Too many expatriates know very little about the culture of their hosts, and Emiratis aren't making enough of an effort to enlighten their guests. To help counter the stereotypes and misunderstandings that pervade Dubai society, Sahary Gate offers a range of workshops and tours that help educate foreigners about the local culture. Arabic calligraphy, cooking, language and jewellery-making are taught in workshops typically lasting between two and four hours, while some of the tours are refreshingly unique. You can visit the palace of a generous Ajman sheikh, who donates all proceeds to charity, or go to the house of a local family for coffee, dates and a light meal. The proceeds for these tours go to City of Hope, a shelter for abused women. Sahary House also runs regular cultural awareness classes and free talks about Islam. If you don't have enough time for a class or a tour, it's still worth popping in to enjoy the beautiful building and courtyard, and a coffee or two in the traditional *majlis.*

'HINDI LANE' Map pp62–3
Behind Grand Mosque, off Ali bin Abi Talib St
If you venture behind the Grand Mosque in Bur Dubai, you'll find evidence of two places of worship behind very modest exteriors – rows of shoes in shelves at the bottom of a couple of sets of stairs. One staircase leads to the Shri Nathje Jayate Temple, also known as the Krishna Mandir (*mandir* is Hindi for temple). Shri Nathji is the main deity of Pushtimarg, a Hindu devotional sect, with its main temple near Udaipur in Rajasthan, India. The other house of worship is identified by a discreet sign, Sikh Gurudaba, which is interesting, because a Sikh place of worship is called a *gurdwara.*

A *guru* is a teacher-guide, and a *dabar* is a cheap lunch stop, but we're not sure if there's a connection. Of most interest to travellers is the small alley that expats refer to as 'Hindi Lane'. Here vendors sell Hindu religious paraphernalia and offerings to take to the temples: baskets of fruit, garlands of flowers, gold-embossed holy images, sacred ash, sandalwood paste and packets of bindis, the little pendants Hindu women stick to their foreheads.

HERITAGE & DIVING VILLAGES
Map pp62–3

☎ 393 7151; Al-Shindagha Rd; ☽ 8am-10pm Sat-Thu, 8-11am & 4-10pm Fri

During the Dubai Shopping Festival (p88), the Heritage and Diving Villages bloom with burqa-clad Emirati women making hot *dosa* (flat, grilled bread made of flour and water), Bedu men offering short-haul camel rides to children, and unusual traditional activities such as rifle-throwing competitions. Unfortunately, for the rest of the year the villages are lifeless, devoid of both tourists and staff, with empty souqs and only a few dreary displays to keep visitors interested. The occasional performance of traditional music or dance takes place outside the shopping festival – it's worth calling in advance and making sure your visit coincides with an event.

GRAND MOSQUE Map pp62–3
Ali bin Abi Talib St, opposite Dubai Museum

This mosque, with the tallest minaret in town, might appear to be as old as the Dubai Museum, but it was actually built in the 1990s. The multi-domed mosque maintains the style of the original Grand Mosque, which dated from 1900 and was knocked down to make way for another mosque in 1960. Its sand-coloured walls and wooden shutters blend in perfectly with the surrounding old quarter of Bur Dubai. As well as being the centre of Dubai's religious and cultural life, the original Grand Mosque was also home to the town's *kuttab* school where children learnt to recite the Quran from memory. Note that it's only possible to admire the mosque from outside – interiors of mosques in Dubai and the UAE are out of bounds to non-Muslims (except for the tour at Jumeirah Mosque; see p75).

CREEKSIDE PARK Map pp64–5

☎ 800 900 (Dubai Municipality); off Riyadh St, btwn Al-Garhoud & Al-Maktoum Bridges; admission Dh5; ☽ 8am-11pm Sat-Wed, 8am-11.30pm Thu-Fri & public holidays, women & children only Wed

This lovely, lush waterfront park is one of the city's largest – running from Al-Garhoud Bridge to Al-Maktoum Bridge – and is one of the favourites. It's very peaceful and has gorgeous views across the Creek. It also offers children's play areas, *abra* rides and *dhow* cruises, kiosks, restaurants, an amphitheatre and beaches (though it's not advisable to swim). On weekends it's like a huge *sheesha* café, with families spread out on blankets, puffing away. There's also a 2.5km cable-car ride (tickets adult/child Dh25/15) 30m above the shore of the Creek, with fabulous vistas. Also situated in a colourful building in the park is Children's City (☎ 334 0808; www.childrencity.ae; adult/child Dh15/10; ☽ 9am-10pm Sat-Thu, 4-10pm Fri). Popular with local and expat kids, it's home to a creative, educational and entertaining kids' activities centre.

DHOW-BUILDING YARD Map p52
Jaddaf, Bur Dubai side of Creek
The gorgeous, traditional old dhows you see on Dubai Creek are still built by hand in the traditional style on the Creek waterfront, in Jaddaf, about 1km south of Al-Garhoud Bridge. Here, craftsmen use basic tools (a hammer, saw, chisel, drill and plane) to curve and fit sturdy teak planks, one on top of the other, before fitting the frame on the inside of the boat. Be impressed: this is in contrast to Western boat-building techniques where the frame is generally built first, and the planks fitted to it. These days, of course, the blokes pop an engine on the back before sliding it into the Creek.

XVA Map pp62–3
☎ 353 5383; www.xvagallery.com; behind Basta Art Café, Al-Musallah Roundabout; ☒ 9am-9pm Sat-Thu, 10am-5pm Fri
A peaceful retreat from the traffic that's less than a block away, XVA is a contemporary art gallery, casual café and boutique hotel (p157) in one of Bastakia's most beautifully restored old courtyard residences. XVA holds regular exhibitions of art, sculpture and design with splashy openings; organises Creek cruises with a difference; has a wonderful little gift shop; and runs a film club offering regular art-house movie screenings and discussions.

MAJLIS GALLERY Map pp62–3
☎ 353 6233; www.majlisgallery.com; Al-Fahidi Roundabout; ☒ 9.30am-8pm Sat-Thu, closed Fri
In a fabulous old house in the Bastakia Quarter, Majlis Gallery is Dubai's oldest commercial gallery, established in the 1970s. Compared to the progressive galleries in Al-Quoz, Majlis is much more traditional and gentle, focusing on paintings and calligraphy by local and regional artists.

ALI BIN ABI TALIB MOSQUE Map pp62–3
Ali bin Abi Talib St
This simple yet striking mosque in the textile area of Bur Dubai Souq is notable for its sensuous, bulbous domes and gently tapering minaret. Its outline is best appreciated at night from Baniyas Rd in Deira, on the opposite side of the Creek, when the mosque and neighbouring wind-towers are beautifully lit up – it makes a postcard-perfect shot.

ZA'ABEEL PARK Map pp64–5
☎ 800 900 (Dubai Municipality); Sheikh Khalifa bin Zayed Rd & Al-Qataiyat Rd; admission Dh5
This 51-hectare park, stretching over three areas, has gorgeous lakes, ponds, a jogging track, sports facilities, a club house, and retail and food facilities – not to mention fabulous views of the Sheikh Zayed Rd skyline. Work is underway on a project called StarGate, a space-themed park-within-a-park where kids can learn about technology.

BUR DUBAI WATERSIDE WALK
Walking Tour
1 Bastakiah Nights Start this heritage walk of Dubai's oldest areas at Bastakiah Nights (p111) restaurant, near Al-Seef Rd. The courtyard house it occupies is lavishly decorated and worth a look inside (staff are happy to show you around). Spend some time wandering the quarter's atmospheric narrow lanes and peeking into the lovingly renovated wind-tower houses.

2 XVA Hotel & Art Gallery A superbly restored courtyard residence in Bastakia, XVA (left) houses an art gallery, a café, a gift shop and a hotel.

3 Majlis Gallery Another marvellous old house in Bastakia, Majlis (left) has paintings and calligraphy from local artists.

ABRA CRUISING

Fifteen thousand people cross Dubai Creek each day on *abras*, the traditional wooden water taxis, for just Dh1 a journey. You can hire an *abra* to do the same trip the cruise companies do, but you'll be at water level, with wind in your hair and seagulls in your face. It's a more interesting experience, especially if the boat captain speaks a little English or you speak Urdu, Hindi or Arabic – you might learn a whole lot more about the Creek and those who work on it. *Abras* can be hired from the *abra* stations along the creek, but try the dock near Al-Seef roundabout, where they cost around Dh40 for 30 minutes or Dh60 for an hour.

BUR DUBAI WALKING TOUR

4 Sahary Gate Learn about Emirati culture at Sahary Gate (p66) or just drop in to and savour Sahary House's lovely architecture.

5 Dubai Museum From Basta Art Café, head along Al-Fahidi St to Dubai Museum (p61). Here you can easily spend an hour engaging in the history, heritage and development of Dubai, and sneaking photos of the kitschy dioramas.

6 Grand Mosque Emerging from the museum, walk down 78A St to admire the reserved architectural details of the multidomed Grand Mosque (p67); make a note when visiting Sheikh Saeed al-Maktoum House (No 14 on this tour) to look for the original Grand Mosque in old photos of Dubai.

7 Shri Nathje Jayate Temple Take the lane to the mosque's right-hand side, passing the humble Hindu Shri Nathje Jayate Temple (p66) on your left.

8 Hindi Lane Continue straight ahead until you get to Hindi Lane (p66), a wonderful, colourful alley lined with tiny stores selling religious paraphernalia.

9 Sikh Gurudaba Along the way, you'll notice rows of shoes at the bottom of stairs that lead up to the Sikh Gurudaba (p66).

10 Bur Dubai Souq At the end of the lane take a right – you are now in Bur Dubai Souq (p66) – but first head towards the waterfront, past the refurbished wooden stores, until you come to a lovely open area. A favourite spot, it's an oasis of calm overlooking the commotion of the Creek. On the Deira side, you'll notice more restored wind-towers at the Spice Souq, while looking back to the Bur Dubai side you'll see some handsome renovated waterfront houses. Head back in the direction you came, turning right into the souq, and continue under the wooden arcades, passing scores of textile shops. Look up the lanes to the left and you'll notice even more revamped wind-towers.

11 Allah Din Shoes When you see the Dubai Old Souq Abra Station on your right, you'll also spot Allah Din Shoes, selling wonderfully colourful curly-toed slippers at bargain prices. Continue through the vibrant souq, which is generally hectic at night (chaotic on Friday evenings) but peaceful in the morning. Exit the souq at its western entrance with the Bur Dubai Abra Station ahead to your right, and walk past the *abras* and along the waterfront, passing Shindagha Tower on your left, until you arrive at a number of wonderful historic buildings.

12 Sheikh Saeed al-Maktoum House Once the residence of Dubai's ruling Maktoum family, Sheikh Saeed al-Maktoum House (p66) is home to a fascinating collection of old images of Dubai. Before reaching the house, have a look at Bin Suroor Mosque, which dates back to 1930 and is frequented by local workers, and the historic Sheikh Juma al-Maktoum House.

13 Heritage & Diving Villages On the walk to the Heritage & Diving Villages (p67) consider stopping and having a look at the Islamic Centre at Sheikh Obaid bin Thani House. If your visit to Dubai coincides with the Dubai Shopping Festival, the villages will be a hive of activity, providing an insight into Emirati traditions. There are occasional traditional music or dance performances at other times of the year.

14 Kan Zaman Grab a waterfront table at Kan Zaman (p112) and relax, sit back and enjoy a tasty Arabic lunch.

Eating p114; Entertainment p125; Shopping p98; Sleeping p157

Sheikh Zayed Rd itself, which connects Dubai to Abu Dhabi, has been around for many years. But the stretch of high-rise apartment blocks, five-star hotels and offices crammed into the space between the World Trade Centre (a 1979 building that looks prehistoric alongside its space-age cohorts) and the Dusit was mostly built in the late '90s. Just to the side of Dubai's favourite speedway, there's the growing district of Al-Quoz, home to innumerable industrial estates and, of greater interest to tourists, some of the Middle East's best art galleries.

DUBAI WILDLIFE & WATERBIRD SANCTUARY Map p52

☎ 223 2323; Oud Metha Rd, Ras al-Khor; admission free; ⏱ 10am-4pm Sat-Thu, closed Fri

Pretty pink flamingos flock to the inland end of the Dubai Creek during the winter months. Also known as Al-Khor Nature Reserve, this sanctuary has platforms that allow visitors to get a close-up view of the birds (with fantastically sharp binoculars) without disturbing them, and the juxtaposition of these elegant birds with the Dubai metropolis is dramatic. Kids love it, and it's a decent outside bet for a quirky date too.

B21 GALLERY Map pp72–3

☎ 340 3965; off Sheikh Zayed Rd, btwn Interchanges 3 & 4, Al-Quoz; ⏱ 11am-7pm Sat-Thu, closed Fri

In this warehouse space, Palestinian artist Jeffar Khaldi shows his own vibrant work, as well as rotating exhibitions of locally produced and regional art, such as Ramin Haerizadeh's distorted photography. It's worth a look if you're in this developing arts neighbourhood, but call first if you're not, as they could be in-between exhibitions.

THIRD LINE Map pp72–3

☎ 341 1367; www.thethirdline.com; off Sheikh Zayed Rd, btwn Interchanges 3 & 4, Al-Quoz; ⏱ 11am-8pm Sat-Thu, closed Fri

One of Dubai's more adventurous art spaces is operated by a couple of talented young curators, Sunny Rahbar and Claudia Cellini, whose exhibitions focus on provocative contemporary art. Their shows often include work that breaks the rules of traditional arts in the region to create fresh new forms, playfully appropriating everything from Pakistani miniatures and Persian calligraphy to traditional clothing. Recent exhibitions have included the arresting op art of Rana Begum and the elaborate paintings of Iranian artist Farhad Moshri.

MEEM GALLERY Map pp72–3

☎ 347 7883; www.meem.ae; Umm Suqeim Rd, off Interchange 4, Al-Quoz; ⏱ 9.30am-6.30pm Sat-Wed, closed Thu, 9.30am-2pm Fri

An ambitious venture by two Emirati business tycoons and British art dealer Charlie Pocock, Meem is dedicated to traditional and contemporary Islamic art. Recent exhibitions have included Ali Omar Ermes' calligraphic paintings and the pop art of Jordan's Jamal Abdul Rahim. If you're interested in learning more about Arabic art, this is a great place to visit and possibly make an acquisition.

COURTYARD Map pp72–3

☎ 347 5050; www.courtyard-uae.com; off Sheikh Zayed Rd, btwn Interchanges 3 & 4, Al-Quoz; ☎ 9am-7pm Sat-Thu

The Courtyard is home to several galleries that hold changing exhibitions of painting, calligraphy, mixed media, miniatures, rare Persian carpets and sculptures by local, Middle Eastern and international artists. The Courtyard also has interior design and handicrafts stores, and a few media/design businesses. Highlights here are Iranian expat artist, Dariush Zandi's Total Arts at The

top picks

FOR KIDS

- Dubai Museum (p61)
- Za'abeel Park (p68)
- Creekside Park & Children's City (p67)
- Ibn Battuta Mall (p101)
- Ski Dubai Snow Park (p142)
- Wild Wadi Waterpark (p78)
- Dubai Wildlife & Waterbird Sanctuary (left)
- Jam Jar (p74)
- Al-Mamzar Park (p58)
- Jumeirah Beach Park (p78)

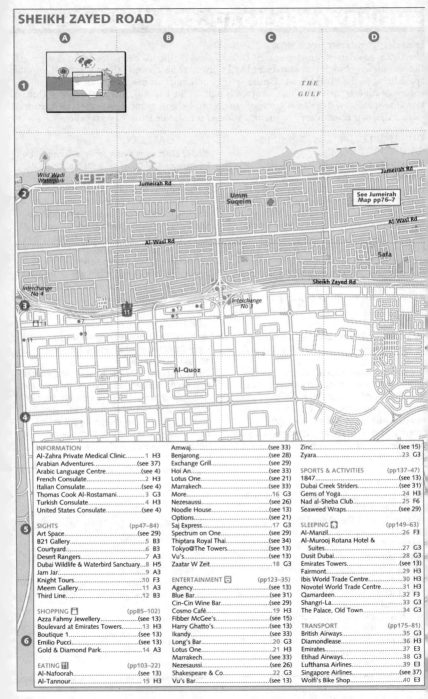

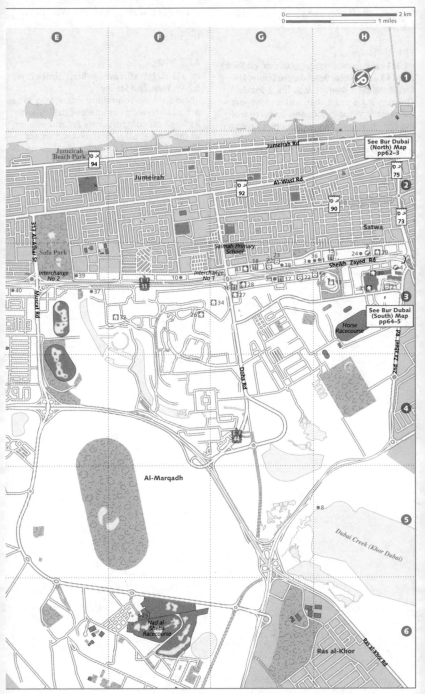

Jumeirah
Beach Park ▯ 94

Jumeirah

Jumeirah Rd

Al-Wasi Rd

Satwa

See Bur Dubai
(North) Map
pp62–3

▯ 75

▯ 92

▯ 90

▯ 73

313 Al-Athar St

Safa Park

Interchange
No 2

● 39

● 40

● 37

Muscat Rd

Salmah Primary
School

Interchange
No 1

Sheikh   Zayed   Rd

23
18   20   38
13   10 ●   16
11   28
27   35   17   22
34
26
32

36
3 ● ● ●   24 ◉   29
30

Horse
Racecourse

See Bur Dubai
(South) Map
pp64–5

Doha Rd

2nd Zaabeel Rd

44

Al-Marqadh

● 8

Dubai Creek (Khor Dubai)

25
Nad al-
Sheba
Racecourse

Ras al-Khor

Ras al-Khor Rd

73

Courtyard (☎ 347 5050) and locally-owned Courtyard Gallery & Café (☎ 347 9090).

JAM JAR Map pp72–3

☎ 341 7303; www.thejamjardubai.com; off Sheikh Zayed Rd exit 39, near Dubai Garden Centre, Al-Barsha; ☎ 10am-9pm Sat, Mon-Thu, 2-9pm Fri

The Jam Jar is more than just another art gallery. It's a studio too, and if you're feeling the creative urge, you can hire an easel, a canvas and all the paint and paper you require to create your own masterpiece.

For those travelling with children, it's an appealing alternative to an afternoon in the mall.

ART SPACE Map pp72–3

☎ 332 5523; 9th fl, Fairmont Hotel, Sheikh Zayed Rd; ☎ 10am-8pm Sat-Thu

There's always something interesting to see at this refreshing commercial gallery with its focus on contemporary art and mission to promote local artists, develop an appreciation for art and grow the local scene.

JUMEIRAH

Eating p117; Entertainment p128; Shopping p99; Sleeping p159
Before you were able to own a private desert island in the shape of your favourite country, Jumeirah was the place where everybody went to realise their Dubai dreams. It's the emirate's answer to Bondi or Malibu, with excellent public beaches, boutique shopping, copious spas and health clubs, and a mix of Mercedes and expensive 4WDs in villa driveways. The far end of Jumeirah is home to some of Dubai's landmark buildings, including the Burj Al Arab and Madinat Jumeirah.

BURJ AL ARAB Map pp76–7
☎ 301 7777; www.burj-al-arab.com; Jumeirah Rd, Umm Suqeim

In its first decade since opening, the Burj Al Arab has been more than just the iconic symbol of a booming city in the sand; it has challenged preconceived ideas of what an Arab country in the Middle East can achieve. The Burj's statistics are certainly impressive. It is built on an artificial island 280m offshore from the Jumeirah Beach Hotel and the sail-shaped building tops out at 321m. These numbers, of course, have been dwarfed by the newer Burj in town, but this five-star hotel (it's best to ignore the nonsense about seven stars) is still worth visiting, if only to gawk at an interior that's every bit as gaudy as the exterior is gorgeous. If you're not staying at the hotel, you need a restaurant reservation to get past the security gates. The most wallet-friendly option is to visit the Skyview Bar (although the price of drinks will induce vertigo before you've even peered out the windows) or book an equally pricey afternoon tea at Sahn Eddar. The unthinkable alternative, however, is travelling all the way to Dubai and then leaving without going inside and forming an opinion on this extraordinary building.

JUMEIRAH MOSQUE Map pp76–7
☎ 353 6666; Jumeira Rd; tour Dh10; ☉ 10am Sat, Sun, Tue & Thu

The splendid, intricately detailed architecture (stunningly lit at night) and the opportunity to have a look inside (normally non-Muslims are not able to enter mosques here) makes Jumeirah Mosque well worth visiting. It is aimed at promoting greater understanding between Muslims and other religions and cultures; the Sheikh Mohammed Centre for Cultural Understanding's 'Open Doors, Open Minds' tour takes visitors through the building describing the architecture of the mosque and introducing them to Islam plus the Emirati culture and traditions. The Q&A session is viewed as a vital part of the visit, so read up a little first (see the boxed text, p41). It's best to prebook, as it's becoming increasingly popular, and make sure to dress modestly (no shorts, cover back and arms, and women should wear a headscarf). You'll also need to remove your shoes before entering.

MADINAT JUMEIRAH Map pp76–7
Al-Sufouh Rd, Jumeirah

The Madinat is a hotel, shopping and entertainment complex that delights and frustrates in equal measures. For starters, it is quite a sight – its exteriors are inspired by the ancient skyscrapers found in Saudi Arabia and Yemen, and the interiors are influenced by old Arabian merchant houses. There are some exquisite details here, so if you see some stairs, take them – they might lead you to a secreted terrace and wind-tower, with a mesmerising vista of the sprawling complex. If you're a hotel guest, or have a restaurant reservation, you can catch the silent *abras* cruising along the Venetian-style canals from one location to the next. If you're a day tripper and non-diner, your progress will be cut short by staff patrolling the walkways to keep the riff-raff from the souq away from the hotels. More a themed shopping mall than a traditional Arabian market, the souq is a bit of a tourist trap. Prices are several times more expensive than they are in real souqs and with a few exceptions, such as Pisces (p118) and the Noodle House (p117), the restaurants overcharge for ordinary fare. The Madinat Theatre (www.madinattheatre.com) hosts musicals, plays, opera, ballet and festivals; and during the cooler winter months, a traditional oud player enchants the *sheesha*-smoking crowd in the souq's central plaza.

JUMEIRAH

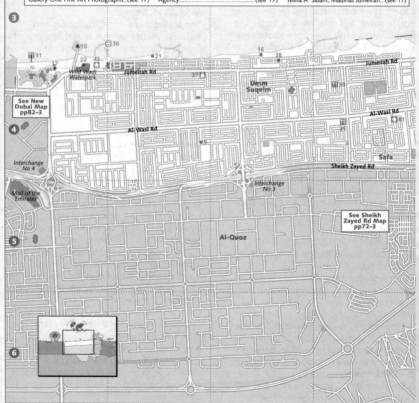

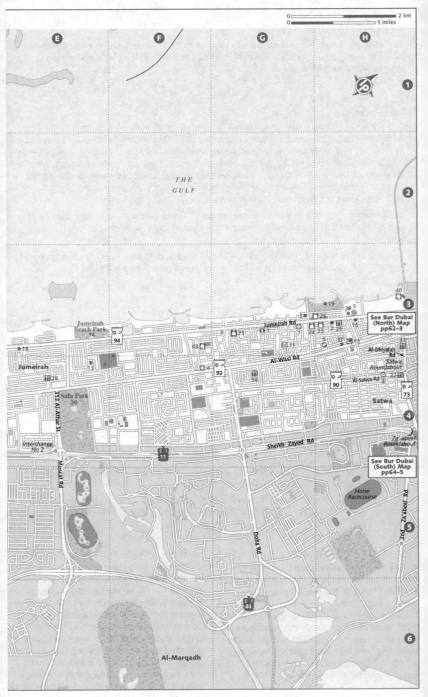

See Bur Dubai (North) Map pp62–3

See Bur Dubai (South) Map pp64–5

THE GULF

0 ——————— 2 km
0 ——————— 1 miles

E   F   G   H

1

2

3

4

5

6

Jumeirah Beach Park
14

94

Jumeirah
28

313 Al-Athar St

Safa Park
20

18

Interchange No 2

Muscat Rd

Al-Marqadh

Sheikh Zayed Rd

Doha Rd

E 11

E 44

Jumeirah Rd

Al-Wasl Rd

43

92

25

1

7

19

3

26

24 23

2 29

6

37

39

90

Al-Dhiyafah Rd

Satwa
Roundabout

Al-Satwa Rd

Satwa

73

40

Za'abeel
Roundabout

Horse
Racecourse

2nd Za'abeel Rd

PUBLIC EXPOSURE

If you're not staying at a five star with access to some sand, and want to be able to say you've swum in the Arabian Sea (or at least dipped your toes in the water), you've got two options: either head to one of Dubai's free public beaches or pay for a day at a beach club.

Dipping Without Dirhams

Dubai's free beaches...

Russian Beach (Map pp76–7; next to Dubai Marine Beach Resort & Spa, Jumeirah) Also known as Open Beach, this is one of Dubai's few truly public spaces. As such, it reflects the multicultural nature of Dubai society and is a great place for a walk, especially on a Friday when most guest workers have the day off and take to picnicking, playing volleyball and splashing around in the ocean. We have reservations about recommending it as a destination for sunbathing. The city still struggles to deal with beach pests, packs of men who head to the beaches at the weekends to stare at and photograph women. Physical harassment is extremely rare, but it's probably worth spending a little extra money or waiting for a women-only day. Showers and kiosk are available.

Kite Beach (Map p52; behind old Wollongong University campus, Umm Suqeim 4) This long pristine beach is a great place to sunbathe, except for the kite surfers (hence the name), whose abilities range from good to good grief. No facilities.

Umm Suqeim Beach (Map p52; btwn Jumeirah Beach Hotel & Kite Beach) This white sandy beach, with fabulous views of the Burj, is popular with Jumeirah families and Western expatriates. Showers and shelter.

Beaches for Bucks

The ones that cost...

Jumeirah Beach Park (pp76–7; per person/car Dh5/20; ✆ 8am-11pm, women & children only Sat & Mon) It's a real treat to take a walk on the grass at this verdant park, as it's a couple of degrees cooler than the beach. Fronting onto a long stretch of Jumeirah Beach, the beach has lifeguards on duty, a children's play area, barbecues, picnic tables, walkways and kiosks.

Khor al-Mamzar (Map p52; per person/car Dh5/30; ✆ 8am-11pm; women & children only Wed) This calm inlet must be one of the prettiest spots to swim, although construction on the Palm Deira is becoming an increasing eyesore. Showers, picnicking facilities and tour groups galore.

One&Only Royal Mirage (p162) If you're not a guest, you have to win a mini-lottery to gain access to this groomed beach and pool with views of the Palm development (adult Dh175). You have to turn up on the day (they don't accept advance bookings) and hope that hotel occupancy is below 80%. Only couples are permitted – no children.

Hilton Dubai Jumeirah (p163) Parents love the non-stop organised kids' activities, water sports and comparatively low prices (adult/child weekdays Dh180/95, weekends Dh250/95).

Le Meridien Mina Seyahi (p163) This good beach and its great pools are popular with a more body-conscious clubbing set (Sunday to Thursday adult/child Dh150/75). The weekends are reserved for hotel guests and members.

WILD WADI WATERPARK Map pp76–7

☎ 348 4444; www.wildwadi.com; Jumeirah Rd, Jumeirah; adult/child Dh180/150; ✆ 11am-6pm Nov-Feb, 11am-7pm Mar-May & Sep-Oct, 11am-9pm Jun-Aug

Wild Wadi seems to satisfy everyone's needs, with dozens of ingeniously interconnected rides based on the legend of Arabian adventurer Juha and his friend, Sinbad the sailor, who are shipwrecked on a lush lagoon, beyond which lies a magical oasis. There are water-safety lessons for children, more sedate rides for young children and nervous adults, two Flowriders (artificial waves) and the truly terrifying near-freefall Jumeirah Sceirah (hold on to your trunks, lads). Many people settle in for a few hours; the body boards and tubes are free, and food and drinks are available via a clever debit card attached to your wrist. It's important to call ahead before you visit: if it isn't closed to men (occasional Thursday night is women-only), there's a remote chance Michael Jackson will book the entire joint to swim in a lycra bodysuit that only reveals his eyes and nose. Rumours are that some lifeguards on duty in 2005 suffered post-traumatic stress disorder after seeing such an event.

MAJLIS GHORFAT UM-AL-SHEEF
Map pp76–7

17 St, near Jumeirah Beach Park; admission Dh1; ⏲ 8.30am-1.30pm & 3.30-8.30pm Sat-Thu, 3.30-8.30pm Fri

It is unusual to find a traditional building still standing so far from the Creek, but this one, south of Jumeirah Beach Park, has been well restored and is worth a visit. The two-storey structure was built in 1955 and was attended in the evenings by Sheikh Rashid bin Saeed al-Maktoum. Here he would listen to his people's complaints, grievances and ideas. The *majlis* also provided a cool retreat from the heat of the day because it is made of gypsum and coral rock, traditional building materials of the Gulf, and the roof is made of palm fronds *(areesh)*. The *majlis* is decorated with cushions, rugs, a coffeepot, pottery and food platters, and is pretty close to the way it would have looked in Sheikh Rashid's day.

GREEN ART GALLERY Map pp76–7
☎ 344 9888; www.gagallery.com; behind Dubai Zoo, Jumeirah; ⏲ 9.30am-1.30pm & 4.30-9pm Sat-Thu

With regular temporary exhibitions and a growing permanent collection concentrating on the work of artists living in the UAE, this small, altruistic commercial gallery is committed to nurturing local talent and developing the art scene. It also helps educate artists about international art distribution and promotion, and the website features selections from upcoming and past exhibitions.

IRANIAN MOSQUE Map pp76–7
Al-Wasl Rd, Satwa

Shiite mosques are noteworthy for their exquisite faïence (green-and-blue-coloured and glazed) tile work covering the façade and main dome. A stunning Dubai example is the Iranian Mosque in Satwa – and the Iranian Hospital, adjacent and opposite, carries this same type of tile work.

JUMEIRAH ARCHAEOLOGICAL SITE
Map pp76–7

Off 27 St (look for a large fenced-in area) near Jumeirah Beach Park, Jumeirah

Only really of interest to archaeology buffs, this is one of the most significant and largest archaeological sites in the UAE, where items dating from the 6th century AD were found and can be seen at Dubai Museum (p61) and the Heritage Village (p67). Surrounded by atmosphere-inhibiting modern villas, the settlement is interesting in that it spans the

---

GET LOST: BUR DUBAI, SHEIKH ZAYED ROAD & JUMEIRAH

Al-Musallah (Map pp62–3) Most people walk down Al-Musallah Rd only to reach Bastakia, but it's a shame not to explore the animated backstreets of this area. The roads behind Dubai Museum are the city's 'Little India', where you'll see lots of textile stores, cheap restaurants, hair salons (amusingly called 'saloons' in the Emirates), and men on the street watching cricket through the windows of cafeterias.

Karama (Map pp64–5) Wandering the gritty backstreets of the lower-income expat community in Karama is interesting, especially if you're sociable and chat to the affable shopkeepers. The district is best known for its laissez-faire attitude towards patents, copyrights and intellectual property – bootleg DVDs, handbags, football shirts and perfumes are widely available here. In most cases you get what you pay for. It's also fantastic for food, with dozens of restaurants serving the assorted cuisines of the Indian subcontinent. At many of the restaurants you can eat well and get change from a Dh20 note.

Satwa (Map pp72–3) In the space between the swanky skyscrapers of Sheikh Zayed Rd and the cosmopolitan swagger of Dubai's best street for eating, Al-Dhiyafha Rd, is this fascinating residential area. The villas here are so odd-looking, uneven and colourful (pink and yellow are popular choices) they look like they've been designed by kids in a classroom. It's quite common for 15 to 20 people to share a single villa; you'll see sofas and even beds on the roof and the road, such is the lack of space. The souq-like main thoroughfare, Satwa Rd, comes alive at night in a riotous blaze of neon. Unless you want a cheap haircut or a new set of keys, it's unlikely many of the shops will appeal, but it's definitely worth refuelling at Ravi (p119). Don't miss Al-Hudaiba Rd, known locally as 'Plant Street'. It's home to a few good florists, a great Filipino supermarket, a couple of excellent fruit and veg shops, and pet shop owners who should thank their lucky stars animal welfare is such a fringe concern in this city.

pre-Islamic and Islamic eras and was once a caravan stop on a route linking Ctesiphon (now Iraq) to northern Oman. Remains from here link it with the Persian Sassanid Empire, dominant in the region from the 3rd to 6th centuries AD, and the Umayyad dynasty in the 7th century, when Islam arrived in the Gulf.

1X1 ART SPACE Map p52
☎ 348 3873; www.1x1artspace.com; Villa 1023, Al-Mahara, Al-Wasl Rd; ☼ 11am-8pm Sat-Thu
Expats from the Indian subcontinent make up a huge chunk of Dubai's population, yet they're under-represented in the city's galleries. 1x1 Art Space aims to redress the imbalance by exhibiting Indian and Pakistani contemporary art in its elegant gallery.

SAFA PARK Map pp76–7
Cnr Al-Wasl Rd & Al-Hadiqa St, Safa; admission Dh5; ☼ 8am-11pm, women & children only Tue
This very popular park stretches for 1km from Al-Wasl Rd to Sheikh Zayed Rd. Lots of cricket is played on the wide grassy expanses at weekends, and after dark the rides (near Al-Wasl Rd) get busy. There are tennis courts, a soccer pitch, barbecues, an artificial waterfall, and a lake where you can hire paddle boats.

NEW DUBAI

Eating p119; Entertainment p130; Shopping p101; Sleeping p162

There's an expat fable about a couple who move into the penthouse suite of a high-rise Marina apartment with amazing views of the Burj Al Arab, the Palm Jumeirah and The World. Feeling smug about the postcard perfection of their dream life in the Emirates, they retire to bed. The following morning they wake up, pull back the curtains, and are devastated to discover a block of apartments entirely obscuring their view.

The couple should consider themselves lucky that only one building materialised from nothing overnight. New Dubai, as it's unimaginatively known, is thought to be the fastest-growing place on earth. The figures are mind-blowing. In a few years time, the combined population of the Palm Jumeirah, Palm Jebel Ali and Dubai Waterfront is expected to be over a million people (with a further million living on the Palm Deira). The Palm Jumeirah will be home to 30 luxury hotels, and the Dubai Waterfront alone will add 800km to the emirate's coastline. It's hard to keep up. In the previous edition of this book we didn't require a separate section for New Dubai. In the next edition we might have to add a further section: New New Dubai?

FORTHCOMING ATTRACTIONS

It's believed that a third of the world's cranes are in Dubai. Here are some of the more ambitious projects underway (for soon-to-open luxury hotels, see the boxed text, p162). You might just spot a theme developing…

Bawadi How's this for ambition? Bawadi will consist of 51 hotels and 60,000 hotel rooms, plus lots of shopping malls, theme parks and restaurants. No half-measures in this city.

Burj Al Alam One of countless skyscrapers in the Business Bay district, Alam is expected to become one of the 10 tallest buildings in the world upon completion.

Culture Village Whaddya mean Dubai has no culture? It's soon to have an entire satellite town dedicated to the clever stuff. Culture Village will feature academies, galleries, workshops, craft studios and, of course, luxury villas.

Dubailand Bawadi, Mall of Arabia, Dubai Sports City and plenty of other developments will all be part of Dubailand, which as far as we can tell, will be significantly bigger – and much more fun – than life itself.

Dubai Waterfront A series of manmade islands forming around the Palm Jebel Ali, Dubai Waterfront will eventually be home to around 400,000 people. It will be the largest manmade development in the world.

Dubai World Central International Airport The planet's biggest airport will also be home to its biggest car park. Now they're just showing off…

Great Dubai Wheel The 185m observation wheel will be – surprise – the biggest in the world. It will offer panoramic views of the city.

Falcon City of Wonders A theme park featuring replicas of the Eiffel Tower, the Taj Mahal and the Leaning Tower of Pisa, among others. Why go anywhere else?

Lyon-Dubai City The rebuilding of the French city of Lyon in the desert is perhaps the single most bonkers Dubai project so far, and there's been no shortage of competition.

Meydan A city-within-a-city dedicated to horse racing. For fans only.

55° Time Dubai The world's first rotating skyscraper to be powered by the sun. And why ever not?

Palm Deira This set of artificial islands, the concluding chapter of the Palm trilogy, will be 10 times larger than the Palm Jumeirah and home to approximately a million people by 2020.

Palm Jebel Ali Expected to burst into life some time around 2010, the second Palm, when seen from above, spells out a verse of poetry written by Sheikh Mohammed: 'Take wisdom from the wise. Not everybody who rides a horse is a jockey. It takes a man of great vision to write on water. Great men rise to great challenges.'

Pentominium The world's tallest residential building has been saddled with one of the world's worst building names. It'll tower over the rest of Dubai Marina.

The Universe Here's how you trump The World. Islands built in the shape of the sun, the moon and the planet of the solar system will fill the gap between the Palm Deira and the Palm Jumeirah. But where do they go from here?

NEW DUBAI

THE GULF

Dubai Marina

To Jebel Ali (16km)
Oud Metha Rd

Interchange No 5

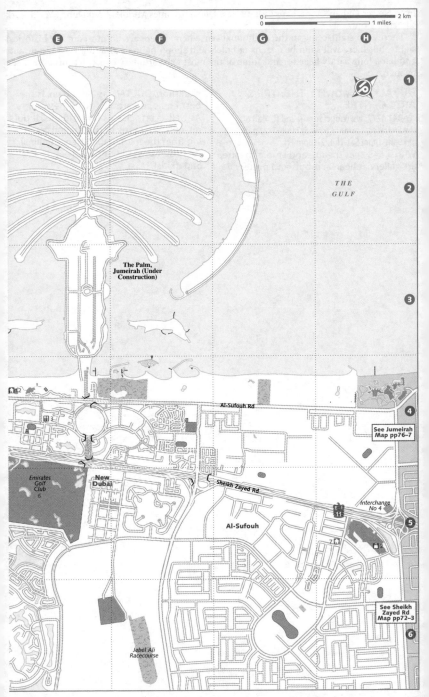

The Palm, Jumeirah (Under Construction)

THE GULF

Al-Sufouh Rd

New Dubai

Sheikh Zayed Rd

Emirates Golf Club

Al-Sufouh

Interchange No 4

Jebel Ali Racecourse

See Jumeirah Map pp76–7

See Sheikh Zayed Rd Map pp72–3

Even Newer Dubai? Or perhaps today's New Dubai becomes Middle-Aged Dubai. We'll work something out…

There's no sightseeing in the traditional sense here. There are no museums or historical sights, but there will soon be dozens of hotels and shopping malls, hundreds of restaurants and bars, long sandy beaches and some of the most extraordinary constructions ever made by man.

DUBAI COMMUNITY THEATRE & ARTS CENTRE

☎ 341 4777; www.ductac.org; 2nd fl, Mall of the Emirates, entrance from Ski Dubai car park; ☉ 9am-10pm Sat-Thu, 2-10pm Fri

With a 543-seat theatre and studio theatre, art gallery, rehearsal rooms and pottery workshop, DUCTAC, as it's known, is the best-equipped arts centre in the country. As well as arts classes for residents, it puts on a diverse range of productions ranging from the memorable (Henry Rollins) to those we would rather forget (Flying Superkids).

top picks

SHOPPING

Dubai loves to shop. With so much money floating around, it only makes sense that there be so many places to spend it. The city has few public spaces; shopping malls are the de facto town commons. Part cultural centre, part entertainment complexes, malls are the primary gathering place in Dubai: when you meet up with friends, you often do so at a mall. And such malls you'll see nowhere else.

The explosion in themed mall architecture took off in 2002 with the opening of Mercato Mall and its preposterous Tuscany-meets-Venice architecture. Now Mercato looks tame. The Souq Madinat Jumeirah reinterprets the classic covered Arabian bazaars of old, with gracefully arching wooden ceilings above a maze of corridors designed to get you lost. Anchoring the complex at either end are two palatial, seaside hotels connected by a series of canals, with the iconic Burj Al Arab hotel looming in the background. Think Disney does Arabia. Nearly 1.5km long, Ibn Battuta Mall is comprised of six interconnected shopping centres, each one styled after a country visited by the eponymous explorer, who travelled from China to Andalusia in the 14th century. Amble beneath faux starry skies, past towering live palms, and into a giant tiled Persian dome with (what else?) a Starbucks at its centre. The China section is the stunner: a life-size junk lies on its side – someone is always posing for pictures in front of it.

The biggest shopping centre in the region until the Dubai Mall opens, Mall of the Emirates and its shiny white-marble corridors, is most famous for its indoor ski slope, Ski Dubai, where snow flies every night. Outside a series of colour-lit fountains blast water into the sky, choreographed to the blaring theme of *Mission Impossible*. The massive Dubai Festival City opened in 2007, with a red-carpet-lined VIP entrance (essentially valet parking). The back of the mall is most impressive: a three-storey-high, origami-inspired marble sculpture, with water running down its faces, doubles as a staircase for shoppers. *Abras* float past on outdoor canals, setting a picturesque if ersatz backdrop for al fresco performances.

With 12 million sq ft of retail, the soon-to-open Dubai Mall will take its place as the world's largest mall, smack dab in the shadow of the Burj Dubai, the world's tallest tower. In true Dubai style – ever in competition with itself – shortly after the Dubai Mall opens in late 2008, the Mall of Arabia will open in 2009 and take the prize as the world's largest. The Guinness judges make a lot of trips to Dubai.

Looked down upon in other parts of the world, air-conditioned malls make sense in Dubai, their trickling fountains and cool marble floors a welcome respite from the oppressive heat. The problem is, every new mall offers more of the same corporate chain stores, repackaged in glitzier format. We've included some of these major style franchises, such as Zara and Marc Jacobs, but have endeavoured to suss out the independent shops, stores like the exotic Mumbai Se and whimsical Ginger and Lace at Ibn Battuta Mall, and the funky Lebanese fashion shop Aizone and Norwegian skincare-shop Pixi at the Mall of the Emirates.

The Dubai shopping scene lacks the dynamism and breadth of major Western cities, such as London and New York, primarily because the city has no significant underground art scene to fuel new ideas. Everything in Dubai is imported, including creativity. That's why you'll be especially happy about two independent boutiques, S*uce and Five Green. While they won't bowl you over if you shop the world, you'll find brands and designs you otherwise wouldn't.

Scouring the souqs (covered outdoor markets) remains the city's quintessential shopping experience and the fastest way to get to the heart of the culture. Nothing compares to the atmosphere and chaos of the souqs – the colours and textures, the cacophony of sounds, the street hawkers barking for customers, and the call to prayer booming down narrow lanes. There's a souq for everything: fish, fruit and vegetables, electronics – there's even a camel souq. But head to sensuous Spice Souq, where you can close your eyes and be carried away by distant culinary memories. Trawl for Bedouin jewellery, Palestinian embroidery, curly-toed Aladdin slippers, Oriental perfumes, frankincense and myrrh, cheap headphones, and camel-shaped clock radios to take home to friends.

Souqs are on either side of Dubai Creek and the backstreets of Karama; malls are scattered about town. Hailing a taxi can take a long time (see p94). Malls have dedicated taxi lines (though they may be over an hour in length). At the souqs you'll simply have to stand in the street; alternatively head to the nearest main drag, or take a bus or *abra*. All malls have food courts, some remarkably good, especially the Mall of the Emirates; they also boast full-service restaurants, some licensed, and ATMs and foreign-exchange offices. Whether they actually have any bargains is another story. Though there are no duties and taxes (see the boxed text, p99), unless you're buying expensive luxury items such as a Rolex, you'll find prices only a bit cheaper than overseas, depending on your home currency. For the best deals, come during one of the shopping festivals (p88).

OPENING HOURS

Malls in Dubai open from 10am to 10pm Sunday to Wednesday, from 10am to midnight Thursday to Saturday (weekends), and later during Dubai Shopping Festival and Ramadan (often until 1am). Traditionally, souqs and non-mall stores close a few hours during the afternoon for prayer, lunch and rest, and don't open on Fridays until late afternoon, but that's changing. These days many remain open all day. Malls get packed Friday nights: if you hate crowds, stay away. Otherwise, the people-watching is great.

BARGAINING

Bargaining is an obsession for some; others do anything to avoid it, immediately accepting the first offer. If you fall into the latter category, bear in mind that the first price suggested by spruikers in souqs is unrealistic; if you accept, you're overpaying and sending a signal to locals that out-of-towners are easy marks. Here's how to handle it. A counter-offer of half is made. The final figure will usually be somewhere about 20% to 50% lower than the shopkeeper's initial offer. Expect additional discounts for buying more than one piece from a vendor. Once the vendor agrees to your figure, you're expected to pay. Continuing to haggle once you've agreed is an insult. Leaving the store empty-handed after you've bargained is impolite. Remember, you may want to return; leaving on good terms will score you bigger discounts next time.

top picks

MALLS

- Dubai Festival City (p102)
- Mall of the Emirates (p101)
- BurJuman Centre (p96)
- Souq Madinat Jumeirah (p101)
- Ibn Battuta Mall (p101)

Confidence comes with practice; having a friend with you helps. Some like to play 'good cop, bad cop', with one feigning disinterest, trying to drag the other away. The shopkeeper will reduce the price rather than lose a sale. You don't typically bargain at chain stores in shopping malls, but at independent stores inside the malls, ask for the 'best price', especially on carpets, perfumes and electronics.

BEST BUYS
Gold & Gems

The City of Gold's glistening reputation grows from low prices and the sheer breadth of selection. There are a whopping 700 jewellery stores in Dubai, with nearly 300 at the Gold Souq and over 100 at the Gold & Diamond Park. Low import duties and no tax mean it's one of the cheapest places in the world at which to buy jewellery. Tradition keeps business booming: in India and the Gulf countries, when you provide gold for a dowry, it must be brand new – and over-the-top, apparently. Windows in the Gold Souq display the ornate necklaces, earrings and headpieces worn by Indian and Arabian brides. This is the jaw-dropping jewellery that you see in tourist-brochure photographs. But the selection inside the stores is significantly more diverse, ranging from intricately patterned pieces to sleek contemporary designs.

Dubai's jewellery shops also carry an impressive array of silver, diamonds, pearls and precious gems. And if you don't find anything you love, have something made. Either way, fear not: what you're buying is authentic. Local laws are very strict. Dubai Municipality makes regular quality checks. Gold traders wouldn't dare risk their reputations in such a competitive environment. Look for the gold-purity hallmark, get a detailed invoice and ask for a Certificate of Authenticity for diamonds and gems. While gold is sold by weight and prices fluctuate, the rate is fixed twice daily, according to international rates, by the Gold and Jewellery Group; check www.dubaicityof gold.com for the current numbers. Prices for fashion jewellery vary depending on several factors, including the intricacy of the design, and whether the piece was made by machine or hand. Regardless, prepare to bargain.

Carpets

Dubai is a carpet-lover's paradise. Fine Persian carpets, colourful Turkish and Kurdish kilims, rough-knotted Bedouin rugs – they're all widely available. Dubai has a reputation in the region for having the highest-quality carpets at the best prices. The only problem is, each year the prices creep up as more visitors come to Dubai to shop. Bargaining is the norm. If you can't secure the price you want, head to another store. There are hundreds of 'em. Dubai's malls have the greatest number of carpet shops; the streets around Baniyas Sq (Map pp56–7) and Sharjah souqs also have a good selection. When you buy a carpet ask for a certificate of authentication guaranteed by the Dubai Chamber of Commerce & Industry, so you can be sure that the carpet actually comes from where the vendor says it does. For more information and what to look for when shopping for rugs, see p90 and right.

Arabian Handicrafts & Souvenirs

Arabian handicrafts are as popular with Dubai visitors as carpets, gold and perfume. The Oriental décor of the city's top-end hotels and restaurants seems to inspire travellers to pack away little pieces of exotica to recreate their own little

BEST CARPET BUYING BOOKS

- *Oriental Rugs Today*, 2nd edition, by Emmett Eiland
- *Persian Rugs and Carpets: Their History and Symbolism*, by Essie Sakhai
- *Oriental Rugs, A Complete Guide*, by Murray L Eiland Jr and Murray Eiland the Third
- *The Carpets, Rugs and Kilims of the World*, by Enza Milanesi
- *Kilims, a Buyer's Guide*, by Lee Allane
- *Tribal Rugs*, by James Opie

genie bottles back home. Head to the souqs for Moroccan coloured lanterns, Syrian rosewood furniture inlaid with mother-of-pearl, Arabian brass coffee pots, Turkish miniature paintings, and embroidered Indian wall-hangings and cushion covers dotted with tiny mirrors. If you're on a budget, use your imagination to create fab home furnishings. Colourful Indian saris make sexy curtains, and Kashmiri shawls look great atop tables and sideboards. Add foldable wooden legs to a decorative metal serving platter for a cool coffee table, or stretch a camel bag over cube-shaped ottomans.

Sheesha pipes (aka hubbly bubblies and nargilehs) make memorable souvenirs. Note: the smaller pipes are decorative and don't work. If you intend to use your pipe, buy a complete *sheesha* kit in an easy-to-carry hard case, which includes all the little accessories you'll need. *Sheesha* pipes and the flavoured tobacco are available from souqs, specialist

DUBAI'S SHOPPING FESTIVALS

Every year from mid-January to mid-February, the month-long Dubai Shopping Festival (www.mydsf.com) draws hoards of bargain-hunting tourists from around the world. This is the best time to visit Dubai: aside from the huge discounts in the souqs and malls, the weather is gorgeous and the city abuzz. Outdoor souqs, amusement rides and food stalls set up in many neighbourhoods, with the best on the Bur Dubai waterfront across from the British Embassy. There are traditional performances and displays at the Heritage and Diving Villages, family entertainment across the city, concerts and events in the parks, and nightly fireworks, best viewed from Creekside Park. Dubai Summer Surprises, a related event, is held during the unbearably hot months of July and August; it mainly attracts visitors from other Gulf countries. NB: For the best bargains at either festival, come during the last week, when retailers slash prices even further to clear out their inventory.

The carnival-like Global Village (www.globalvillage.ae; Dubailand; adult/family Dh5/15; 4pm-midnight) runs from December to March in Dubailand (off Map p52). Think of it as a sort of World Fair for shoppers. Each of the 30-something pavilions showcases a specific nation's culture and – of course – products. Some favourites: the Afghanistan pavilion for fretwork-bordered stone pendants and beaded-silver earrings; Palestine for traditional cross-stitch *kandouras* (casual shirt-dresses) and ever-popular cushion covers; Yemen for its authentic *khanjars* (Bedouin daggers); India for spangly fabrics and slippers; and Kenya for its kitsch bottle-top handbags. Dig the earnest entertainment, from Chinese opera to Turkish whirling dervishes. Organizers claim this is to be a permanent installation at Dubailand, but as of this writing it was still seasonal. Check the web.

CLOTHING SIZES

Women's clothing

Aus/UK	8	10	12	14	16	18
Europe	36	38	40	42	44	46
Japan	5	7	9	11	13	15
USA	6	8	10	12	14	16

Women's shoes

Aus/USA	5	6	7	8	9	10
Europe	35	36	37	38	39	40
France only	35	36	38	39	40	42
Japan	22	23	24	25	26	27
UK	3½	4½	5½	6½	7½	8½

Men's clothing

Aus	92	96	100	104	108	112
Europe	46	48	50	52	54	56
Japan	S		M	M		L
UK/USA	35	36	37	38	39	40

Men's shirts (collar sizes)

Aus/Japan	38	39	40	41	42	43
Europe	38	39	40	41	42	43
UK/USA	15	15½	16	16½	17	17½

Men's shoes

Aus/UK	7	8	9	10	11	12
Europe	41	42	43	44½	46	47
Japan	26	27	27½	28	29	30
USA	7½	8½	9½	10½	11½	12½

Measurements approximate only, try before you buy

stores, tobacconists, supermarkets and souvenir shops. (See p134 for a lesson in how to use your new pipe.)

If you're shopping for family and friends, look for silver prayer holders, inlaid wooden boxes, tinted-glass perfume bottles and kitsch souvenirs (see right). Dad may appreciate a framed *khanjar* or silver gunpowder horn. Mum will definitely love a new pashmina (see p98). Kids will love a cuddly camel; some even play Arabian music when you squeeze them. Camel Company (p99) has the best selection of camel toys. For older kids, look for brightly painted pencil holders and boxes with Emirati scenes rendered in naïve style, from Gifts and Souvenirs at Karama Shopping Centre (p97). Julia Johnston's illustrated story books also make great gifts; find them at Magrudy's (p93).

For the best-quality souvenirs and handicrafts, head to Deira City Centre, Mall of the Emirates and Souq Madinat Jumeirah. For the best prices, head to Karama Shopping Centre (aka Karama Souq), Bur Dubai and Deira Souqs. Also check out the stalls at the Heritage & Diving Villages (p67).

Kitsch Souvenirs

The ultimate kitsch souvenir used to be a colourful mosque clock with an irritating call-to-prayer alarm. Now the souqs and souvenir shops overflow with wacky, kitsch gifts – glass Burj Al Arab paperweights, wooden Russian dolls painted as Emiratis, Barbie and Ken dolls in Emirati dress, key rings strung with miniature towers, camel-crossing-sign fridge magnets, and coffee mugs and baseball caps with Sheikh Zayed or Sheikh Mohammed waving to the crowd. Karama Shopping Centre (p97) is where you'll find the most bizarre stuff, but it's more fun to wander around Deira, especially at night, near the *abra* station.

Bedouin Jewellery

Bedouin jewellery is brilliant in Dubai and with the rise of bo-ho ethnic chic, it makes a great gift. Look for elaborate silver necklaces and pendants, chunky earrings and rings, and wedding belts, many of which incorporate coral, turquoise and semiprecious stones. Some of the older Bedouin jewellery comes from the Emirates, but most is from Oman, Yemen and Afghanistan. General guidelines are: Omani jewellery is produced with good-quality silver and is more intricate of detail and design; Yemeni jewellery is elaborate and chunkier; Afghani jewellery looks cheap, but it's the most fun and often comes embellished with coloured beads, ribbon and tiny mirrors. Like gold, silver jewellery is sold by weight. You'll pay more for intricate workmanship and quality, but the shopkeeper usually sets a fixed price on these items. There's also a lot of 'Bedouin-inspired' and other ethnic beaded-silver jewellery made in India; you'll pay a lot less for this stuff in Dubai than you will at boutiques in London or New York. Keep an eye out for necklaces, bracelets and earrings embellished with beads, charms and trinkets. You can also buy Bedouin jewellery displayed (a la *khanjars*) in glass-covered picture frames, or frame it yourself when you get home.

Perfume & Incense

Attars (Arabian perfumes) are spicy and strong. Historically this was a necessity: with precious little water, washing was a

CARPET-BUYING 101

Due diligence is essential for prospective carpet-buyers. Though you may only want a piece to match your curtains, you'll save a lot of time and money if you do a little homework. Your first order of business: Read *Oriental Rugs Today* (2nd edition), by Emmett Eiland, an excellent primer on buying new Oriental rugs.

In the early 1900s, rug makers started using fast-acting chemicals and machines to streamline the arduous processes of carding, washing, dying, and spinning wool into thread, leaving only the actual weaving to be done by hand. One hundred years later, traditional cultures have been decimated, and the market flooded with bad rugs destined to depreciate in value.

A rug's quality depends entirely on how the wool was processed. It doesn't matter if the rug was hand-knotted if the wool is lousy. The best comes from sheep at high altitudes, which produce impenetrably thick, long-staple fleece, heavy with lanolin. No acids should ever be applied; otherwise the lanolin washes away. Lanolin yields naturally stain-resistant, lustrous fibre that doesn't shed. The dye should be vegetal-based pigment. This guarantees saturated, rich colour tones with a depth and vibrancy unattainable with chemicals.

The dyed wool is hand-spun into thread, which by nature has occasional lumps and challenges the craftsmanship of the weavers, forcing them to compensate for the lumps by occasionally changing the shape, size, or position of a knot. These subtle variations in a finished carpet's pattern – visible only upon close inspection – give the carpet its character, and actually make the rug more valuable.

Dealers will hype knot-density, weave-quality and country of origin, but really, they don't matter. The crucial thing to find out is how the wool was treated. A rug made with acid-treated wool will never look as good as it did the day you bought it. Conversely, a properly made rug will grow more lustrous in colour over time and will last centuries.

Here's a quick test. Stand atop the rug with rubber-soled shoes, and do the twist. Grind the fibres underfoot. If they shed, it's lousy wool. You can also spill water onto the rug. See how fast it absorbs. Ideally it should puddle for an instant, indicating a high presence of lanolin. Best of all, red wine will not stain lanolin-rich wool.

We've endeavoured to list good dealers, but you'll be taking your chances in Dubai if you're looking for an investment piece. But if you're looking for a gorgeous pattern that will look great in your living room, pack a few fabric swatches from your sofa and draperies, and go for it. Patterns range from simple four-colour tribal designs in wool to wildly ornate, lustrous multicoloured silk carpets that shimmer under the light. Look through books before you leave home to get a sense of what you like. Once in the stores, plan to linger long with dealers, slowly sipping tea while they unfurl dozens of carpets. The process is great fun. Just don't get too enthusiastic or the dealer won't as readily bargain.

If you're serious about becoming a collector, hold off. Read Emmett Eiland's book; Google 'DOBAG', a Turkish-rug-making cultural-survival project; and check out www.yayla.com for other reliable background info. Follow links to nonprofit organisations (such as DOBAG) that not only help reconstruct rug-making cultures decimated by modernisation, but also help to educate, house and feed the people of these cultures, giving them a voice in an age of industrial domination. And you'll get a fantastic carpet to boot.

sometimes-thing, so women smothered themselves in *attars* and incense. The tradition continues. As you walk past Emirati women, catch a whiff of their exotic perfume. You can find Arabian-perfume shops in all Dubai's malls, but we highly recommend you visit the Perfume Souq (p60), a small stretch lined with perfume stores along Sikkat al-Khail St in Deira, just east of the Gold Souq. Shopkeepers will daub you senseless with myriad scents, and if you buy a few (remember to bargain), you'll also receive a bag of tiny samples. Perfume is sold by the *tolah* (12mL or 12g) and prices vary, depending on the perfume. The expensive concentrated scents are made from agar wood from Malaysia. Perfume shops also sell a range of incense in the form of *oud* (wood), rock, crystals or compressed powder. Frankincense (*luban* in Arabic) is the most common form.

Quality varies; the best comes from the Dhofar region of southern Oman.

To burn incense, you have three options: an electric incense burner; heat beads; or a traditional burner and a box of Magic Coal charcoal, a long-lasting Japanese coal sold in a black box. Set charcoal or heat beads over a gas burner or hotplate until they glow red, then put a piece of frankincense on top. Frankincense burned alone may remind you of church, but add *oud* for a sweet, rich, log-fire smell. The colourful burners themselves make great souvenirs, and many shops sell all-inclusive gift sets.

Textiles

Vendors at Bur Dubai Souq and along nearby Al-Fahidi St carry vibrant, colourful textiles from the Indian subcontinent and Southeast Asia. They're remarkably cheap, but quality varies. Silk, cotton and linen represent the best value. Dubai's tailors work quickly, and their rates are very reasonable. Prices start around Dh35 for a shirt or skirt. Draperies may cost as little as Dh10 apiece.

Exotic Delicacies

Fragrant Iranian and Spanish saffron costs far less than back home. Buy it in the spice souq or supermarkets. Honey from Saudi Arabia and Oman is scrumptious. Look for it in specialty shops in Satwa, in the Spice Souq and in supermarkets. Its colour ranges from light gold to almost black. The most expensive varieties are collected by hand from remote areas in the mountains and deserts of Oman. As much as we love good caviar, because of over fishing and pollution in the Caspian Sea, we cannot advocate the purchase of Iranian roe.

Electronics

If it plugs into a wall you can buy it in Dubai. Because of minimal duties, Dubai is the cheapest place in the region to buy electronics and digital technology. The selection is huge. Research products of interest before hitting the stores; sales staff don't always know enough. For the lowest prices and no-name brands, head to Al-Fahidi St in Bur Dubai and the area around Al-Sabkha and Al-Maktoum Hospital Rds, near Baniyas Sq, known as the Electronics Souq (Map pp54–5; test items before you buy). If you want an international warranty, shell out the extra money and head to a mall, Carrefour or Plug-Ins. Prices on multiregion DVD players, digital cameras, PDAs and mobile phones vary hugely, but will probably be cheaper than back home. For software and hardware, head to Khalid bin al-Waleed Rd (Bank St; aka Computer Street) in Bur Dubai between Al-Mankhool Rd and the Falcon Roundabout.

Perfume Shopping: Clearing Your Palate

Perfume-shopping can wear out your sense of smell. If you're in the market for Arabian scents, do what top perfumiers do to neutralize their olfactory palate: close your mouth and make three forceful exhalations through your nose. Blast the air hard, in short bursts, using your diaphragm. But be careful, lest boogers come flying out (blow your nose first, if you're worried). Some people incorrectly say to smell coffee grounds, but this numbs your sense of smell, effectively deadening it.

For iPods and other Apple products try the Mac Store (at Ibn Battuta Mall, p101) or Virgin. Compare prices before you buy.

DEIRA

AJMAL Map pp56–7   Cosmetics
☎ 295 3580; Deira City Centre; ◷ 10am-10pm
The place for traditional Arabian perfumes, Ajmal caters to well-heeled Emirati women. The fancy jewel-encrusted bottles are as impressive as the scents.

AL-GHURAIR CITY Map pp54–5   Shopping Centre
☎ 223 2333; cnr Al-Rigga & Omar ibn al-Khattab Rds; ◷ 10am-10pm Sat-Thu, 2-10pm Fri
If seeing all those flowing robes has made you want your own checked *keffiyah* (or *gutra,* as they're called in the Gulf), grab yours at Al-Ghurair City, the place to shop for national dress, offering stylish *abayas* and *shaylas,* quality leather sandals, and *dishdashas* in chocolate and slate (popular for winter). Be forewarned: the floorplan is confusing.

AMINIAN PERSIAN CARPETS
Map pp56–7   Carpets
☎ 295 5379; Deira City Centre; ◷ 10am-10pm Sun-Wed, 10am-midnight Thu-Sat

KHANJARS

Visit the Al-Ain Camel Souq or the bullfights at Fujairah and you'll see old Emirati men wearing *khanjars* over their *dishdashas* (men's shirt-dress). Traditionally, *khanjar* handles were made from rhino horn; today they are often made of wood. Regular *khanjars* have two rings where the belt is attached, and their scabbards are decorated with thin silver wire. The intricacy of the wire thread pattern and its workmanship determine value. Sayidi *khanjars* have five rings and are often covered entirely in silver sheet, with little or no wire, and their quality is assessed by weight and craftsmanship. A *khanjar* ought to feel heavy when you pick it up. Don't believe anyone who tells you a specific *khanjar* is 'very old' – few will be more than 30 to 40 years old. If you're in the market, there's an especially good selection at Lata's (p100), Showcase Antiques (p100) and at Global Village (p88).

SOUVENIR SUGGESTIONS

Traditional Take-Homes

If you can't resist taking home gold, carpets, perfume and the like, here are some helpful hints:

Carpets Go for Persian; better value and finer quality than anywhere except Iran.

Gold Assuming you don't buy at its peak, you'll feel smug once it's valued back home.

Perfume No tax means French brands are cheaper than in Paris, but check the packaging to make sure they're authentic.

Pashminas Fakes are found all over the world, but in Dubai you'll find bargains on real, silky-soft 100% pashmina shawls. For tips on buying, see p98.

Oriental music Sure, you want to shimmy like a belly dancer on your desert safari, but listen before you buy – some are excruciating.

Cool Keepsakes

These Dubai-designed, home-grown and lesser-known regional products make more original mementos:

Colourful camel bags Make groovy ottoman covers.

Azza Fahmy Jewellery Impress your friends by explaining the Arabic inscriptions and imagery. Be prepared to pay retail.

Arabian attars (essential oils) You can be confident no other woman in the room will be wearing the same scent.

A Pink Sushi piece Funky feminine fashion made from the traditional *gutra* (red-and-white-checked men's head-dress) by an Emirati designer. They may be hard to find; call Five Green (p97), S*uce (p100) and Amzaan (p96).

Lemonada or Blue Bedouin CDs Kick back to Arabian lounge and chill-out music made in Dubai.

This trusted Iranian-carpet specialist offers great service and stocks a wide selection of classic Persian carpets and colourful tribal kilims. Plan to linger long: the collection is far bigger than it first appears.

BOOK CORNER Map pp54–5 Books
☎ 228 2835; Al-Ghurair City, cnr Omar ibn al-Khattab & Al-Rigga Rds; ☽ 10am-10pm Sat-Thu, 2-10pm Fri
The number of English and Arabic titles is astounding, but the best reason to come is for travel-related and children's products. Look for the 'Quran Challenge Game', a wacky souvenir. NB: if you're buying travel books, check the publication dates (the store stocks out-of-date titles as well as new ones).

top picks

GOLD & JEWELLERY

- Gold Souq (p53)
- Azza Fahmy Jewellery (p98)
- Gold & Diamond Park (p99)
- Damas Jewellery (right)

CARREFOUR Map pp56–7 Supermarket
☎ 295 1010; Deira City Centre; ☽ 10am-10pm Sat-Tue, 10am-midnight Wed-Fri
This enormous French hypermarket draws big crowds of Emiratis and European ex-pats for its off-the-jet-fresh seafood, foie gras, stinky cheeses, fresh-baked bread and plump Arabian olives. It also stocks an excellent selection of well-priced mobile phones, digital cameras and electronics.

DAMAS Map pp56–7 Jewellery
☎ 295 3848; Deira City Centre; ☽ 10am-10pm Sun-Wed, 10am-midnight Thu-Sat
Damas may not be the most innovative jeweller in Dubai, but with over 50 stores, it's the most trusted. Among the diamonds and gold, look for classic pieces and big-designer names like Fabergé and Tiffany.

DEIRA CITY CENTRE
Map pp56–7 Shopping Centre
☎ 295 1010; Al-Garhoud Rd; ☽ 10am-10pm Sun-Wed, 10am-midnight Thu-Sat
Though other malls are bigger and flashier, Deira City Centre remains a stalwart for its logical layout and wide selection of shops, from big-name chain stores like H&M and Zara to independent shops carrying good

SOUQ TO SOUQ

Bur Dubai Souq (Map pp62–3) Scores of stalls carry textiles, souvenir T-shirts, faux antiques and mosque alarm clocks. The selection of shops is nothing remarkable; it's the structure of the souq itself that's cool. Open-sided wooden arcades with graceful archways extend for blocks, just a stone's throw from the Creek. Linger by the *abra* station and strike up conversations with Indian expats, watch the boats load up, then duck up narrow side streets of the adjacent Indian neighbourhood to try on saris, bargain for electronics and browse Bollywood CDs. Don't miss the tiniest, most-atmospheric alley of all, Hindi Lane (p66), between the Hindu and Sikh temples, where you can wander into tiny shops chock-a-block with religious paraphernalia, colourful Buddhas, bindis and incense.

Deira Covered Souq (Map pp54–5) Deira's souqs are the most dynamic and exciting in Dubai, and they're best visited in the evening when buzzing neon signs light up throngs of Indians crowding the busy sidewalks. A labyrinth of sprawling markets and narrow alleyways, Deira's souqs aren't as straightforward as the one in Bur Dubai: plan to get lost. The covered Naif Souq (between Naif South St, 9A St and Deira St) is easier to navigate than the Deira Covered Souq (between Al-Sabkha Rd, 67 St and Naif Rd), which isn't really covered, but consists of warrens of tiny shops on narrow lanes and dead-end arcades. When you get turned around, find your way back to the Creek to get oriented. Even if you're not keen on cheap textiles, knock-off Dior scarves, *kandouras* and kitchenware, you're sure to be wowed by the high-energy street scene.

Deira Gold Souq (Map pp54–5) The most famous of Dubai's souqs is a grimy place, considering the high value of the goods carried in the cheek-by-jowl shops. Giant dust-covered ceiling fans hang from the arching wooden arcades, whirring loudly above mobs of gawkers whose attention is squarely riveted on the spot-lit bling glittering in windows. Though you'll see some impossibly overwrought solid-gold headdresses and medallion-encrusted belts destined for an Indian bride's dowry or the set of a Bollywood musical, most of the stuff is rather ordinary – pins, pendants, earrings and necklaces. You may find something to buy, but really it's the spectacle that's so mesmerising. Keep an eye out for the well-fed wives of Russian oligarchs – their frenzies are highly entertaining.

Deira Spice Souq (Map pp54–5) The narrow alleyways leading to the Spice Souq (aka Deira Old Souq) are lined with the usual made-in-China plastics, polyester and porcelain, but forge ahead and you'll suddenly catch a whiff of pungent spices perfuming the air. Once you glimpse the narrow alleyway and its stalls brimming with giant bags of spices, stop and close your eyes: this is one place in Dubai where vision is a distraction. See if you can't pick out the scents of saffron, rose, cinnamon, cardamom, vanilla and cumin. Even if you don't purchase a pouch of pulverised roots or leaves, do seek out the essential buy: frankincense. If you're not sure what to do with it, pick up a beginner's incense kit, which includes a small burner, *oud* and coal. (Tip: 'Magic Coal' brand lasts longer than others.)

Marina Market, Dubai Marina (Map pp82–3; ☎ 050 244 5795; New Dubai; ☯ 11am-7pm Fri & Sat Oct-Apr, 2-10pm during Ramadan) Marina Market is a crowd-pleaser not so much for its local and international arts and crafts, ethnic jewellery and home-grown fashion, but for its sunny waterside location. Plan to snap pictures as you stroll the promenade. When it's time to buy, Sara Moseley's photographs of Dubai make original souvenirs; market-organiser Roslynne Bargugnan's cheeky 'Made in Dubai' and 'Expat Brat' T-shirts sell like beer at a ballgame. Egyptian Rania El-Farouki's textiles resurrect the ancient Nubian art of *talli*, with delicate gold- and silver-threaded kaftans, scarves and shawls; every design tells a story, and your purchase supports a disappearing art form.

carpets, souvenirs and handicrafts. You'll also find the city's best supermarket (Carrefour), good food courts and a cinema. Some say it's *the* place on a Thursday night. Not true. Crowds are unbearable, rife with screaming teens; the taxi line is over an hour long; and traffic outside is abominable.

EARLY LEARNING CENTRE
Map pp56–7   Children's Toys
☎ 295 1548; Deira City Centre; ☯ 10am-10pm Sun-Wed, 10am-midnight Thu-Sat
Parents: if you're travelling with little ones and failed to pack enough toys to keep them entertained, fret not. Early Learning

Centre stocks great games designed to get kids thinking and develop key learning skills. And because they're not always easy to figure out, they'll keep children busy for hours.

MAGRUDY'S Map pp56–7   Books
☎ 295 7744; Deira City Centre; ☯ 10am-10pm Sun-Wed, 10am-midnight Thu-Sat
Of Magrudy's Dubai branches, this one's the best. It stocks a wide selection of English-language books, with a stand-out collection of travel, language and children's titles; intriguing books on Middle East history and politics; and a complete selection

JUMPING THE TAXI QUEUE

Hailing a taxi at a mall on a weekend can take well over an hour. Different malls have different systems. At some, you've no choice but to queue up, as at Deira City Centre – the worst of the lot – where the snaking line of people can easily exceed 200 tired shoppers. To avoid it, wander around the corner to the adjacent Sofitel and tip the doorman Dh5. (Consolidate or hide your shopping bags; the hotel's doormen aren't supposed to hail taxis for shoppers.) At Dubai Festival City, the system is more civilized: the doorman hands you a number telling you where you are in the queue (don't be surprised to learn that 100 people are ahead of you). The upside of this system is that you can plan your shopping around the wait: once you're nearly done, pick up your number, then head back inside and hit the stores near the taxi door. Alternatively, head to the adjacent InterContinental Hotel, at the far end of the mall, where you'll have to pony up extra for a hotel taxi, but will rarely wait. (Again, tip the doorman.) At Mall of the Emirates, avoid the long queue by heading to the front door of the Kempinski Hotel, adjoining Ski Dubai, where there's always a line of non-hotel taxis waiting. If there's a queue at Wafi City, head to Raffles Dubai and pony up the extra cash for a hotel taxi. At other malls, you'll just have to brave the wait. If you're shameless and really pressed, you can cheat and catch an arriving taxi before he pulls into the lot, but the taxi attendant will make a fuss. Be discreet.

of coffee-table books on Dubai. Alas, the magazine selection is weak.

MIKYAJY Map pp56–7 — Cosmetics
☎ 295 7844; Deira City Centre; ☽ 10am-10pm
You feel like you're walking into a candy gift-box at tiny Mikyajy, the Gulf's home-grown make-up brand. Developed to suit the colouring of Arabian girls, its popularity now includes foreigners who appreciate vibrant colours like turquoise and tangerine.

PLUG-INS Map pp56–7 — Electronics
☎ 295 1010; Deira City Centre; ☽ 10am-10pm
If you left your digital camera on the back seat of a taxi, Plug-Ins carries a big selection of tiny digital cameras, as well as MP3 players, hand-held organizers and home-theatre systems. Prices are competitive, but you may do better at Carrefour.

PRIDE OF KASHMIR
Map pp56–7 — Carpets & Handicrafts
☎ 295 0655; Deira City Centre; ☽ 10am-10pm
The high-knot-density Kashmiri and Persian silk carpets are lovely, but you'll especially enjoy the selection of silky pashmina shawls and home furnishings like velvet patchwork bedspreads, embroidered throws and sequined cushion covers. Look for branches at Souq Madinat Jumeirah (p101), Mall of the Emirates (p101) and Mercato Mall (p100).

RITUALS Map pp56–7 — Cosmetics
☎ 294 1432; Deira City Centre; ☽ 10am-10pm
Rituals' natural products seek to make quotidian chores more sensuous. Though you probably won't want to weigh down your

luggage with minty dishwashing soap, you may appreciate the invigorating mandarin-and-mint shower gel, lotus-flower massage oil, or ginger-and-basil shaving balm, all available in travel sizes.

VIRGIN MEGASTORE Map pp56–7 — Music
☎ 295 8599; Deira City Centre; ☽ 10am-10pm
The enthusiastic sales staff is great at suggesting Middle Eastern music to take back home, from traditional oud to Oriental chill-out. The selection is huge. Also check out the Arabian and Iranian DVDs. The Mall of the Emirates store is bigger, but for Middle Eastern tunes, this one's best. Also carries MP3 players.

WOMEN'S SECRET
Map pp56–7 — Women's Clothing
☎ 295 9665; Deira City Centre; ☽ 10am-10pm Sun-Wed, 10am-midnight Thu-Sat
This sassy Spanish label thrills girls with its global-pop-art-inspired underwear, swimwear and nightwear. Expect anything from cute Mexican cross-stitched bra and pants sets to Moroccan-style kaftan-like nightdresses. There are other branches, but this is the best.

ZARA Map pp56–7 — Clothing
☎ 294 0839; Deira City Centre; ☽ 10am-10pm
Stylish Spain-based Zara has stores all over Dubai, but this is the original and still has the biggest selection of smart-looking affordable clothes and accessories. They never stray from their black, white and grey colour palette, but their cuts and styling feel very now and look expensive – even if the tailoring is cheap.

TOP SHOPPING & EATS STREETS

When it's cool enough to be outdoors, escape the monotony of the shopping malls and hit the street. Though generally grimy, Dubai's commercial streets are chock-a-block with stores and restaurants, and each has its own flavour. Some are specific to a particular type of consumer good, others to a particular culture and its food. Since shopping and eating go hand-in-hand, we've crafted a short-list of our favourite areas to do a bit of both. For the best people-watching and liveliest atmosphere, come in the evening. Note that many shops close in the afternoon.

Khalid bin al-Waleed Rd (Bank St), Bur Dubai (Map pp62–3) Nicknamed Computer Street, Bank St's crowded sidewalks are lined with shops selling software, hardware, laptops, personal organisers and computer accessories. (Never mind the occasional hooker.) Go for inexpensive Sri Lankan cooking at Curry Leaf (p113), inside the computer-mall Al-Mussalla Tower.

Al-Fahidi St, Bur Dubai (Map pp62–3) A bustling Indian 'hood great for textiles, saris, digital cameras and electronics, with myriad tailor shops and luggage dealers; it's also good for snacks at hole-in-the-wall Indian joints that serve strong black tea cut with milk.

Al-Hisn St and 73 St, Bur Dubai (Map pp62–3) Another predominantly Indian area with impossibly narrow sidewalks and buzzing neon, here you'll find sari shops, sequinned slippers, and Bollywood music and movies. Head to Rangoli (p113), which makes great all-veg curries and gooey-delicious sweets.

Al-Rigga Rd, Rigga (Map pp54–5) A wide boulevard with broad sidewalks, Al-Rigga is good for specialist *sheesha* shops, discount gifts, internet cafés and traditional Emirati dress (head to Al-Ghurair City). Stop for Syrian and Iranian sweets along the way, but for a meal walk around the corner to Aroos Damascus (p109).

Al-Dhiyafah, Satwa, between Al-Satwa Rd and Al-Mina Rd (Map pp76–7) A favourite walking street for its wide sidewalks, cultural diversity, and mix of day-to-day and specialty shops, Al-Dhiyafah is good for books, *sheesha*-pipe stores and Syrian handicrafts. But the standout attraction here is the bevy of great Lebanese food. For mezze visit Sidra (p118); for shawarma, try Al-Mallah (p113) or Beirut (p119).

Al-Satwa Rd, Satwa, between Al-Dhiyafah Rd and Al-Hudheiba Rd (Map pp76–7) This thoroughfare feels anonymous but it is the place to buy low-cost luggage, cheap *kandouras* (robes) and textiles. Munch on Indian sweets at little cafés, or follow the Pakistani workers and five-star chefs to Ravi (p119).

BUR DUBAI

2000 HORIZON ANTIQUES
Map pp64–5   Handicrafts & Souvenirs
☎ 335 3544; Block T, Karama Shopping Centre, Karama; ☯ 9am-10pm Sat-Thu, 9-11am & 4-10pm Fri
These guys offer the best prices in Karama Shopping Centre – and that's before you even start bargaining. The selection may be small, but you'll still find enough Orientalia to recreate the Arabian look at home. The friendly no-nonsense service is a welcome respite from the irritating spruikers outside.

AJMAL Map pp62–3   Cosmetics
☎ 269 0102; BurJuman Centre, cnr Khalid bin al-Waleed (Bank St) & Sheikh Khalifa bin Zayed Rds; ☯ 10am-10pm Sat-Thu, 2-10pm Fri
The most popular maker of heady Arabian *attars* (perfumes and essential oils) in the region, Ajmal custom-blends its earthy scents. These aren't fancy French colognes – they're woody and pungent perfumes. Look for 'Zikra Al Nawaaem', a spicy sandalwood based scent in an ornate gold bottle.

AL-AIN SHOPPING CENTRE
Map pp62–3   Computers
☎ 351 6914; Al-Mankhool Rd; ☯ 10am-2.30pm & 4.30-10pm Sat-Thu, 4.30-10pm Fri
Jam-packed with small shops selling every kind of software, hardware and accessory for PCs, this computer and electronics mall also has a good range of digital cameras. There is an internet café and fast-food outlets on the ground floor. Across the street, Al-Khaleej Centre has similar (but fewer) stores.

AL-OROOBA ORIENTAL Map pp62–3 Carpets
☎ 351 0919; BurJuman Centre; ☯ 10am-10pm Sat-Thu, 2-10pm Fri

DID YOU KNOW?

It may be pushing 40°C outside, but Dubai's shopping malls are freezing: they're notoriously over air-conditioned. The worst offender? BurJuman Center. If you didn't pack a lightweight wrap for your shoulders, you now have extra incentive to shell out for that new pashmina you've been eyeing.

top picks

HANDICRAFTS & SOUVENIR SHOPS

- Lata's (p100)
- Al-Jaber Gallery (p101)
- Al-Orooba Oriental (p95)
- Gift World (opposite)
- Showcase Antiques, Arts & Frames (p100)

You'll have to decide whether to enjoy the ritual of unfurling fine carpets or combing over the cool collection of Bedouin jewellery, prayer beads, ceramics and *khanjars* – you won't have time for both: this is high-quality stuff that merits careful attention.

AMZAAN Map pp64–5   Boutique
☎ 324 6754; Wafi City Mall; ☾ 10am-10pm Sat-Thu, 4pm-midnight Fri
Sharjah princess Sheikha Maisa al-Qassimi's funky little boutique specializes in local and out-of-town designers, with an ever-changing line-up of labels. Ones to look for: Manoush, Free for Humanity, and Dubai brands you won't find anywhere else.

BATEEL Map pp2–3   Food
☎ 355 2853; BurJuman Centre; ☾ 10am-10pm Sat-Thu, 2-10pm Fri
Old-style traditional Arabian hospitality meant dates and camel milk. Now Emiratis offer their guests Bateel's scrumptious date chocolates and truffles, made from 120 varieties using European chocolate-making

techniques. Try the sparkling date drink and take home some date jam. For more on Bateel, see below. Other locations: Deira City Centre and Jumeirah Town Centre.

BURJUMAN CENTRE
Map pp62–3   Shopping Centre
☎ 352 0222; cnr Khalid bin al-Waleed (Bank St) & Trade Centre Rds; ☾ 10am-10pm Sat-Thu, 2-10pm Fri
Dubai's answer to Beverly Hills, BurJuman has one of the highest concentrations of high-end labels and an easy-to-navigate floorplan with wide expanses of shiny marble. Too bad it's freezing inside. Max out your credit card at Saks Fifth Avenue, Dolce and Gabbana, Donna Karan, Kenzo, Calvin Klein, Etro, Christian Lacroix, Cartier and Tiffany.

ETRO Map pp62–3   Women's Clothing
☎ 351 3737; BurJuman Centre; ☾ 10am-10pm Sat-Thu, 2-10pm Fri
Italian designer Jacopo Etro's exuberant paisley designs are inspired by his travels. Borrowing ideas from around the globe, his exotic collections have featured richly coloured chiffon kaftans, Rasta shawls and textured ponchos, patchwork and mirrored skirts, sari-style tops, and embroidered belts and handbags.

FACES Map pp62–3   Cosmetics
☎ 352 1441; BurJuman Centre; ☾ 10am-10pm Sat-Thu, 2-10pm Fri
Before Faces opened, women had to fly to Paris to purchase hard-to-find cosmetic and fragrance brands. No more. Sniff out Serge Lutens, L'Artisan Parfumer and Annick Goutal, among others.

BATEEL DATES

The de rigueur gift for any proper gourmet, Bateel dates are the ultimate luxury food of Arabia. At first glance, Bateel looks like a jewellery store, with polished-glass display cases and halogen pin spots illuminating the goods. A closer look reveals perfectly aligned pyramids of dates – thousands of them. Bateel plays to its audience with gorgeous packaging that might leave the recipient of your gift expecting gold or silver within: the fancy boxes of lacquered hardwood are worth far more than their contents. Alas, they're manufactured in China, but not the dates. These come from Saudi Arabia, which has the ideal growing conditions: sandy, alkaline soil and extreme heat. Quality control is tight: Bateel has its own farms and production equipment. The dates sold here are big and fat, with gooey-moist centers. Because they have a 70% sugar content, dates technically have unlimited shelf life, but you'll find they taste best around the autumn harvest. If agwa dates are available during your visit, buy them – you may not have another opportunity. Agwa trees only yield every few years, so they're considered a delicacy. Look for them in September; other varieties arrive in November. The stuffed dates make a great gift – love the candied orange peel and caramelized almonds. If you miss your chance in town, you can stock up at the airport as you leave Dubai. A cardboard box will set you back Dh100 per kilo, a fancy box Dh200, and a little beribboned sampler of five or seven perfect dates around Dh25.

SUPERMARKET SOUVENIRS

Happiness is shopping at Spinneys, Carrefour and Choithram (p105) – the shelves are positively packed with international foodstuffs. Here are a few favourites.

Cardamon-flavoured condensed milk Worth weighing down the luggage for, this provides a taste of Arabia when you return home. Great in coffee.

Natco rose syrup Wow your dinner-party guests by pouring rose syrup over sorbet or vanilla ice cream.

Zaatar and sumac Add zaatar (a blend of thyme, sesame, marjoram and oregano) to your soups, salads or stews; add sumac (a sour, cherry-red spice) and lemon to a chopped salad to recall some of the fabulous Lebanese meals you ate in Dubai.

Saffron You won't find cheaper back home. Soak it in hot cooking water or broth to extract its aroma before adding it to the pot.

Indian tea Unlike in the West, Indian tea is powdered and instantly dissolves in hot water. Cut it with full-cream milk to evoke memories of Dubai's Indian-sweets sidewalk bakeries.

FIVE GREEN Map pp64–5   Boutique
☎ 336 4100; www.fivegreen.com; Garden Home, Oud Metha; ⊙ 10am-11pm Sat-Thu, 4-11pm Fri
You may get lost trying to find the city's leading indie boutique and concept store, but it's worth it to meet the cool kids of Dubai's retail scene. Aside from art installations and kick-ass international magazines, Five Green carries cool unisex labels like Fidel, Paul Frank, BoxFresh, Xlarge, and Upper Playground. It also stocks Pink Sushi, our fave local designer because of its fantastic bags and skirts made from checked *gutras* (men's headcloths). Check the website for upcoming installations and shows.

GIFT WORLD Map pp64–5   Handicrafts & Souvenirs
☎ 335 8097; Block T, Karama Shopping Centre; ⊙ 9am-10.30pm Sat-Thu, 4-10.30pm Fri
Imagine yourself in Aladdin's Cave as you bump your head on the hanging Moroccan and Syrian lamps while rummaging through Oriental bric-a-brac, ranging from Bedouin jewellery and beads, to sequined bedspreads and dizzyingly patterned camel cushion covers. It's around the corner from 2000 Horizon Antique.

INTERNATIONAL ALLADIN SHOES
Map pp62–3   Handicrafts & Souvenirs
☎ 050-515 4351; Bur Dubai Souq abra station; ⊙ 10am-10pm Sat-Thu, 10am-noon & 2-10pm Fri
Every souvenir shop in Dubai sells colourful sequined slippers and gold-threaded curly-toed shoes from Pakistan and Afghanistan, but Alladin was the first and still has the best quality, selection and prices.

The teeny-tiny slippers are a hit at baby showers.

KARAMA SHOPPING CENTRE
Map pp64–5   Shopping Centre
Karama, Bur Dubai; ⊙ 9am-10.30pm Sat-Thu, 9-11am & 4-10.30pm Fri
An ugly concrete souq, Karama's bustling backstreet shopping area has dozens of little shops selling handicrafts and souvenirs, 'genuine fakes' and cheap clothes. Prices are low, but bargaining lowers them further – be aggressive: the spruikers are accustomed to tourists. Listen for the cries of hucksters hawking pirated copies: 'Dee-vee-dees! Bloo moovees!' The municipality seems to look the other way.

MOTHERCARE Map pp64–5   Children's Clothing
☎ 335 9999; Lamcy Plaza, Oud Metha, Bur Dubai; ⊙ 10am-10pm
Out of the way, but open Friday mornings, Mothercare is one of the most popular and affordable shops for kid's necessities, from cute clothes and cuddly toys to baby carriers and car seats. There are other branches, but this one's close to several other children's shops at slightly downmarket Lamcy Plaza.

OHM RECORDS Map pp64–5   Music
☎ 397 3728; just behind Trade Centre Rd, opposite BurJuman Centre; ⊙ noon-9pm
DJs dig Ohm, the first Dubai shop to carry vinyl. There's a discerning selection of house, trance, hip-hop, trip-hop and drum 'n' bass, as well as DJ equipment and accessories. It's been responsible for bringing

PASHMINA: TELLING REAL FROM FAKE

Women around the world adore pashminas, those feather-light cashmere shawls worn by the Middle East's best-dressed ladies. If you're shopping for a girlfriend or your mother, you can never go wrong with a pashmina. They come in hundreds of colours and styles, some beaded and embroidered, others with pompon edging – you'll have no trouble finding one you like. But aside from setting it afire to make sure it doesn't melt (as polyester does), how can you be sure it's real? Here's the trick. Hold the fabric at its corner. Loop your index finger around it and squeeze hard. Now pull the fabric through. If it's polyester, it won't budge. If it's cashmere, it'll pull through – though the friction may give you a mild case of rope burn. Try it at home with a thin piece of polyester before you hit the shops; then try it with cashmere. You'll never be fooled again.

some of the more interesting DJs to Dubai. If you spin, check 'em out.

PRAIAS Map pp62–3   Women's Clothing
☎ 351 1338; BurJuman Centre; ☾ 10am-10pm Sat-Thu, 2-10pm Fri
Emirati women wouldn't be caught dead wearing Praias' skimpy candy-coloured bikinis and swirly-patterned beach dresses in public. Perhaps you shouldn't either, unless you've first gotten a Brazilian wax job.

TAPE À L'OEIL Map pp62–3   Children's Clothing
☎ 352 3223; BurJuman Centre; ☾ 10am-10pm Sat-Thu, 2-10pm Fri
A refreshing alternative to Gap Kids, Tape à l'Oeil carries fun kids' clothes that look like miniature adult wear. Denim features prominently, as do skirts and sweaters that look best on kids who keep their hair combed.

TOPSHOP Map pp64–5   Boutique
☎ 327 9929; Wafi City Mall; ☾ 10am-10pm Sat-Wed, 10am-midnight Thu & Fri
The jewel in the crown of British high street fashion, Topshop's snappy ready-to-wear should be your first choice if Emirates lost your luggage in transit. The diverse selection runs from denim and jumpers to handbags and jazzy earrings.

WAFI CITY Map pp64–5   Food
☎ 324 4555; Wafi City Mall, Al-Qataiyat Rd, near Al-Garhoud Bridge; ☾ 10am-10pm Sat-Wed, 10am-midnight Thu & Fri
Westerners mistakenly bypass palatial Wafi in favour of the behemoth shopping malls, which explains why it's so quiet. Their loss. It may have once resembled a third-rate airport terminal, but the new wing's stained-glass pyramids are stunning (come before sunset). Emirati women love Wafi's fancy French stores like Chanel and Givenchy,

but you may well prefer the lesser-known regional designers showcased in smaller boutiques. Come after sunset for great bars and restaurants like Asha's (p112), and to snap pix of the entry court's giant illuminated sphinx and brilliant crystal chandeliers. If you're feeling swish and look sharp, head for the grandest pyramid of all, the adjoining Raffles Dubai (p156), see its rooftop botanical garden and fantastical poolside water clock, then sip champagne at the top-floor New Asia Bar (p127).

WAFI GOURMET Map pp64–5   Food
☎ 324 4555; Wafi City Mall, Al-Qataiyat Rd, near Al-Garhoud Bridge; ☾ 10am-10pm
Dubai's best Arabian deli counter brims with juicy olives, pickles, peppers and cheeses, velvety hummus, *muttabal* and tabouleh, and crispy Lebanese pastries. This is the place to pack a picnic in the cooler months: assemble a mezze plate and head to the Creek. Any of the packaged foods make great gifts, but particularly good to take home are the dried fruits and baklava, which both keep well for several months.

WHISTLES Map pp62–3   Boutique
☎ 351 5070; BurJuman Centre; ☾ 10am-10pm Sat-Thu, 2-10pm Fri
An antidote to Dubai's overly glam-focused shopping scene, Whistles carries smart, understatedly sexy women's wear – think outfits for a girls' night on the town.

SHEIKH ZAYED ROAD
AZZA FAHMY JEWELLERY
Map pp72–3   Jewellery
☎ 330 0346; Blvd at Emirates Towers, Sheikh Zayed Rd; ☾ 10am-10pm Sat-Thu, 2-10pm Fri
Egyptian Azza Fahmy crafts jewellery inlaid with precious gemstones and fine calligraphy of classical Arabic poetry and spiritual

sayings that express core values of Islam. Even if you're not a believer, there's no disputing the elegant simplicity and beauty of these unique pieces.

BOULEVARD AT EMIRATES TOWERS

Map pp72–3   Shopping Centre

☎ 330 0000, 319 8999; Sheikh Zayed Rd; ☽ 10am-10pm Sat-Thu, 2-10pm Fri

If you feel like you're being watched, you are. Emirates Towers is the location of Sheikh Mohammed's office, and the secret police are everywhere. Dress appropriately and keep your voice down as you window-shop exclusive designer boutiques like Bulgari, Cartier, Zegna, Armani, Gucci, Jimmy Choo, Pucci and the fabulous Boutique 1 (below). Don't miss the wearable art of Azza Fahmy Jewellery (opposite). At day's end, sip chardonnay at Agency (p127), sing karaoke at Harry Ghatto's (p128), and refuel at the ever-popular Noodle House (p117)

BOUTIQUE 1 Map pp72–3   Designerwear

☎ 330 4555; Blvd at Emirates Towers; ☽ 10am-10pm Sat-Thu, 4-10pm Fri

Ground zero for prêt-à-porter straight off the runways of Paris and Milan, Boutique 1 is the pinnacle of Dubai's fashion scene with designers like Missoni and Yves St Laurent. If you're a fashionista but don't want to drop Dh10,000 on a new outfit, pop in for a preview of next season's new looks, go home and recast them using thrift-shop finds, and you may find yourself featured in the *New York Times* 'On the Street' fashion page.

EMILIO PUCCI Map pp72–3   Designerwear

☎ 330 0660; Blvd at Emirates Towers, Sheikh Zayed Rd; ☽ 10am-10pm Sat-Thu, 2-10pm Fri

Emilio may be dead, but the signature swirly, colour-saturated paisleys he made famous in the 1960s live on. The tailoring is exquisite, the fabric's drape elegant and the psychedelic prints acid-trip ready.

GOLD & DIAMOND PARK

Map pp72–3   Jewellery

☎ 347 7788; Sheikh Zayed Rd, near Interchange No 4; ☽ 10am-10pm Sat-Thu, 4-10pm Fri

A cooler alternative to the Gold Souq in the hot summer months, the air-conditioned Gold and Diamond Park houses over 30 retailers and 120 manufacturers in a traditional Arabian-style building, and there's a lovely café. Too bad it's in the middle of nowhere. Plan to bargain.

ORGANIC FOODS & CAFÉ Map pp62–3 Food

☎ 398 9410; Al-Mankhool Rd, near Satwa Roundabout, Satwa; ☽ 8am-10pm

Despite the massive amounts of jet fuel required to ship them in, the fruits and veggies are 100% organic at Dubai's first natural supermarket, providing a refreshing, much-needed alternative to the flavourless produce sold elsewhere and in restaurants. Also on offer are an onsite bakery, fresh-roasted coffee and an extensive selection of gluten-free products you won't find anywhere else in town.

JUMEIRAH

BLUE CACTUS Map pp76–7   Boutique

☎ 344 7734; Jumeirah Centre; ☽ 10am-9pm Sat-Thu, 4.30-9pm Fri

The buyer is from Mexico at this upstairs boutique, and boy, does she have an eye for brilliant colour and sexy lines. The va-va-voom fashions are mostly American, and range from sleek long dresses with gorgeous drapings to sassy separates that look hot on a dance floor. NB: the downstairs shop carries cool Mexican silver jewellery.

CAMEL COMPANY

Map pp76–7   Handicrafts & Souvenirs

☎ 368 6048; Souq Madinat Jumeirah, Al-Sufouh Rd, Jumeirah; ☽ 10am-11pm

TAX-FREE DUBAI: WHAT IT MEANS

When people talk about Dubai being tax-free, they're referring to personal income tax on wages. There are however import duties. Recently there's been talk of creating a consumer tax, but as of this writing there was still none. Does this mean that a new Donna Karan suit will cost less here than in Milan, New York, or London? Not necessarily. If you're shopping for mid- and low-cost goods, depending on your home currency, you may not see much difference. But you will on luxury goods and cars. If you're in the market for, say, a new Rolex, you'll save a bundle in Dubai. Otherwise don't be lulled by the tax-free promise. Find what you want at home, then price it in Dubai. You may pay more in overweight-luggage charges than you wind up saving in the first place. Caveat emptor.

If you can slap a camel on it, Camel Company has it. This hands-down best spot for camel souvenirs carries plush stuffed camels that sing when you squeeze them, camels in Hawaiian shirts, on T-shirts, coffee cups, mouse-pads, notebooks, greeting cards and of course fridge magnets.

FLEURT Map pp76–7   Boutique
☎ 342 0906; Mercato Mall; ⏰ 10am-10pm Thu-Sat, 2-10pm Fri
Comb the racks for funky-smart fashions by Betsey Johnson and Soul Revival, among other progressives. The collection is refreshingly offbeat, with spangles and sequins, curve-hugging lines, and cheeky party frocks.

GALLERY ONE FINE ART PHOTOGRAPHS Map pp76–7   Souvenirs
☎ 368 6055; Souq Madinat Jumeirah; ⏰ 10am-11pm
For an arty souvenir, consider a colourful Arabian abstract image, pop-art screen print (say, maybe a camel-crossing road sign), or a black-and-white photograph of Dubai's bustling Creek scene or famous wind-towers. The problem will be choosing which you like best.

LATA'S Map pp76–7   Souvenirs
☎ 368 6216; Souq Madinat Jumeirah; ⏰ 10am-11pm
Our favourite one-stop shop for Arabian and Middle Eastern souvenirs, such as Moroccan lamps, brass coffee tables, khanjars, and silver prayer holders. It also stocks some fabulous silver jewellery, and some not-so-fabulous costume pieces. Tell the staff what you're after, and they'll steer you right.

LE STOCK Map pp76–7   Boutique
☎ 342 0211; Jumeirah Plaza; ⏰ 10am-9pm
If you're not above wearing last season's fashions, hit this clearinghouse for overstock from Le Stock's main branch (Wafi City Mall, p98). Look for designer gear by the likes of Tata-Naka, Juicy Couture and Willow – all marked down 50% to 90%.

MERCATO MALL Map pp76–7   Shopping Centre
☎ 344 4161; Jumeirah Rd; ⏰ 10am-10pm Sat-Thu, 2-10pm Fri
At first glance Mercato looks like a European train station with an arched glass

---

CAMEL CRAZY

Here are our top five camel gifts:
- Stuffed camels that play Arabic music when cuddled.
- *Camelspotting* CD – cool Mid East music.
- Julia Johnston's *Camel-o-shy* kids books.
- A camel road-crossing-sign fridge magnet.
- Eye-poppingly intricate camel-patterned cushion covers.

---

ceiling. A closer look reveals fake façades of *palazzos* and soaring murals of Venice, leaving you wondering, why? (Ah, Dubai.) Still it's fun to wander between the brick colonnades, and the compact size makes shopping here easy. The mall offers a good selection of stylish boutiques like Fleurt (left), a small Topshop, a Virgin Megastore, and some interesting carpet and curio shops. The taxi line is a nightmare at peak periods; expect to wait.

TEHRAN PERSIAN CARPET & ANTIQUES Map pp76–7   Carpets
☎ 345 6687; Mercato Mall; ⏰ 10am-10pm Thu-Sat, 2-10pm Fri
The largest carpet retailer in the country, Tehran carries a big selection of handmade Persian carpets and Oriental rugs from Turkey, Afghanistan, Pakistan, India and Kashmir. The antiques selection, though small, includes some cool old gramophones, radios and telephones. There's a bigger branch, called Persian Carpet House, on Sheikh Zayed Rd in the Crowne Plaza Hotel.

S*UCE Map pp76–7   Boutique
☎ 344 7270; Village Mall, Jumeirah Rd; ⏰ 10am-10pm Thu-Sat, 4.30-10pm Fri
S*uce was the first of an increasing number of eclectic, independently owned boutiques in Dubai. Loyal customers flock here for idiosyncratic women's fashion – think skirts trimmed with ribbons and pompons, and bubblegum mini-kaftans – from Nicola Finetti, Third Millenium, Tata-Naka, Sass and Bide, Ashish and local designer Essa. Check out the quirky accessories – funky beads, baubles and crocheted flowers on chains.

SHOWCASE ANTIQUES, ART & FRAMES Map pp76–7   Art & Antiques
☎ 348 8797; Jumeirah Rd, Umm Suqeim; ⏰ 9am-8pm Sat-Thu

Browse this three-storey Jumeirah villa for antique *khanjars,* firearms, Arabian coffee pots, Bedouin jewellery and costumes. It's one of few places in Dubai to carry quality collectables and antiques, with certificates of authenticity to back them up.

SOUQ MADINAT JUMEIRAH
Map pp76–7   Shopping Centre
☎ 348 8797; Madinat Jumeirah; ☼ 10am-11pm
The ersatz Arabian architecture with its arched wooden ceilings feel very Disney-esque, but it's entirely worth a look to see how the enormous Madinat Jumeirah fits together. Outside, *abras* float by on man-made canals; dozens of al fresco bars and restaurants overlook the scene. The floor-plan is intentionally confusing: the PR people say it's to recreate a real souq, but others think it's to keep you trapped and lull you into emptying your wallet at the overpriced shops. It's chaotic on a weekend night; stay away if you don't like crowds.

NEW DUBAI

AIZONE Map pp82–3   Boutique
☎ 347 9333; Mall of the Emirates; ☼ 10am-10pm Sun-Wed, 10am-midnight Thu-Sat
Lose yourself for hours in this enormous Lebanese fashion emporium, with hard-to-find labels and snappy drag for twirling on the dance floor. Prices skew high, but wow, what a collection.

AL-JABER GALLERY
Map pp82–3   Handicrafts & Souvenirs
☎ 341 4103; Mall of the Emirates; ☼ 10am-10pm Sun-Wed, 10am-midnight Thu-Sat
Look past the tacky souvenirs to find some quality handicrafts, including colourfully embroidered Indian tapestries spangled with beads and cool hand-of-Fatima mirrors. If you're intrigued by the idea of henna tattoos, pick up a starter kit here and design your own.

CHARLES & KEITH Map pp82–3   Shoes
☎ 341 0408; Mall of the Emirates; ☼ 10am-10pm Sun-Wed, 10am-midnight Thu-Sat
Just this side of a discount show boutique, Charles & Keith is a refreshing change from ubiquitous Prada. The girly collection of shoes ranges from easy-wear clogs to strappy sandals ideal for Dubai's heat.

FIDEL Map pp82–3   Boutique
☎ 368 5600; Ibn Battuta Mall; ☼ 10am-10pm Sat-Tue, 10am-midnight Wed-Fri
Fidel's minimalist flagship Dubai store stocks little else but funky Fidel T-shirts, t-shirts, hoodies and club-kid sneakers. The look is very back-to-school in the OC. If you're over 30, you may feel old.

FOREVER 21 Map pp82–3   Boutique
☎ 341 3412; Mall of the Emirates; ☼ 10am-10pm Sun-Wed, 10am-midnight Thu-Sat
Cutting in on H&M for affordable style and selection, this is one of Dubai's largest stores, with a big range of youthful, afford-able fashion and accessories.

GINGER & LACE Map pp82–3   Boutique
☎ 368 5109; Ibn Battuta Mall; ☼ 10am-10pm Sat-Tue, 10am-midnight Wed-Fri
Ginger & Lace stocks an eclectic selection of colourful, whimsical fashion by high-spirited New York designers Anna Sui and Betsey Johnson; German-bred Ingwa; Melero – love those sexy halter-top dresses; Tibi for Capri-style chic; Indian cult-label Ananya for signature bejewelled kaftans – a favourite of Madonna; and Australian brands Wheels and Doll Baby for the clos-est to rocker-bitch drag you'll find in Dubai. There's another at Wafi City.

IBN BATTUTA MALL
Map pp82–3   Shopping Centre
☎ 362 1900; Sheikh Zayed Rd; ☼ 10am-10pm Sat-Tue, 10am-midnight Wed-Fri
The 14th-century Arab scholar Ibn Battuta travelled 75,000 miles over 30 years. You'll have a better idea how he felt after trekking from one end of this behemoth mall to the other. The architectural theme and decora-tive elements reflect his trip from China to Andalusia; look for a full-size Chinese junk and a fabulous Persian tiled dome. If you're too exhausted to walk back, hop on the golf-cart shuttle (Dh5). Our hands-down fave shop? Mumbai Se (p102). The food courts could be better, but you won't go hungry.

MALL OF THE EMIRATES
Map pp82–3   Shopping Centre
☎ 409 9000; Sheikh Zayed Rd; ☼ 10am-midnight
The most popular mall in Dubai – and formerly the biggest – sprawls with acres of polished white marble. The curiosity of Ski

Dubai (p142) is a major draw, as are the remarkably good food court and Dubai's best cinema, Gold Class (p135). The major drawback is crowds at peak periods. Along with the usual brands, there's also a Harvey Nichols and a great big Borders with an awesome selection of travel books (be nice and they may show you the banned-book list).

MUMBAI SE Map pp82–3 — Boutique
☎ 366 9855; Ibn Battuta Mall; ⌚ 10am-10pm Sat-Tue, 10am-midnight Wed-Fri

Star in your own Bollywood movie with Mumbai Se's cool Indian-inspired collection. Styles combine contemporary elements with classic designs, like kaftans adorned with Indian beading and seashell trim, bejewelled mandarin tunics, and tiny hand-crafted bags embellished with semiprecious stones, spiritual emblems, and engravings.

PIXI Map pp82–3 — Cosmetics
☎ 341 3833; Mall of the Emirates, Sheikh Zayed Rd, New Dubai; ⌚ 10am-midnight

This Swedish make-up and skincare line offers sublime cosmetics and beauty products. Try the honey-almond polish, beauty serum with evening primrose, cucumber-juice toner or the quick-fix mask, a five-minute revival treatment after a night on the town.

RECTANGLE JAUNE Map pp82–3 Men's Clothing
☎ 341 0288; Mall of the Emirates; ⌚ 10am-10pm Sun-Wed, 10am-midnight Thu-Sat

Finally a store for men, with a terrific selection of dress shirts in snappy stripes and bold patterns by a Lebanese team of fashion-savvy designers. This is the only branch outside Lebanon.

OTHER NEIGHBOURHOODS

CONVERSE Map p52 — Shoes
☎ 232 5906; Festival City; ⌚ 10am-10pm

Stock up on canvas All-Stars in a full palette of colours. Who cares if there's no arch support when your sneakers just look so cool?

DUBAI FESTIVAL CITY
Map p52 — Shopping Centre
☎ 213 6213; Dubai Festival City; ⌚ 10am-10pm

Billed as an 'urban retail resort', Festival City is so massive that you half expect to see a 747 parked outside. It encompasses a whopping 2.8 million sq ft and includes 600 stores – 25 of them 'anchor stores' – 100 restaurants and cafés, outdoor performance spaces, and three enormous hotels, including an InterContinental and a new Four Seasons golf resort. While the manmade canals and *abra* rides are cute, the real showstopper is the origami-inspired cubist fountain that doubles as a grand staircase. Wear sensible shoes – you're gonna need 'em.

MARC BY MARC JACOBS Map p52 Boutique
☎ 232 6118; Dubai Festival City; ⌚ 10am-10pm

The famous designer's diffusion line features downscaled, democratised sportswear by the reigning king of prêt-à-porter. But it ain't cheap: a T-shirt may set you back Dh700.

PAUL & JOE Map p52 — Boutique
☎ 232 6898; Dubai Festival City; ⌚ 10am-10pm

Named for the proprietor's sons, Paul & Joe's French clothing is playfully postmodern – think coat dresses and flouncy peasant blouses – and a welcome change from standard mall fashions.

TOYS-R-US Map p52 — Toys
☎ 206 6552; Dubai Festival City; ⌚ 10am-10pm

You won't believe the size of this warehouse-like toy store. But the best reason to come is to see the Burj Al Arab built entirely of Lego.

VINTAGE 55 Map p52 — Boutique
☎ 232 6616; Dubai Festival City; ⌚ 10am-10pm

Dress like dead celebrities in replicas of clothing they made famous. Vintage 55 creates limited-edition sets of drag worn by the likes of Marilyn Monroe and James Dean. Love those vintage Nikes.

top picks

- **Verre by Gordon Ramsay** (p107)
- **Al-Qasr on Thursday** (p117)
- **Fire & Ice** (p110)
- **Nina** (p121)
- **Hoi An** (p115)
- **Pisces** (p118)
- **BiCE** (p120)
- **Al-Mallah for shawarma** (p119)
- **Deira's cheap eats** (p109)
- **Bastakiah Nights** (p111)

EATING

Dubai's culinary landscape mirrors the imported expat population – Indian, Thai, Chinese, African, Lebanese – not local Emirati culture. In fact, you'll be hard pressed to find anything indigenous. Unless you score an invitation to a wedding, you're unlikely ever to sample the local specialty, *khouzi,* a whole roasted lamb or baby camel stuffed with rice and spices. You might come across chicken, lamb or shrimp *mashbous* – spiced meat served with equally spicy rice – but they're nothing fabulous, mostly a mass of protein and starch. Blame it on tradition: the Bedouin diet once consisted only of fish, dates, camel meat and camel milk – tasty, yes, but even the Emiratis hardly eat it anymore. Now you spot them lining up at the fast food chains with great frequency, indifferent to the major increase in Type II diabetes locally.

The best food is Middle Eastern, and includes Lebanese, Persian (Iranian) and Syrian. The cooking of the Indian subcontinent is also superb, with nearly 30 distinct subtypes available in Dubai. Asian cooking varies: you'll find good Thai and lots of Japanese (especially sushi), but Chinese is lacking. Likewise European: though Italian restaurants draw big crowds, few merit a critical look. Seafood is wildly popular and the favourite local fish is the tender and meaty *hammour,* a member of the grouper family, which you'll find on nearly every menu.

There are two types of restaurant in Dubai: the hotel restaurant and the independent. Only hotels are licensed to serve alcohol, which is why they house the city's top dining rooms. Alas, many of these top-end spots lack the individuality and eccentricity you'd find in a first-class Western restaurant because they fall under the umbrellas of giant corporate hotel chains with strict S&P (standards-and-procedures) manuals that effectively flatten individuality. Creativity doesn't flourish in Dubai. Yes, there are standout exceptions, such as Gordon Ramsay's Verre, but even this is part of a small empire run from overseas. Head to the independent restaurants when you want ethnic authenticity and don't mind slumming it; head to the hotels when you want splash and panache – and a big glass of vino to wash it down.

Opening Hours & Meal Times

Restaurant hours are generally noon to 3pm and 7.30pm to midnight; inexpensive café-restaurants are generally open 9am to midnight. Shawarma joints open in the late afternoon and stay open well past midnight. Most restaurants open seven days a week, with the exception of Friday lunch, when some smaller local eateries close. In top-end restaurants, most locals book an 8.30pm or 9pm table. For Arabic and Lebanese restaurants with live music, an 11pm booking is the norm, as entertainment usually starts at 10pm and continues until 3am; book earlier for quiet conversation.

How Much?

Street food, such as shawarma, costs around Dh4; an inexpensive curry at a cheap Indian restaurant runs about Dh10. At midrange restaurants, mains run Dh25 to Dh40, at top-end spots Dh65 to Dh150. Alcohol will spike your cheque sky-high. Because booze is only sold in bars and restaurants attached to hotels (generally three-star or better), and a few stand-alone clubs, prices are outrageous (see p126). Expect to pay Dh20 for a beer or glass of wine, more at a club. If you're on a budget, pick up duty-free booze on your flight in. We wish we could tell you to carry a hip flask into clubs, but it's illegal.

Booking Tables

Make reservations for hotel restaurants; at the indies, it's generally not necessary. Be prepared to give your mobile number, and expect a call if you're late. Make weekend bookings – Thursday and Friday nights, and Friday brunch – for top tables at least a week ahead. Some restaurants have one-off nights geared to foodies; check *Time Out* magazine to see what's doing during your visit.

Tipping

Tipping is a tricky business in Dubai. Many restaurants, particularly in hotels, tack on a 10% service charge, but depending on the hotel, the employees may never see this money. Service is weak in Dubai not because the waiters are being obnoxious, but because employers in Dubai are cheap. They hire poor people from developing countries and don't spend the money to train them properly. Many workers had never set foot in a five-star hotel before working in one. Don't hold their inexperience against them. The average hotel waiter works six days a week and makes Dh900 to Dh1000 per month, including housing; they have no access to their own passports or their own money because employers lock up the staff's travel documents and pay into savings accounts, not checking accounts. Can you imagine living in Dubai with no pocket money and no escape route? Waiters at independent restaurants make Dh2000 per month, but must pay for their own housing. A studio apartment in Dubai costs at least Dh4000 a month. This means that waiters leave home and wind up sharing a studio with four or more strangers, just to make ends meet. Frankly, we don't know how they remain so cheerful.

When it comes to the tip, leave an additional 10% to 15% in cash, under the ticket, particularly at low-end restaurants – some unethical bosses will take the money away from the waiter if they see it. If you must tip on your credit card, first ask the waiter if the manager will pay out the money that night or not. If not, then pony up cash. If service is perfunctory, it's okay to leave a mere 5%. But if you really feel pushed around by your waiter or otherwise badly treated, leave nothing.

Self-Catering

The small grocery stores around Dubai are good for a box of washing powder, but

lonelyplanet.com

VEGETARIAN EATS

Good news: restaurants with poor vegetarian selections are the exception in Dubai. Blame it on all that cooking from the Subcontinent, the Middle East and Thailand. The city's many Indian restaurants do fantastic things with spiced vegetables, potatoes and rice. At any Lebanese restaurant, you can fill the table with all-veg mezze for a small feast. At Thai places plan to eat rice dishes and coconut curries. Vegans may have to ask more questions, but will be surprised by the choices. Alas, Dubai has barely started to catch on to the idea of organics; plan to eat conventional produce or shop for yourself at Organic Foods & Café (p99). Here's a list of all-vegetarian restaurants so you won't have to endure even a whiff of meat.

- Magnolia (p118)
- XVA Cafe (p113)
- Govinda's (p113)
- Rangoli (p113)

they're not much fun to browse if you're a foodie trying to suss out Dubai's culinary landscape. The closest thing you'll find to a farmers market is the Shindagha Market (Map pp62–3; ⏰ 7am-11pm), where there are daily fish and meat markets. If you're buying, plan to bargain. Further up Al-Khaleej Rd, near Hamriya Port, the Wholesale Market (Map pp54–5; ⏰ 7am-11pm) is even cheaper, but most sales are in bulk. The huge parking area is full of trucks hauling produce from Oman. It feels very industrial, but this is the mainline source of Dubai's food.

The best consumer shopping is at the major grocery stores. The expat favourite is Spinneys (⏰ 8am-midnight). It's the most expensive, but wow, what a selection, from frozen Oregon raspberries to South African oranges. And they carry pork. Carrefour and Géant (⏰ 10am-10pm, to midnight Wed-Fri), the French-based hypermarket chains, are great for stinky cheeses

EATING TIPPING

CHILD-FRIENDLY RESTAURANTS

Emiratis prize the family. While you can take kids to most restaurants in Dubai, we've indicated with the 🐥 icon restaurants especially good for families. What this means is that your kids can safely 1) scream without freaking anyone out; 2) have fun; 3) possibly meet other children; and 4) find something on the menu to please them, if only a plate of noodles, that longstanding favourite of kids everywhere. If you're not sure where to eat, malls are a sure bet; most listed in this book have surprisingly good food courts. Though all hotels have at least one restaurant good for families, those we've selected in resort-heavy New Dubai (p119) are best for adults. But if you show up at the hotel during meal times and ask the front desk, they'll direct you to the most appropriate dining room. In short, fear not. Your hardest task will be strapping the kids into the taxi, not finding something to eat.

RAMADAN & IFTAR

Muslims are required to fast during Ramadan, and everyone, regardless of religion, is expected to observe the fast when in public. That means no eating, drinking or smoking during daylight hours. Some hotels still serve breakfast and lunch, but this is in specially designated rooms; most of the time eating during the day means room service or self-catering. Non-Muslims offered coffee or tea when meeting a Muslim during the fast should initially refuse politely. If your host insists, and repeats the offer several times, you should accept, so long as it doesn't look as though you're going to anger anyone else present who may be fasting.

Ramadan would seem to be the ideal time to lose weight, yet a lot of locals pile on the pounds. For many, avoiding food from dawn to dusk results in immense hunger come sunset, and with hundreds of restaurants putting on good-value Iftar buffets, the temptation to overindulge is everywhere. Iftar, the meal that breaks the fast, is traditionally very light – just a couple of dates, some *jallab* (date drink) and a bowl of lentil soup. But Dubai's commercially savvy restaurants have turned Iftar into an all-you-can-eat glutton-fest. From huge spreads at the Burj Al Arab to bottomless buckets at KFC, there are plenty of ways to catch up on missed meals.

Ironically those with a passion for Middle Eastern cuisine will find Ramadan a great time to visit. Restaurants may be closed during the day, but in the evenings they're at their busiest, liveliest and cheapest: this is the chance for Muslims to socialise with family and friends. Many hotels set up Ramadan tents for the entire month. They're often superbly situated beachside and serve Lebanese mezze and *sheesha* until the wee hours. Here are our favourite hotels to take in the action:

- Le Royal Meridien (p162)
- Emirates Towers (p158)
- One&Only Royal Mirage (p162)
- Grand Hyatt Hotel (p156)
- Ritz-Carlton Hotel (p120)

and European imports. Choithram caters to Indian and Pakistani communities. While we recommend buying curry at the Spice Souq, you can pick it up here at a pinch. For organic produce and groceries, there's one choice: Organic Foods & Café (p99). The selection is limited, but it's huge for Dubai.

Spinneys locations:

Abu Baker al-Siddiq Rd (Map pp54–5) **In Deira.**

Al-Mankhool Rd (Map pp62–3) **Opposite Al-Rolla Rd .**

Sheikh Khalifa bin Zayed Rd (Map pp62–3) **Near Kuwait St.**

Jumeirah Rd (Map pp76–7)

Al-Wasl Rd (Map pp76–7) **In Safa.**

Mercato Mall (pp76–7) **On Jumeirah Rd.**

Carrefour locations:

Bur Dubai (Map pp62–3)

Deira City Centre (pp56–7)

Mall of the Emirates (pp82–3).

Ibn Battuta Mall (pp82–3)

Choithram locations:

Al-Rolla & Al-Mankhool Rds (Map pp62–3) **Next to Al-Khaleej Shopping Centre.**

Al-Wasl Rd (Map pp76–7) **Jumeirah, near Safa Park.**

DEIRA

Deira has a great street scene: snag a sidewalk table beneath flickering neon and soak up the colour. Deira is where many poor people live, and here you eat their food – Chinese, Arabic, African and especially Indian. With several notable exceptions, most of them listed below, Deira lacks upmarket restaurants; for a white-tablecloth dinner with wine, head to the beach. If you're on a budget, you can do well for under Dh20 (see the boxed text, p109). But even if you're not, an unpretentious dinner in conservative Dubai can be as special as a fancy meal at home.

CAFÉ CHIC Map pp56–7   French $$$

☎ 217 0000; Le Meridien Dubai, Airport Rd, Al-Garhoud; lunch set-menu/dinner mains Dh110/180; ⏱ lunch Sat-Thu 12.30-3.30pm, dinner nightly 8-11.30pm

Two-star Michelin-rated chef Philippe Gauvreau oversees Café Chic, a stalwart of haute-contemporary French cuisine. Top ingredients are flown in daily from France – line-caught fish from Brittany, Red Label guinea hen, Valrhona chocolate – and they're transformed into art by executive-chef Pierrick Cizéron. Go for a set menu, and request the sommelier pair wines – his list is one of Dubai's best. The room is dated, but the culinary acumen is spot-on. Come at lunch for a three-course set menu, with wine, for a mere Dh110.

VERRE BY GORDON RAMSAY

Map pp54–5   Fine Dining $$$

☎ 212 7551; Hilton Dubai Creek, Baniyas Rd; mains Dh175; ⌚ 7pm-midnight

The pinnacle of Dubai's culinary scene, Verre stands out for embracing the gentile *art de la table* in all its sensuality – from your first sip of champagne to your last bite of chocolate, this is one meal you won't soon forget. Verre plays to European sophisticates who recognize subtlety, not to Dubai's ubiquitous parvenu: there are no distracting gimmicks, no silly flourishes and no dumbing down of the West's great culinary traditions. Near-perfect executions of French-inspired classics are served with choreographed precision in an austere white-tablecloth dining room. Expect lovely surprises from the chef, such as an *amuse* of finger-sized *pithiviers* of quail and foie gras; and a plate of *mignardises* with lip-smacking *fruit-gelées* and dense truffles after dessert. In between, it's up to you – everything is heartily recommend. One of the city's foremost sommeliers oversees the heady wine list, and an ambassadorial maître d' keeps the ballet in synch. If you're serious about eating, don't miss Verre.

JW'S STEAKHOUSE Map pp56–7   Steak $$$

☎ 262 4444; JW Marriott Hotel, Abu Baker Al-Siddique Rd; mains Dh150; ⌚ noon-midnight

In the classic American tradition, the dimly lit JW's is done in dark-wood panelling with green-leather Queen Anne wing chairs. The menu is equally orthodox, with succulent fat-man-sized steaks and chops, best preceded by Scotch and followed by cigars. Expats know JW's best as the home of the 12-hour Friday brunch, the longest in town (note: no alcohol served between 4pm and 6pm; call for details).

SHABESTAN Map pp54–5   Persian $$$

☎ 222 7171; Radisson SAS Hotel, Baniyas St; mains Dh90; ⌚ 12.30-3.15pm & 7.30-11.15pm

Shabestan is Dubai's top Persian restaurant. But don't take our word for it. Ask Sheikh Mohammed, who regularly pops in for lunch. But go at dinner time, when the window-lined dining room reveals a panorama of glittering lights over the Creek (book a window table). Hot fresh bread and homemade yoghurt hit the table as you arrive. Mountains of perfumed rice accompany melt-off-the-bone braised lamb. Save room for vermicelli ice cream with saffron and rose water. The Persian house band is first-rate.

MIYAKO Map pp54–5   Japanese $$$

☎ 209 1222; Hyatt Regency, off Al-Khaleej Rd; mains from Dh90; ⌚ 12.30-3pm & 7pm-midnight

The coolly minimalist, compact dining room of Dubai's best Japanese eatery narrowly escapes being bland, but feels very Tokyo, with sleek surfaces of stainless steel and glass-enclosed *shoji* screens. The sushi is stellar (as are its prices), but this is a place to branch out. *Shabu shabu* is superb, made with tender and tasty beef; the crumbed fried oysters and braised pork belly *(kakuni)* merit a special trip. The drawback? Traffic. Avoid coming during evening rush hour; book after 9pm or on the weekend.

SUMIBIYA Map pp54–5   Japanese Grill $$$

☎ 222 7171; Radisson SAS Hotel, Baniyas St; mains Dh80; ⌚ 12–3pm & 7-11pm

Japanese BBQ-grill cooking (aka Yakiniku) is the specialty at Sumibiya, and every table has a recessed fire grill. Though the Wagyu beef and seafood run high (Dh100+), the set menus of various meat-and-veggie combos are a relative bargain. There's nothing romantic about the narrow window-less room, but it's great fun for families or groups of foodie friends. If you can't bear to cook your own dinner, fried-rice dishes spare you the trouble.

ASHIANA Map pp54–5   Indian $$$

☎ 228 1707; Sheraton Dubai Creek; mains Dh80; ⌚ 12.30-3pm & 7.30pm-midnight

In a town that knows good Indian, Ashiana's stands out as one of the best. Presentations of the northern Indian fare are brilliant: *dum biryani* is cooked in a pot sealed with bread, elegantly perfuming the meat. Sophisticated, complex curries justify the prices, as do the solicitous service, atmospheric dining room and live sitar music. Plan to linger long. Good vegetarian food too.

EATING DEIRA

FARSI FOOD By Matthew Lee

Relations between the UAE and Iran haven't always been congenial – they're still disputing the ownership of three tiny islands in the Gulf. But the Iranian contribution to the success of the United Arab Emirates shouldn't be understated. Large numbers of Iranian migrants moved to Dubai in the 1920s and 1930s and some of today's most influential and wealthy Emirati families have Iranian roots. There was another brief period of mass migration when thousands moved to Dubai to flee the Islamic Revolution of 1979. There are Persian buildings all over the city, such as the beautiful Iranian Hospital, and, of course, lots of fantastic restaurants. Dubai is a great place to sample this deeply underrated cuisine.

At most Persian restaurants in Dubai, your meal will begin with *noon-o-panir-o-sabzi*, or bread, cheese and herbs – roll the cheese and herbs together in the hot bread that waiting staff deliver – soft, puffy, warm-from-the-oven – to the table every few minutes. It's hard to resist filling up on it. Soup, or *ash*, is also a staple of a traditional Persian meal, and at some restaurants a bowl of barley soup (*ash-e-jow*) comes with every order. It's also worth trying *kashk-e-bademjan*. *Bademjan* is aubergine in Farsi and *kashk* is a type of whey; the result is an alluringly creamy and smoky dip.

The preparation of rice becomes an art form in the Iranian kitchen, from the fluffy and light *chelo* rice to the herb-saturated *pollo* rice and the sticky *kateh* rice. Even the burnt rice at the bottom of the pan is wondrous – it's called *tahdig* and is buttery, crunchy and zinging with saffron. The closest thing Iran has to a national dish is the *chelo kebab* (meaning 'kebab with rice'), a simple portion of grilled lamb or chicken usually marinated in lime and onion. There are also plenty of hearty lamb stews on the Persian menu; expect subtle spices and combinations of okra, aubergine and spinach. You can wash everything down with *dogh*, a yoghurt drink like the Indian *lassi*, and finish your meal with *falooda*, an icy dessert of frozen vermicelli noodles, rosewater and cherry syrup.

For a Persian dining experience so authentic it's got the stamp of approval from Tehran, lunch at the Iranian Club (p114), where women have to cover their heads and a portrait of the Ayatollah greets you on arrival. If you're not in touch with your conservative side, you can't go wrong with a meal at Shabestan (p107); Golestan (☎ 282-8007; near Computer College, Al-Garhoud; mains Dh35; noon-midnight); or Special Ostadi (☎ 397-1933; Al-Mussallah Rd, Bur Dubai; mains Dh30; noon-4pm, 6.30pm-1am)

EATING DEIRA

KIKU Map pp56–7 Japanese $$$
☎ 217 0000; Le Meridien Dubai, Airport Rd, Al-Garhoud; mains Dh75; 12.30-2.45pm & 7-11.30pm

It's a good sign when the patrons in a Japanese restaurant are Japanese. Sushi is Kiku's primary focus, with *fugu* the signature, and here they're done right, with thick slices of off-the-boat-fresh fish. The classic shoji-screen decor is crisp and clean, but reserve a tatami room for more elbow room and maximum romance. For drama – and hot food – book a teppanyaki table.

AL-MIJANA Map pp56–7 Lebanese $$$
☎ 282 4040; Le Meridien Dubai, Airport Rd, Al-Garhoud; mains Dh75; noon-3pm & 8pm-12.30am

The wooden ceiling, keyhole windows and sweeping arches lend the dining room an abbey-like simplicity, but the Lebanese party scene is anything but subdued. Book a 10pm table, just before the belly dancer arrives, and fill the table with mezze and kebabs; if you're an intrepid foodie, order the pomegranate-lemon sauté of sparrows. The food's great, but the real reason to come is to whoop it up, spontaneously

dance, and laugh too loud. Even the waiters join in.

CASA MIA Map pp56–7 Italian $$$
☎ 702 2506; Le Meridien Dubai, Airport Rd, Al-Garhoud; mains Dh75; 12.30-2.45pm & 8-11.30pm

Though one of the most dependable Italian joints in town, Casa Mia is well off the beaten path in Le Meridien Village. Friendly service and reliable cooking justify the trek. Start with beef carpaccio, then move on to wood-fired pizza or housemade pasta – soak up the sauce with fresh-baked bread. Mains run high, upwards of Dh130 for a steak (albeit properly juicy and tender); stick to starch i you're on a budget.

CREEKSIDE Map pp54–5 Japanese $$$
☎ 207 1750; Sheraton Dubai Creek, Baniyas Rd, Deira; mains Dh70; 12.30-3pm & 6.30pm-midnight

Despite its name, there are no Creek views at this austere Japanese restaurant with overly bright lighting. But sushi cuts are thick and hearty, the chef's signature rolls inventive, and the tepanyaki table great

DEIRA'S BEST CHEAP ETHNIC EATS

If you want to sample some of Dubai's best ethnic cooking, hit the backstreets of Deira, and eat beside the working-class expat workers who've imported their culinary traditions to Dubai. The following are for adventurous travellers, not the skirt-and-sweater crowd. At first glance, some might look scary – Westerners don't usually wander into these joints – but we've sampled all of them: they're the real deal. In a city that embraces artificiality, it's refreshing to find authenticity. Best of all, you'll likely get change on your Dh50 note. No credit cards.

Aroos Damascus (Map pp54–5; ☎ 227-0202; Al-Muraqabat St, at Al-Jazeira St; mains Dh20; ⏰ 6am-3am; 🏃) Syrian food is similar to Lebanese, but they use more cumin in the fatoush and spice in the kebabs. Our favourite dish: *arayees* – Syrian bread stuffed with ground lamb and grilled. The sweetness of the bread plays off the gamey flavour of the meat. Great tabouleh, fantastic fresh-from-the-oven bread, huge outdoor patio, cool flickering neon.

Abesinian Restaurant (Map pp54–5; ☎ 273-7429; 10 St (Somali St), near 23 St junction; mains Dh15; ⏰ 10am-midnight) The staff is welcoming and warm at this homey Ethiopian restaurant, where the big platters of curry and stews are best sopped-up with *injera*, spongy flat bread of native grain. Tricky to find but worth it.

Al-Baghdadi Home (Map pp54–5; ☎ 273-7069; Al-Mateena St, opposite Dubai Palm Hotel; mains Dh40; ⏰ noon-3am) In Little Iraq, on one of Dubai's best, lesser-known walking streets, Al-Baghdadi spit-roasts whole fish beside an open fire (the traditional preparation) in the restaurant's window, and serves it with bread and lentil salad. (NB: don't order randomly – *patchaa* is sheep's head.)

Afghan Kebab House (Map pp54–5; ☎ 222-3292; behind Naif Mosque, off Deira St; mains Dh15; ⏰ noon-3pm, 6pm-midnight) Big hunks of meat – lamb, beef, chicken – charred on foot-long skewers come served with rice and bread. That's it. Think caveman food. Eat with your hands. Tricky to find, but locals can direct you.

Pinoy Grill (Map pp54–5; ☎ 222-2225; Al-Rigga Rd at Al-Jazeira St; dishes Dh18; ⏰ noon-2am; 🏃) A friendly and welcoming intro to the weird, wonderful world of Filipino cuisine, which borrows from Spanish, Indonesian and French, mixing pungent ingredients, like garlic and chillies, in sweet and savoury combinations not always tastebud-friendly to foreigners. But the menu is in English, and the super-fun staff will guide you.

Xia Wei Yang (Map pp54–5; ☎ 221-7177; Baniyas Rd; hot pots Dh40; ⏰ noon-2am; 🏃) Chinese hot-pot restaurant. Order everything raw, then boil it at the table. Begin with veggies to enrich the broth, then add the meat – they have everything from meat- and fish-balls to tendons, hearts and testicles (fear not: they also serve beef and chicken). Hardly anyone speaks English: plan to point.

---

fun for watching chefs throw knives as they cook. The expansive bento box is great at lunchtime (Dh90), but at dinner the service needs help.

CHINA CLUB Map pp54–5 Contemporary Chinese $$
☎ 222 7171; Radisson SAS Hotel, Baniyas Rd; mains Dh60; ⏰ 12–2.45pm & 7.30-10.45pm
Lunchtime yum cha – especially on Fridays – is the big draw at this red-silk-fancy dining room that's an aesthetically smart, but faded holdover from the *Dynasty* era. At dinner, the classics are spot-on, including a standout Szechuan-style boiled lamb and a crispy-delicious Peking duck carved and rolled tableside. Private dining rooms are ideal for a group, with lazy susans in the middle of the tables.

THAI KITCHEN Map pp56–7 Thai $$
☎ 602 1234; Park Hyatt Dubai; mains Dh60, brunch with/without alcohol Dh180/120; ⏰ 7pm-midnight, brunch 12.30-4pm Fri

The decor is decidedly un-Thai, with black-lacquer tables, a swooping wave-form ceiling, and not a branch of bamboo, but the two open kitchens dominating the room are run entirely by Thai nationals. This is the real deal: dishes are based on Bangkok street eats, served tapas-style. Come for Friday brunch and sample the entire menu. Standouts: prawns in pandan leaves, and crispy catfish in baconlike strips with green-mango salad. One complaint: they under-spice. Ask for it hot!

GLASSHOUSE MEDITERRANEAN BRASSERIE Map pp54–5 Modern Mediterranean $$
☎ 227 1111; Hilton Dubai Creek, Baniyas Rd; mains Dh50; ⏰ 7am–midnight
It must be hard for the folk at Glasshouse not to want to throw stones at their neighbouring restaurant, Gordon Ramsay's Verre (p107). While Verre gets all the media attention, Glasshouse has quietly reinvented itself as one of Dubai's most accomplished

brasserie-style restaurants. The British-heavy comfort-food menu lists dishes like risotto with mushrooms, and rib-eye steak with chips. It's executed with style, unlike the service, alas. Great wines by the glass.

CELLAR Map pp56–7 Fusion $$
☎ 282 9333; Aviation Club; mains Dh50; ☽ noon-2am
Known best for its Friday brunch, this casual expat favourite serves gastro-pub fare, British classics with a contemporary twist. The braised lamb shoulder in filo pastry is tender and juicy, a solid choice. Order simple: sometimes the kitchen over styles. The crowd loves to party.

YUM! Map pp54–5 Noodle Bar $$
☎ 222 7171; Radisson SAS Deira, Baniyas Rd; mains Dh42; ☽ noon-1am; ⏱
Though not as dynamic as Noodle House (p117), it's a good pick for a quick bowl of noodles when you're wandering along the Creek – and you can be in and out in half an hour.

GRAND ABU SHAKRA Map pp54–5 Egyptian $$
☎ 222 9900; Al-Maktoum Rd, next to Al-Khaleej Palace Hotel; mains Dh35; ☽ 7am-3am
Black-and-white TVs show classics (sound off) from the golden age of Egyptian cinema, a fitting backdrop for Dubai's best-known Egyptian restaurant. Come at lunchtime on Tuesday or Thursday for the classic carb-rich koshary, a combination of rice, lentils and pasta, with chilli sauce, lemon and fried onion. The adventurous should order the charred whole pigeon (Dh90), but be forewarned: it's unboned – and still has its head. The red, gamey meat is richly flavourful, but boy, it's a struggle to get at it. If you're hungry, stick to the fava-bean falafel instead.

BOMBAY Map pp54–5 Indian $$
☎ 272 0000; Marco Polo Hotel, Al-Mateena St; mains Dh30; ☽ 7pm-midnight
It's worth a detour deep into Deira for Bombay's orthodox North Indian cooking. Come hungry and start with the kebab sampler (mutton, chicken, fish) then move on to mint-marinated fish cooked tandoori style, or a cardamom-rich saag gosht (lamb and spinach). There's lots for vegetarians. The French-style service by tuxedo-clad waiters is a surprise at this price, but we're not arguing. We're just happy they serve beer.

CAFÉ HAVANA Map pp56–7 Café $
☎ 295 5238; Level II, Deira City Centre; coffee Dh12; ☽ 8am-midnight
The coffee's okay and the food nothing special; it's the people-watching that's great – Emirati men kick back here for hours on end, providing a rare opportunity to rub shoulders with them.

BUR DUBAI
Possibly the most eclectic eating area of Dubai, restaurants here run the gamut from dirt-cheap curry joints to white-tablecloth restaurants worthy of a Michelin star.

FIRE & ICE Map pp64–5 Contemporary European $$$
☎ 341 8888; Raffles Dubai, Wafi City Mall; mains Dh200, tasting menu from Dh550; ☽ 7-11pm
If Michelin gave stars in Dubai, they'd surely consider bestowing one on Fire & Ice, Raffles Dubai's floor-to-ceiling-brick dining room that feels strangely like a styled-out New York warehouse. The menu plays on opposites (hot-cold, sweet-sour etc), and though the highly composed presentations can get too theatrical (think pop rocks on torchon de foie gras), the culinary acumen is spot-on. Using French technique, the chef expertly explores the delicate balance point between Eastern and Western ingredients. A tasting menu (Dh550+) might include yellow-fin sashimi with tomato salsa, ponzu jelly and wasabi foam, or Wagyu sirloin with pan-fried pistachio-polenta and vanilla jus. Service is among Dubai's best, comparable to top tables in London; likewise the sommelier, who oversees a fantastic collection of New World wines you won't find elsewhere in the Middle East.

IZ Map pp64–5 Contemporary Indian $$$
☎ 317 1234; Grand Hyatt Dubai, Al-Qataiyat Rd; dishes Dh40; ☽ 12.30-3pm & 7pm-1am, to 2am Thu & Fri
The modernist-feeling wood-and-stone dining room glows by candlelight at this tapas-style contemporary Indian eatery. The tandoori-oven specialties are perfectly executed – order the always-succulent skewered roasted prawns – as are classics like murgha tikka, aka butter chicken in a creamy tomato sauce perfect for sopping up with the fresh-from-the-oven bread. Sit at the open kitchen's counter and watch the chef's theatrics. One drawback: all

LEBANESE FOOD LINGO 101

Break the hummus habit and try something new. Here's a primer to help you navigate some lesser-known dishes on Dubai's ubiquitous Lebanese menus. Spellings may vary.

Baklava The Lebanese use pistachios and almonds, not walnuts, in this classic honeyed pastry. Say bak-la-WAH or nobody will understand you.

Bastirma Air-cured beef (think pastrami).

Fattoush Chopped salad topped with fried Arabic bread and a dressing of olive oil, lemon and sumac.

Falafel Deep-fried balls of seasoned, mashed chickpeas, best served with tahini sauce.

Kofta Grilled skewers of spicy minced lamb.

Kibbeh Balls of minced lamb and onion, rolled in cracked wheat and fried. These are the measure of a good Lebanese kitchen; they should be golden-brown and nongreasy outside, warm and juicy inside.

Kibbeh Nayeh Ground raw lamb served with egg and condiments.

Labneh Thick, strained yoghurt spreadable like cream cheese.

Mujadara Seasoned lentils and bulghur topped with caramelised onions.

Muhammara Paste of red-bell pepper, ground nuts, bread crumbs and pomegranate.

Sambusak Pastries stuffed with ground lamb or cheese.

Shawarma Rotisserie-cooked seasoned lamb or chicken, carved onto flatbread and rolled up with salad and sauce.

Shish Taouk Spiced chunks of char-grilled chicken.

Sujok Heavily spiced, air-dried beef sausage.

Tabouleh Parsley salad with cracked wheat, tomato, mint, onion, lemon and olive oil.

Tahini Pulverized sesame seeds, often used to enhance dips or thinned into a sauce for falafel.

Warak Enab Rice-stuffed grape leaves (*dolmas* in Greece).

those little plates add up fast. Plan Dh300 a head.

AWTAR Map pp64–5 · Lebanese $$$
☎ 317 1234; Grand Hyatt Dubai, Al-Qataiyat Rd; mains Dh65; ⏰ 12.30-3pm & 7.30pm-3am, closed Sat

Emiratis love the opulent Bedouin tent–like atmosphere and warm welcome of this formal Lebanese restaurant, complete with a Brazilian belly dancer and blaring Lebanese pop – it's not uncommon for women to stand up, clap and sway to the music. The menu lists the usual mezze and kebabs, as well as a full page of raw-meat dishes, all served in mountainous portions. If you're loath to shout, book at 8pm, but for maximum fun round up a posse and come at 10pm when the scene gets rockin'. Request one of the swoop-backed booths for the best views.

BASTAKIAH NIGHTS Map pp62–3 · Arabian $$
☎ 353 7772; near the Rulers Court, off Al-Fahidi St, Bastakia; mains Dh60, set menu Dh138; ⏰ 12.30-11.30pm

One of the city's most romantic restaurants, Bastakiah Nights occupies a restored home in this historic district, and the old Arabian-style atmosphere is fabulous. It also includes a few Emirati dishes on its Lebanese-based menu. Though you can order á la carte, we recommend the set menu, which includes soup, copious mezze,

top picks

ORIENTALIST'S DELIGHT

In a city that's always reinventing itself, old-guard *Thousand and One Nights*-style dining rooms can be hard to find. Here are our top picks to indulge your Arabian fantasies.

- Awtar (left) Fancy, fabric-draped Lebanese.
- Bastakiah Nights (left) Restored, historic old-Arabia-style house.
- Al-Qasr (p117) The Lebanese big night out.
- Shabestan (p107) Old Persia with a view.
- Tagine (p121) Fez-wearing waiters and moody Moroccan atmosphere.

and choice of entrées, such as mixed grill or lamb stew. It's not the best food in town and service is sometimes weak, but on a balmy evening, the candlelit courtyard, with the indigo night sky overhead, can't be beat. No alcohol.

TROYKA Map pp62–3   Russian $$

. ☎ 359 5908; **Ascot Hotel, Khalid bin al-Waleed Rd (Bank St); mains Dh55;** ❤ noon-3pm & 7pm-3am
A little slice of Moscow for the ever-increasing number of Russian tourists in Dubai, Troyka has everything you need for a night on the town: copious amounts of vodka, caviar, hearty mains (try the tongue), and best of all a fabulously camp floorshow that would do Bob Fosse proud. Arrive around 10pm.

ASHA'S Map pp64–5   Contemporary Indian $$

☎ 324 4100; **Pyramids, Wafi City Mall, Al-Qataiyat Rd; mains Dh55;** ❤ 12.30-3.30pm & 7.30pm-12.30am
Namesake of owner Asha Bhosle of Bollywood fame, Asha's packs a see-and-be-seen crowd of rich Indian expats into its sexy, low-light, tandoori-orange dining room, with ethnic-fusion dance music playing in the background. On our last visit, we had a gorgeous meal of spicy-ginger-garlic marinated prawns, followed by a gorgeous *muscat gosht* (tomato-and-butter-braised spicy lamb) – both Asha's personal recipes. Some complain that the cooking occasionally misses (think foie gras and lentils), but all agree that this is a fab place to party.

THAI CHI Map pp64–5   Thai & Chinese $$

☎ 324 0000; **Pyramids, Wafi City Mall, Al-Qataiyat Rd; mains Dh50;** ❤ 12.30-3pm & 7pm-midnight
We're generally sceptical of restaurants that serve two differing cuisines, but Thai Chi does Thai and Chinese right – probably because it has two separate kitchens. The extensive Thai menu does great things with prawns; the Chinese menu stands out for its irresistible Peking duck and wok specialties. A solid choice for a midrange meal at Wafi.

ANTIQUE BAZAAR Map pp62–3   Indian $$

☎ 397 7444; **Four Points Sheraton, Khalid bin al-Waleed Rd (Bank St); mains Dh50;** ❤ 12.30-3.30pm & 7.30pm-3am
As the name suggests, this deservedly popular Indian eatery resembles a wildly coloured antique bazaar, with dynamic Indian cooking to match. The preparations are classics, and they're deftly prepared. What really makes this place special is the combination of the food, raucous house band and Indian dancer. Note: bring earplugs if you're sensitive to noise.

LEMONGRASS Map pp64–5   Thai $$

☎ 334 2325; **near Lamcy Plaza; mains Dh35;** ❤ noon-midnight; ⓰
Though pricey for an independent, Lemongrass's soothing lime-coloured dining room, brightly flavoured cooking, and solicitous service make it one of Dubai's best for Thai. Pad Thai is presented in an omelette wrapper – a nice touch – and curries have marvellous depth of flavour. If you like spicy, say so; the kitchen is shy with the heat. Good for vegetarians. Note: the toilets are shared with the building and not maintained by the restaurant. Pee before you come.

COCONUT GROVE Map pp62–3 South Indian $$

☎ 398 3800; **Rydges Plaza Hotel, Al-Diyafah St, Satwa Roundabout, Satwa; mains Dh35;** ❤ noon-3pm & 7pm-12.30am
Fragrant curries and biryani pack in regulars who love the authentic Keralan and Goan cooking – the Goan fish curry is thick, creamy and spicy, with hunks of supple and tender fish. Alas, waiters are pushy, always trying to upsell and force more beer on you. Overlook this in favour of the stellar rooftop views and reasonable prices. Call early to book a window table.

PAUL Map pp62–3   French Café $$

☎ 351 7009; **BurJuman Centre, Trade Centre Rd; mains Dh35;** ❤ 9am-midnight; ⓰
European expats flock here in droves on Thursday and Friday nights to linger over French pastries and dream of home. By day, it's a good spot to refuel on *salade Niçoise* and quiche while shopping in the BurJuman Centre.

KAN ZAMAN Map pp62–3   Arabic $

☎ 393 9913; **Heritage Village, Al-Shindagha; mains Dh27;** ❤ 11am-3am
While on a trip to Heritage Village, stop by this Creekside favourite to munch on mezze and grills and watch the passing parade of boats. During the cooler months, sit on the big outdoor patio and puff on a *sheesha* pipe.

GAZEBO Map pp64–5   Indian $

☎ 397 9930; Sheikh Khalifa bin Zayed Rd (Trade Centre Rd), opposite Spinneys; mains Dh22; ☽ 10am-3.30pm & 7pm-midnight

You'll forgive the unexciting interior when you taste the brilliant North Indian cooking. Standouts on the huge menu include a great tawa lobster masala, with succulent chunks of lobster, black pepper, tomato and rich masala sauce; Banjara Gosht, mutton in masala gravy, rose petals, cashew nuts and tomato; and Gosht Achari, mutton in coriander, tomato and pomegranate. Good value. Note: vegetarians should hop next door to Kamat, its sister restaurant.

KWALITY Map pp62–3   Indian $

☎ 393 6563; near Ascot Hotel, Khalid bin al-Waleed Rd (Bank St); mains Dh20; ☽ 12.30-3pm & 7-11.30pm

The food is dependable and the service swift at this long-standing Indian restaurant (though the walls need a good scrubbing; sit upstairs). It's hard to go wrong with hearty portions of favourites like chicken makhani (butter chicken) or rogan josh (lamb curry). Good vegetarian options and tandoori too.

BASTA ART CAFÉ Map pp62–3   Café $

☎ 353 5071; Al-Fahidi St, Bastakia; mains Dh20; ☽ 8am-9pm; ♿

A cool respite while exploring the Bastakia, this café occupies a garden courtyard outside an old Dubai house. The food is respectable café fare – the salads are refreshing on a hot day – but it's the sun-dappled garden that makes this place special. Good breakfasts. No credit cards.

XVA CAFÉ Map pp62–3   Café $

☎ 353 5383; behind Basta Art Café, Al-Musallah Roundabout; mains Dh20; ☽ 9am-9pm Sat-Thu, 9am-6pm Fri

For a respite from Dubai's chaotic street scene, seek out this hidden gallery-cum-café in the courtyard of a 120-year-old house in the Bastakia Quarter. The all-veg cooking lists a mishmash of salads and grain-based dishes with vaguely Southeast Asian overtones. You'll especially like the *mojardara* (rice topped with sautéed veggies and yogurt) and the dense-green mint-lemonade – a must-order.

AL-MALLAH Map pp62–3   Lebanese $

☎ 398 4723; Al-Dhiyafah St, Satwa; mains Dh20; ☽ 6am-4am; ♿

Local-favourite Al-Mallah gets packed on its outdoor seating area, even during the scorching summer. The things to order: shawarma (served after 4pm), wrapped or on a plate; falafel dripping in tahini; and fresh juice. Skip the mezze (go to Sidra p118, across the road). Great for people-watching after a night drinking. No credit cards.

GOVINDA'S Map pp64–5   Indian-Vegan $

☎ 396 0088; off Trade Centre Rd, two blocks behind Regent Palace Hotel; mains Dh15; ☽ noon-3.30pm & 7pm-midnight Sat-Thu, 1.30-3pm & 7pm-midnight Fri; ♿

Jains (no-kill-anything) run this Gujarati-Indian restaurant that uses no onion or garlic in its all-vegan food, but the cooking is rich in character, with intense flavours and heady perfumes. The staff couldn't be friendlier. Save room for homemade ice cream from the adjacent, affiliated ice-cream parlour.

CURRY LEAF Map pp62–3   Sri Lankan $

☎ 397 8940; Al-Mussalla Tower, Bank St; mains Dh15; ☽ 8am-12.30pm; ♿

Hoppers – crispy rice-flour pancakes with fried egg – best accompany the smoky-hot, spice-rich curries at this food-court Sri Lankan place in an electronics mall. A few Dutch colonial dishes round out the menu; try the *lumpries* (spiced rice with meat, egg and aubergine). There's zero atmosphere, but kids love to play in the adjacent fountain.

RANGOLI Map pp62–3   Indian-Vegetarian $

☎ 351 5873; Meena Bazaar; mains Dh12; ☽ 8.30am-3pm, 5pm-midnight

There's not a Westerner in the house at this all-vegetarian Gujarati Indian eatery, with a take-away window on the sidewalk. Inside there's a tiny cafeteria jammed with tables. Fill your tray with rice, daal (lentil broth), potatoes, curry and bread – filling, satisfying, cheap. Afterward, wander the hub of Dubai's Indian community and shop for fabric and spices. NB: tricky to find, but locals will direct you. No credit cards.

KARACHI DARBAR Map pp64–5   Pakistani $

☎ 334 7272; Karama Shopping Centre & various locations; mains Dh12; ☽ 4am-2am

LET'S DO BRUNCH...

The workweek in Dubai runs Sunday through Thursday, which means (nearly) everyone is off on Friday. An expat institution, Friday brunch is a major element of the Dubai social scene – particularly among Bacchanalian revellers – and every hotel-restaurant in town sets up an all-you-can-eat buffet with an option for unlimited champagne or wine. Some smaller, independent restaurants also serve brunch, but without alcohol, making them popular with local families. Here's a very short selection of some of the best brunches in town.

Spectrum on One (Map pp72–3; ☎ 332 5555; Fairmont Hotel; buffet with alcohol Dh400; ☟ noon-3pm) The most popular brunch in town includes free-flowing bubbly and eight different buffets with six different cuisines. Phenomenal sushi. Book weeks ahead.

Glasshouse Mediterranean Brasserie (Map pp54–5; ☎ 227 1111; Hilton Dubai Creek; brunch incl bubbly and cocktails Dh195; ☟ from 12.30pm) After Spectrum on One at the Fairmont, Glasshouse tops many European-expats' lists – blame it on the bloodies, Pimm's and smart British-brasserie fare.

Yalumba (Map pp56–7; ☎ 217 0000; Le Meridien Dubai, Airport Rd; nonvintage/vintage champagne Dh366/700; ☟ 12.30-3.30pm) One of the few to offer an á la carte menu so you won't have to schlep plates. Go whole-hog with vintage Bollinger champagne.

Thai Kitchen (Map pp56–7; ☎ 602 1234; Park Hyatt Dubai; per person with soft drinks/beer & wine Dh120/180; ☟ 12.30-4pm) Sample an enormous repertoire of Thai cooking, served tapas-style. Mellow scene, good for non-drinkers.

Waxy O'Conner's (Map pp62–3; ☎ 352 0900; Ascot Hotel; with beer Dh65; ☟ from 12.30pm) For the hungry, hard-drinkin' pub crowd. Includes a full fry-up, five pints, and carvery dinner in a windowless bar.

Iranian Club (Map pp64–5; ☎ 336 7700; Oud Metha Rd; brunch Dh60; ☟ 1-4pm) Feast at this Persian-cuisine showcase owned by the Iranian government. Start by rolling cheese and mint in hot bread, then sample soups and marinated salads, followed by tender kebabs and stews from an enormous buffet. Pace yourself. Women must wear headscarves, men long pants, and there's no alcohol, but it's worth altering your habits – especially if you're American – for a culturally rich afternoon and the chance to glimpse Iranians at table.

A favourite of guest workers and expats with an eye for a biryani bargain, Karachi Darbar keeps 'em well fed with a huge menu of Pakistani, Indian and Chinese specialities – but stick to the Pakistani. Point to what others are eating and order – it's the only way to know what you're going to get. Fear not: it'll be good. Don't do Chinese or Indian here. No credit cards.

SHEIKH ZAYED ROAD

The tower hotels lining the Sheikh Zayed strip are the psychological centrepoint of Dubai. Dinner here positions you well to travel elsewhere afterward, but with so many nearby hotels bars and nightclubs, you may as well stick around. But good luck crossing the road: there's only one pedestrian overpass. Take a taxi instead.

AMWAJ Map pp72–3   Contemporary European $$$
☎ 343 8888; Shangri-La hotel; mains Dh150;
☟ Sun-Fri 12.30-3pm, 7.30pm-midnight
It's rare in Dubai to find an adroit kitchen staff properly schooled in classic European

technique, which is exactly why we love Amwaj. Seafood is the specialty on the French-derivative menu. Dishes may include torchon de foie gras with warm brioche toast, sautéed scallops fanned on the plate and topped with an elegant saffron-orange foam, or rack of lamb on eggplant compote with black-olive sauce. The only drawback is the dining room: it overhangs a hotel lobby, and sound echoes upward. Request a table away from the railing. Vegetarians: look for the all-veg tasting menu.

THIPTARA ROYAL THAI Map pp72–3   Thai $$$
☎ 428 7888; The Palace Old Town hotel, downtown Burj Dubai; mains Dh150; ☟ 7-11.45pm
The prices are as high as the adjacent Burj Dubai, but if you're looking for a reason to linger long beneath the world's tallest tower, Thiptara's elegant interpretations of classic Thai dishes and its location in a lakeside Thai-style pagoda provide just the excuse. The note-perfect som tum (green-papaya salad) is as good as we've had in Bangkok; the smoky-hot ka pohn nau (beef in spicy brown sauce) is intensely spiced

top picks

MEALS WITH A VIEW

Dubai has restaurants with breathtaking views. Here's our top five:

- Pierchic (p118) Off-shore views of the dramatic Burj Al Arab and the moody Madinat Jumeirah.
- Vu's (below) Top-of-the-world vistas from Emirates Towers.
- Shabestan (p107) Gaze at the ballet of dhows on the Creek.
- Thiptara Royal Thai (opposite) Dine on a lakeview deck beneath the world's tallest tower.
- Magnolia (p118) Sit outside and watch silent *abras* floating by.

with on-the-vine peppercorns. Alas, the interior is too austere (sit on the deck) and the plates look chain-store cheap, but the solicitous service by an all-Thai staff and the exceptional cooking make up for it. Note: budgeteers, order the Dh50 pad Thai.

EXCHANGE GRILL Map pp72–3   Steakhouse $$$
☎ 311 8000; Fairmont hotel, Sheikh Zayed Rd; mains Dh150; ☽ 7pm-midnight
Dubai's top steakhouse has a clubby feel, with oversized leather arm chairs at giant linen-draped tables, and big picture windows overlooking the glittering strip. The classic American menu features Wagyu beef, which may sound attractive, but is more than twice the price of the more-flavourful USDA prime: save your dirhams. Seafood rounds out the menu, but really, beef is the big draw – and it's fabulous here. The wine list is mind-bogglingly extensive, and the service exemplary. Can't wait to return.

VU'S Map pp72–3   European-Fusion $$$
☎ 319 8771; Emirates Towers, Sheikh Zayed Rd; mains Dh130; ☽ 12.30-3pm & 7.30pm-midnight
As the name implies, the views are stellar from this gorgeous tower-top white-tablecloth dining room, a favourite of wheeler-dealers celebrating the closing of a multi-million-dollar contract. The Australian chef weaves Asian overtones into his Franco-Italian-inspired cooking, and while it's solidly good, the kitchen lacks discipline: some dishes clash or miss entirely – inexcusable at this price. Service is slightly pretentious and drinks are wickedly

overpriced, but oh! those views. Save this one for an expense account, or if nothing you can do will impress your spoiled-rotten girlfriend. Note: jackets required, no jeans.

TOKYO@THETOWERS
Map pp72–3   Japanese $$$
☎ 330 0000; Emirates Towers, Sheikh Zayed Rd; mains Dh125; ☽ 12.30-3pm & 7.30pm-midnight, Sun lunch 1-3pm
We're torn about T@T. While it serves brilliant sashimi and some of the freshest, perkiest, shiniest sushi in town, the prices are ridiculous, there's too much din and the views from the corridor-like dining room are of a shopping mall – a big letdown when you consider its location in one of Dubai's iconic towers. Try Kiku (p108) first, but keep this in your back pocket if they're booked.

HOI AN Map pp72–3   French -Vietnamese $$$
☎ 343 8888; Shangri-La hotel; mains Dh100; ☽ 7.30pm-1am
Teak latticework, plantation shutters, and spinning wooden ceiling fans evoke a *très civilisé* Colonial-era Vietnam at this upmarket French-Vietnamese restaurant. The flavours are lively and bright. Start with the crispy crab rolls, then move on to the signatures: lotus-wrapped sea bass with ginger-lemon sauce, or tamarind-spiced rack of lamb. Deliciously low lighting and genteel service make this an ideal place for a third date.

MARRAKECH Map pp72–3   Moroccan $$$
☎ 343 8888; Shangri-La hotel; mains Dh85; ☽ 1-3pm & 8pm-midnight
A languid counterpoint to Dubai's go-go scene, Marrakech feels more like a hammam than a high-rise, with key-hole doorways, north-African wall tiles and flickering candle lanterns casting moody shadows. The subtle and earthy cooking includes *harira*, a coriander-spiced lamb soup; the Moroccan signature dish *pastilla* (pigeon pie); and of course couscous royale and tagine – we recommend the melt-off-the-bone lamb shank with preserved lemon. One caveat: book a table inside the main dining room (ideally in view of the soulful Fez-wearing oud player), not on the balcony overlooking the office-tower-like hotel lobby.

BENJARONG Map pp72–3   Thai $$$
☎ 343 3333; Dusit Dubai; mains Dh70; ☽ 7.30pm-midnight

EATING SHEIKH ZAYED ROAD

115

Gold-leafed columns, drop-dead views and a carved wooden ceiling make quiet Benjarong the prettiest Thai restaurant in town, ideal for a tête-à-tête with your paramour. Start with *gung hom sabai* (deep-fried prawns in egg noodles) or *tom yam goong* (spicy prawn soup with lime, lemongrass and chilli), then move on to the specialty: coconut curry – red or green – best served with duck and pineapple. For maximum atmosphere, book the tatami-style Ayotoya room and sit on cushions on the floor.

AL-TANNOUR Map pp72–3   Lebanese $$
☎ 331 1111; Crowne Plaza Hotel, Sheikh Zayed Rd; mains Dh60; ⏰ 8.30pm-3am
While its traditional village-style décor doesn't excite, the smell of freshly baked bread does. So does the rest of the food – this is some of the most authentic Lebanese food in Dubai. Go with a group that likes to get noisy, and fill the table with mezze from the unusually long list; round out the meal with a couple of grilled dishes (try the chicken). Book for around 10.30pm for maximum fun, when the band and belly dancer really get going.

SPECTRUM ON ONE
Map pp72–3   International $$
☎ 332 5555; Fairmont hotel, Sheikh Zayed Rd; mains Dh60; ⏰ 7pm-1am; 🖢
Ideal for families and groups that can't decide where to go, Spectrum on One is the classic jack of all trades, master of none. The food is solidly good, with no disappointments from its eight kitchens, which feature six distinct cuisines from around the world, but don't expect to be wowed. Still, kids love it, as do big tables of Dionysian revellers who flock here for Friday brunch.

LOTUS ONE Map pp72–3   Fusion $$
☎ 329 3200; Dubai International Convention Centre, off Sheik Zayed Rd; mains Dh55; ⏰ noon-2am
The cool lounge beats, bamboo-ceilinged dining room and high-backed velvet chairs create an invitingly lush backdrop for drinks and dinner at Lotus One, known better for its candy-coloured cocktails than its Asian-fusion menu. An English chef took over in late 2007, promising to reinvigorate the once overly ambitious menu. The jury's out, but if you like to get dolled up, linger over dinner, then hit the bars for a night of dancing, Lotus One sets the right mood for you.

OPTIONS Map pp72–3   Contemporary Indian $$
☎ 329 3293; Dubai International Convention Centre, off Sheik Zayed Rd; mains Dh50; ⏰ noon-2.45pm & 7-11.45pm
Beaded glass curtains, tufted red-vinyl walls, and glittering crystal chandeliers set a Subcontinent-fancy mood at Indian celeb-chef Sanjeer Kapoors' Options. Though noteworthy for consistency, the kitchen's real excellence lies in the chef's exquisite spicing. Standouts include tandoori-grilled citrus-marinated prawns with green cardamom, cream and cashew paste; chicken tikka with saffron gravy and rose petals; and vegetarian slow-cooked black lentils with pomegranate, finished with housemade butter.

NEZESAUSSI
Map pp72–3   Australian-South African $$
☎ 428 5888; Al-Manzil hotel, Burj Dubai Blvd; mains Dh45; ⏰ 6pm-2am Sun-Thu, noon-2am Fri & Sat; 🖢
The name is an amalgam of New Zealand, South Africa and Australia, and the menu plays on those countries' classics. Standouts include dynamite slow-cooked five-spice pork ribs, giant Monte Cristo sandwiches, and grilled New Zealand lamb. Portions are huge. The place is basically a high-end sports bar, where football fans throw back VBs and holler, but the heavy flatware, linen napkins and solicitous service make this a worthwhile dining destination as well. Plan to shout across the table on match nights.

AL-NAFOORAH Map pp72–3   Lebanese $$
☎ 319 8088; Emirates Towers, Sheikh Zayed Rd; mains Dh35; ⏰ 12.30-3pm & 8pm-midnight
Tucked at the base of Emirates Towers, Al-Nafoorah's clubby, wood-panelled dining room feels like a Wall St power-lunch spot. The mezze stand out – try the *kibbeh* (raw lamb) – more than the kebabs on the classic Lebanese menu, but really, the kitchen does everything very well, if not beautifully. It's quieter and more formal than most Lebanese restaurants (to wit, dessert pastries come on three-tiered stands, like at a fancy tea party), making this a great choice for a dressy-casual night out without the noisy fanfare of the big Lebanese party places.

RELIGION ON THE PLATE

You may never realize just how much you like pork until you travel to Dubai and are rarely allowed any. As an alternative to pork bacon, some supermarkets sell beef- and turkey-bacon, both poor substitutes for the real thing. To serve pork in a restaurant, you must have a pork license. Likewise alcohol, which is generally only served in hotels. If an item on a restaurant menu has been prepared with either alcohol or pork, it must be clearly marked.

Muslims never eat pork: it is *haram*, forbidden by Islam – purely for health reasons, as pigs were considered disease-carrying animals. Alcohol is forbidden, not for health, but because it makes followers forgetful of God and prayer. The other major dietary restriction applies to meat: it must be *halal*, meaning religiously suitable or permitted. The animal must be drained of its blood at the time of slaughter by having its throat cut. This is why much of the red meat slaughtered and sold locally is very pale in colour. In restaurants you'll easily find non-*halal* beef – just don't expect your tenderloin to be wrapped in a fatty strip of bacon before it's grilled. If it is, savour it.

NOODLE HOUSE Map pp72–3 Asian $$
☎ 319 8757; Emirates Towers, Sheikh Zayed Rd; mains Dh30; ☻ noon-11.30pm; ♿

Sheikh Mohammed sometimes lunches at this reliably good, always-packed pan-Asian noodle joint at the base of Emirates Towers. The concept is simple: everyone sits on long wooden communal benches and orders by ticking dishes on a tear-off menu pad. There's great variety – curry laksa to duck pancakes – to please disparate tastes, and there are good wines by the glass and several Asian beers, including Tiger on tap. Plan to wait at peak times: leave your mobile number and head next door to Agency (p127) for pre-dinner drinks.

MORE Map pp72–3 Café $$
☎ 343 3779; Doha Rd, next to Al-Murooj Rotana Suites; mains Dh30; ☻ 8am-11pm; ♿

An industrial-like space with poured concrete floors, More feels like the giant café-restaurants of the West, which explains why European expats flock here in droves for brunch. There's a little of everything on the menu – Thai curries, Italian pastas, good burgers and great eggs Benedict. Portions are huge: one dish is enough. The execution is okay, but not everything works: if it looks experimental, skip it. Save room for homemade ice cream. Free wi-fi.

ZAATAR W ZEIT Map pp72–3 Lebanese $
☎ 343 1259, 343 6265; near Shangri-La hotel, Sheikh Zayed Rd; mains Dh15; ☻ 24hr; ♿

Pick the spicing on your flatbread at this Lebanese fast-food joint: top with cheese, tomatoes, minced meats, or of course zaatar (thyme, sumac and sesame). Think Lebanese pizza. *Labneh* (salted yoghurt drink) goes best with 'em, not cola. Sit outside and gaze up at the towers.

SAJ EXPRESS Map pp72–3 Lebanese $
☎ 321 1191; Sheikh Zayed Rd; mains Dh15; ☻ 9am-2am; ♿

Saj Express is one of Sheikh Zayed Rd's top fast-food joints, and the fresh bread (cooked on the *saj*, a curved, iron dome-topped oven) is what makes the shawarmas here so special. The rest of the menu doesn't excite, but pair a shawarma with one of the fresh juices and you can't go wrong.

JUMEIRAH

The restaurants in Dubai's low-rise, high-rent district draw wealthy locals and tourists on holiday. Though the beach is never far away, it's barely visible from some of the following eateries: for ocean views, head to New Dubai or the Madinat Jumeirah. The restaurants at Madinat Jumeirah are generally good, entirely touristy and overpriced, but they're some of the most scenic – never mind the vague feeling of dining at Disneyland Arabia. Note: Al-Diyafah St, though not technically in Jumeirah, is the best walking street in the city and is tops for a late-night shawarma.

AL-QASR Map pp76–7 Lebanese $$$
☎ 336 1111; Dubai Marine Beach Resort; set menu Dh200; ☻ 7.30am-8pm

For the full-on Lebanese big night out, book an evening – ideally Thursday – at Al-Qasr. The meal starts with bread and veggies, followed by a dozen cold mezze and half a dozen hot. Then comes the meat… the meal goes on for hours. Show up after 10pm, when the noisy-fun Lebanese pop band plays and an enthusiastic belly dancer flutters, twirls and spins. By evening's end, the whole place joins in, clapping, dancing and singing. For a quieter meal, sit outside or come before 10pm. This is one of just a few places that carries Al-Maza Beer, which you should drink copiously.

PISCES & P2 BRASSERIE

Map pp76–7   Seafood $$$

☎ 366 8888; Souq Madinat Jumeirah; mains Pisces/Brasserie Dh180/90; ⏲ 7-11.30pm
Stylish and slick Pisces is Dubai's top table for seafood. The chef has a knack for eking out intensely bright flavours from his ingredients; dishes are elegantly light and melt on the palate. We're not too keen on his overdependence on foams and nages, but with talent this good, we can forgive a few idiosyncrasies. The understated dining room echoes the colours of the sea: wear blue-grey Armani and blend right in. (No sneakers.) Note: there's a cheaper, more accessible menu upstairs at the adjoining less-formal French brasserie. Think duck confit and mussels marinière.

ZHENG HE'S

Map pp76–7   Contemporary Chinese $$$

☎ 366 8888; Mina A'Salam, Madinat Jumeirah; mains Dh95; ⏲ noon-3pm & 7-11.30pm; ⓖ
An army of 20 clatters pans and fires woks behind the glass of the open kitchen at Zheng He's, the spectacular contemporary Chinese restaurant known for its fresh, light dim sum and stellar seafood specials (many diners go for the live tank, but others prefer the wasabi prawns with black pepper). The Sino-chic room is gorgeous, with a pagoda-style ceiling and good symmetry; alas, the hard surfaces mean high decibels, and the location at Madinat Jumeirah means high prices. The sea-view deck is great at lunch, but overlit at night with compact fluorescents; sit inside. Book well ahead.

MAGNOLIA Map pp76–7   Vegetarian $$$

☎ 366 6730; Al-Qasr, Madinat Jumeirah; mains Dh80; ⏲ noon-2.30pm & 7-11.30pm
Dubai's only high-end vegetarian restaurant, Magnolia overlooks the canals at the Madinat Jumeirah, and if you make reservations, you can arrive by *abra*. The so-called 'well-being' cooking takes itself a bit too seriously in its emulation of haute cuisine and lacks resonance on the palate, but the elegant presentations, romantic setting and top-end ingredients make up for the pretence and price – provided you're a vegetarian.

PIERCHIC Map pp76–7   Seafood $$$

☎ 366 6730; Al-Qasr, Madinat Jumeirah; mains Dh80; ⏲ noon-3pm & 7-11.30pm
Looking for a place to drop a ring into a glass of champagne? Make reservations for access to this stunning seafood house at the end of a long pier jutting out to sea. The best tables line the outdoor decks and provide drop-dead-gorgeous vistas of the Burj Al Arab and the Madinat Jumeirah. The food is solidly good, but the overambitious menu gets a little heavy-handed with its ingredient combinations; order simple and you'll do better. But with so much romance, you'll hardly notice what you're eating. Note: sitting inside defeats the purpose of coming here.

BELLA DONNA Map pp76–7   Italian $$

☎ 344 7710; Mercato Mall, Jumeirah Rd; mains Dh45; ⏲ 11am-11pm; ⓖ
Skip the overlit dining room in favour of the big outdoor terrace and glimpse the sea across Jumeirah Rd at this midrange Italian restaurant, good for tender-crusted thin pizzas and house-made pastas at great prices (for Dubai). The strong coffee will jack you up for shopping in the adjoining Mercato Mall.

SMILING BKK Map pp76–7   Thai $$

☎ 349 6677; Jumeirah 1; mains Dh30; ⏲ 11am-12:12am
Locals will kill us for including this indie hole-in-the-wall Thai gem, but it's too good not to share. The walls of the cheek-by-jowl space are covered with hipster mishmash (think Van Gogh paint-by-numbers, postcards, and a moustached Mona-Lisa), and scratchy rock-and-roll blares on the speakers (sit outside for quiet conversation). A Thai national cooks your dinner. The food is good, sometimes very good, but what's great is the adventure of finding an underground bo-ho hangout hidden in this vast cultural wasteland. (It's just west of Jumeirah post office, behind the petrol station, off 2a Street, which runs perpendicular to the alley where the restaurant sits.)

SIDRA Map pp76–7   Lebanese $

☎ 398 4723; Al-Dhiyafah St, Satwa; mains Dh22; ⏲ 24hr; ⓖ
The top pick for mezze on Al-Dhiyafah St – Dubai's best walking street – Sidra does a

SHAWARMA SHOOTOUT

Shawarma is the snack food of the Middle East and the *de rigueur* snack after a night of drinking. Dubai is blessed with an enormous number of shawarma joints, so to help you enjoy this ingenious snack we undertook a massive research project involving countless late-night tastings to present you our favourite shawarmas.

Al-Mallah (p113) Our favourite in Dubai. Both the chicken and lamb shawarmas are sublime here. The juicy chicken is loaded with pungent garlic sauce and jammed with pickles; lamb is tender with tons of fresh tomato, parsley, pickles and hummus.

Ashwaq Cafeteria (Map pp54–5; cnr Al-Soor & Sikkat al-Khail Sts, Deira; ⏲ noon-11pm) Everyone's favourite stop on a Gold Souq shopping excursion. The chicken is best, with a light spread of garlic sauce and fresh lettuce.

Beirut (Map pp62-3; ☎ 398 9822; Al-Dhiyafah St, Satwa; mains Dh20; ⏲ noon-2am) Beirut is one of the major shawarma joints on Al-Dhiyafah St and battles with Al-Mallah for the title of best lamb shawarma. Available in two sizes.

Lebanese Village (Map pp62-3; ☎ 352 2522; Al-Mankhool Rd; mains Dh22; ⏲ noon-3am) The lamb shawarmas are zesty with onion, parsley, pickles and tomato. The falafel is good too, but skip everything else.

Saj Express (p117) The excellent fresh bread makes these shawarmas special. Try the delicious chicken.

great *moutabbal* (eggplant dip), creamy-rich hummus, tangy tabouleh and fantastic fresh, hot bread. The kebabs are okay, but the dips are what's best. Inside is ugly; sit on the sidewalk and soak up the street scene. Ideal after a night out.

MARIA BONITA'S TACO SHOP
Map pp76–7   Mexican $
☎ 395 5576; Umm al-Sheif St, Umm Suqeim; mains Dh20; ⏲ 7.30am-8pm; ♿
Maria Bonita's is Dubai's only real Mexican restaurant, and the only one in town that's not Tex-Mex. The burritos could be fatter, but the flavours are spot-on – spicy, smoky and deep. Okay, so the squawking parrots and gimmicky, tableside guacamole service are a bit much without any alcohol on offer to soften the edges, but it's great coming here just the same.

LIME TREE CAFÉ Map pp76–7   Café $
☎ 349 8498; near Jumeirah Mosque, Jumeira Rd; mains Dh20; ⏲ 7.30am-8pm; ♿
You forget you're in traffic-snarled Dubai on the upstairs waterview balcony of this mellow café on the Jumeirah strip, the best spot to spot shopping-bag-toting 'Jumeirah Janes' (rich expats' wives). Best too is its use of clean ingredients, including some organics, and its healthful cooking (it's great at labelling dairy-free and low-fat options). Salads figure prominently, as do toasted paninis and wraps (the goat-cheese variety is fab) and brilliant smoothies (try the blueberry). Portions are generous, prices good. Best carrot cake in town.

RAVI Map pp76–7   Pakistani $
☎ 331 5353; Al-Satwa Rd, Satwa; mains Dh12; ⏲ 24hr; ♿
Five-star chefs reference this legendary Pakistani cafeteria as their favourite day-off eatery. It ain't fancy – au contraire: expect to share your table with burly men. The kebabs are good, as are the simple curries, biryani and (especially) fresh-baked bread, best washed down with yoghurt drink. Alas, the meat is tough (think mutton, not lamb); order chicken. No credit cards.

NEW DUBAI

The city's sprawling beach resorts, with their many top-end restaurants, happening bars and popular nightclubs, dominate New Dubai. If you're not staying at a resort, spend an evening at one. They're far from the chaos of inner Dubai, and you won't have to hail a taxi till it's time to go home. This section also includes several restaurants at Mall of the Emirates.

RHODES MEZZANINE
Map pp82–3   Modern British $$$
☎ 399 8888; Dubai Marina, Grosvenor House, Jumeirah; mains Dh150; ⏲ 7pm-midnight
British cuisine is no longer an oxymoron at Rhodes Mezzanine. Celebrity-chef Gary Rhodes breathes new life into traditional dishes like shepherd's pie, toad in the hole, oxtail, Yorkshire pudding – even roly poly. The emphasis is on freshness of ingredients and bold flavours. Unlike its competitor Verre (p107), there's nothing understated

about the room, which looks more like a High Street hair salon than a top-end restaurant, with bright-white mirror-polished floors, lipstick-red velvet accents, French-baroque chairs and transparent room dividers of coloured Lucite. Austin Powers could walk in the door at any moment – but with food this compelling, your attention squarely on your plate, you probably wouldn't notice.

EAUZONE Map pp82–3 — Fine Dining $$$

☎ 399 9999; One&Only Royal Mirage; mains Dh130; ☾ noon-3.30pm & 7.30pm-midnight

The premier dining room at a favourite resort sits atop a vast free-form swimming pool, with decks jutting out over illuminated blue water like little islands. (Sit outside. Period.) The menu is decidedly California-Asian, incorporating European technique and drawing heavily on the flavours of the Pacific Rim. This is smart cooking, some of the best in Dubai. The four-course tasting menu (Dh450) is the way to go. Dishes may include saffron-sautéed scallops with pineapple gazpacho; a perfect *torchon de foie gras;* or green-tea-and-salt-seasoned lamb with truffled mashed potatoes. Make reservations.

INDEGO Map pp82–3 — Contemporary Indian $$$

☎ 399 8888; Dubai Marina, Grosvenor House, Jumeirah; mains Dh120; ☾ 7.30pm-midnight Sun-Fri

Michelin-starred Vineet Bhatia is the consulting chef at this gracious Indian restaurant with a spacious and open dining room, lorded over by big brass Natraj sculptures. Though the recipes are traditional, the ingredients and style veer toward European. You might find a house-smoked tandoori salmon; pan-grilled sea bass with tomato and coconut; or samosas with chocolate and nuts. Note: unlike most Indian cooking, here plates are delicately composed and not designed for sharing.

BUDDHA BAR Map pp82–3 — Asian $$$

☎ 399 8888; Grosvenor House, Dubai Marina, Jumeirah; mains Dh120; ☾ 8pm-2am

At last a restaurant that knows the power of good lighting. So what if it's too dark and the bmm-bmm music requires you to shout over the table? You're in the shadow of a giant Buddha, rubbing shoulders with Dubai's beautiful crowd, and you look fabulous in that new outfit. Oh, the food? It

(nearly) measures up to the room – a mishmash of Thai and Japanese with a dash of Chinese – but really, who cares? Like I said, you look a-m-a-z-i-n-g. Uh, you didn't forget your platinum card, did you? And I hope you have a condom (or two) if you plan on sticking around past midnight when the beautiful people abound.

GRAND GRILL Map pp82–3 — Steak $$$

☎ 399 4221; Habtoor Grand Hotel; mains Dh120; ☾ noon-3pm & 7pm-midnight

Wine racks line the walls of this South African steakhouse, a favourite of carnivores in search of half-kilo slabs of perfectly grilled meat and *boerewors* sausage. Detractors point to disappointing appetisers and overly inventive mains that just don't work, but there's no denying the pleasure of biting into a juicy steak the size of a fat man's thigh.

BICE Map pp82–3 — Italian $$$

☎ 399 1111; Hilton Dubai Jumeirah; mains Dh120; ☾ noon-3pm & 7pm-midnight

Expats from Italy call BiCE the best Italian restaurant in town. We can't disagree. In the classic tradition, the cooking is clean. The chef uses just a few top-quality ingredients and lets them shine. The recipes are traditional – beef carpaccio, veal Milanese, house-made pasta, wild-mushroom risotto – but this is not your grandmother's Italian cooking. Dishes are presented with a contemporary style that matches the splashy, always-packed dining room. Book well ahead or eat at the bar. Save room for the exceptional cheese or tiramisu.

SPLENDIDO Map pp82–3 — Fine Dining $$$

☎ 399 4000; Ritz-Carlton Hotel; mains Dh120; ☾ 7-11pm, closed Sun

Tall palms sway in the breeze around the outdoor patio at the Ritz-Carlton's northern Italian restaurant, an ideal spot to hold hands by candlelight. It's not as formal as you'd expect – linens are cream, not white – and the cooking is more trattoria style, earthy and rich as in the morel-and-porcini-mushroom ravioli in a pan-reduced brown sauce. Pastas are perfectly al dente, and the tiramisu feather-light. Some of the flourishes are unnecessary, like the waiters' 3ft-long pepper grinder, but for an al fresco dinner in a tropical garden, it's hard to beat Splendido.

top picks

FOR SERVICE

Bad service is all too common in Dubai, but not at these stellar standouts:

- Fire & Ice (p110)
- Verre (p107)
- Exchange Grill (p115)
- Nezesaussi (p116)
- Pisces (p118)
- Hoi An (p115)

TANG Map pp82–3   Experimental $$$

☎ 399 3333; Le Meridien Mina Seyahi; mains Dh100; ⏲ 7-11pm Sun-Fri

Tang raises the level of culinary discourse in Dubai, but does it feed you dinner? The chef is more scientist than cook – he unabashedly calls his cooking style 'molecular' – fetishising food for its atomic structure, not for its sustenance. This amounts to a lot of complicated (and expensive) cryogenics: instead of a hunk of tomato with basil, you may get a paper-thin tulip made from tomato purée blasted with liquid nitrogen, then garnished with a crumbled, flash-frozen basil leaf. Portions are miniscule, and service is abysmally slow: after four excruciating hours, we wound up stopping for shawarma on the way home. Save this one for an expense-account dinner, and don't come hungry.

CERTO Map pp82–3   Italian $$$

☎ 366 9111; Radisson SAS Dubai Media City; mains Dh85; ⏲ noon-3.30pm & 7pm-midnight

Overlook the dining room which is reminiscent of an office-tower lobby, and just enjoy the house-made pastas, properly cooked al dente, and tender thin-crusted pizzas with inventive toppings. But the real standouts are the mains – go for the lamb *alla bracce*, four chops with wilted romaine, fava beans and pancetta. Some dishes fall flat – if a dish sounds too starchy, it is – but it's worth coming if only for the succulent prosciutto, a rare treat in pork-shy Dubai.

TAGINE Map pp82–3   Moroccan $$$

☎ 399 9999; One&Only Royal Mirage; mains Dh75; ⏲ 7-11pm

You feel like you're in Tangiers at Tagine. Cozy up between throw pillows at a low-slung table in the shadowy-dim dining room, and tap your toe to the live Moroccan band. Fez-capped waiters jump in and dance (sometimes neglecting your table) between runs to the kitchen for big platters of tagine and couscous. This is the real deal. Book ahead, and request a table near the band.

ALMAZ BY MOMO Map pp82–3   Moroccan $$$

☎ 409 8877; Harvey Nichols, Mall of the Emirates; mains Dh65; ⏲ noon-midnight

Though it lacks the celeb factor of Momo's London flagship, high-energy Almaz draws party-hearty Emiratis who guzzle nonalcoholic champagne by the bottleful. Hardly any Westerners come here for dinner for the very reason Emiratis do: there's no booze. Don't be deterred. The moody-dark dining room, with its dizzying *zelaeg*-tile floor, feels like a cool Kasbah Lounge. Tender-sweet pigeon pastilla has great depth of flavour. The succulent Almaz lamb tagine melts off the bone. And the honey-sweet Moroccan pastries go down easy with the nose-tickling cinnamon tea.

NINA Map pp82–3   Contemporary Indian $$

☎ 399 9999; Arabian Court, One&Only Royal Mirage; mains Dh60; ⏲ 7-11.30pm

Floor-to-ceiling purple fabric, lush red-orange light, and beaded curtains set a seductive backdrop for Nina's dynamic cooking. The chef combines Indian with a touch of Thai, and tempers it with European technique. The results are heady: rich spicing means flavours develop slowly on the palate with an elegant complexity that demands savouring. Choose the chef's selection of starters (Dh45) and curries (Dh85) for a sense of his broad repertoire. Though the ethnic beats thump too loudly, Nina remains a favourite spot for a date.

KARAM BEIRUT Map pp82–3   Lebanese $$

☎ 341 2202; Mall of the Emirates; mains Dh55; ⏲ noon-midnight

Outpost of the famous Beirut restaurant, Karam's extensive menu showcases everything you'll find in Lebanon, including its most ambitious dishes – even lamb's brain – all meticulously presented. There are six types of *kibbeh* (raw lamb), stellar mezze including a velvety hummus, and creative kebabs, one flavoured with pistachio and white cheese. The room's look is decidedly upmarket

EATING NEW DUBAI

(comb your hair), but a wall of windows overlooking Ski Dubai adds levity (call ahead for a window table; bring a sweater). Full bar. Note: service is erratic and the kitchen sends everything at once; order piecemeal.

ROYAL ORCHID Map pp82–3   Chinese/Thai $$
☎ 367 4040; Marina Walk, Dubai Marina; mains Dh40; 🕙 10am-midnight; 🚸

It's an institution in neighbouring Abu Dhabi, but Royal Orchid's Dubai branch is heavier on Thai than Chinese. Though the Peking duck is a standout, it's probably a good idea to stick to Thai here, including the fun build-your-own curry. The food, while tasty, won't win any awards, but the marina views are lovely on a balmy evening.

ENTERTAINMENT

top picks

ENTERTAINMENT

A night on the town is a big deal in Dubai, and despite the municipality's efforts to curtail excessive noise, every night of the week you'll find a place to whoop it up. The big nights are Thursday and Friday – Dubai's weekend nights – when expats burn off steam from their 12-hour-a-day work weeks. And boy, do they like to drink. Plan to head to hotels which, along with major sporting venues, are the only places licensed to serve alcohol. This concentration of bars in hotels by definition makes them touristy. In Dubai there's no such thing as an independent, out-of-the-way neighbourhood pub that nobody knows about.

Finding the right bar can be tricky. Dubai is a city of new money and playground of the parvenu, as much as it's a city of expat workers trying to advance their careers and save some tax-free cash. You're in Dubai either to dump your wallet or fill it. Choosing an appropriate bar depends on the people with whom you want to rub shoulders. Wanna get a sense of the social lives of resident workers? Follow the expats. Wanna feature that new Marc Jacobs outfit you just bought? Follow the glam crowd. And then there are the niche bars, places frequented by, say, Russian oligarchs or British footballers. Wherever you wander, don't expect to strike up many conversations; most people in Dubai stick to their cliques. Occasionally you'll spot a random *dishdasha*-clad local breaking ranks with his countrymen (and the law) by drinking alongside Westerners, but this is an anomaly. We've endeavoured in our reviews to paint a picture of who frequents which bars and clubs to help you choose, but we highly recommend you stray from your comfort zone and visit a few of each to get a representative sampling of what Dubai's nightlife is all about.

DJs spin nearly every night of the week (except during Ramadan), with regular one-off dance events. The repertoire is global – funk, soul, house (lots of house), trip-hop, hip-hop, R&B, African, Arabic and Latino. Though most hotels engage full-time ensembles, they're basically cover bands: there's a lack of innovative local musical talent.

Nights can be long, but they never end at dawn. Clubs and bars officially close by 3am, smaller venues at 1am. Start early with sunset cocktails, head to dinner, then follow up with post-dinner drinks before hitting a dance club. Afterward soak up the booze with a late-night shawarma. The fancy-pants bars are concentrated around Jumeirah and New Dubai. The seedy places are at cheap hotels in Bur Dubai and Deira; working girls are common – too common – but there are also some gritty-fun ethnic bars here worth a visit.

Alcohol is expensive (see boxed text, p126) but that doesn't stop rowdy Westerners from downing pint after shot after pint. Nurse your drinks or you'll shell out a lot of dirhams. The irony is, it can be hard – really hard – to catch the eye of a bartender. Long waits at the rail are common at crowded venues. Conversely, waiters are trained to upsell guests (though not usually trained in the fine art of service). If you hear, 'Would you like another round?' make clear exactly who at the table wants one or you may wind up with a full table of glasses – and a hefty bill. Likewise if you order a bottle of wine; waiters often empty a bottle into one person's glass, rather than divvy the last of it up between everyone's, then look at those whose glasses are empty and ask, 'Another bottle?' Don't be duped. When there's not much left in the bottle, keep it out of the waiter's hand.

If you're not up for drinking, plan to hit the mellow *sheesha* cafés and play a game of backgammon. This is where you'll spot locals. Emiratis don't like to be around alcohol, but they sure love coffee. You could also take in a movie, but we've got our reservations about cinemas in Dubai. For more on the subject, see p135.

It's best not to criss-cross the city on a weekend; traffic is abominable on Thursday and Friday nights, and taxis can be hard to come by. Stick to a particular area or two, such as New Dubai and Jumeirah, or Deira and Bur Dubai. And under no circumstance should you *ever* get behind the wheel of a car if you've had even one drink. The authorities will lock you up and throw away the key. Seriously.

BARS & CLUBS

Multicultural Dubai has a range of bars and pubs to match your mood, from gritty to glam. Though they're touristy, plan to visit a beach bar in New Dubai to see the sun set over the gulf – a quintessential Dubai experience; a fancy spot, whether it be a dance club or a

NIGHTS ON THE TOWN

It's wise – and cost-effective – to stick to one area of town for a night out. There's no better buzz-kill than Dubai's weekend traffic. Here are some favourite nights out, by neighbourhood.

Bur Dubai

Wafi City and the Grand Hyatt hotel are solid options for a night out because they're within walking distance of each other and provide a varied selection of bars and restaurants. At Wafi, you could start with wine and cheese at Vintage (p127) or soak up the views over fancy cocktails atop Raffles hotel at New Asia Bar (p127). For dinner consider the Indian party scene at Asha's (p112) or the Asian cooking at Thai Chi (p112). For a serious splurge, book a table at Fire & Ice (p110). You could pep it up with post-dinner drinks at Ginseng (p126). Or head to the Grand Hyatt for something mellower. There's a good selection of wines at the Grand's mellow Vinoteca. For a sexy Indian tandoori dinner, head to Iz (p110) or book a table (late) at Lebanese Awtar (p111), which can turn into its own big night out. To dance to Arab pop and live DJs, hit the dance floor at MIX (p132), but the hands-down best club is a short taxi ride from either Wafi or the Grand: Chi@The Lodge (p131).

Deira

Begin with a quiet pre-dinner drink at Issimo (p126), before having the ultimate top-end dinner at Gordon Ramsay's Verre (p107). Alternatively book a window table for Persian at Shabestan (p107) and tap your toe to the fantastic all-Iranian band. If you're feeling mellow after dinner, stroll along the waterfront and watch dockworkers loading the *dhows*. To coo with your date over a snifter of brandy, head to intimate, sometimes lively Ku-Bu (p126), or sink into a sofa and time-travel back to the 1970s at the often-empty Velvet Lounge (p126).

Sheikh Zayed Road

Start the evening with a glass of wine at the Emirates Towers location of Agency (p127) – it's beside the escalators of the Boulevard shopping centre – or a fancy cocktail high in the sky at Vu's (p128). Have a casual supper at Noodle House (p117) or a Lebanese feast at stately Al-Nafoorah (p116). If it's a weekend and you're in the mood for live music, pop over to the Novotel for jazz and Belgian beer at Blue Bar (p133). If you're featuring a new ensemble and want to show it off, sip French champagne at glittering Cin-Cin (p128). For something in between, consider cocktails with the mixed crowd at thump-thump Lotus One (p128).

Jumeirah & New Dubai

Chill out with sunset drinks on the veranda at Bahri Bar (p128) or swill margaritas at Maya (p130). For maximum splash, book pre-sunset drinks at the Skyview Bar (p129) atop the Burj Al Arab (reservations essential). Sup at one of the Royal Mirage's stellar restaurants – Tagine (p121), Eauzone (p120) or Nina (p121) – then swill post-dinner drinks at the Rooftop Bar (p130) or recline on cushions at the atmospheric Sheesha Courtyard (p134). If you're up for a trip around the dance floor, head to the Moroccan club Kasbar (p132). If drinking and dancing are your top priorities, skip a sit-down meal and start at Madinat Jumeirah's Agency (p128) for vino and tapas, followed by drinks at the lounge-y Left Bank (p129), and live music and more snacks at the bar of Jam Base (p133). If you prefer to stay in Jumeirah, start out at Sho Cho (p129), then throw back tequila and salsa-dance at Malecon (p129). Once the clock strikes 1am, turn it out on the dance floor at swanky Boudoir (p131).

lounge, to giggle at arrivistes in impossibly high heels; and an expat bar to catch a buzz with overworked Westerners laughing too loudly. If you like to make your own discoveries, put down your guidebook and wander the ethnic backstreets of Deira, find a bar in a no-star hotel, maybe an Iranian or Filipino club, and soak up the colour (for a headstart, check the low-end listings in the Sleeping chapter, p151). Don't overlook your own hotel bar, even if – especially if – you're staying in a dive; you may be surprised by a goofy house band and wacky floorshow.

Bars are open until 1am or 3am; alcohol service is illegal between 4pm and 6pm Fridays and Saturdays. Drink prices are ridiculous (see the boxed text, p126). You could pay anything from Dh20 to Dh40 for a pint of beer or Dh25 to Dh100+ for a glass of wine, depending on quality and vintage. Hotels usually add a 10% service charge. Tip a few dirhams per round. Take heart: nearly all bars in Dubai offer drink specials at nonpeak times, happy hours, and ladies' nights when women drink free. (Dubai's population is 75% male; bars are desperate to pad the room with gals.) For current specials, check Mumtazz (www.mumtazz .com). Some bars accept reservations for tables; call ahead.

WHY ALCOHOL COSTS SO MUCH: THE TAX FORMULA

Alcohol costs a small fortune in Dubai because it's forbidden by Islam. Understanding the importance of booze to tourism, the municipality allows it, but slaps on a hefty *haram* tax — in short, a sin tax. Here's the formula.

A bottle of California plonk that costs US$10 wholesale automatically incurs a 50% import tax, upping the importer's price to $15. Add a 33% profit for the importer, and now it costs $20. The Dubai-based purchaser (ie, the hotel that sells it to the consumer) pays a 30% tax. Now it costs US$26 — at wholesale. The hotel then marks up the price 200% to make its profit and pay its employees. Now it costs about $75. At the moment of sale, the public pays an additional 20%, jacking up the final retail price to a whopping $90.

Prices aren't going to come down anytime soon: a duopoly controls all the alcohol sales in Dubai. If drinking is important to you, buy your alcohol at duty-free before leaving the airport. Otherwise, you may get the jitters when you see your bar bill.

DEIRA

ISSIMO Map pp54–5

☎ 227 1111; Hilton Dubai Creek, Baniyas Rd;
🕙 7am-1am

Illuminated blue flooring, black-leather sofas and sleek chrome finishing lend a James Bond look to this sports-and-martini bar, popular with middle-aged men. If you're not into sports – or TV – you may find the giant-screen TVs distracting. Good for drinks before dining at Verre by Gordon Ramsay (p107).

JULES BAR Map pp56–7

☎ 282 4040; Le Meridien Dubai, Al-Garhoud; weekend cover including two drinks Dh80;
🕙 11am-3am

The six-piece Filipino house band kicks, twirls and belts out top-40 hits, while an odd mix of oil workers, southeast Asians and European flight crews (especially on Fridays) grind shoulder-to-shoulder on the floor. If you're over 40, you'll hate it – unless you're as hammered as everyone else – but you just have to dig those charcoal portraits of Whitney and Mariah. The outdoor terrace is way mellower and charges no cover.

KU-BU Map pp54–5

☎ 222 7171; Radisson SAS Dubai, Baniyas Rd;
🕙 6pm-3am

A DJ spins funky tunes at this small, dark, sultry bar that has African-inspired interiors and secluded nooks that are made even more private with plush draperies. If you're alone, you may get hit on. Still, it's a good choice for drinks before or after dinner at the Radisson SAS's terrific restaurants.

TERRACE Map pp64–5

☎ 602 1234; Park Hyatt Dubai; 🕙 noon-1am

Specialising in French oysters, caviar, champagne and vodka, the Terrace is one of Dubai's smartest waterside lounge bars. Resident British DJ Lady Red sets just the right mood with sensual chill-out beats. The dramatically lit interior is stylin', but it doesn't compare with sitting on the outdoor deck and watching the bobbing boats moored in the marina.

VELVET LOUNGE Map pp54–5

☎ 227 8206; Al-Khaleej Palace Hotel; 🕙 7pm-1am

Miles from the glam-slam New Dubai scene, in an unfashionable hotel, the accidentally fabulous Velvet Lounge is stuck in a baroque 1970s time warp with smoked-mirror ceilings, velour sofas and red-velvet draperies. And it's often empty, making it a top spot for a *tête-à-tête* with your paramour.

BUR DUBAI

GINSENG Map pp64–5

☎ 324 8200; Wafi City Mall, Al-Qataiyat Rd;
🕙 7pm-2am Tue-Fri, 7pm-1am Sat-Mon

A good spot to start the evening, Ginseng makes brilliant cocktails with everything from champagne to espresso. The faux-Asian décor needs a fluff job and too many hard surfaces mean high decibel levels when it fills up. Come early – and bring a wrap to deal with the too-cold air-con.

KEVA Map pp64–5

☎ 334 4159; Al-Nasr Leisureland, Oud Metha;
🕙 noon-3am

Keva's Eurasia-meets-join-by-numbers decor goes a bit overboard with fake grass

TOP YE OLDE PUBS

Dubai's old English-style pubs were the lifeblood of expats before the city boomed – informal social clubs where you could meet others with a love of bad food and warm beer. These days most foreign residents stick to their cliques. But not at the pubs. When you want to strike up a conversation and down a few ales with new friends, pop into a pub.

Fibber Magee's (Map pp72–3; ☎ 332 2400; Sheikh Zayed Rd, behind the Crowne Plaza Hotel; ❍ noon-2am) Dubai's most authentic Irish pub is a scruffy boozer with great ales and stouts. Tuesday is quiz night (arrive by 8pm). Great fun on match nights.

Carter's (Map pp64–5; ☎ 324 0000; Wafi City Mall, Al-Qataiyat Rd; ❍ noon-2am) For better or worse, Carter's is a Dubai institution. Love that kitsch Egyptian décor. Happy hour from 6pm to 8pm Saturday to Thursday.

Dubliners (Map pp56–7; ☎ 282 4040; behind Le Meridien Dubai, Airport Rd, Al-Garhoud; ❍ noon-2am) A friendly, boozy Irish bar with reliable pub grub and Guinness. Packed on match nights; happy hour 5pm to 8pm. Try the pies.

Irish Village (Map pp56–7; ☎ 282 4750; Aviation Club, Dubai Tennis Stadium, Al-Garhoud Rd, Deira; ❍ 11am-1.30am) An Irish pub popular with expats for its pond-side 'beer garden'. No happy hour, but there's Guinness and Kilkenny draft.

Long's Bar (Map pp72–3; ☎ 312 2202; Tower Rotana Hotel, Sheikh Zayed Rd; ❍ noon-3am) The longest bar in town, live bands, cheap drinks and a late closure keeps this American-style bar-and-grill hoppin'. Number-one bar choice during Ramadan. Happy hour, noon to 8pm, till midnight Friday.

walls in the ladies' toilets, but the low-slung seating, moody lighting, live DJ and big menu of surprisingly great bar nibbles make it ideal before twirling on the dance floor of the adjoining Lodge (p131).

MAHARLIKA Map pp64–5

☎ 334 6565; President Hotel, Sheikh Khalifa bin Zayed Rd, Karama; ❍ 6pm-3am

The black-box cabaret feels like a speakeasy at this all-Filipino club, revealing a glimpse of the culture of service-industry expats who cook your hotel breakfast. The vibrant floorshow is awesome – think nine-piece high-energy bands with wacky names like Elvis Presley Asia.

NEW ASIA BAR & CLUB Map pp64–5

☎ 324 8888; Raffles Dubai, Wafi City Mall, Al-Qataiyt Rd; ❍ 7pm-3am

High atop the pyramid of the ultra-plush Raffles hotel, dynamic New Asia draws a slick crowd for its fancy Asian-inspired cocktails and drop-dead views. We like the outdoor terrace, but the black-marble-and-leather interiors make a better backdrop for that hot little Betsy Johnson dress you just bought. Stay late to shimmy to high-energy house.

TROYKA Map pp62–3

☎ 359 5908; Ascot Hotel, Khalid bin al-Waleed Rd (Bank St); drink minimum Dh100; ❍ 7pm-3am, floor show 11.30pm-1.30am

If you're into Bob Fosse musical numbers (think *Chicago* and *Sweet Charity*), make a beeline to Troyka for an extraordinarily camp floor show by sequin-spangled Russian dancers who twirl, dip, and kick higher than a young Shirley Maclaine. In between, a three-piece house band plays mournful Russian ballads. Stunning. Scope the crowd for oligarchs ignoring the show. Come for dinner (p112) and make a night of it.

VINTAGE Map pp64–5

☎ 324 0000; Wafi City Mall, Al-Qataiyt Rd; ❍ 6pm-1.30am

A favourite of Dubai wine aficionados for its impressive wine list and wide range of varietals, Vintage also serves superb fondue, cheeses, charcuterie meats and fantastic cheesecake. The living-room-like interior is well lit – a boon if your eyesight is failing – but its small size means tables fill up fast. Arrive early.

SHEIKH ZAYED ROAD

AGENCY Map pp72–3

☎ 330 0000; Boulevard at Emirates Towers, Sheikh Zayed Rd; ❍ noon-3am, Sun-Thu, 3pm-3am Fri & Sat

A cosmopolitan wine bar frequented by older businessmen, Agency is a civilized spot for a glass of French wine. (Skip the New World wines; they're strictly grocery-store labels.) Alas, it's in an office tower and

top picks

VIEW BARS

- Bar 44 (p130)
- Koubba (opposite)
- Skyview Bar (opposite)
- Vu's (right)
- New Asia Bar (p127)

feels like it. Focus your attention on the interesting varietals; go for a flight of four half pours (Dh110). Good cheese fondue and finger foods like fried calamari.

CIN-CIN WINE BAR Map pp72–3

☎ 332 5555; Fairmont Hotel, Sheikh Zayed Rd;
🕙 6pm-2am

You'd be hard-pressed to find a more impressive wine-and-spirits list than the one at this sleek bar, styled out with blue light, deep leather club chairs, and illuminating changing-colour ice buckets. The list is dizzying, with over 400 wines – 48 by the glass – 50 vodkas and 26 Scotches. Prices skew high, but you'll find good French vintages in the Dh300 range. Shine your shoes.

HARRY GHATTO'S Map pp72–3

☎ 319 8088; Boulevard at Emirates Towers;
🕙 8pm-3am

Grab a posse of friends and belt out your favourites at this shoebox-sized karaoke bar. Drinks are expensive and service gruff, but we love the odd mix of people drawn here, including the occasional *dishdasha*-clad local.

IKANDY Map pp72–3

☎ 343 8888; Shangri-La hotel, Sheikh Zayed Rd;
🕙 6pm-2am

Wear white to Ikandy and your clothes will glow in the diffuse hot-pink light reflecting off the diaphanous fabric hanging from the palm trees. Think Ibiza pool party, only it's set on the 4th-floor pool deck of the Shangri-La hotel instead of the Balearics. Stellar views of the Burj Dubai. Note: open October to March only.

LOTUS ONE Map pp72–3

☎ 329 3200; World Trade Convention Centre, off Sheik Zayed Rd; 🕙 noon-2am

Sitting on Lucite stools over glass flooring or in the '60s-throwback swinging chairs may throw off your equilibrium by your third round, but fret not. You wouldn't be the first to stumble out of this Asian-inspired scenester bar with a cosmo spilled down your pant leg. Wear black, not white.

NEZESAUSSI Map pp72–3

☎ 428 5888; Al-Manzil Hotel, Burj Dubai Blvd;
🕙 Sun-Thu 6pm-2am, Fri & Sat noon-2am

Throw back pints with your mates at this high-end sports bar, just a stone's throw from the world's tallest tower. Great food (see p116). The huge round bar lets you watch both the match and the mainly Aussie, Kiwi and South African crowd.

VU'S BAR Map pp72–3

☎ 330 0000; Emirates Towers Hotel, Sheikh Zayed Rd; 🕙 6pm-2am

The tower-top views over Sheikh Zayed Rd are as breathtaking as the prices at this sophisticated restaurant-bar, 51 storeys in the sky. If conversation lags, bury your nose in the encyclopaedic cocktail list. Look sharp: no jeans or sneakers allowed.

JUMEIRAH

AGENCY Map pp76–7

☎ 366 6320; Souq Madinat Jumeirah, Al-Sufouh Rd; 🕙 noon-1am

The Agency wine bar at Souq Madinat Jumeirah gets packed with khaki-clad tourists and expats. As at its sister branch at Emirates Towers (p127), the wine list includes unusual varietals (skip the New World wines in favour of better French labels), but here there's a terrace overlooking the canals of the Madinat where you can glimpse the Burj Al Arab. Good luck snagging a table at peak times.

BAHRI BAR Map pp76–7

☎ 366 8888; Mina A' Salam, Madinat Jumeirah, Jumeirah; 🕙 noon-2am

One of our first-choice spots in winter, Bahri has a fabulous 2nd-floor veranda laid with Persian carpets and big cane sofas where you can drink in gorgeous views of the Burj Al Arab. It's the kind of place you take your visiting parents for after-dinner drinks. Inside is less impressive and way too crowded on weekends, but the cocktails are strong – if overpriced. For a touristy treat, order the camel-milk mocktail.

DUBAI'S NEW SMOKING LAWS

In November 2007, a smoking ban was issued by the Dubai municipality. But because of vague language, it's not clear the extent to which it will be enforced. Hotel managers are scratching their heads, trying to figure out how to implement the loophole-riddled legislation. Can you imagine smokers' corners outside 'lifestyle hotels'? How untidy. Here's what we've been able figure out for sure. Smoking is no longer allowed in hotel public areas, but it is permitted indoors at hotel bars and nightclubs provided the establishment builds a depressurised room to keep smoke from wafting into the nonsmoking areas. Lighting up on outdoor terraces remains legal. When in doubt, look for ashtrays or ask the bartender if there's a designated smoking area.

BARZAR Map pp76–7

☎ 366 6348; Souq Madinat Jumeirah, Al-Sufouh Rd; ☾ noon-1am

Barzar is a bit of a pickup joint, but it's good for pre-club cocktails. Sit outside (never inside: the cheesy cover band plays too loudly) in the relative comfort of beanbag chairs and sip killer cosmos while overlooking the water.

KOUBBA Map pp76–7

☎ 366 8888; Al-Qasr, Souq Madinat Jumeirah, Al-Sufouh Rd; ☾ noon-2am

Score a candlelit table on the outdoor terrace overlooking the Madinat and Burj, and you'll instantly know you've found one of the most tranquil and romantic spots in all Dubai. The interior is nearly as compelling, with plush red velvet and Oriental cushions for you to lie against as you chill out to live Arabian-lounge music. Too bad it's illegal to lock lips in public.

LEFT BANK Map pp76–7

☎ 368 6171; Souq Madinat Jumeirah, Al-Sufouh Rd; ☾ noon-2am

We love the waterside tables, with *abras* floating past, but the real party is inside the dark bar, where moody lighting, giant mirrors, leather club chairs and chill beats create a dynamic lounge scene. Put your name on the list for a table; expect to wait. Good food, too, especially steaks.

MAI TAI LOUNGE Map pp76–7

☎ 366 5646; Souq Madinat Jumeirah, Al-Sufouh Rd; ☾ 6pm-1.30am

The tiki bar at Trader Vic's mixes lethal cocktails served in pineapples with paper umbrellas – the ultimate in kitsch. It's great fun once you've downed your second round and the salsa band gets going, usually at 9.30pm. Unlike its sister branch at the Crowne Plaza on Sheikh Zayed Rd, here there's room to dance.

MALECON Map pp76–7

☎ 304 8281; Dubai Marine Beach Resort & Spa, Jumeirah Rd; ☾ 6.30pm-3am

Tequila is the essential drink at Malecon, an important stopover for the party crowd. Tipping its hat to Havana's graffiti-walled Bodeguita del Medio, this Latino-inspired bar is the place to hit late – do shots and twirl with a Cuban heel. Look sharp; though unpretentious, the crowd appreciates nice gear. Inquire about the ever-fun salsa classes.

SHO CHO Map pp76–7

☎ 346 1111; Dubai Marine Beach Resort & Spa, Jumeirah Rd; ☾ 7pm-3am

The cool minimalist interior, with its blue lights and wall-mounted fish tanks, may draw you in, but the beachside deck is where it's at. Join the white-pants-wearing Lebanese party people for sunset martinis. The sushi is merely average, but the cocktails are awesome. Great on Mondays and Wednesday, when you can reserve an outdoor table. Sundays and Tuesdays it's packed.

SKYVIEW BAR Map pp76–7

☎ 301 7438; Burj Al Arab, Jumeirah Rd, Umm Suqeim; ☾ 11am-2am

Cocktails or afternoon tea on the 27th floor of the Burj Al Arab tops most tourists' must-do lists, and with good reason: the views are breathtaking, plus you gain access to the world's most garish hotel lobby (for more, see p159). Arrive before sunset or don't bother. But you *must* book ahead. The per-person minimum is Dh250. As for the Liberace-meets-*Star Trek* interiors, all we can say is, welcome to the Burj.

360° Map pp76–7

☎ 352 3500; Jumeirah Beach Hotel, Jumeirah Rd, Umm Suqeim; ☾ 5pm-2am

Wander out the long pier to this rooftop with a circular outdoor bar offering sublime views of the Burj Al Arab. A shiny-shiny crowd of scenesters packs the place on Fridays; expect to deal with bouncers at the rope. Alas, the outdoor music ban imposed in 2007 means no more live DJs or dancing. But ask around. We've a feeling they'll come up with a solution, possibly by hosting DJs inside the downstairs restaurant. Expect s-l-o-w bar service – don't come thirsty. But oh, what a view.

NEW DUBAI

APRÈS Map pp82–3

☎ 341 2575; Mall of the Emirates, Sheikh Zayed Rd; ☾ noon-2am

After four hours shopping at the Mall of the Emirates, a triple-berry cocktail becomes a very novel idea. The crowd at Après feels very expatty – loud and raucous – the polar opposite of what you see out the windows: Emiratis stumbling in the snow at Ski Dubai. Great chocolate-Cointreau fondue.

BAR 44 Map pp82–3

☎ 399 8888; Grosvenor West Marina Beach by Le Meridien, Jumeirah; ☾ 6pm-2am

The champagne lounge on the 44th floor of the Grosvenor House has extraordinary views of New Dubai's skyscrapers and the burgeoning marina. Done in a retro-1970s chic, with high-backed tufted-velvet banquettes and buttery-soft leather tub chairs, this is the spot to kick up your (high) heels with local swankers and raise a glass to excess. Good backup if Buddha Bar is full.

BARASTI BAR Map pp82–3

☎ 399 3333; Le Meridien Mina Seyahi Beach Resort & Marina, Al-Sufouh Rd; ☾ 6pm-2am

Seaside Barasti is the locals' top spot for laid-back sundowners on a hot afternoon. No need to dress up – you can head straight here after a day at the beach, provided you look sexy in a sarong: the crowd is very body-conscious. DJs play indoors, but it's generally better to sit outside within ear shot of the sea.

BUDDHA BAR Map pp82–3

☎ 399 8888; Grosvenor West Marina Beach by Le Meridien, Jumeirah; ☾ 7pm-3am

If there are celebs in town, they'll show up at Buddha Bar, where the dramatic Asian-inspired interiors are decked out with gorgeous chandeliers, a wall of reflective sheer glass, and an enormous Buddha lording

over the heathens. The bartenders put on quite a show with their impressive shakes (think Tom Cruise in *Cocktail*). Because the deep-red lighting is so central to the atmosphere, the bar opens only after dark. Arrive early or wait in line; otherwise book dinner for guaranteed admission. For more, see p120.

LIBRARY BAR Map pp82–3

☎ 399 4000; Ritz-Carlton Hotel lobby; ☾ 3pm-1am

When you're craving a Glenfiddich and a Cuban cigar, steer your luxury sedan to the Ritz-Carlton. A pianist and singer play easy-on-the-ear jazz standards to set the mood. If you're under 50 and still have your vision, you'll be in the minority.

MAYA Map pp82–3

☎ 316 5550; Le Royal Meridien, Al-Sufouh Rd; ☾ 6pm-2am Mon-Sat

Arrive an hour before sunset to snag one of the Gulf-view tables on the rooftop bar of this upmarket Mexican at the Royal Meridien, and swill top-shelf margaritas as the sun slips into the sea. Order a plate of the succulent duck enchiladas to soak up the booze.

ROOFTOP BAR Map pp82–3

☎ 399 9999; Arabian Court, One&Only Royal Mirage, Al-Sufouh Rd; ☾ 5.30pm-1am

The fabric-draped nooks, cushioned banquettes, Moroccan lanterns and Oriental carpets make this candle-lit outdoor rooftop bar one of Dubai's most sublime spots. Come at sunset to watch the sky change colours – but not earlier; the bar doesn't pick up till evening. The new Palm Jumeirah diminishes the views, but the moody lighting and romantic vibe make it easy to overlook any unsightliness. An ideal spot to present a gift-wrapped jewellery box.

DANCE CLUBS

Clubbers come out in force when big-name DJs like Pierre Ravan, Roger Sanchez and Joey Negro jet in for the weekend, but even on a regular old Tuesday, you can find ardent club kids twirling beneath disco balls to house music, the preferred sound in Dubai. Wednesday through Friday are the big nights out, when marauding expats join gyrating tourists on the dance floor. The scene remains segregated. Not only are Dubai's clubs rife with

OUTDOOR DANCING? FORGET IT

In late 2007, the Dubai municipality banned outdoor dancing and amplified music, effectively curbing the fun at some of the city's major DJ-dance venues. The leading bars once beloved for their outdoor scenes – Barasti Bar, 360° – could no longer blare music outside or allow patrons to dance beneath the stars. Hotel owners were left scrambling to reconfigure their spaces; some simply ripped out their dance floors. It's hard to know for sure how this is going to play out over time, but one thing's certain: if you dance outdoors at a bar, even to your own inner beat, you'll be thrown out. Ask locals for an update or Google 'Dubai outdoor music ban'.

racism (p31), but cliques of club-goers keep to themselves. Don't go out expecting to meet new friends at a Dubai dance club.

The scene starts late – around 1am – just two hours before clubs are required to close, and queues are sometimes preposterous. It's best to arrive early to snag seats and load up on drinks before the line forms, then hit the dance floor when others arrive.

Dubai's dance floors reveal engrossing sociological studies and vignettes. The city's population is made up of well over 100 different nationalities, and everyone grooves differently. The Lebanese are the reigning kings of the club world. Western expatriates look down on them, tackily whispering things like, 'That guy is such a Lebanese poser.' But damn, do they dress sharp and dance hard. Others don't move at all, endlessly looking for something to look for, frozen at the edge of the parquet floor, cell phones in hand, desperately texting potential partners. Most people meander on and off the floor, some featuring their outfits, others their moves.

Cover charges range from Dh50 to Dh300, depending on whether there's a big-name DJ spinning; call ahead. Groups of men aren't always allowed admission on busy nights; bring a girl. Some club nights, like the roving Peppermint Club, remain perennially popular, others disappear after only a month. As of this writing, the ever-fun iBo had closed, but promised to reopen. Check out www.mumtazz.com, www.timeoutdubai.com and promoters' sites such as www.9714.com and www.fluidproduction.com, for up-to-date details on what's happening in the club world. And not to be alarmist, but many clubs have terrible emergency-exit signage. Spot the ways out on your way in.

APARTMENT Map pp76–7

☎ 406 8000; Jumeirah Beach Hotel, Jumeirah Rd, Umm Suqeim; ⏰ 7pm-1.30am
You're going to hear about this place anyway, so here's the lowdown. The tight windowless space feels like an underground bunker, but that doesn't stop throngs of self-conscious twenty-somethings from flocking here, hormones raging, every weekend. Come with people you like or risk isolation. The saving grace is the better-than-average DJs, but the tiled dance floor is too small (and sometimes slick) to cut loose, and the so-called VIP area blocks movement around the club, resulting in a lot of drinking, instead of dancing, to the music. Free before midnight.

BOUDOIR Map pp76–7

☎ 345 5995; Dubai Marine Beach Resort & Spa, Jumeirah Rd; ⏰ 7.30pm-4am
Though snooty expats distance themselves from the tight-pants-and-straightened-hair Lebanese crowd at Boudoir, we love the look of the place. Tufted red-velvet booths, beaded curtains and tasselled draperies lend a super-model vibe – indeed, you may spot one among the wannabes – and the circular layout is perfect for twirling away from the occasional unwanted advance by a Lothario. High on the chic-o-meter. Look sharp or be ostracised.

CHI@THE LODGE Map pp64–5

☎ 337 9470; Al-Nasr Leisureland, Oud Metha; cover charge varies; ⏰ 8pm-3am
The shiny-shiny fave of young expats, Chi sometimes hosts live music, but the big draws are its kick-ass DJs playing funk, house and hip-hop; ever-popular theme nights (think retro-80s, skool disco, Halloween); velvet-plush surroundings; and big semi-outdoor dance floor and garden. Two sound systems and four big rooms mean that once you've worn out your legs, you can chill in a cushioned lounge or VIP cabana (provided you've made reservations and purchased a Dh500-or-so bottle of booze). Two white-suit-clad Indian little people greet your arrival; they're sometimes placed on the DJ booth and made to dance – offensive, yes, but you can't help but stare. The big fun makes up for the organisers' little transgressions. Arrive early to beat the queue.

GETTING OUT WITH THE IN CROWD

For entertainment listings, buy the weekly *Time Out* and glance through *7 Days*. Look for free guides and leaflets promoting clubs, dance parties and gigs; find them at bars, cafés, Virgin Megastore and Ohm Records.

There's okay stuff on the web, but Dubai sites aren't the fastest to load – or the most complete. The best (by far) is www.timeoutdubai.com. Also check www.7days.ae, and try the club guides on www.mumtazz.com (click on the UAE flag for Dubai) and www.fluidproduction.com, which is the main site for the roving Peppermint Club (below). For tickets to concerts and major events at Dubai Media City, the Tennis Stadium and Madinat Jumeirah, phone the Time Out ticketline on ☎ 800-4669 (☎ +971-4-210-8567 from overseas). Or buy online at either www.timeouttickets.com or www.boxofficeme.com.

KASBAR Map pp82–3

☎ 399 9999; One&Only Royal Mirage, Al-Sufouh Rd; cover charge Dh50; 9.30pm-3am Mon-Sat

Kasbar can be inconsistent – one night it's packed, the next it's dead – but we highly recommend you check out this sexy three-storey Moroccan-themed club, with glittering crystal chandeliers, a coffered ceiling, and big black-and-white-tiled dance floor. Call ahead to reserve a table on the mezzanine and take in the scene from above. Or forego the thump-thump scene in favour of a game of billiards on the quiet lower floor – a godsend for nondancing men whose dates want to twirl. When there's Arabian-fusion playing on the decks, don't miss it. Cover includes one drink.

MIX Map pp82–3

☎ 317 2570; Grand Hyatt; 9pm-3am, closed Sat

Big with the Middle Eastern crowd, Mix was Dubai's first super-club and it's still going strong. Every night is different, but you can generally expect hip-hop, R&B, house and Arabic pop, made better when a top international DJ spins. Things to like are the raised bar, huge dance floor, podium dancers, bongo players and stellar people-watching. Cover charge for DJ events. Ask about all-you-can-drink nights.

PEPPERMINT CLUB Map pp82–3

☎ 332 0037, 050-343 3909; Habtoor Grand Hotel; cover charge Dh120; 10pm-3am Fri

If you're a serious dancer, seek out the location of Dubai's ultimate Friday-night party. Promoter Fluid Production imports some of the biggest international DJs (Paul Van Dyk, Steve Lawler, James Lavelle etc) to wear out the insatiable, sweaty throngs. A mixed crowd of over 2000 clubbers packs the democratised dance floor. If you don't dance, don't come. Inquire about occasionally weekend-long events that begin on

Thursday. Admission charge for men, but women often get in free. Look hot, but dress light: the floor gets overheated. The above location was accurate as of this writing, but is likely to change.

ZINC Map pp72–3

☎ 331 1111; Crowne Plaza Hotel, Sheikh Zayed Rd; 7pm-3am

Once you've got past the metal detector, old reliable Zinc plays crowd-pleasing popular tunes everyone knows. Though some uppity expats call it trashy, Zinc is good because people don't seem to care who you are; they're here to dance and drink, not show off. Wednesday's Kinky Malinki night draws house-spinning London DJs. Saturday before midnight is salsa night; lessons start at 8pm. The concrete floors are hard to dance on with rubber soles; wear leather (but no open-toes are allowed). Bar service is quick – well, for Dubai. Men pay cover, women don't. Flight crews get discounted drinks and flock here Thursday and Friday.

LIVE MUSIC

Though on the upswing, Dubai's live-music scene is still in its nascent years. Only a handful of indie bands are doing anything innovative; generally you'll hear cover bands. Don't get us wrong, there's some cool music to be heard and some pretty good musicians, but Dubai is a boom town, not a cultural capital. Still, you'll occasionally find great music in unexpected places, particularly hotel restaurants which nearly all employ full-time house bands that play six nights a week. Arena concerts are a different story, when international acts like Moby or Black Eyed Peas swing through town on their world tours, but they're one-off performances not specific to Dubai. Instead keep an eye out for major-name Middle Eastern and

Subcontinental stars. When you see big posters and hear multiple radio ads for acts you're unfamiliar with, do a quick Google search to find out where they're from. There's a reason they're so popular. You'd be amazed by some of the acts that draw big crowds of expat locals – Lebanese, Indian, Pakistani, Persian. This is the stuff you can't hear at home. Check *Time Out* and *7 Days* magazines, as well as the ticket hotlines (opposite). If you're adventurous, ditch your guidebook, comb the streets of Deira, and pop into no-name hotels to check out the ethnic acts in the house bars. (Tip: for a head start, poke around the budget and midrange listings in the Deira section of the Sleeping chapter, p151.) From mullet-headed Russian boy bands to jangly Persian belly dancers, you never know what you might turn up.

BLUE BAR Map pp72–3
☎ 310 8124; Novotel World Trade Centre; ☽ noon-1am

The best thing about Blue Bar is its stand-out selection of beers on tap. It hosts live jazz and blues 10pm to 1am Wednesday through Friday, and though the bands are hit or miss, the scene is mellow. It's a minimalist bar and lounge with floor-to-ceiling wood-panelled walls and scattered cocktail tables – a good place for the 40+ crowd. When there's no band, 'smooth jazz' (read: fake jazz) blares on the sound system.

JAM BASE Map pp76–7
☎ 366 6730; Souq Madinat Jumeirah, Al-Sufouh Rd; ☽ 7pm-2am Mon-Sat, to 3am Thu & Fri

Early in the evening, Jam Base is a moody supper club, with low lighting, hearty Creole-inspired cooking and jazzy music beginning at 7.30pm. At 10pm it becomes a dance club. Tables are cleared away and the over-30 crowd shimmies to live soul, R&B and Motown hits. This is when it's most fun, though you may have to endure getting your foot stepped on by a drunk or her beefy banker boyfriend. Biggish-name bands sometimes play here, too.

MARRAKECH Map pp72–3
☎ 343 8888; Shangri-La hotel, Sheikh Zayed Rd; ☽ 1-3pm & 7.30pm-1am

When you want to go out, but prefer hushed tones to amplified music, this is just the spot. Though it's first a restaurant (p115) and second a bar, Marrakech is rarely crowded, meaning you can snag one of the low-slung tables draped in lace and take in the haunting sounds of a two-piece Moroccan oud and hand-drum player while luxuriating in upholstered armchairs with mint tea and pastries or a fine cognac. *Très civilisé.*

PEANUT BUTTER JAM Map pp64–5
☎ 324 4100; Wafi City Mall, Al-Qataiyat Rd; ☽ 8pm-midnight Fri, except summer

You never know what you're going to hear at PBJ. Sink into a beanbag in the rooftop gardens of Wafi City Mall and munch on barbecued goodies while you take in that night's acts. The thing is, anyone can walk up to the mic and perform. Much of it is amateurish, a couple of steps up from karaoke, but you may be surprised. Go ahead and sing – we dare you.

ROCK BOTTOM CAFÉ Map pp64–5
☎ 396 3888; Regent Palace Hotel, Sheikh Khalifa bin Zayed Rd; ☽ 10am-3am

It's with reservation that we mention this Dubai institution, but since you may wind up in the back of a taxi with your new best friends insisting you simply must end the night here, it figured that you should be filled in. US GIs on leave from Iraq – and the women who hope to love them – pack the ersatz-American roadhouse, while a cheesy cover band blares top-40 hits and scantily clad women dance. No self-respecting woman would come here alone, but with a mob of friends and a bottle of tequila gone, it's the quintessential ending to a messy night on the town in Dubai.

SHEESHA CAFÉS

Dubai's *sheesha* cafés give great insight into local culture. Even if you don't smoke, it's worth sampling a puff to better understand this traditional Middle Eastern pastime; for more details, see p134. The future of *sheesha* cafés is uncertain (see the boxed text, p129) but because they're so ingrained in the culture, doubtless they're not going away. *Sheesha* cafés are open till after midnight, later during winter months when the city's population spends their evenings outdoors. The going rate is Dh15 to Dh30 for all you can inhale.

COSMO CAFÉ Map pp72–3
☎ 332 6569; The Tower, Sheikh Zayed Rd; ☽ 8.30am-1am

SHEESHA: A PRIMER

Sheesha pipes are packed with flavoured tobacco, such as apple, anise, strawberry, vanilla and coffee – the range of flavours is endless. Good *sheesha* cafés, like good wine bars, pride themselves on the variety they offer.

The *sheesha* pipes used in Dubai are similar to those found in Lebanon and Egypt, and are available in the souqs, specialty shops and even some supermarkets. If, like many visitors to Dubai, you decide to take one home as a souvenir and forget the instructions the shopkeeper gave you, here's a primer on how to use one:

- First fill the glass bowl with water and fix the metal turret into it, ensuring that the tube is underwater with the rubber stopper holding it in position.
- Next, return the metal plate to the top of the turret and put your small ceramic or clay bowl on top of it.
- Fill the bowl with some loose *sheesha* tobacco and cover it tightly with a small piece of foil, before poking about five holes into it with a skewer or fork.
- Using tongs, heat up some Magic Coal on a stove or a hot plate or over a gas burner, then pop it on top of the foil. (Magic Coal is the preferred brand of charcoal because it burns the longest. It's from Japan and comes in a black box. Check the souqs.)
- Lastly, place the pipe into the hole on the side of the *sheesha* pipe, pop a disposable plastic mouthpiece on the end if you're planning to share, and take a long hard puff on the pipe. Recline on the Oriental cushions you bought at the souqs and remember your time in Dubai.

The sleek metal-and-glass façade looks more Manhattan than Middle East, but if you're looking for a toehold on Arab expat life, you can glimpse beautiful, mainly Lebanese people sucking on *sheesha* at this stylish spot. Pretty good food, too.

QD'S Map pp56–7

☎ 295 6000; Dubai Creek Golf & Yacht Club, Deira; ⏰ 6pm-2am

Smoke beneath the stars at this always-fun outdoor Creekside bar, and watch the ballet of lighted *dhows* floating by. Shaped in a giant circle, the main action is on the (very public) raised centre ring, where Oriental carpets and cushions set an inviting mood. For privacy, score a table on the vast wooden deck jutting over the water, or book a cabana. Avoid tables by the bar; ugly fluorescent light bleeds from the kitchen, ruining the aesthetic. Highly recommended for *sheesha*, but skip the food.

SHAKESPEARE & COMPANY Map pp72–3

☎ 331 1757; opposite KFC, just behind Sheikh Zayed Rd in Al-Attar Tower; ⏰ 7am-1am

Linger long and puff *sheesha* under a big outdoor tent at this woman- and child-friendly hangout with mismatched velvet sofas, wicker chairs and big wooden tables. Perfect for a game of backgammon. The Lebanese-French menu is good for a nosh between smokes – think *croque monsieur*, crêpes and pizzas, all around Dh30. Good breakfasts, too.

SHEESHA COURTYARD Map pp82–3

☎ 399 9999; One&Only Royal Mirage, Jumeirah; ⏰ 7pm-1am

The Royal Mirage does it right. Reclining on beaded cushions and Oriental carpets in an Arabian palm courtyard is the ultimate way to enjoy a *sheesha*. Though it would take a connoisseur to appreciate the 20 different flavours on offer, you can't go wrong with the sweet aroma of apple. Highly recommended.

SOUQ MADINAT JUMEIRAH Map pp76–7

☎ 366 8888; Central Plaza, Souq Madinat Jumeirah, Al-Sufouh Rd; ⏰ 10am-11pm

The Madinat's *sheesha* courtyard is good for a smoke if you're staying nearby. The views are lovely – manmade canals dotted with floating *abras*, stately (if ersatz) wind-towers and views of the Burj – but because *sheesha* is a traditional Middle Eastern pastime, it's always better to get under the skin of Dubai and puff with the locals at one of the other spots, unless you're already staying at one of the Madinat's hotels.

TCHÉ TCHÉ Map pp62–3

☎ 355 7575; Khalid bin al-Waleed Rd (Bank St), near BurJuman Centre; ⏰ 10am-2am Sat-Thu, 3pm-2am Fri

If you're over the *Arabian Nights* tourist trip, hit this plain-Jane neighbourhood *sheesha* café with Arabian pop and a blaring TV reverberating off too many hard surfaces. It's interesting because it's frequented mostly by Emiratis and other Arabs, along with the occasional expat. Good place to bone up on your Arabic.

ZYARA Map pp72–3

☎ 343 5454; behind National Bank of Abu Dhabi, Sheikh Zayed Rd; ☽ 8am-1am

Puff in the shadow of giant skyscrapers at this convivial bo-ho-cool Lebanese café. The colourful dollhouse-like interior is great for booze-free socializing over a game of cards or backgammon. The *sheesha* is presented outdoors where you sit at living-room-like clusters of bright-orange sofas on a palm-lined patio while you gaze up at the impossibly tall towers.

CINEMAS

The first thing you need to know if you're considering catching the latest Hollywood blockbuster at a mall in Dubai is that Emiratis don't view the cinema as a cultural institution, but as a social scene. At mainstream cinemas, kids run up and down the aisles while adults talk on their cell phones. It's excruciating. There's one exception: Gold Class (read on).

The Dubai International Film Festival (www.dubaifilm fest.com), usually held in December, is arguably the cultural highlight of the year. The other 51 weeks of the calendar can be disheartening. The only independent cinemas are dedicated to Tamil, Hindi and Malayalam films, so English-language films are restricted to the unadventurous multiplexes. Occasionally a good film manages to sneak its way onto the schedules alongside the endless action movies, horror flicks and romantic comedies, but most of the time it's all too predictable. The festival's success suggests there's a market for independent and world film, and for years we've been hearing murmurs that an art-house cinema will open its doors to deprived cinemagoers. In the absence of quality programming at the multiplexes, art galleries such as the Third Line and XVA occasionally hold film screenings. These are free and pro-

moted in listings magazines such as *Time Out Dubai*. Also check out the Alliance Française (Map pp64–5; ☎ 335 8712), which shows weekly films in French and occasionally hosts festivals.

For pure-fluff value and a glimpse of local culture, consider taking in a Bollywood film instead – really, how often do you get the chance? They're pure spectacle, packed with melodrama, romance and action, and punctuated by song and dance numbers. Plots are hardly complicated, so you'll be able to get the gist if the films haven't subtitles. If you're not up for Hindi, look for free outdoor movie nights – a big draw for European expats.

GOLD CLASS Map pp82–3

☎ 341 4999; Cinestar, Mall of the Emirates, Sheikh Zayed Rd; tickets Dh100

The ultimate way to see a movie, Gold Class is more of a small screening room than a cinema, but you'll hardly care. The seats are enormous recliners and waiters bring you blankets, popcorn in silver bowls and drinks in glass goblets. Best of all, everyone pays attention to the film. Reservations essential.

LAMCY Map pp64–5

☎ 336 8808; Lamcy Plaza, Al-Qataiyat Rd; tickets Dh25

The two-screen complex is one of the few remaining theatres showing Hindi, Malayalam and Tamil films. If you've never seen a Bollywood movie on the big screen, do it in Dubai on a Friday, the only day off for most Asian expatriates. You're in for a memorable experience.

MOVIES UNDER THE STARS Map pp64–5

☎ 324 0000; Wafi City Rooftop Gardens, Al-Qataiyat Rd; ☽ 8pm-midnight Sun

Settle into a beanbag on a balmy winter's night with a bucket of beers and watch a themed double-feature of vintage-modern films. Even if you don't appreciate, say, Tom Cruise night, it's hard to argue when admission is free.

SPORTS & ACTIVITIES

top picks

Before the boom, Emiratis spent their free time watching camel races, riding horses and boating. Now that expats have shown up, sports in Dubai have broadened to reflect the new population. Europeans brought golf, tennis and rugby. Cricket is huge, owing to the enormous Subcontinental communities. Emiratis have a new-found fondness for the world-popular game of football (aka soccer). Visitors generally take it easier, sticking to the Gulf's placid, bathtub-warm waters. You could spend an afternoon skittering across the surf on a kiteboard or diving in the shallow gulf on a scuba expedition. If you can't stand the sweltering heat, there's always Ski Dubai, the ultimate expression of Dubai excess. Or you could stay indoors; as you might expect in such a money-rich land of tourism and luxury hotels, spas and fitness clubs are big business. Spectator sports provide an occasional glimpse into Emirati life or the lives of expat workers. From the lowly game of cricket played out on a sandy lot by Indian and Pakistani labourers to the grand display of sheikhs rooting for their prize thoroughbreds, sports in Dubai unite its various subcultures. If you want to get under the skin of one in particular, keep an eye out for the games its people play.

HEALTH & FITNESS

The health-and-fitness set is comprised primarily of Western expats. While Emiratis grow large beneath their robes, Westerners shed the hummus at health clubs, yoga studios and fitness centres. With so many people working so hard to continue wearing their skinny jeans, there are lots of sore muscles in Dubai. Consequently, massage and beauty-treatment schedules at day spas fill up fast: book ahead. If you prefer swimming in salt water instead of chlorine, check out the beach listings on p78.

GYMS

Nearly every hotel in Dubai has a gym, but the equipment is sometimes chosen by people who don't work out. The worst have only a few stationary bikes and a cumbersome all-in-one machine with too many cables and pulleys that constantly need adjusting. The best have a full complement of top-end circuit- and weight-training equipment, including Smith racks, cable-crossovers and the hottest new gadget, a Power Plate. If it really matters, call the hotel and ask to speak to the fitness-centre manager. Because labour is so cheap in Dubai, many hotels have onsite trainers to help you tighten up. Some hotels sell memberships to nonguests, effectively packing them in during after-work hours; if you don't like crowds when you work out, avoid hitting the gym in the early evening. Admission to gyms generally costs about Dh100 for a one-day pass, twice that at a top-end hotel, but you'll gain access to the resort's grounds, tennis courts and swimming pool. If you're going to a hotel gym, get your money's worth by making a day of it.

AVIATION CLUB Map pp64–5

☎ 282 4141; www.aviationclub.ae; Dubai Tennis Stadium, Al-Garhoud Rd, Deira; Sun-Thu Dh80, Fri & Sat Dh95; ⏰ 6am-11pm

Packed after work and on weekends – and with good reason – the Aviation Club has killer body pump and spinning classes, and a big selection of weights and circuit training for a pre-cardio workout or before a lap-swim in the half-Olympic-size pool. This is where the Dubai Tennis Championships are held; the club's five tennis courts – four side courts and one centre – are available only by reservation.

FITNESS FIRST Map pp62–3

☎ 397 4117; www.fitnessfirst.com; Al-Mussalla Tower; Dh100; ⏰ 6am-11pm

All the fitness junkies in Dubai are signing up for the hot new gym. Multiple locations mean easy access. There's a great line-up of classes – as many as 80 per week – from belly dancing and salsa to yoga and kick-boxing, and a full complement of free weights, racks, barbells and dumbbells, and benches. Onsite trainers hone your skills. Check the web for the list of locations. Fitness First have another Bur Dubai branch (Map pp62–3; ☎ 351-0044; BurJuman Centre, New BurJuman Bldg S-3) around the corner from this one. Though inconveniently located, we especially like the mammoth 27,000-sq-ft branch (Map p52; ☎ 375-0177; Dubai Festival City) at Festival

top picks

HOTEL GYMS

- Grand Hyatt (p156)
- Shangri-La (p158)
- Radisson SAS (p152)
- Dubai Marine Beach Resort (p160)
- Ramada Hotel (p156)
- Le Royal Meridien (p162)

City. Also consider the Ibn Battuta mall branch (Map pp82–3; ☎ 366-9933; Ibn Battuta Mall).

GRAND HYATT Map pp64–5

☎ 317 1234; www.hyatt.com; Al-Qataiyat Rd; Sun-Thu Dh200, Fri & Sat Dh250; ⏰ 6am-11pm
The top-notch equipment includes Smith racks, cable-crossover racks, and full circuit-training equipment. The gym also offers aerobics, yoga and onsite trainers to guide your workout. Justify the expense by spending the afternoon inside with a treatment at the glittering spa or outside by Dubai's biggest swimming pool. Also outdoors you'll find a meandering 450m running track beneath tall palms and four tennis courts. Kids have their own pool.

INTER-FITNESS Map pp54–5

☎ 222 7171; www.interfitness.com; Radisson SAS Hotel; Dh77; ⏰ 6am-11pm
For serious lifting, Inter-Fitness has two smallish rooms full of equipment. It feels a bit grungy, like an old YMCA, but the equipment is in good shape and the location convenient to both sides of the Creek. No aerobics classes; this is a place to grunt with iron, then dive into the pool.

PHARAOHS CLUB Map pp64–5

☎ 324 0000; fax 324 4611; www.wafi.com; Wafi City Mall, Al-Qataiyat Rd; weekly membership including pool use Dh 450, pool per day Dh100
Other than Fitness First (opposite), this is the closest you'll find to an LA-style club, with some serious weight-lifting equipment (including 100lb dumbbells) for juiced-up grunters, a climbing wall, squash courts and multiple fitness classes (some for women only) including body pump, yoga, aikido, mat Pilates and step. The best amenity is the enormous, free-form 'lazy-river' rooftop swimming pool; kids love it. One caveat: temporary memberships are a nuisance to acquire. You must set one up, via fax or in person, at least three days prior to your week's membership; passport required. Don't bother if you're not staying nearby. The pool (⏰ 9am-10pm), by contrast, is open for one-day drop-ins.

YOGA & PILATES

CLUB STRETCH Map pp62–3

☎ 345 2131; www.clubstretch.ae; next to Capitol Hotel, Al-Mina Rd; per class Dh70; ⏰ 8.30am-8.30pm by reservation
An independent studio great for Pilates and Bikram (hot-room) yoga, Club Stretch's

---

DUBAI'S TOP SPA TREATMENTS

Oriental Hammam (p141) Impeccable re-creation of a Moroccan bathhouse. Not to be missed.

Couples' Massage (Amara, p140) Reignite your romance behind a walled garden.

Pure Awakening Package (Talise, p141) Get over your jetlag in 50 minutes – or at least feel somewhat refreshed.

Maya's Secret (Sensasia, p141) Indulge your olfactory senses with a sandalwood-and-myrrh body scrub – or opt for the dry-skin-reviving Sunrise Body Treatment, a moisturising olive-oil body scrub and massage.

Seaweed Wraps (Map p158, Willow Stream Spa, Fairmont hotel) Great for marine-inspired treatments and exfoliating rubs. Two pools mean you can chase the sun from morning till evening.

Rasul Mud Treatment (Map pp82–3; ☎ 399 8888; www.grosvenorhouse.lemeridien.com; Retreat, Grosvenor House) Soak in a hydrotherapy tub before getting slathered in detoxifying mud.

Food-based Body Scrubs (Map pp82–3; ☎ 318 6184; www.ritzcarlton.com; The Spa, Ritz-Carlton, Al-Sufouh Rd) If you're into food-body treatments, the Ritz does them well – think wild-berry body bath and cinnamon body glow.

Hopi Ear Candling (Map pp64–5; ☎ 324 7700; www.waficity.com; Cleopatra's Spa, Wafi Pyramids, Wafi City Mall, Bur Dubai) If your ears didn't unplug after your flight, ear candles may help by drawing out excess wax. Women only.

SAVING FACE IN DUBAI

Dubai does a roaring trade in plastic surgery, rivalling surface-deep Los Angeles for rhinoplasty, liposuction and breast augmentation. One local cosmetic-surgery clinic announces on its website, 'Stem cell technique could help women grow their own breast implants.' DIY breasts. Who'd have thought? Plastic surgery in Dubai makes sense because afterward you have to hide out, vanish from the social scene for a couple of weeks and heal. No self-respecting socialite would dare appear the next day at a cocktail party with two black eyes. Botox is one thing; broken bones are another. In Los Angeles, celebs get their faces smashed around, then disappear to Palm Springs to recover poolside, in total privacy, behind bougainvillea-covered walls. Palm Springs is to the States as Dubai is to the world: a hiding place for the nipped and tucked. Think about it. Geographically speaking, Dubai is in the middle of nowhere, halfway between London and Singapore, and most of the world's airlines fly here. London matrons and wives of Russian oligarchs can jet here in a few hours and remain totally anonymous while they get their faces done, a world away from their normal social circles. And all that high-end shopping means they can also build new wardrobes to match their new noses, with zero fear of running into their girlfriends in the boutiques. After all, the point of plastic surgery is not to let anyone know you've had it. Keying in to a need for good care in a region that once had none, the American Academy for Cosmetic Surgery has set up shop at the new Dubai Healthcare City, guaranteeing its international clientele the same high standard of medical care they'd find in the States, the birthplace of the craft. If you're staying at a five-star beach resort, one of the self-contained compounds that guests need never leave before they fly back home, keep an eye out for oversized black sunglasses worn by women too old to be so thin. Chances are there are a couple of big, fat shiners turning purple beneath those Gucci frames.

Dh120 one-week introductory package is a bargain for hard-core yogis. Reservations essential. Also offers individual Pilates sessions on a reformer.

GEMS OF YOGA Map pp72–3
☎ 331 5161, 331 1328; www.gemsofyogadubai .com; 17th fl above KFC, near the Fairmont Hotel, Sheikh Zayed Rd; introductory class Dh50; ⏱ 6.30am-10pm Sat-Thu, 10am-8pm Fri
These guys are serious about their yoga. The challenging hourly classes include Hatha, as well as power-yoga (a combination of aerobics and yoga) and occasional outdoor classes in local parks; call ahead for schedules. Dh50 buys you an introductory one-hour class.

DAY SPAS & MASSAGE
Though you can get a good rubdown at most sports clubs, for the proper treatment book a dedicated spa. Dubai's spas like to incorporate food into their treatments – berries, chocolate, even gingerbread at Christmas. You may disagree, but we remain unconvinced of their merit. If you're dubious, stick to the tried-and-true, not the out-of-the-blue. Make reservations as far in advance as possible; for top spas such as Amara and the Oriental Hammam, book weeks ahead. Ask if a spa treatment includes use of the pool and grounds; if it does, make a day of it – arrive early and lollygag poolside. If you're considering a facial and you like to sun, book an afternoon appointment

– say, 5pm – following your tanning session. If you receive the treatment in the morning, your skin will be too sensitive for sun exposure that afternoon. Note: facials look best the next day, so if you have a fancy dinner engagement and want to look great, get the treatment the day before. Spas are generally open from 10am to 10pm Saturday through Thursday; on Fridays, most open only in the afternoon. Most spas offer manicure-pedicures; if you want a dedicated nail salon, a first choice is Nail Spa Mercato Mall (Map pp76–7; ☎ 349 7766; Jumeirah); Aviation Club (Map pp56–7; ☎ 282 1617; Al-Garhoud); and Ibn Battuta Mall (Map pp82–3; ☎ 368 5070).

AMARA Map pp56–7
☎ 602 1234; www.dubai.park.hyatt.com; Dubai Creek Golf & Yacht Club
Dubai's top spa has eight treatment rooms, including three couples' rooms, all with their own totally private walled gardens complete with outdoor showers – the only ones to be found in Dubai. Instead of traipsing around in a robe from the locker room, you're escorted directly to your own beautifully lit private garden suite, where the entire treatment takes place. You even choose your own background music. First comes a luxurious foot bath, then your selected treatment. Best of all, afterward you're not shoved out the door, but instead are served tea and allowed time to relax and enjoy the tranquillity. Reserve well ahead.

1847 Map pp72–3
☎ 330 1847; Boulevard at Emirates Towers, Sheikh Zayed Rd

Men: if you're lucky enough to be able to grow a good-looking beard, we highly recommend you do so while in Dubai. The Arabs will approve and be ever-so-slightly more accepting of you. (It worked for us.) However, many expats prefer to keep a hairless visage; the dandies among them indulge in an old-fashioned straight-razor shave – complete with hot towels beforehand – at the clubby men-only 'grooming salon' 1847. Ask about packages, including mani-pedis and massages. Good haircuts, too. There's another branch at the Grosvenor House (p162) in New Dubai.

GIVENCHY SPA Map pp82–3
☎ 315 2140; www.oneandonlyresorts.com; One&Only Royal Mirage

Clean, elegant and straightforward, Givenchy exclusively uses its eponymous products in its 12 treatment rooms. The lighting is a bit yellow, but it's the kind of place you can go with your conservative mother who prefers sensibility to excess. Hot-stone massage is the specialty.

JET SET Map pp82–3
☎ 399 8888; www.grosvenorhouse.lemeridien.com; Grosvenor House, Dubai Marina

The ladies-only salon at Grosvenor House is vaguely reminiscent of the beauty parlour in the 1939 film *The Women* – if only one could speak Arabic to keep up on the gossip. Great for a wash-and-set and mani-pedi before a big night out.

SENSASIA Map pp76–7
☎ 349 8850; www.sensasiaspas.com; The Village, Jumeirah Rd, Jumeirah

Detox treatments, facials and massage are the specialties at this independent Jumeirah spa done in a fancy Far East–meets–Middle East style. For a splurge, book the Queen for a Day treatment (Dh1350), a 4½-hour indulgence. There are no grounds to roam afterward; instead plan to lunch at Lime Tree Café (p119), then hit the boutiques – just like the Jumeirah Janes do.

SOFTTOUCH SPA Map pp82–3
☎ 341 0000; www.kempinski-dubai.com; Kempinski Hotel, Mall of the Emirates

Conveniently located for a post–Ski Dubai rubdown, Softtouch specialises in Ayurvedic oil-drip treatments as well as massages. While you'll love the Asian-minimalist look – slate floors, Thai-silk walls, orange hanging lamps – the changing rooms are upstairs, meaning you have to walk through the hotel's public areas in a robe. There's no sense of exclusivity, but after shooshing down the slopes, it's a great choice.

TALISE SPA Map pp76–7
☎ 366 6818; www.madinatjumeirah.com/spa; Madinat Jumeirah

Arrive by *abra* at the Madinat Jumeirah's Arabian-themed spa, which has 28 gorgeous free-standing temple-like treatment rooms complete with altars laden with quartz crystal – they're like the inside of a genie's bottle. The only problem is, once your treatment is over, you can't enjoy the sumptuous surroundings because you're hustled out the door to make room for the next appointment. Still, the treatments are top-notch – a blend of Eastern and Western, from Ayurvedic cupping to Swedish massage – and convenient if you're staying at the Madinat. Otherwise, think about trying Amara (opposite).

THE ROYAL TREATMENT

In a city built on ersatz facsimiles and Disney-esque gimmicks, the not-to-be-missed Oriental Hammam (Map pp82–3; ☎ 315 2140; www.oneandonlyresorts.com; One&Only Royal Mirage) stands out as the hands-down best re-creation of another country's cultural institution: a Moroccan bathhouse. Moroccan-born attendants walk you into a giant, echoey, steamy marble room lit by stained-glass lanterns, where they wrap you in muslin, bathe you on a marble bench from a running hot-water fountain, then lay you down on an enormous, heated marble cube – head-to-toe with three other women (or men, depending on the day) – and scrub your entire body with exfoliating coarse gloves. Next they bathe you again then lead you to a steam room where you relax before receiving a sensuous mud body mask and honey facial, a brief massage and your final rinse. Afterward, you're wrapped in dry muslin and escorted to a meditative relaxation room, where you drift to sleep beneath a blanket and awaken to hot mint tea and dates – just like in Morocco. If you visit only one spa in Dubai, make it the Oriental Hammam.

HENNA

Henna body tattooing is a long-standing tradition dating back 6000 years, when central-Turkish women began painting their hands in homage to the Mother Goddess. The practice spread throughout the regions around the eastern Mediterranean, where the henna shrub grows wild. Today, Emirati women continue the tradition by decorating their hands, nails and feet for special events, particularly weddings. A few nights before the nuptials, brides-to-be are honoured with *layyat al-henna* or henna night. This is a women-only affair, part of a week of festivities leading up to the big day. The bride is depilated, anointed head-to-toe with perfumes and oils, and shampooed with henna, jasmine or perfume. Her hands, wrists, ankles and feet are then tattooed with intricate floral designs, which typically last around six weeks. Lore has it, the duration of the tattoos is an indication to the mother-in-law of what kind of wife the bride will become. If she's a hard worker – and thus a more desirable daughter-in-law – the henna will penetrate deeper and remain longer.

Want to give it a try? Henna tents are all over the city. Look for signs depicting henna-painted hands in Deira City Centre (p92), BurJuman Centre (p96), Souq Madinat Jumeirah (p101), Emirates Towers (p99) and hotel lobbies. Just don't show your mother-in-law; she may disapprove.

RUNNING

The winter months are cool enough for running nearly anytime during the day; in summer you've got to get up with the sun to jog with no fear of heatstroke. The following groups meet regularly. If you're into the more social aspects of running (read: drinking afterward), look into Dubai's 'hashing' clubs at www.creekhash.net. There's also a marathon in January (see p15).

DUBAI CREEK STRIDERS Map pp72–3

☎ 321 1999; www.dubaicreekstriders.com; meet at Trade Centre car park opposite Exhibition Hall 4, Sheikh Zayed Rd

The Striders meet for weekly training runs on Friday mornings at 7am opposite the Novotel (check the web for an aerial image). The run's length varies depending on the season, but it's generally 10km. Contact the club to register before turning up. Free.

DUBAI ROAD RUNNERS Map pp76–7

☎ 050-624 3213; www.dubai-road-runners.com; north entrance to Safa Park, Al-Wasl Rd; per adult Dh5; ☽ 6.30pm Sat

The club welcomes runners of all ages and abilities to run one or two laps of the park (3.4km per lap). Runners predict how long it will take them to run the course; the one closest wins a prize. Fun and communal.

'WINTER' SPORTS

Ice Skating

AL-NASR LEISURELAND Map pp64–5

☎ 337 1234; www.alnasrll.com; off Oud Metha Rd, Oud Metha; incl boot hire Dh10; ☽ 2hr sessions at 10am, 1pm, 4pm & 7.30pm

Though Leisureland sporting facility is dated, it's got a bit of character, and the rink here is bigger than the sad-looking one at the Hyatt Regency (p152). If the kids tire of the ice, there's a bowling alley next door. Look for the Indian restaurant Khazana; it's the best of the onsite food options.

Skiing & Snowboarding

SKI DUBAI Map pp82–3

☎ 409 4000; www.skidxb.com; Mall of the Emirates; Snow Park admission adult/child Dh85/70; Ski Slope per 2hr Dh180/150; ☽ 10am-11pm Sat-Tue, 10am-midnight Wed-Fri

Dubai's most famous attraction, Ski Dubai draws gawkers to the plate-glass windows of the Mall of the Emirates, where they peek inside a faux winter wonderland, complete with ice sculptures, a tiny sledding hill and a 400m ski run. Gulf Arabs are fascinated by this display of a winter they've néver seen before, but they typically restrict themselves to the walk-through Snow Park, passing through a colour-lit igloo filled with carved-ice penguins and dragons, then sledding down a little hill in plastic toboggans. Here is one of the rare opportunities to spot Emiratis openly guffawing. Skiers and boarders are kept separate from the Snow Park and instead whiz down a forking slope – one side for beginners, one for intermediates. The 58m (190ft) vertical drop is an ant hill when compared with a real ski mountain, and the chairlift is s-l-o-w, but if you've never skied or boarded before, it's a good place to learn basics. Advanced skiers quickly weary of the too-short runs (think 30 seconds at a good clip) but generally everybody is pleasantly surprised by the velvety snow. Conditions are ideal: at night, the interior is chilled to -10°C, and snow guns blow feather-light powder; during operation, it warms to a perfect -1°C. The operators spent a lot on this place, and managed to get the snow right, but we're disappointed with the upper hill's appearance – a giant Fly Emirates advertisement dominates the ugly baby-blue gymnasium-like walls. A *trompe l'oeil* sky-and-mountain scene would go a long way toward creating a compelling illusion. (After all, isn't illusion the point?) Though weekends are more crowded, Ski Dubai operates a faster-moving secondary lift, a rope tow, that significantly shortens the ride uphill, giving you more runs per hour than you can get riding the chair. Everything you need is provided, from socks to skis. (Note: you *must* wear the ski clothes they provide; if you wear your own gear you'll be barred admission until you've changed clothing.) Bring gloves and a hat, or buy them cheap in the adjoining ski shop; gloves start around Dh10, hats Dh30.

DIVING

The waters around Dubai are home to small coral reefs, tropical marine life and a few shipwrecks, but visibility is lousy, due in large part to underwater construction of the Palms and the World islands, which are being built with little regard to the environmental impact they're having on marine environments. If you want to dive, get far away. Dive companies will zip you up to the East Coast to dive between Khor Fakkan and Dibba, or off the east coast of the Musandam Peninsula, in Oman. For more information on diving on the East Coast, see p173. Not including equipment hire, a day's diving includes two dives and costs between Dh200 and Dh500. No experience is required, but if you are uncertified, here's your chance to take a course; ask the concessionaires for details.

The Emirates Diving Association is the UAE's official diving body. It takes a strong interest in environmental matters – whether anyone in Dubai is listening is another matter. The association runs a good website: www .emiratesdiving.com. Also look for the 180-page *UAE Underwater Explorer*, which provides details on 30 dive sites.

AL BOOM DIVING Map pp76–7
☎ 342 2993; www.alboomdiving.com; Al-Wasl Rd, Jumeirah, just south of the Iranian Mosque

Al Boom's staff is experienced and PADI certified; they teach courses and guide dives in Dubai, off the East Coast in Fujairah, and at Musandam. They also provide air-tank fill-ups and equipment maintenance.

SCUBATEC DIVING CENTRE Map pp64–5
☎ 334 8988; Sana Bldg, cnr Sheikh Khalifa bin Zayed & Al-Adhid Rds, Karama

Scubatec runs classes for PADI certification, rents equipment to experienced divers, and leads two-dive trips off Khor Fakkan. With a few days' notice staff can also arrange dives to the Gulf's pearl beds.

OTHER WATERSPORTS

The hot sun, warm sea and high volume of tourists make water sports big business in Dubai. Most facilities are at major beach hotels and private clubs, meaning prices skew high for the following activities. Calm waters mean lousy surfing – indeed there are no major surfing concessionaires because of it – but the placid conditions are ideal for beginners in the sports of kite boarding and water skiing.

Kite-surfers congregate at Wollongong Beach, aka Kite Beach (Map pp76–7), where there's a designated launch and recovery area. You must have a licence to kite-surf on Dubai's beaches; the Dubai Kite Club (www.dubaikiteclub.com) regulates the sport. Visit its website for details on temporary licences. Note: use only the instructors it recommends – there's been reports of phoney (and unlicensed) teachers. Rent kites and seek advice at Fatima Sports (Map pp76–7; ☎ 050-618 0612; www.fatimasport.com; Kite Beach).

When the kids start whining about the heat and grow weary of your hotel pool, give them a big treat: a visit to Wild Wadi Waterpark (Map pp76–7; ☎ 348 4444; www.wildwadi.com; Jumeirah Rd, near the Jumeirah Beach Hotel; adult/child Dh180/150; ☼ 11am-6pm Nov-Feb, 11am-7pm Mar-May & Sep-Oct, 11am-9pm Jun-Aug) Wild Wadi is an American-style waterpark with 14 interconnected rides, including a big-wave pool, a white-water rapids 'river' and a 33m-high slide that drops you at a speed of 80km/h, resulting in a serious wedgie. Little kids have their own dedicated play areas. Rides follow a vague theme about an Arabian adventurer named Juha, and his friend Sinbad the sailor who get shipwrecked together, but it lacks the seamless perfection of Disneyland's attractions. But really, who cares when there's so much fun to be had splashing around? Come on weekdays to avoid long queues.

DID YOU KNOW?

The white metal crosspieces at the top of the Burj Al Arab form what is said to be largest cross in the Middle East – but it's only visible from the sea. Some say the Western designer did it on purpose. Regardless, by the time it was discovered, it was too late to redesign the tower even if the owner, the venerable Sheikh Mohammed, had wanted to – the hotel already had put Dubai on the map and become *the* icon for the city. Jumeirah Properties' PR people downplay it saying that it's not a cross, but an architectural detail. What do you think? Go see it on a boat charter and decide for yourself. You won't believe the scale of it.

Water-skiing in the polluted Dubai Creek is not recommended. Instead head to New Dubai or Abu Dhabi. Water-skiing at a Gulf-front five-star hotel with its own beach club costs around Dh140 for 20 minutes – which, if you've never water-skied, is a long time. Nonguests must also pay a daily admission fee for access to the hotel grounds and beach club (usually about Dh75 to Dh250). Try Le Meridien Mina Seyahi (p163), where beach access costs Dh150 and water-skiing Dh140.

Dubai's waterfront is growing like mad. To get perspective on just how far the city now stretches, see it from the water. While there's a location for the following charter service at Dubai Marina, we recommend starting from the Creek and yachting past Deira and Bur Dubai – the original city – then into the Gulf and up the coast to New Dubai. Along the way, you'll pass the Palm Jumeirah and get to see the Burj Al Arab – and its accidental Christian symbolism (above) – from the sea.

For boat charters starting at Dh700 per hour, with a one-hour minimum, visit Dubai Creek Golf & Yacht Club (Map pp56–7; ☎ 205 4646; www .dubaigolf.com; near Deira side of Al-Garhoud Bridge) The skippered vessels range from a 30ft fishing boat with room for six to an 88ft yacht with room for 28 people. Plan three to four hours to make it to the Palm and Burj, then back again. Ask about food-and-drink packages.

GOLF

Dubai has become a big golfing destination over the past few years and will continue to grow, especially with Tiger Woods lending his cachet to a new planned golf community scheduled for completion in late 2009. Dubai has several challenging courses designed by other big names. Fear not: Dubai's clubs don't require memberships; however, greens fees at top clubs soar to nearly Dh800 for 18 holes. Proper attire is essential. If you're serious about golf, reserve your tee times as soon as you book your hotel and flight.

ARABIAN RANCHES off Map p52
☎ 884 6777; www.thedesertcoursedubai.com; Arabian Ranches, cnr Umm Suqeim St & Emirates Ring Rds; per 18 holes Thu-Sat Dh600, Sun-Wed Dh510 (cart Dh55)
If you've golfed in the American southwest (ie Palm Springs or Scottsdale) you'll feel right at home on this 18-hole desert-style course designed by former golf champion Ian Baker-Finch. Nine-hole play also available.

DUBAI CREEK GOLF & YACHT CLUB Map pp56–7
☎ 295 6000; www.dubaigolf.com; near Deira side of Al-Garhoud Bridge; per 18 holes Thu-Sat Dh760, Sun-Wed Dh715
The former host course of the Dubai Desert Classic has been redesigned by a former winner of the tournament, Thomas Björn. The Creekside location is gorgeous. Serious golfers should stay at the neighbouring Park Hyatt (p152), within walking distance of the greens. There's also a par-three floodlit course for evening play, but the driving range is pricey – Dh30 for a bucket of 50 balls.

EMIRATES GOLF CLUB Map pp82–3
☎ 347 3222; www.dubaigolf.com; Interchange No 5, Sheikh Zayed Rd; 18-hole Majlis course Dh825
The first grass course in the Middle East is home to the Dubai Desert Classic (www.dubai desertclassic.com), a major tourney on the PGA circuit; compare your tee-offs to Tiger Woods'. The way-cool Bedouin-style tents set a striking backdrop for the 19th hole.

FOUR SEASONS GOLF CLUB off Map p52
☎ 601 0101; www.fourseasons.com/dubaigolf/; Al-Rebat St, Al-Badia, at Festival City; Sun-Thu Dh685, Fri & Sat Dh725, includes cart & driving range
The hot new course in Dubai is a pleasure to play – impeccably manicured and well laid out with challenging land features and hazards. Reserve well ahead. The changing rooms are like a mini-spa, complete with sauna and Jacuzzi. The driving range is pricey – Dh100 – but includes unlimited balls. There's a good spikes bar for after-play drinks. As of this writing, the hotel

hadn't yet opened; check the website. It promises to become the new premier golf-hotel in Dubai.

SPECTATOR SPORT

Rumour has it, Dubai is gearing up to make a bid for the Olympics, probably in 2020, and they're building like mad at Dubai Sports City in Dubailand. While it may not offer much in the way of individual activities until it's completed, it will bring enormous stadiums and race tracks expressly built to host world-famous sporting events.

The single-biggest sporting event among elite Emiratis is horse-racing. The Nad Al-Sheba racetrack had temporarily closed for renovations as of this writing so that the track and clubhouse could be rebuilt to put the Dubai World Cup on par with the Royal Ascot and Kentucky Derby. By the time you read this, there should be a glittering, brand-spanking-new facility. If you score tickets to the Dubai World Cup, you may even glimpse Sheikh Mohammed himself, with a rare big grin on his face.

Expats turn out in force for the Dubai Rugby 7s, when you may spot more drunken Brits in one place than at any other time during the year.

And then there's cricket, the biggest single sport among Indians and Pakistanis. Emirates airlines teamed up with the International Cricket Council, and after nearly a century at Lord's in London, the council is now based in the UAE, much to the delight of the city's cricket fans. During any of these events, there's palpable excitement in the air; when a favourite team wins, people drive around blowing their car horns and waving flags.

This isn't the case when Tiger Woods wins the Desert Classic golf tournament or Roger Federer the Dubai Tennis Championships, but spectators still show up from around the world to cheer them on while they play.

You could plan an entire trip around any of these events. Keep an eye out for more big-name international competitions over the coming years. This is Dubai, after all. You never know what's coming down the pike.

HORSE-RACING

NAD AL-SHEBA CLUB Map pp72–3
☎ 336 3666; www.dubairacingclub.com; Nad al-Sheba District, 5km southeast of Dubai centre; general admission free

A passionate love of Arabian thorough-breds courses through the blood of Emiratis, and the Dubai-based Godolphin (www.godolphin.com) stables are well known to horse-racing enthusiasts worldwide. Though racing season officially starts in November, the Dubai International Racing Carnival (late January through March) is when things really heat up. But it's not the white-linen set that packs these weekly races. It's the not-so-civilised drunk expats in shorts and T-shirts – at least in the public areas. For access to the stands, you must wear a 'lounge suit', basically a jacket and trousers. The season culminates in the Dubai World Cup (www.dubaiworldcup.com), the world's richest horse race, with prize money of a dizzying US$6 million and a total purse for the event of over US$20 million. If you attend, dress to the nines.

Nad al-Sheba's races are held at night from about 7pm. Don a hat and make an evening of it. The stands are licensed, and there are various food and beverage packages available from Dh275 (for details, see www.dubairacingclub.com; click on 'hospitality'). Check the website of the Emirates Racing Association (www.emiratesracing.com) for the exact dates of race meetings throughout

---

UAE FOOTBALL

On winter weeknights, neighbourhood stadiums in Dubai are packed out with up to 10,000 spectators – mostly young Emirati men – passionately barracking for their favourite football teams. Surprisingly most foreigners, be they expats or visitors, hardly attend the matches. And they're rarely covered by the local English-language press. If you're a football fan, attend a match once and you may be hooked; the carnival atmosphere is electric. Fans dress up in colour-coordinated outfits, and a singer and band of drummers lead song-and-dance routines to inspire their teams. If you're curious, catch a match between the old rivals, Al-Ahli, Sheikh Mohammed's red-and-white jersey team, and the purple-clad Al-Ain. Watch out: tempers may flare post-match; it's not uncommon for police on horseback to charge the stadium and set off smoke bombs to restore order. Keep your distance. (Remember, Emiratis' legal rights *always* trump yours.) For the latest, check *Emirates Today* or the official UAE Football Association (☎ 316-0101; www.uaefootball.org).

the year. Even if you don't like horse-racing, attending a race presents great people-watching opportunities.

CAMEL RACING

DUBAI CAMEL RACECOURSE

☎ 338 8170; Lisaili, Al-Ain Rd exit 37, approx 40km from Dubai

The traditional sport of the UAE, camel-racing was originally practised only at weddings and special events. These days it's big business, with races held every Thursday, Friday, Sunday and sometimes Monday mornings, October to April. Races usually start around 7am and continue until about 9am. But in classic Emirati style, no schedule is set in stone. Other races are held exclusively for Emiratis. Call ahead before you drive an hour out of town.

The use of child jockeys at races has been a contentious issue in the past. International human-rights groups decried the practice, and the Emiratis acquiesced in July 2005; public races no longer exploit children.

Watching these mighty animals race at speeds of up to 60km/h is quite a sight. So is the erratic driving of their owners, who race around the inside track cheering on their camels. If you miss out on a race meeting, you can usually catch training sessions on each of the above-mentioned mornings at roughly the same time, and again around 5.30pm. The sheer number of camels is shocking. Bring your camera.

MOTOR RACING
Desert Rallying

Motor sports are exceedingly popular with Emiratis. The Emirates Motor Sports Federation holds events throughout the year, with the important ones scheduled during the cooler months. A round of the FIA Cross-Country Rally World Cup, the UAE Desert Challenge (www.uaedesertchallenge.com), attracts top rally drivers from around the world. Held in November, it starts in Abu Dhabi and ends in Dubai. There are a number of smaller rallies during February and March, including the 1000 Dunes Rally and the Spring Desert Rally, which are both 4WD events. Visit the website of the Emirates Motor Sports Federation (www.emsfuae.com) for more details.

DUBAI AUTODROME off Map p52

☎ 367 8700; www.dubaiautodrome.com; off Emirates Rd (take Interchange No 4 on Sheikh Zayed Rd), south of Dubai centre

The best place to catch live motor sport is at the Dubai Autodrome. This 5.39km circuit and complex is host to a round of the burgeoning A1 Grand Prix circuit (www.a1gp.com), where drivers compete as representatives of their country. Oddly, despite it being a Dubai initiative, there's no UAE team on the circuit – the nearest local team is Team Lebanon, which only occasionally scores well. Things may soon change: a new Formula One track is under construction in Abu Dhabi, due for completion at the end of 2009. The Dubai Autodrome has an adequate track, but the facilities aren't up to snuff for the calibre of events the UAE wants to attract. Keep an eye out.

GOLF

EMIRATES GOLF CLUB Map pp82–3

☎ 347 3222; www.dubaigolf.com; Interchange No 5, Sheikh Zayed Rd

The Dubai Desert Classic (www.dubaidesertclassic.com) attracts some of the world's best golfers.

CRICKET CRAZY

The enormous Indian and Pakistani communities l-o-v-e cricket. You'll see them playing on sandy lots between buildings during their lunch breaks, in parks on their days off, and late at night in empty car parks. By contrast, you won't see Emiratis playing: cricket in Dubai belongs to the Subcontinental nationalities. If you want to get under the skin of the game, talk to taxi drivers – you can be sure most of them have posters of their favourite players Scotch-taped to their bedroom walls. But first ask where your driver is from – there's disdain between Pakistanis and Indians. Each will tell you that his country's team is the best, then explain at length why. (Some drivers need a bit of cajoling; show enthusiasm and you'll get the whole story.) When Pakistan plays India, the city lights up. Remember, these two nationalities account for about 45% of Dubai's population, far outnumbering Emiratis. Because most of them can't afford the price of satellite TV, they meet up outside their local eateries in Deira or Bur Dubai to watch the match. Throngs of riveted fans swarm the sidewalks beneath the crackling neon – it's a sight to behold.

So popular is the event that some expat aficionados take the entire week off work to view international players tackling the local course. The event, which is held in late February or early March at Emirates Golf Club, has seen some thrilling finishes over the past couple of years – the 18th hole has become legendary on the PGA circuit. Tickets run at Dh175 per day for adults; you can purchase them online until the event draws near, but then you can only buy them at outlets in Dubai.

CRICKET

SHARJAH CRICKET STADIUM
off Map p52
☎ 06-542 2991, 06-543 0067; 2nd Industrial Rd, Industrial Area 5, Sharjah
Cricket lovers surely know about the surprising move of the International Cricket Council to Dubai after 96 years at Lord's, the home of cricket. However, at present, international cricket in the UAE is held in nearby Sharjah (and also in Abu Dhabi), where matches are hosted over the winter months. At present the sport hasn't entirely taken off. This will change once Dubai Sports City is complete and a new stadium constructed. Keep your ear to the ground.

RUGBY

DUBAI EXILES RUGBY CLUB
☎ 333 1198; www.dubaiexiles.com
The club hosts one of Dubai's biggest annual events, the Dubai Rugby Sevens (www.dubairugby7s.com). Held in early December, the final of this three-day Bacchanalian jamboree of sport and booze hosts over 30,000 spectators, all crammed into a temporary stadium built expressly for the 7s. If you're a rugby fan, don't miss it. Book well ahead. Tickets are scarce in the final days leading up to the event.

TENNIS

DUBAI TENNIS STADIUM Map pp56–7
☎ 216 6444; www.dubaitennischampionships.com; Al-Garhoud
Big-name players like Roger Federer and Justine Henin compete at the Dubai Tennis Championships. Held over two weeks from late February to early March, the tournament consists of a Women's Tennis Association (WTA) event followed by an Association of Tennis Professionals (ATP) event. The intimate stadium provides up-close views of the world's best hitters in action, a breathtaking sight.

SLEEPING

top picks

- **XVA Art Hotel** (p157)
- **Raffles Dubai** (p156)
- **Hilton Dubai Creek** (p152)
- **Emirates Towers** (p158)
- **One&Only Royal Mirage** (p162)
- **The Palace, Old Town** (p157)
- **Al-Qasr** (p159)
- **Shangri-La** (p158)
- **La Maison d'Hôtes** (p160)
- **Al-Hijaz Heritage Motel** (p154)

SLEEPING

Make no mistake, Dubai is a luxury-travel destination. Your biggest expense will be your hotel. In order to accommodate the vast amounts of wealth pouring into the city, five-star hotels have been opening nearly every month – and there still aren't enough to satisfy demand. Likewise for midrange accommodation, where rates hover around Dh1000. New chains are arriving to meet tourist demand; brands like Four Points, Holiday Inn Express and Easy Hotel all plan to open in 2008, but these will cost around Dh700 a night at best. If you're on budget, the least you'll pay is Dh400 a night, making Dubai a bad choice for backpackers. Alternatively, if you can bear 50ºC heat, come during the summer, when you can often score deep discounts.

Accommodation in this chapter is listed by neighbourhood, with listings sorted by the price, from highest to lowest, of a double room.

ACCOMODATION STYLES

There are two types of hotel in Dubai: the city hotel and beach resort. City hotels range from one star to five, while the beach resorts are generally all five-stars. Though there are no official camping sites in Dubai, some residents spend weekends camping on beaches or in the desert, but given the temperatures and lack of facilities, camping is neither a reliable nor popular option for a Dubai holiday.

Before you choose a hotel, determine what you want from your holiday. If you like to drink, make sure your hotel isn't dry. City hotels are ideal for jaunts to shopping malls, souqs and historic areas. Beach resorts tend to be more lavish, with expansive grounds, swim-up bars and sandy shores, but they're 30 minutes from Dubai centre; when the traffic's good, a taxi costs Dh50. Most resort guests do the sights in a day and spend the rest of their time soaking up the sun.

Top-end hotels are cities unto themselves, with multiple restaurants, bars and nightclubs. Alcohol is generally only served in hotels, which means expats flock to them in droves. At a good hotel, the party comes to you. Conversely, if you're at a low-end hotel, you'll wind up travelling to the big hotels for fun.

PRICE GUIDE

$$$	over Dh1200
$$	Dh700-1200
$	under Dh700

CHECK-IN & CHECK-OUT TIMES

Because flights arrive in Dubai at all hours, it's crucial to confirm your check-in time with the hotel prior to arrival. Get a confirmation number when you book, and present it at check-in; it's shocking how many reservations get lost. Check-in is generally at 3pm. It's sometimes possible to arrive earlier, but this is never a given unless you pay for the previous night. Check-out is 11am or noon. Here's a little trick to score a late check-out: on the morning of departure, call the front desk and ask, 'How late can I check out?' Don't give them the option to say no by asking, 'Can I check out late?' If you don't get the answer you want, speak to the manager on duty, who will give you the final word. If you absolutely must keep the room until the evening, inquire about a day rate, which is usually half the overnight rate.

LONGER-TERM RENTALS

The Bur Dubai area is full of longer-term rentals; many hotels throughout the city also rent furnished apartments. The chief advantages are the kitchen and washing machine. Prices start around Dh700 for a studio in one of the midrange hotel apartments in Bur Dubai, and prices often drop for stays longer than a week. At top-end hotel apartments, rates skyrocket. Dubai Tourism (www.dubaitourism.ae) has a full listing.

STRAIGHT TALK ABOUT ROOM RATES

We visited every hotel listed in this chapter and inquired directly about rates. Some hoteliers were upfront and told us what the average guest pays; others were cagey and quoted numbers *higher* than rack rates. We were left scratching our heads, wondering what to quote to readers. Understand that the numbers listed in this chapter are to be used as a guide for comparison only. You can often score better, but you may pay more. Visiting Dubai was once dirt cheap. No more. It's now one of the world's most expensive cities.

Fear not: unless you're coming in November or December, when occupancy is highest, or for a major conference or event, you'll nearly always find rates that are lower than racks. Shop around – a little research goes a long way. Even if the words 'package tour' send a chill up your spine, keep in mind that airlines and tour companies often offer the best deals available – especially for resort hotels.

RESERVATIONS

Most major hotel chains have online booking engines, saving you expensive telephone calls. Smaller hotels sometimes offer online booking, but they don't always use a secured server; verify the site's security certificate (use an up-to-date browser; Firefox has good security) before sending your account number. When reserving a hotel that you can't book online, expect miscommunications via email. Pick up the phone and expect to stumble through conversations with people who don't fully understand English. Once reserved, the reservation must be guaranteed with a fax-copy of your credit card, along with a signed guarantee. Upon sending the fax, verify receipt of it by telephone. Keep your fax-confirmation page, and get a reservation number: bring them both with you. This detail is crucial. You may need proof of your reservation on a sold-out night. You will seriously bum out if you arrive at your hotel at 3am, following a too-long flight, only to learn you've nowhere to lay your head or have a shower. Don't let it happen to you. (We actually saw this transpire at our hotel in Dubai. The guy was a wreck.)

Hunt for specials on hotels' proprietary websites (if none is available, it typically means occupancy is high). Expedia (www.expedia.com) is pretty good, as is Lastminute (www.lastminute.com); both often have good deals in Dubai. We really like Let's Go (www.reservations.bookhostels.com/letsgo) for finding budget hotels.

NB: Dubai's occupancy rates are the highest in the world, with an annual average of 86% – and that factors in the miserable months of summer. For peak periods (read: winter), book well ahead. If you arrive and need accommodation, there's an office to your left after you pass through customs – but you may be SOL (out of luck).

ROOM RATES

Rates we've quoted are generally rack rates – standard, published, high-season rates. Expect to pay these at peak times and during major events; during city-wide sell-outs, prices spike higher, sometimes as much as 50%. Always ask for the 'best price' or whether there are any specials – generally the hotels won't say unless you ask. If you work for a big company, presenting a business card may qualify you as a corporate client and earn you a substantial discount.

Nearly all hotels in Dubai have private baths; all have air-conditioning. Budget rooms are tiny and have only the basics, with wafer-thin pillows and closet-size bathrooms. Midrange hotel rooms are big enough to unpack two suitcases, and usually have tea- and coffee-making facilities, minibars and extras like flat-panel TVs. Top-end hotels have enough space to throw a cocktail party and inevitably have huge marble bathrooms – some very sexy – with amenities like rainfall showerheads and freestanding oversize bathtubs. Ablutions are a cornerstone of Arab culture: Emiratis love their bathrooms. Even at a two-star, they're usually spotless.

Expect to present your passport at check-in. Hotels are legally required to scan them and file a copy with the CID, Dubai's secret police, so they can track your movements if they want to (welcome to Dubai). Hotels also require you to leave a credit-card authorisation of about Dh500 per night for incidentals. If you don't have a credit card, you must leave a cash deposit.

Hotels charge 20% tax: 10% municipal tax, plus 10% service charge.

DEIRA

Deira is the city's grittiest, most colourful area. Near the neon-lit chaos of the souqs, it's fun for getting lost in back alleys, but horrible for

top picks

VIEWS

- Burj Al Arab (p159)
- Hilton Dubai Creek (below)
- Shangri-La (p158)
- Park Hyatt Dubai (below)
- Jumeirah Beach Hotel (p160)
- Mina A' Salam, Madinat Jumeirah (p160)
- Al-Qasr, Madinat Jumeirah (p159)

taxis. The best hotels front the Creek. Budget hotels are tucked inland along narrow streets. Many hotels provide airport, mall and beach shuttles; inquire when you book. You'll find great deals in Deira, but if you have business elsewhere, you'll be slowed (way) down by traffic; choose Bur Dubai instead.

PARK HYATT DUBAI Map pp56–7 Hotel $$$

☎ 602 1234; www.dubai.park.hyatt.com; Dubai Creek Golf & Yacht Club; s/d Dh2350/2550; 🖥 🖩

Discretion is the watchword at this sprawling low-rise golf resort, where every huge room has a Creek-view balcony. Park is Hyatt's luxury brand, and it's evident in the details: rooms are austerely and artfully styled in greige tones, sand-dune-inspired wave-patterned textiles and Moroccan-led archways. By night, the lobby glows by candlelight. The open-floor-plan bathroom has a giant two-person tub at its centre and a detached enormous shower stall with a waterfall showerhead – ideal for a romantic retreat, but lacking in privacy for shy couples. Downstairs is Dubai's top spa, Amara (p140), and the Dubai Creek Golf Club (p144) surrounds the hotel.

HILTON DUBAI CREEK Map pp54–5 Hotel $$$

☎ 227 1111; www.hilton.com; Baniyas Rd, Rigga; r from Dh1440; 🖥 🖩

These sexy city digs are the best of Deira's accommodation, with swooping wood-panelled walls, leather-padded headboards, grey-granite baths, and fabulous beds with feather-light duvets. The floor-to-ceiling windows provide amazing Creek views – request a no-additional-charge corner room. There's stellar in-room gadgetry (think iPod docking stations) and the ultra-modern design offers a smart alternative to the in-your-face white-marble opulence of

Dubai's other luxury hotels. Its restaurant, Verre by Gordon Ramsay (p107), is Dubai's top table. Fabulous rooftop pool.

HYATT REGENCY DUBAI

Map pp54–5 Hotel $$$

☎ 209 1234; www.dubai.regency.hyatt.com; off Al-Khaleej Rd; r from Dh1200; 🖥 🖩

The granddaddy of Dubai's five-stars opened in 1980. All 414 spiffy guestrooms have sumptuous beds with ultrasoft high-thread-count linens, and giant picture windows overlooking the Palm Deira. Primarily geared toward business travellers, the hotel also has family activities, including mini-golf, tennis, and indoor ice-skating. Traffic is the biggest drawback to staying here.

RADISSON SAS DUBAI Map pp54–5 Hotel $$$

☎ 222 7171; www.dubai.radissonsas.com; Baniyas Rd; s/d from Dh1200; 🖥 🖩

This Creekside stalwart is the city's first five-star. It commands a great location, within walking distance of the souqs and dhow wharves. The Soviet-era-cellblock high-rise architecture is dated, but the rooms (however small) recently got a much-needed renovation and all the basic business-class amenities are in place. The biggest selling point is the restaurants – Sumibiya (p107) for Korean-Japanese, China Club (p109), Shabestan (p107) for Persian and Yum! (p110) for noodles. Great gym too. For these prices you can do better, but this is a solid backup.

AL-BUSTAN ROTANA Map pp56–7 Hotel $$$

☎ 282 0000; www.rotana.com; Casablanca Rd, Al-Garhoud; s/d Dh1150/1200; 🖥 🖩 🏊

The atrium lobby is vintage-1990s, but the spacious rooms are up to date and surprisingly decked-out at this airport hotel, catering primarily to business travellers. Wall-mounted LCD screens, big desks, spotless baths, good mattresses and an oversized pool justify the price, but the location is inconvenient unless you've got an early flight.

SHERATON DEIRA Map pp54–5 Hotel $$

☎ 268 8888; www.starwood.com; Al-Mateena St; s/d 950/1050; 🖥 🖩

Rates are reasonable for the better-than-average business-class amenities at this off-the-beaten-path five-star in Little Iraq. It got a facelift in 2007, and the spiffy decor is fresh, if predictably pastel. Go for the junior suites, if you can score a good rate; they're extra-spacious, with big marble bathrooms and giant tubs. Good service too.

SHERATON DUBAI CREEK
Map pp54–5   Hotel $$

☎ 228 1111; www.starwood.com; Baniyas Rd; s/d Dh950/1050; 🖳 🏊

Floor-to-ceiling windows provide mesmerising Creek vistas at this traditional business-class chain property. There's nothing risky to the beige design scheme, but amenities like flat-panel TVs, DVD players, cushy bed linens and marble baths provide extra comfort. The best views are from tower floors; the food is good, too, especially at Indian Ashiana (p107) and Japanese Creekside (p108).

SUN AND SANDS HOTEL
Map pp56–7   Hotel $$

☎ 223 9000; http://sunandsandsdubai.com; 37 St; s/d Dh900/1000; 🖳 🏊

Better than others in this three-star ghetto of anonymous concrete-block hotels, the Sun and Sands is nonetheless a three-star, which automatically implies quirkier furnishings and so-so service compared to the four- and five-stars listed above. Still, this is a good choice for its price range. Though heavy on chintz, rooms are fresh and well-kept – management takes great care of the place. Bathrooms are the weak point: tiles need re-grouting and fans hum too loudly. Still, it's worth spending the extra Dh200 for the vastly better service and facilities.

CARLTON TOWER HOTEL
Map pp54–5   Hotel $$

☎ 222 7111; www.carltontower.net; Baniyas Rd; s/d/ste Dh800/900/1300, Creek view extra Dh100; 🖳 🏊

Fave of Russian tour groups, this stately hotel has a picturesque Creekside location – pony up Dh100 for a view. Rooms are decorated with blonde-wood and glass-topped furniture; bathrooms are spacious, but tiles need replacing. Still, rates are terrific, the souqs walkable, and the pool refreshing. The nightclubs are cheesy, but there's a great belly dancer in the restaurant.

MARCO POLO HOTEL
Map pp54–5   Hotel $$

☎ 272 0000; www.marcopolohotel.net; Al-Mateena St; s/d Dh 800/900; 🖳 🏊

The off-the-beaten-path Marco Polo is good for exploring the backstreets of Little Iraq. The tourist-class digs are well kept, if simple, and though pillows are lumpy, the white linens are spotless and fresh. Minibar prices are great – only Dh15 for a beer, half the Dubai average. Alas, the pool gets no direct sun in winter; if you're out for a tan, look elsewhere.

RIVIERA HOTEL
Map pp54–5   Hotel $$

☎ 222 2131; www.rivierahotel-dubai.com; Baniyas Rd; s/d Dh700/775, Creek view 750/850; 🖳

The Indian-fancy chintz decor may be dated and tired, but the Creekside location can't be beat. Bathrooms are immaculate, and beds even have down pillows. Aesthetes may bemoan the recessed fluorescent lighting, but splurge on a Creek view and you'll hardly notice. Note: no alcohol.

MOSCOW HOTEL
Map pp56–7   Hotel $$

☎ 228 8222; www.moscowhoteldubai.com; Al-Maktoum Rd; s/d 700/800; 🖳 🏊

An eye-poppingly kitsch slice of Moscow, the lobby sports an over-the-top Bolshoi Theatre–styled dome, a nod to the upwardly mobile Russian tourists it caters to. Rooms are big and colourful, but furnishings border on tacky (think French provincial chairs with vinyl seats). The Russian-by-the-Creek theme continues throughout, with the crowning touch the Red Square nightclub and its mullet-headed Russian rock band.

LANDMARK HOTEL
Map pp54–5   Hotel $$

☎ 228 6666; www.landmarkhotel-dubai.com; just off Baniyas Sq; s/d Dh600/800; 🖳 🏊

Along with its sister, the Landmark Plaza, this is the best of the hotels around Baniyas (or Al-Nasser) Sq, an Indian business district. Rooms are furnished in mass-market blonde wood, but they're clean and have satellite TV and enough room to unpack. The tiny rooftop pool has no loungers, but reveals a delicious panorama of Deira, especially during the call to prayer, when mosques' loudspeakers compete in a blaring cacophony.

ORCHID HOTEL
Map pp56–7   Hotel $

☎ 295 6999; www.orchidhoteldubai.com; off 37 St; s/d Dh500/600; 🏊

The Orchid is popular with Russian and Arab travellers. Rooms are unexceptionally decorated with plain-Jane wood-laminate furniture, and are smaller than at other neighbouring hotels, but service is better here. Rooms are clean, if not immaculate; bar fridges and satellite TV sweeten the deal. Alas, the rooftop pool is t-i-n-y and closes at 6pm but you'll dig the hotel's international club scene – African, Arabic and Indian – all with live bands nightly.

LORDS HOTEL Map pp54–5 Hotel $
☎ 228 9977; lords@emirates.net.ae; Al-Jazeira St; s/d Dh500/600; 🖳 🖭
The pool gets all-day sun at this lacklustre Deira hotel, which is otherwise only notable for its clean rooms, good-size bathrooms and convenient location for souq shopping raids. Rooms are furnished with mass-produced wood-laminate furniture and mismatched fabrics. Keep it on your backup list when other hotels are full, but it's not worth seeking out first. Note: no alcohol.

AL-HIJAZ HERITAGE MOTEL
Map pp54–5 Hotel $
☎ 225 0085; www.alhijazmotel.com; next to Al-Ahmadiya School; s/d/q Dh350/420/650; 🖳
Our favourite budget Deira hotel is run by warm and welcoming innkeepers. Next to Al-Ahmadiya School (p58) and Heritage House (p58), Al-Hijaz occupies a historic building with rooms on two floors surrounding a central courtyard. Rooms are spotless with tiled floors, satellite TV and some charming details like carved wooden armoires and embroidery-edged pillowcases. Suites are huge. The call to prayer from the adjacent mosque is atmospheric, but really loud; bring earplugs. Note: no alcohol.

RAMEE INTERNATIONAL HOTEL
Map pp54–5 Hotel $
☎ 224 0222; rameedxb@emirates.net.ae; 9C St; s/d Dh350/450
This busy hotel off bustling Baniyas Sq attracts tour groups doing Dubai on a budget. It's the usual bland three-star, with dreary hallways and bad lighting, but the rooms are basically clean (though on our last visit, pillows were lumpy and the tub grout black with mildew). Extras include satellite TV, bar fridges and 24-hour room service. Pop in to see the fun Indian bars downstairs.

FLORIDA HOTEL Map pp54–5 Hotel $
☎ 226 8888; www.floridahotels.co.ae; Al-Sabkha Rd; s/d 300/400
The front door opens onto the chaos of Deira's souqs, but inside all is calm and quiet. Rooms are surprisingly clean (evidence, the plastic-wrapped lampshades) and have a few spiffy amenities like stitched-leather side chairs. The carpet needs replacing and bathrooms have dim fluorescent lighting and the occasional mildew spot, but face it, the Florida offers overall good value. Budgeteers: put this one high on your list.

PACIFIC HOTEL Map pp54–5 Hotel $
☎ 227 6700; www.pacifichotel-dubai.com; 115 Al-Sabkha Rd, opposite Sabakha bus station; s/d/tr Dh360/440/520; 🖳
The best things about the Pacific Hotel are firstly, its location near the Creek and secondly, its balconies overlooking the neon-lit hordes roaming the souqs below you. Alas, the lobby is dumpy – expect to see an Indian man napping on the sofa – and rooms are clean but run-down. The paper-thin sheets are scratchy; you'll be happier if you bring your own pillow case. However, friendly management makes up for the shortcomings, as does the wall-mounted satellite TV.

DEIRA PALACE HOTEL Map pp54–5 Hotel $
☎ 229 0120; alkhadari_2010@yahoo.com; 67 St; s/d Dh250/380
Don't be fooled: there's nothing palatial about this bare-bones hotel, though the recently remodelled bathrooms are surprisingly clean. Now it's time to redo the bedrooms and replace the ratty low-pile carpeting and beat-up furniture. But you can't argue about the rock-bottom prices. Bring earplugs: people shout in the echoey marble hallways. Most guests are Africans doing business in the souqs, or backpackers looking for Dubai's gritty underbelly. No visitors after 9pm.

TAXI SIR?
Many four- and five-star hotels in Dubai offer guests dedicated taxi service in chauffeur-driven sedans under contract with the hotel. These 'taxis' have no signage, though they do have meters (if not, don't get in) and generally cost about Dh5 more than a regular taxi, provided there's no slowdown. But when you're stuck in heavy traffic, the meter ticks fast: expect to pay nearly double the fee of a regular cab. If you object to paying more, tell the bell captain you want a regular taxi (you might have to insist). But if you are pressed for time and there are no other cabs available, you'll be grateful for the wheels.

THE CALL TO PRAYER

If you're staying in the older areas of Deira or Bur Dubai, you may be awoken around 4.30am by the inimitable wailing of the *azan*, the Muslim call to prayer, through speakers positioned on the minaret of nearby mosques. It's jarring, to be sure, but there's a haunting beauty to the sound, one that you'll only hear in the Middle East.

Muslims pray five times a day: at dawn; when the sun is directly overhead; when the sun is in the position that creates shadows the same length as the object shadowed; at the beginning of sunset; and at twilight, when the last light of the day disappears over the horizon. The exact times are printed in the daily newspapers and on websites. Once the call has been made, Muslims have half an hour to pray. An exception is made at dawn: after the call they have about 80 minutes in which to wake up, wash and pray, before the sun has risen.

Muslims needn't be near a mosque to pray; they need only face Mecca. If devotees cannot get to a mosque, they'll stop wherever they are and drop to their knees. If you see someone praying, be as unobtrusive as possible, and avoid walking in front of the person. All public buildings, including government departments, libraries, shopping centres and airports, have designated prayer rooms. You'll find a *qibla* (a niche indicating the direction of Mecca) in every hotel room in Dubai, either on the ceiling, desk or bedside table. Better hotels provide prayer rugs with a built-in compass.

When you hear the call to prayer, listen for the phrasing. First comes *Allah-u-akbar*, which means 'God is Great'. This is repeated four times. Next comes *Ashhadu an la illallah ha-illaah* (I testify there is no god but God). This is repeated twice, as is the next line, *Asshadu anna muhammadan rasuulu-ilaah* (I testify that Mohammed is His messenger). Then come two shorter lines, also sung twice: *Hayya ala as-salaah* (Come to prayer) and *Hayya ala al-falaah* (Come to salvation). *Allah-u-akbar* is repeated twice more, before the closing line *Laa ilaah illa allah* (There is no god but God).

The only variation on this standard format is at the dawn call. In this *azan*, after the exhortation to come to salvation, comes the gently nudging, repeated line *As-salaatu khayrun min al nawn*, which translates to 'It is better to pray than to sleep'.

If you're not in a hotel where you can hear the call to prayer, stop by the souqs in Deira and pick up a mosque alarm clock – it's the perfect tchotchke to take home to friends.

HOTEL DELHI DARBAR Map pp54–5   Hotel $
☎ 273 3555; Naif Rd; s/d Dh220/325

There always seems to be luggage piled in the lobby of this Indian-run, budget-basic hotel, but accommodations are better than most you'll find in Deira's neon-lit commercial centre. Though rooms feel a tad run-down, they're spacious and clean, have fridge and TV, and overlook the vibrant street scene. Bathrooms smell vaguely of mildew, with asylum-yellow fluorescent lighting, but they're clean – even if the tubs need reglazing. There's a popular Indian restaurant on the ground floor, and the souqs are a stone's throw away.

DUBAI YOUTH HOSTEL Map p52   Hostel $
☎ 298 8151/61; uaeyha@emirates.net.ae; 39 Al-Nahda Rd; YHA members/nonmembers dm Dh80/90, s Dh170/190, d Dh200/230; 🖳

The only hostel in town has far better facilities than you'd expect. The new wing, with spotless single and double rooms, beats the Deira and Bur Dubai zero-star hotels hands down for comfort. The dorm rooms are more like pre-teen bedrooms, the New House rooms are excellent value – provided you're a YHA member (Dh200 per annum). If you're not a member, it may be more economical to stay in a better-positioned chea-

pie in Deira (particularly considering taxi fares, though you can take the bus too). Still, you won't match the facilities: a pool and a gym, sauna, spa, Jacuzzi, tennis court and billiards room. Catch buses 3, 13, 17 or 31.

BUR DUBAI

Bur Dubai's heritage sights – Bastakia and Bur Dubai Souq – should be on every traveller's list, and the closer you stay to them, the richer your experience of Dubai will be. Alas, with the exception of the dynamic Indian quarter between Khalid bin al-Waleed Rd and Al-Fahidi St, the rest of Bur Dubai feels soulless, full of low-rise concrete-block apartments. There are lots of apartment-hotels here, but few you'd get excited about recommending; Golden Sands (opposite) dominates the market.

top picks

ON A BUDGET

- Al-Hijaz Heritage Motel (opposite)
- Fusion Hotel (p161)
- XVA Art Hotel (p157)

top picks
SWIMMING POOLS

- **One&Only Royal Mirage** (p162)
- **The Palace, Old Town** (opposite)
- **Shangri-La** (p158)
- **Fairmont** (p158)
- **Grand Hyatt** (right)
- **Hilton Dubai Creek** (p152)

RAFFLES DUBAI Map pp64–5   Hotel $$$

☎ 324 8888; www.dubai.raffles.com; Wafi City Mall, Al-Qataiyat Rd; r from Dh3500; 🖵 🖲

Finally a luxury hotel that lives up to the moniker, with service and amenities on a par with the world's top hotels. Built in the shape of a giant pyramid, Raffles is a new Dubai icon. Its magnificent rooms are done in the colours of a Moroccan kilim – deep-blue, burgundy-red and sandy-taupe. Bathrooms are of limestone and sandstone imported from Egypt, with giant sunken tubs and Dubai's biggest rainfall showerheads. Luxury is in the details: complimentary coffee presented with your wake-up call, lighting controlled from a bedside console, Spiegelau-crystal glassware and Bose CD-stereos – the pool deck is even refrigerated. The palatial limestone lobby is ground-zero for spotting Sheikhs feasting at tables spilling over with chocolates and dates. Don't miss the Michelin-star-worthy Fire & Ice (p110) or New Asia Bar (p127), the view lounge at the top of the pyramid.

MÖVENPICK HOTEL BUR DUBAI
Map pp64–5   Hotel $$$

☎ 336 6000; www.movenpick-hotels.com; 19 St; s/d Dh1140/1380; 🖵 🖲

The garish lobby looks like it was decorated by a court jester, with red-leather walls, faux gold-leaf ceilings and a sweeping staircase. Rooms however are midrange business generic, but crisp white duvets and feather pillows compensate for the blandness; spacious bathrooms provide plenty of room. The rooftop pool is good for laps, with grand views from its spacious deck, and the gym has extensive equipment. Note: choose a city-view room or overlook the sunless atrium.

GRAND HYATT DUBAI Map p52   Hotel $$$

☎ 317 1234; www.dubai.grand.hyatt.com; Al-Qataiyat Rd; s/d from Dh1200/1350; 🖵 🖲

The vast white-marble lobby at this behemoth destination resort recreates a tropical rainforest, with dhow hulls hanging from the ceiling. Rooms are more staid, with dark-wood furniture and tasselled draperies, but have all top-end business-class amenities, from robes and slippers to ultrasoft pillow cases of filigreed cotton. Facilities are impressive and include Dubai's biggest swimming pool, extensive palm-tree-studded gardens, a kids' club, tennis courts, a fantastic gym, and several excellent restaurants. Skip the bland suites.

RAMADA HOTEL Map pp62–3   Hotel $$

☎ 351 9999; www.ramadadubai.com; Al-Mankhool Rd; s/d Dh960/1080; 🖵 🖲

The most notable feature of this mid-budget hotel is its striking late-1970s stained-glass feature stretching 10 storeys up the atrium. The 172 split-level rooms are spacious and good for business travellers, but there's nothing compelling about the generic furnishings. Still, visitors like the Ramada for its oversized rooms, central location and excellent in-house gym.

ORIENT GUEST HOUSE
Map pp62–3   Boutique Hotel $$

☎ 351 9111; www.orientguesthouse.com; Al-Fahidi St; r from Dh1000

Tucked down a hidden pedestrian alley in the historic Bastakia Quarter, the Orient captures the feeling of old Dubai. Rooms in the former home surround a central courtyard; each is styled with carved wooden headboards, delicate chandeliers and velvety-soft jewel-tone fabrics. Alas, the bathrooms are tiny and the pillows thin,

top picks
HOTELS FOR SHOPPING

- **Kempinski** (p163)
- **Raffles Dubai** (left)
- **The Palace, Old Town** (opposite)
- **InterContinental** (☎ 701 1111; www.intercontinental.com; Festival City; r from Dh1800; 🖵 🖲)

but the charming service and romantic vibe more than compensate.

CAPITOL HOTEL Map pp62–3 — Hotel $$
☎ 346 0111; www.capitol-hotel.com; Al-Mina Rd, Satwa; s/d Dh800/900; 🖳 🐾
The Capitol stands out for its anonymity: you've seen these rooms a hundred times at airport business-class hotels – comfortable, clean and entirely forgettable. Still, it's a solid back-up choice and well-located near Al-Dhiyafah St, Dubai's best walking street. Request an outside room, or face the sunless atrium. The gym is good, but the rooftop pool gets no afternoon winter sun: tan in the morning.

FOUR POINTS SHERATON DOWNTOWN Map pp62–3 — Hotel $$
☎ 354 3333; www.starwood.com; 4C St, off Mankhool Rd; s/d 800/850; 🖳 🐾
The hyper-masculine, stark-white chrome-and-marble lobby can't quite decide what it's trying to be – contemporary Italian, 1950s modern, or 1970s disco – but rooms at this new mid-budget hotel are spacious enough for a small family. The look is sterile, but extras such as comfy mattresses, big flat-screen TVs, and rooftop gym and pool make up for it. Good value.

GOLDEN SANDS HOTEL APARTMENTS
Map pp62–3 — Apartment Hotel $$
☎ 355 5553; www.goldensandsdubai.com; multiple locations off Mankhool Rd; studio apt from Dh700; 🖳 🐾
Golden Sands has possibly the biggest inventory of hotel-apartments in Dubai. The 12 stand-alone buildings, all boxy concrete structures, see a lot of wear and tear from business travellers. The efficiency-style kitchens are tiny, but include a washer. Alas, not all buildings are wired for high-speed internet, and those that are share a central modem, meaning slow connections; likewise in the business centre. Furnishings are utilitarian and bland. Still, this is a satisfactory landing pad for expats.

FOUR POINTS SHERATON BUR DUBAI
Map pp62–3 — Hotel $$
☎ 397 7444; www.starwood.com; Khalid bin al-Waleed Rd; s/d from Dh700; 🖳 🐾
Despite the gritty sidewalk scene out front, this Four Points (one of three in Dubai) is a reliable business address.

top picks
FOR ROMANCE

- One&Only Royal Mirage (p162)
- XVA Art Hotel (below)
- Raffles Dubai (opposite)
- Park Hyatt Dubai (p152)
- Al-Qasr, Madinat Jumeirah (p159)

Slated for renovation in 2008, rooms at the time of writing were respectably decorated, if small, but furnishings were old. The bed linens were exceptionally good – crisp white cotton duvet covers with plump feather pillows – a rarity in this price range. You'll find an adequate gym, a small pool, a hot tub and a British pub downstairs. The location is convenient for sightseeing, but taxis are hard to hail. Don't miss the excellent on-site Antique Bazaar (p112) Indian restaurant.

XVA ART HOTEL Map pp62–3 — Boutique Hotel $$
☎ 353 5383; www.xvagallery.com; behind Basta Art Café, Al-Musallah Roundabout; s/d/ste Dh650/700/800
Dubai's first guest house occupies a 100-year-old villa, complete with original windtowers, in the heart of the historic Bastakia Quarter. Rooms open onto a courtyard doubling as a gallery and café. Each one is different, but all are decked out with local artwork, arabesque flourishes and rich colours. Best of all, you get the feeling of staying in a real Arabian guest house. Put XVA at the top of your list. No TVs. No alcohol.

SHEIKH ZAYED ROAD
Lined with giant towers, Sheikh Zayed Rd's biggest selling point is location: it's at the city's geographic centrepoint, making it great for exploring. Rates skew high, but fluctuate wildly with demand. Alas, rush-hour traffic is terrible.

THE PALACE, OLD TOWN
Map pp72–3 — Hotel $$$
☎ 428 7888; www.sofitel.com; Old Town, Downtown Burj Dubai; r from Dh2200; 🖳 🐾
In the shadow of the Burj Dubai, the Palace is among the city's top new luxury hotels.

Silk-clad hostesses greet you with cool towels and fresh juice; a white-gloved butler escorts you to your room. Styled in soothing earth tones, the look is chic and understated – a refreshing change from Dubai's usual hit-you-over-the-head aesthetic. Bathrooms have inlaid marble floors, mother-of-pearl soap dishes, and Frisbee-sized rainfall showerheads. Plan to linger long by the vast palm-lined swimming pool while gazing up at the world's tallest tower.

FAIRMONT Map pp72–3   Hotel $$$
☎ 332 5555; www.fairmont.com; Sheikh Zayed Rd; s/d Dh2000/2200; 🖵 🌊

The Fairmont is a distinctive sight at night when its four-poster towers are illuminated by changing coloured lights. There's nothing understated about this place, from the chrome-and-marble lobby to the white-leather desk chairs that recall Joan Collins' office in *Dynasty* (a renovation is slated for 2008). Still, it's a landmark hotel, with amenities to match, including float-away beds, Bose wave radios and deep bathtubs. The outlets are exceptional, especially the Exchange Grill (p115).

EMIRATES TOWERS Map pp72–3   Hotel $$$
☎ 330 0000; www.emiratestowershotel.com; Sheikh Zayed Rd; d from Dh2160; 🖵 🌊

Arguably the top business hotel in the Middle East, Emirates Towers is one of Dubai's iconic hotels. The black-and-grey aesthetic is ultra-masculine and heavy on angular lines, and like the Shangri-La (right), the room layout is sleek and functional with fabulous in-room gadgets, chief among them a Bang & Olufsen TV. Club-executive rooms even have a radio-frequency USB plug to broadcast tunes from your computer to the TV. Alas, lower-floor bathrooms are disappointingly small. Solo women travellers should book the Chopard ladies' floor, where pink replaces grey and in-bath fridges let you chill your thousand-dollar face creams. Service is among Dubai's best.

QAMARDEEN Map pp72–3   Hotel $$$
☎ 428 6888; www.southernsun.com; Burj Dubai Blvd, Downtown Burj Dubai; s/d Dh1950/2000; 🖵 🌊

Sister to the Al-Manzil, the Qamardeen manages to be hip but not overbearing, with bold splashes of colour in its soaring

lobby and big rooms. The look borders on chain-store modern, but it's fresh, with ultra-suede upholstery, bright-white linens and zero clutter. The palm-lined, blue-tiled pool is fab. Like its sister – both of them four-stars – it's not worth Dh2000, but you can often score way better rates.

AL-MANZIL Map pp72–3   Hotel $$$
☎ 428 5888; www.southernsun.com; Old Town, Downtown Burj Dubai; s/d Dh1950/2000; 🖵 🌊

Arabesque meets mid-century modern at Al-Manzil. The open-floor-plan rooms (read: no wall between the bed and bath) are sexy, but not for shy couples. Baths sport giant rainfall showerheads and big soaking tubs surrounded by glass walls; beds have soft down duvets and crisp white-cotton sheets. The colour scheme is pure Dubai: ten shades of off-white. You'll love the 24-hour pool, but the deck needs more loungers.

AL-MUROOJ ROTANA HOTEL & SUITES Map pp72–3   Hotel/Apartment-Hotel $$$
☎ 321 1111; www.rotana.com; Al-Saffa St; s/d 1300/1500; hotel apt from Dh2000; 🖵 🌊

The overdone lobby clashes with itself and rooms can't decide whether they're formal-fancy or trendy, but overlook these sins in favour of location and in-room comforts like oversized tubs and big desks, a boon for business travellers. Note: book a 'complex view' overlooking the swimming pool, or deal with construction noise. The next-door hotel-apartments are sterile in design, but functional.

DUSIT DUBAI Map pp72–3   Hotel $$$
☎ 343 3333; www.dusit.com; Sheikh Zayed Rd, next to Interchange No 1; s/d Dh1500/1600; 🖵 🌊

Shaped like an upside-down tuning fork, this is one of Dubai's most architecturally dramatic towers. The target market is the business traveller; rooms have big desks and oversized leather chairs, and the usual high-end amenities, like feather-light down pillows. Upper-floor views are stellar. The rooftop pool is good for laps (though overhead trusses partially block the sun). Onsite Benjarong (p115) is one of the city's top Thai tables.

SHANGRI-LA Map pp72–3   Hotel $$
☎ 343 8888; www.shangri-la.com; Sheikh Zayed Rd; s/d from Dh1100/1200; 🖵 🌊

Celebrities favour the Shangri-La. The understatedly sexy rooms in the 43-storey tower are like a Ferrari: everything is perfectly placed. The bedside console lets you adjust the lighting, set the a/c and do everything but close the curtains. Art is the focal point opposite the bed, not a giant flat-screen TV, and marble is conspicuously absent in the bath, replaced by smart grey-granite tiles. The rooftop pool is a happening gathering place for rich locals, and the stellar French-Vietnamese Hoi An (p115) merits a special trip. Great gym.

NOVOTEL WORLD TRADE CENTRE
Map pp72–3   Hotel $$
☎ 332 0000; www.novotel.com; behind World Trade Centre, Sheikh Zayed Rd; d from Dh860; 🖳 🕾
The no-nonsense Novotel, behind the Sheikh Zayed strip, adjoins the convention centre. Rooms are smallish, but there's lots of desk space and a sofa. Furnishings are dated and amenities limited (no washcloths in the bath, wafer-thin soap, lumpy pillows), but the location is central and service friendly. The rectangular swimming pool is sufficient for laps, and there's a pretty good gym with circuit-training equipment.

IBIS WORLD TRADE CENTRE
Map pp72–3   Hotel $
☎ 332 4444; www.ibishotel.com; behind World Trade Centre, Sheikh Zayed Rd; d from Dh450; 🖳
Surprisingly stylish, this hotel's lobby makes promises the small rooms can't keep. But at this price and location, it's the best-value digs in Dubai. Sure, it'll probably be filled with convention-goers here for a plastics conference, and there are no views or a pool, but if our next cancelled flight sees us shuttled to an Ibis as good as this, we'll sleep happy.

top picks
HOTEL DINING
- Shangri-La (opposite)
- One&Only Royal Mirage (p162)
- Radisson SAS Dubai (p152)
- Grosvenor House (p162)
- Hilton Dubai Creek (p152)

JUMEIRAH

The primary advantage of staying in Jumeirah is its oh-so-civilized and calm beachside location. This is where Emiratis live in big villas. Note: heritage sights lie a good 20 minutes away.

BURJ AL ARAB Map pp76–7   Hotel $$$
☎ 301 7111; www.burj-al-arab.com; Jumeirah Rd, Umm Suqeim; r from Dh8500; 🖳 🕾
We adore the exterior of Dubai's iconic sail-shaped hotel, but when we first saw the interior, we laughed and nicknamed it the Bourgeois à l'Arabe. Decorated in the Sheik's favourite colours – gold (of course), royal blue and blood red – it's the first-choice hotel of billionaire Russians of dubious background (one such guest was murdered in his suite here; Google 'murder at the Burj'). Rooms are l-u-s-h, with moiré silk walls, mirrored ceilings over the beds, curlicue high-backed velvet chairs, and inlaid bathroom tiles displaying scenes of Venice. But as for this seven-star-hotel business, we disagree: despite a six-to-one employee-guest ratio, the doormen didn't even hold the door on our last visit. Okay, okay – there are advantages to staying here, like being whisked through customs at the airport and the Rolls Royce limousine-transfer service, but if you can afford to stay here, you probably already have a Bentley. We suggest you stay at Raffles (p156) and come for drinks in the Star Trek-meets-Liberace Skyview Bar (reservations required but good luck getting an operator to pick up) and drop a hundred dollars on drinks instead of two thousand on a room.

AL-QASR, MADINAT JUMEIRAH
Map pp76–7   Resort $$$
☎ 366 8888; www.madinatjumeirah.com; Al-Sufouh Rd, Umm Suqeim; d from Dh3400; 🖳 🕾
Sister to Mina A' Salam (p160) Al-Qasr was styled after an Arabian summer palace. Details are extraordinary, like the lobby's Austrian-crystal chandeliers reflecting rainbows onto mirror-polished inlaid-marble floors. Rooms are styled with heavy arabesque architectural flourishes, rich colours, and cushy furnishings, including sumptuous beds and his-and-her bathroom amenities. The side-by-side balconies lack privacy, but overlook the grand display of the Madinat (p75). Excellent service, great beach.

DESERT DREAMS

Just an hour from the traffic jams, construction sites and megamalls are two stellar desert resorts. If you're craving a little peace and quiet, and are prepared to spend some serious money, these hotels will show you a calmer, less-hurried side of Dubai.

Bab al-Shams Desert Resort & Spa (Map p167; ☎ 832 6699; near Endurance Villlage; r from 2400) Bab al-Shams resort is the tonic for tourists seeking to indulge their *Arabian Nights* fantasies. While the Al-Hadheerah restaurant whirls dervishes, flies falcons, paints henna and rides camels in a production of Disneyesque proportions, the hotel is more restrained; it's a labyrinthine layout displaying both Gulf and Moorish influences. Rooms are gorgeous, spacious and evocatively earthy, with pillars, lanterns, paintings of desert landscapes and prettily patterned Bedouin-style cushions. Beyond desert tours, there's not a lot to do but cosy up with a book in hidden coves and alluring courtyards. There's a wonderful infinity pool where the water appears to merge with the desertscape; the luscious, if expensive, Satori Spa; an archery range; and Sinbad's Club, which entertains kids from 9am to 6pm. We've heard murmurs that service is occasionally less than attentive, but if you get a good rate, a short stay will add dimension to your Dubai break.

Al Maha Desert Resort & Spa (Map p167; ☎ 303 4222; on Dubai–Al-Ain Rd; ste from Dh6170) When you really want to escape, book the most exclusive hotel in the emirate. Al-Maha is in the Dubai Desert Conservation Reserve (p166), where there's nothing for miles but rolling dunes. Privacy is the watchword: children under 12 and visitors aren't allowed; every suite comes with its own pool; and a three-to-one staff-to-guest ratio ensures proper pampering. Several outdoor activities are included in the room rate, including desert tours and camel rides; a conservation expert is on-hand to answer questions about the reserve. The 40 suites are like small houses, with elegant furnishings and intricate design flourishes, and the spa is tailor-made for sustained luxuriating. Dine on private verandas while looking at peach-coloured dunes, punctuated by mountains and grazing white oryx and gazelles. Paint, paper and easels are in your suite should you be inspired to sit on your balcony and capture the scene. Expect to shell out big money for the privilege of staying here.

MINA A' SALAM, MADINAT JUMEIRAH
Map pp76–7   Resort $$$

☎ 366 8888; www.madinatjumeirah.com; Al-Sufouh Rd; r from Dh3000; 🖳 🛋
The entry-level hotel at the behemoth Madinat Jumeirah resort (which also includes Al-Qasr and Dar al-Masyaf) feels less palatial than its sisters (eg gold paint instead of gold leaf) but every spacious room has a private sea-facing balcony and the same luxe bed linens as the other properties. The best thing about staying at the Madinat (p75) is the sense of place. Yes, it's Disneyesque, but it's the only megaproject in Dubai that's actually finished.

JUMEIRAH BEACH HOTEL
Map pp76–7   Resort $$$

☎ 348 0000; www.jumeirahbeachhotel.com; Jumeirah Rd, Umm Suqeim; s/d Dh2900/3000; 🖳 🛋
The most family-friendly of the Jumeirah Properties is shaped like a giant wave. The beach is huge (nearly 1km long), but the rooms need help: their bland pastel colour scheme is tired, as are their furnishings. Stellar Gulf views make up for some of the designer's missteps, as does the better-than-average service. Kids go nuts for the adjoining Wild Wadi Waterpark (p143).

DUBAI MARINE BEACH RESORT & SPA
Map pp76–7   Resort $$$

☎ 346 1111; www.dxbmarine.com; Jumeirah Rd, Jumeirah; r from Dh2000; 🖳 🛋
You'll forgive the vintage-1980s condo box architecture when you consider the convenience of staying halfway between Deira and New Dubai at this compact beachside resort with meandering gardens, terrific restaurants and nightclubs, three pools, a well-equipped gym and a small sandy beach. Rooms are comfy, but display bland business-class design – it's the facilities that are great.

LA MAISON D'HÔTES
Map pp76–7   Boutique Hotel $$

☎ 344 1838; www.lamaisondhotesdubai.com; 83B St, off Al-Urouba; s/d Dh850/950, family ste Dh950/1050; 🖳 🛋
At last Dubai has a real boutique hotel, where you can live like a rich local at budget prices. In a residential neighbourhood near Jumeirah's shops, La Maison's quietly sophisticated, Arabian-style villas sit behind bougainvillea-covered walls, offering a great alternative to Dubai's behemoth hotels. Rooms are individually styled with oriental rugs, canopy beds and rich fabrics; mani-

cured gardens surround both swimming pools. Marvellous privacy and sense of place. Good onsite country-French restaurant.

RYDGES PLAZA Map pp62–3 Hotel $$
☎ 398 2222; www.rydges.com; Satwa Roundabout; s/d Dh650/750; ⬚ ⬚
Along Al-Dhiyafah Rd, Dubai's most dynamic walking street, Rydges Plaza stands out for its respectable English-style dark-wood decor, an aesthetic soothing to squeamish travellers. The sheets are thin, but bathrooms have big showerheads and oversized shower stalls. The location is central – a quick hop to the beach or Deira – and taxis are plentiful in the off hours. The health club has great circuit-training machines; the pool is good for laps.

FUSION HOTEL Map pp76–7 Boutique Hotel $
☎ 478 7539; www.fusionhotels.com; off Al-Wasl Rd; s/d Dh450/550; ⬚

DEBUNKING THE FIVE-STAR MYTH: WHEN BUSINESS CLASS MASQUERADES AS FIRST John A Vlahides

From the iconic sail-shaped Burj Al Arab to the pyramid-shaped Raffles, Dubai is home to some of the world's most instantly recognisable hotels. But does the service measure up to the facilities? Some come close, but no Dubai hotel I found merits the rarefied ranking of a real five-star.

What constitutes true five-star service? In short, the primary difference between four- and five-star service lies in the anticipation of a guest's needs: a good hotel provides you with what you want before you know you want it. Here's an example. You're staying at a city hotel, say, in London and you step outside just as it starts to rain. Before you even ask, the doorman offers you an umbrella. Sure, any good four-star hotel stocks umbrellas, but only the five-star will thrust one into your hand at the exact moment that you need it, without you having to ask.

Dubai's hotels are staffed by inexperienced youths from developing countries, many of whom had never set foot inside a luxury hotel before working in one. Few employees speak the same language and are forced to communicate in English, their second or even third language. They can't rely on shared cultural gestures and nonverbal cues: misunderstandings constantly occur. Employees don't know basic hotel lingo, such as 'feather pillow' or 'alarm clock', let alone 'iPod docking station' or 'ethernet cable'.

Dubai Tourism and Commerce Marketing (DTCM) determines the star level of the city's hotels, but the system is based entirely on facilities. Thus, many hotels in Dubai are classed as five-stars. However, classification systems used elsewhere in the world, by organisations such as Michelin (in Europe, the UK and elsewhere) and Mobil Travel Guides (in North America), are based on anonymous visits by inspectors, as well as facilities. This makes the third Michelin star, or the fifth Mobil star, hard to get.

When I visited the hotels reviewed in this guidebook, I worked like a Michelin or Mobil inspector, considering service as well as facilities. I gave each hotel the benefit of the doubt by assuming it a five-star until it proved itself otherwise. Then I deducted points. I deducted a lot of points in Dubai.

Let's take the Burj Al Arab, the hotel most famous for hyping itself as the world's only 'seven-star' hotel. Psha, say I. To my eye, it's a four-star. Why? The doorman was missing in action, and nobody held the door for me when I arrived, even though a battalion of valets stood by as I approached, one within arm's distance of the front door. He smiled at me, then stood with his arms at his sides and watched as I opened the door myself. A small detail, yes, but the fifth star is entirely about small details. And at US$2500 a night, there's no room for a mistake such as this, one which a demanding guest would consider a discourtesy.

The reason the valet didn't hold the door is at the heart of why Dubai's five-star-hotel service is weak: hotel employees live in fear of losing their employer-sponsored work visas, so they dare not go off script. The valet is hired to park cars, not open doors. But at a proper five-star, employees must be nimble, take initiative: honour first the guest, then the employee handbook.

The true measure of a hotel's service lies in how it handles problems. Anyone can steer a ship in calm seas, but only a master can navigate a gale. Thus, I present complex service requests when I visit a hotel. I won't reveal tactics, but I will say which hotels responded best. The number-one property I found in Dubai is Raffles Dubai (p156). Others that placed include Emirates Towers (p158); One&Only Royal Mirage (p162); The Palace, Old Town (p157); Burj Al Arab (p159); Al-Qasr (p159); and Shangri-La (p158). Fear not. You probably won't have any problems with the service at your hotel, unless you're particularly demanding, in which case, please take notes and send them my way.

Before becoming a guidebook writer, John A Vlahides was a senior concierge at a luxury hotel, and a member of Les Clefs d'Or, the international union of the world's elite concierges.

DUBAI'S DRAWING BOARD...

Five-star hotel openings in Dubai are as common as fashion shows in Paris – and they're greeted with nearly as much fanfare: Sheikh Mohammed himself personally inspects every one. Here's a short list of the big-name projects that are under way.

Armani Hotel (www.armanihotels.com) Another feather in Dubai's cap, Giorgio Armani will open his first hotel in the world's tallest tower, the Burj Dubai. The colour scheme in the mock-ups looks bland (how many shades of brown are there, anyway?) but with views like these, you'll hardly notice the furniture. Due 2008.

Hydropolis (www.hydropolis.com) If rumour is any indicator, the world's first underwater hotel seems a little too...er, fishy for us to believe. The date keeps getting pushed further back, and we'll be surprised if the hotel ever actually materialises. Opening TBA.

Palazzo Versace (www.palazzoversace.ae) Versace made its first foray into hotels on the glitzy Gold Coast, so it's fitting that the brand's second property should be located in Dubai, on the oil coast. The pedicured toes of guests will be spared the city's notoriously hot sands: plans are afoot for temperature-controlled sand. Due 2008.

Palm Trump International Hotel Publicity-magnet and developer Donald Trump is a natural for Dubai. So is his gold tulip-shaped hotel on the Palm Jumeirah, which actually looks more like several upended cockroaches covered in gold leaf. Opening TBA.

Atlantis The Palm (www.atlantisthepalm.com) This is one project we can't get behind. Also on the Palm Jumeirah, the Atlantis hauled 28 live dolphins 30 hours by air from the Solomon Islands to entertain guests in its new water park, despite protestations from environmental groups. Think twice before spending your money here. Opening 2008.

Live like a local at this remarkably well-priced B&B villa in a residential area. Though some of the austerely decorated rooms could use some upgrades, like armoires instead of clothes racks, rates are terrific for what you get – privacy, space, breakfast and, best of all, the sense that you're a guest in someone's home.

NEW DUBAI

The furthermost reaches of the city, New Dubai is where the beach hotels are concentrated. Inland lie several enormous malls and hotels good for shopping holidays.

ONE&ONLY ROYAL MIRAGE

Map pp82–3   Resort $$$

☎ 399 9999; www.oneandonlyresorts.com; Al-Sufouh Rd; Palace/Arabian Court r from Dh2670/2930, Residence & Spa r from Dh4260; 🖳 🖳

Our favourite beach resort, the Royal Mirage consists of three parts: the Palace, done in Moorish style; the Arabian Court, which is more pan-Arabian; and the Residence & Spa, with its majestic spa and *hammam*. All the rooms face the sea, and though cushy, they lack the wow-factor of some of Dubai's flashier hotels, which is just why we like them: they're tasteful. Spend your days meandering through the lush palm-lined gardens, lollygagging in a cabana beside the giant pool, or strolling the 1km private

beach. You may never leave the grounds. The bars and restaurants are among Dubai's best. Note: score the best rates through tour operators and consolidators.

GROSVENOR HOUSE   Map pp82–3   Hotel $$$

☎ 399 8888; www.grosvenorhouse.lemeridien .com; Dubai Marina; r from Dh2500; 🖳 🖳

Grosvenor House was the first hotel to open among the jumble of the Marina's sky-punching towers. Though there is a disconcerting amount of building still going on around the hotel, all rooms have drop-dead views over The Palm development, a fascinating sight. The look is sleek and angular, with black-wood and chrome furniture, giant flat-panel TVs and lots of high-tech gadgetry. Beds have zillion-thread-count linens and even come with a pillow menu. Downstairs is the famous Buddha Bar (p130). One drawback: the beach is across the road and shared with Le Royal Meridien – if screaming kids don't factor into your holiday vision, choose the Royal Mirage or Westin.

LE ROYAL MERIDIEN   Map pp82–3   Resort $$$

☎ 399 5555; www.leroyalmeridien-dubai.com; Al-Sufouh Rd; r from Dh2350; 🖳 🖳

A giant stretch of beach and extensive gardens are the standout features of this tower-hotel resort with three swimming pools, spa, top-notch health-club facilities, numerous restaurants and a bar every 50m. Though kids have their own dedicated pool, they're everywhere: this is not a place for honeymooning couples, but families are very happy.

RITZ-CARLTON DUBAI Map pp82–3 Hotel $$$
☎ 399 4000; www.ritzcarlton.com; Al-Sufouh Rd; r from Dh2300; 🖥 🏊

The first Ritz-Carlton in the Middle East opened in 1998, when New Dubai was still the middle of nowhere. Now high-rises loom above, but the mature gardens and tall palms create a visual berm. The Mediterranean villa–style resort is typical of the chain's restrained and elegant European style – conservative, but cushy – with plush fabrics, marble foyers and Colonial-style hardwood furniture. All 138 rooms face the gardens and sea beyond. Spend the day by one of three pools or the expansive beach.

WESTIN MINA SEYAHI Map pp82–3 Resort $$$
☎ 399 4141; www.starwood.com; Al-Sufouh Rd; r from Dh2000; 🖥 🏊

The top choice for water-sports enthusiasts, this spiffy beach resort sits smack next to the yacht harbour and aesthetically appears like a cross between a Sheikh's summer palace and an Italian palazzo – big and angular, topped with Arabian-style wind-towers, and surrounded by expansive beachfront grounds. The oversized, hyper-masculine rooms look sharp – clean lines, chunky furniture, and chocolate-brown and charcoal-grey accents. Oversized desks reveal that this is also a business hotel. As at all Westins, the biggest selling point is the ultracush Heavenly Bed. Baths have enough marble to sink the QE2, which will moor permanently in view of the ocean-view rooms. The hotel shares facilities with the neighbouring Le Meridien Mina Seyahi (right).

top picks

BOUTIQUE HOTELS

- XVA Art Hotel (p157)
- La Maison d'Hôtes (p160)
- Orient Guest House (p156)
- Fusion Hotel (p161)

LE MERIDIEN MINA SEYAHI RESORT
Map pp82–3 Resort $$$
☎ 399 3333, watersports centre 318 1372; www.lemeridien-minaseyahi.com; Al-Sufouh Rd; r from Dh1800, with sea view Dh2000; 🖥 🏊

Families love this beachfront hotel for its extensive activities, from diving to tennis. It has a giant freeform pool, meandering palm-tree-lined gardens and a big beach. All 210 rooms are in an ugly, dated tower; they're comfortable enough, but frankly need renovating. Better to choose the neighbouring Westin, which shares facilities.

KEMPINSKI Map pp82–3 Hotel $$$
☎ 341 0000; www.kempinski-dubai.com; Al-Barsha; r from Dh1600; 🖥 🏊

Adjoining the Mall of the Emirates, the Kempinski is tops for a shopping holiday. The cavernous white-marble lobby is predictable. What stands out are the rooms' bathrooms: tubs are enormous, as are the travertine, sit-down shower stalls and their rainfall showerheads. Pretend you're in Aspen in the premium 'Ski Chalet' rooms overlooking Ski Dubai; alas, they get no sun. Good gym. Great beds.

HILTON DUBAI JUMEIRAH
Map pp82–3 Resort $$$
☎ 399 1111; www.hilton.com; Al-Sufouh Rd; r from Dh1500; 🖥 🏊

Though overshadowed by the massive Jumeirah Beach Residence on its inland side, the Hilton remains a good choice for a family vacation. Rooms are nothing special – think pastel boxes – but most face the sea, and it has a generous stretch of beach, a playground, baby-sitting, casual eateries and kids' activities. The hotel's top restaurant, BiCE (p120), serves the most authentic Italian in Dubai.

CORP EXECUTIVE HOTEL
Map pp82–3 Apartment Hotel $
☎ 341 7474; www.boutiquehotelsandresorts.com; Al-Barsha; r from Dh600; 🖥 🏊

Despite the lobby's annoying stadium lighting, the Corp is a solid, if sterile, place to stay when you need an apartment hotel in the middle of Dubai's ever-extending city limits. Appliances are new, beds comfy and the washing machine a godsend. And it's right next to the Mall of the Emirates. Tip: hail taxis at the nearby Kempinski Hotel.

DESERT SAFARIS & DAY TRIPS

DESERT SAFARIS

It may be one of the most urbanised countries in the world, but the United Arab Emirates is extremely proud of its Bedouin heritage and its people retain a strong affinity for the desert.

In the pre-oil age, life was harsh for Bedouin tribes in what was then the Trucial States. Food and water were difficult to obtain and living conditions were very simple, and uncomfortable at the height of summer. Bedouins would live in tents made from goat or camel hair, dig for water, and use falcons to hunt for birds and hares to supplement their basic diet of dates and camel milk. Those living on settlements had to pool their resources in order to survive, and a sense of community spirit imbued Bedouins with the qualities of hospitality and generosity. Soon after the discovery of oil, the government built modern houses, roads, schools and hospitals for Dubai's desert-dwellers, but the traditions and culture of life in the desert – from falconry to song and dance – remain intact.

A trip to the desert is an essential part of any Dubai holiday. If you can get some distance from the main road, the emptiness, enormity and tranquillity of the landscape can be breathtaking, with the yellow ochre dunes rippling gently in the wind and undulating as far as the eye can see. The country's biggest sand dune, Moreeb Hill, is in Liwa, on the edge of the vast expanse known as Rub' Al-Khali, the Empty Quarter. If you've read *Arabian Sands,* Wilfred Thesiger's mesmerising account of his journeys across the Empty Quarter and experiences living with nomadic Bedouins, a trip to Liwa will bring the book to life. That middle-of-nowhere satisfaction offered by the Empty Quarter is harder to come by when you're close to Dubai, although there are plenty of quiet spots alongside the road to Hatta.

Many organised desert safaris are a little disappointing. The tour operators usually hire drivers rather than guides and they often know next to nothing about Bedouin culture or the desert environment. It's dispiriting, but don't let this put you off. Even a personality-free tour of the desert will show you what's underneath all the new developments, and emphasise just how remarkable the city's rapid growth has been.

ACTIVITIES
Camping

There are no commercial campsites in Dubai but pitching up in the desert is a popular local pastime and great fun. If you've got a 4WD, the possibilities are fantastic. You can head to the windswept sand dunes of Liwa, the wadis near Hatta, the mountains of Ras al-Khaimah or the beaches of Fujairah. If you don't have a 4WD, you can still find some beautiful spots within walking distance of well-paved roads.

DUBAI DESERT CONSERVATION RESERVE

Move over Dubailand – the largest project in Dubai to date, at least in terms of square kilometres, is one we hear practically nothing about. At 225 sq km, the Dubai Desert Conservation Reserve (www.ddcr.org) accounts for five percent of the emirate's total land. It's a national park, where the primary goal is to protect the desert's biodiversity.

Dubai's approach to environmentalism is characteristically commercial. The DDCR is managed and funded by an airline – a major supplier of climate change – and its super-luxurious resort inside the reserve. But Emirates, who initiated the project, have done a spectacularly good job on the DDCR and now other countries are studying Al-Maha as a model for luxury sector eco-tourism. Since its establishment in 1999, the reserve has reintroduced mountain gazelles and sand gazelles to Dubai's desert, and the Arabian oryx, which almost disappeared completely a few decades ago, now number over 300 and love nothing more than sitting next to Al-Maha's infinity pools.

The DDCR is divided into four zones. In the first zone, all human intervention is prohibited, and in the second only very limited operations are allowed to take place. The third zone is only open to resort guests and the fourth is open to a small number of desert tour operators including Arabian Adventures (p169), Alpha Tours (p169) and Lama Dubai (p170). If you can't afford a villa at Al-Maha – and very few people can – going on a tour with one of these companies is the only way you'll get in.

THE FRAGILE DESERT

An unfortunate consequence of the rapid growth of Dubai's tourism industry is that the desert is being damaged. It is an extremely fragile ecosystem and home to hundreds of species. In the parts of the desert where topsoil has been damaged by 4WDs, very little lives or grows. The Bedouin people have always had a huge amount of respect for the desert, but the desert is getting scarcer as the development of Dubai continues apace. The biggest problem is pollution. Hundreds of camels die every year due to eating plastic bags carelessly dumped in the desert. The lumps of calcified plastic frequently found in the stomachs of dead camels can weigh up to 60kg.

By supporting the Dubai Desert Conservation Reserve (p166) and limiting the area that desert safari companies can operate in to the environs of Al-Awir, the government is taking important steps to protect the environment. To do your bit, stick to tracks wherever possible when driving off-road and avoid damaging vegetation. Don't drive in *wadis* because these are important sources of drinking water and can be polluted by oil and grease from cars. And take your rubbish home with you.

It should go without saying that a camping trip between May and September is likely to be extremely uncomfortable – summer nights in the Emirates are hot and humid. Make sure you are adequately equipped. You should carry a fully-charged mobile phone for your safety, all the necessary maps (and navigation equipment if you're going off-road), sunscreen, insect repellent and plenty of water. If you go camping in December or January, make sure you're prepared for cold night-time weather.

Some of the best destinations for camping are Huwaylat, a tiny village surrounded by wadis; Qarn Nazwa, a rocky outcrop in the desert; Jebel Rawdah, a mountain near the Omani border in an area known as 'Death Valley'; and Khor Khalba, renowned for its beautiful mangrove forests and excellent bird-watching. It's worth picking up Dariush Zandi's excellent guide *Off-Road in the Emirates*. It has the most accurate, up-to-date and detailed directions of any of the guides around.

Off-Road Driving

Off-road driving in the desert, sometimes known as dune-bashing, is hugely popular in Dubai. At weekends, the city's traffic-tired workers zip down the Dubai–Hatta road and unleash their pent-up energy on the nearby sand dunes. The best known of these dunes has been nicknamed 'Big Red', and this ruby-red heap of sand halfway to Hatta is heaven for petrolheads. Pitting your 2½ tonnes of machinery against this giant clenched fist of a dune is thrilling, although you won't be doing the environment any favours (see boxed text, above).

All the major car hire companies (p179) can provide 4WD vehicles. Expect to pay in the region of Dh800 for 24 hours in the company of a Toyota Land Cruiser or a Jeep Cherokee, plus CDW (Collision Damage Waiver) of Dh100, an extra Dh20 for personal insurance, and an extra Dh50 if you require comprehensive insurance. For more information on car insurance, see p179.

If you're driving off-road for the first time, you should ideally travel as part of an entourage, with other cars and drivers providing safety in numbers. You'll also need up-to-date maps (Explorer Publishing's *Off-Road Map*, Dh30, is as detailed as they get), a tow rope, a spade, a shovel and plenty of water. Don't be overambitious – even if you're an expert off-road driver, your car may not be able to handle the biggest bumps.

We strongly recommend a few hours of training before you drive off-road for the first time. Knowledge of the basics will give you the confidence to drive safely on unpredictable terrain.

OFF-ROAD DRIVING INSTRUCTION

On all courses drivers must be over 25 and hold an appropriate driving licence that is valid for at least another year.

Al Futtaim Training Centre (Map pp56–7; ☎ 285 0455; www.traininguae.com; Al-Garhoud, Deira) One-day desert driving courses are Dh300 per person or Dh450 for two people. Additional passengers are charged at Dh150 per person. The centre doesn't provide training vehicles, so you'll need your own car.

Arabian Adventures (Map pp72–3; ☎ 303 4888; www.arabian-adventures.com; Emirates Holidays Bldg, Sheikh Zayed Rd) This company runs desert driving courses to help get you off the road safely. A half-day course taught by an experienced desert driver costs Dh1990 and a full-day is Dh2890, and these prices cover four people in the vehicle.

Emirates Driving Institute (Map pp56–7; ☎ 263 1100; www.edi-uae.com; Near Al-Bustan Center, Al-Qusais, Deira) The EDI's desert driving courses are very thorough nd offer fantastic value for money. A full-day course in ne of its vehicles costs Dh200 (Dh250 on Fridays) and includes lunch. There's a maximum of four students per class.

Camel Riding

f you're on your first trip to the Middle East, a short camel ride is pretty much compulsory. It's cheesy, clichéd and ever-so-slightly ncomfortable, but a souvenir shot of you nd your humped pal will delight your family ack home and do wonders for your Facebook rofile. If you visit during the Dubai Shopping Festival, it's likely you'll find a couple of sad sack camels moping around Heritage Village (p58) to provide tourists with photo pportunities. Pretty much all the desert safari perators, as well as Al-Hadheerah restaurant t Bab al-Shams (p160), can arrange for you to pend a couple of minutes on a camel's back. f you'd like to develop a more meaningful elationship with a camel, many of the tour perators listed in Organised Tours (below) can rrange one-hour rides in the desert.

Sand Boarding/Skiing

Where else in the world can you ski on snow in he morning and ski on sand in the afternoon? andboarding and sand-skiing are very similar o snowboarding and skiing, only slower, slipperier and scratchier. While sand-skiing has et to really take off, sandboarding now has ts own world championships – do a search on YouTube for the dazzling highlights.

To start sand-slaloming, Desert Rangers (Map p72–3; ☎ 340 2408; www.desertrangers.com; Dubai Garden entre, Sheikh Zayed Rd) organises sandboarding saaris (adult/child Dh195/135) most mornings of the week. Net Tours & Travels (Map pp56–7; ☎ 266 655; www.nettoursdubai.com; Al-Bakhit Centre, Abu Baker aliddiq Rd) runs regular sand-skiing trips (adult/ hild Dh190/165).

ORGANISED TOURS

At first glance, there's little to choose between most of the desert safari operators in Dubai. They all offer daily half-day trips that begin n the middle of the afternoon and end at round 10pm. These rarely stray from a timeested formula: an hour or so of dune driving, visit to a camel farm, and a buffet dinner with all the anticipated extras – belly dancing, heesha, henna tattoos and camel rides. Most ompanies also offer full-day tours, adding the lajar Mountains or Hatta to the usual half-

day schedule. If the weather's pleasant, we suggest you spend a little extra (but much less than the cost of a night in a hotel in Dubai) and opt for an overnight safari – there's nothing like sleeping under the stars.

Although tour operators require a licence from the DTCM (Department of Tourism and Commerce Marketing), sometimes it feels like everybody with a 4WD is whizzing people across the dunes near Al-Awir. There are so many operators now it's possible to find desert safaris for under Dh150, but be warned – you hear stories about bigger problems than merely chewy kebabs and ungainly Eastern European belly dancers, which, by the way, are both to be wholly expected. If you opt for a cut-price tour, you're likely to return home in one piece (although you might want to check when booking that the driver has passed the off-road test and been certified by the police), but you're very unlikely to have any burning questions about Bedouin culture satisfactorily answered.

Knight Tours is the best option if you want to learn about Bedouin life. It can arrange falconry demonstrations on request. Otherwise Alpha Tours, Arabian Adventures and Lama Dubai have the edge over the competition because they have access to the less crowded sands of the Dubai Desert Conservation Reserve. The following tour operators are all reputable.

Alpha Tours (☎ 294 9888; www.alphatoursdubai.com) Alpha Tours is one of the few operators allowed access to the Dubai Desert Conservation Reserve and its Bedouin camps are particularly well maintained. It offers halfday (adult/child Dh260/190) and overnight (adult/child Dh350/250, minimum five people) tours, which both include dune driving, a visit to a camel farm, and dinner with belly dancing, sheesha and henna painting.

Arabian Adventures (Map p72–3; ☎ 303 4888; www.arabian-adventures.com; Emirates Holidays Bldg, Sheikh Zayed Rd) Part of the Emirates group, Arabian Adventures is one of the most dependable tour operators in town, although it doesn't offer discounted prices for children. The standard desert safari (Dh310) kicks off at 2.30pm daily and includes a visit to a camel farm, a brief dune drive, access to the Dubai Desert Conservation Reserve, and a dinner including sheesha, camel rides and a belly dancer. The full-day desert safari (Dh325) departs on Tuesday and Friday and covers the wadis of the Hajar Mountains as well as Fossil Rock. The overnight safari (Dh450) includes everything

BEATING THE DRUM

Here's an environmentally friendly, social and entertaining way of seeing the desert – join a drum circle. Dubai Drums (www.dubaidrums.com) hosts regular full-moon drum circles (adult/child Dh150/50) in desert camps. These sessions are led by Atsu, a Ghanaian master drummer, and usually last several hours and occasionally until the early hours of the morning – look out for the near-legendary all-nighter events. Drums and a BBQ dinner are provided.

offered in the standard desert-safari package, plus tents, sleeping bags and breakfast the following morning.

Hormuz Tourism (Map pp54–5; ☎ 228 0668; www.hormuz tourism.com; Bin Jarsh Bldg, Fish Roundabout, Deira) Most companies run three or four different tours. Hormuz offers no fewer than 48 Dubai days out, so if you fancy crab hunting, hot air ballooning or horse riding you're in luck. The bestseller, of course, remains the bog-standard desert safari (adult/child Dh180/130), but the company also does overnight safaris (adult/child Dh350/275), camel riding (adult/child Dh225/150) and sand-skiing (adult/child Dh160/120).

Knight Tours (Map pp72–3; ☎ 04-343 7725; www.knight tours.co.ae; Al-Wadi Bldg, Sheikh Zayed Rd) Knight Tours is the only operator we could find that employs Emirati guides. The company's owner is a UAE national with Bedouin roots and his company's philosophy of giving tourists an authentic experience can make a real difference if you want to learn about activities such as falconry and camel breeding. Half-day (adult/child Dh220/110) and full-day (adult/child Dh450/225, minimum four people) tours end up at Knight's attractive 'Bedouin Village', where guests can smoke *sheesha*, get henna tattoos and try on traditional dress. Knight earns bonus points for ditching the belly dancing – it's never been part of the culture in this part of the world and doesn't belong in a Bedouin camp.

Lama Tours (Map pp64–5; ☎ 334 4330; www.lama.ae; Al-Sayegh Bldg, Oud Metha Rd, Bur Dubai) Lama provides the full gamut of desert tours and has access to the Dubai Desert Conservation Reserve. Its safari (adult/child Dh245/185) includes dune driving, camel rides, *sheesha* and a buffet dinner. The company also offers overnight desert safaris (adult/child Dh380/220), tours of the Hajar Mountains (adult/child Dh280/220) and east coast trips (adult/child Dh200/100).

Net Tours & Travels (Map pp56–7; ☎ 266 6655; www.net toursdubai.com; Al-Bakhit Centre, Abu Baker al-Siddiq Rd) One of the longest-established tour operators in the region, Net Tours offer sand-skiing (adult/child Dh190/165) and half-day camel treks (adult/child Dh330/240), as well as the usual half-day (adult/child Dh275/200), full-day (adult/child Dh320/220) and overnight (adult/child Dh425/330) desert tours. The overnight trips include breakfast and a Hatta excursion.

Orient Tours (Map pp56–7; ☎ 282 8238; www.orienttours .ae; Al-Garhoud Rd, Deira) Having been around for quarter of a century, Orient is the granddaddy of the Dubai tourism industry and can be relied upon for an efficient, if predictable, whiz around the desert. It's one of the few Dubai operators that organises trips to Liwa upon request (Dh1800 per car, minimum two cars per trip). The half-day (adult/child Dh290/205) desert safari includes the usual dune drive, camel farm, sand boarding and dinner, while every Tuesday a full-day trip (adult/child Dh310/230) includes a visit to the village of Falaj al-Mualla.

DAY TRIPS

Dubai's relentless drive to create the tallest, longest, biggest and best versions of just about everything has made it the pin-up boy of 21st-century urban development. But while the mad scientists of the city get ever closer to complete domination of the Guinness Book of Records, some of the villages and towns a short drive away resemble the dioramas of yesteryear at the Dubai Museum. Get some distance from the city and pass tiny roadside mosques, date palms burdened with fruit, camels wandering down the middle of highways, and pristine white-sand beaches with barely a hotel in sight.

These couple of day trips are selected to add another dimension to your Dubai experience. To the southeast, Al-Ain is a temperate, convivial and verdantly green city, and to the east, the coastal road between Dibba and Fujairah boasts some of the most spectacular scenery in the Emirates. To find out more about what the United Arab Emirates has to offer visitors, see Lonely Planet's *Oman, UAE & Arabian Peninsula* guide.

THE OASIS RETREAT

The UAE's third city is a breath of fresh air. Compared to Dubai, life in Al-Ain seems uncomplicated and unrushed. There are no skyscrapers here, no megaprojects, no big shopping malls – and no attitude. People are genuinely friendly and welcoming and are determined to show visitors why they are so proud of their city.

It's the birthplace of Sheikh Zayed, and Al-Ain has benefited from his patronage and passion for greening the desert; it's famed for its lush gardens and date palm oases, as well as its myriad forts, fascinating museums and lively markets. The desert is never far from this capital of the eastern region of Abu Dhabi emirate. The winding road up Jebel Hafeet – considered one of the best roads for driving in the world – offers a magnificent view of the Empty Quarter in Saudi Arabia, as well as a hotel perched on a precipice. In summer, temperatures up here can be as much as 10°C lower than the temperature in Dubai. Buraimi is across the border in Oman and is nowhere near as affluent, a telling indicator of what the presence of ample reserves of oil can do for a national economy.

If you visit Al-Ain in early summer, one of the things you will be struck by is the enormous number of date clusters hanging off the palms that line many of the streets and parks. The ubiquitous date palm has always held a vital place in the life of Emiratis. For centuries dates were one of the staple foods of the Bedouin, along with fish, camel meat and camel milk. Not a great deal of variety you might think, but consider the fact that there are over 80 different kinds of dates in the UAE. Dates are roughly 70% sugar, which prevents them from rotting, making them edible for longer than other fruits. Apart from providing a major foodstuff, the date palm was also used to make all kinds of useful items. Its trunk was used to make columns and ceilings for houses, while its fronds (called *areesh*) were used to make roofs and walls.

Al-Ain can be confusing for the visitor to navigate. Its small population is thinly spread over a large area and it can take up to an hour to drive across the city. There's never any traffic, but all the streets look the same and there are an absurd number of roundabouts – hundreds of them – hindering your progress every hundred yards or so. To make matters a little easier, the local authorities have erected brown signs throughout the town directing traffic to hotels and major tourist attractions.

The Al-Ain Palace Museum (☎ 03-764 1595; Zayed ibn Sultan St; admission Dh3; ❧ 8.30am-7.30pm Tue-Sun, 3-7.30pm Fri), situated on the edge of the Al-Ain oasis in the centre of town, is a good place to start your exploration of the city. The majestic fort was the birthplace of the UAE's late president, Sheikh Zayed, and is one of the best museums in the country. Don't miss Sheikh Zayed's *majlis*, and be sure to check out the display of photographs of Al-Ain in the 1960s – it's unrecognisable. There are many splendid rooms, decorated as they probably used to be, and beautiful, verdant gardens.

It's also worth briefly visiting the charmingly old-fashioned Al-Ain National Museum (☎ 03-764 1595; Zayed ibn Sultan St; admission Dh3; ❧ 8.30am-7.30pm Tue-Sun, 3-7.30pm Fri). Highlights include impressive archaeological displays and artefacts from the 3rd millennium BC tombs at Hili and Umm al-Nar. There are also some black-and-white photos tracing the development of Al-Ain, Abu Dhabi and Liwa from 1962 to the present day, beautiful silver Bedouin jewellery, traditional costumes and a beguiling circumcision display.

A wander through the atmospheric Al-Ain Oasis is a highlight of a visit to the city. With its shady stands of date palms, labyrinthine paths and traditional *falaj* systems, it's a great place to spend an hour or so, particularly in hot weather, when it stays deliciously cool. It's also a great place to relax, as the only thing disturbing the extraordinary tranquillity of the oasis is the regular call to prayer from the small mosques within its boundaries. Note that the entrance to the oasis that is near the museum and fort closes at sunset; you will need to use one of the two other entrances after this time.

Don't leave Al-Ain without driving up Jebel Hafeet. This majestic, jagged 1160m limestone mountain rears out of the plain south of Al-Ain. Near the top of the mountain is the Mercure Grand Hotel (☎ 03-783 8888; www.mercure.com), where the views are great but the food is lousy. To get to the mountain, head south from the clocktower roundabout and turn right at Khalid ibn Sultan St, then follow the signs.

On your way back to Dubai, pop into the Hili Gardens & Archaeological Park in Al-Ain. The main attraction is the Round Structure, a building dating from the 3rd millennium BC. It has two porthole entrances and is decorated with relief carvings of animals and people. Although this structure is locally referred to as a tomb, it may not have been a tomb at all. No bones were ever found here, just remnants of pottery, and there are suggestions that it may have been a temple. The

TRANSPORT: AL-AIN

Distance from Dubai 160km

Direction Southeast

Travel time 90 minutes

Car From the centre of Dubai, take the exit next to the World Trade Centre in the direction of Za'abeel. From here, there are plenty of signs directing you all the way to Al-Ain.

Public transport Al-Ghazal run minibuses between Al-Ain (Dh20) and Bur Dubai Bus Station (p178) every hour from 6.30am to 11.30pm. Al-Ain's bus station is off the Al-Murabba (coffeepot) roundabout opposite the Lulu Centre. A taxi to or from Dubai will cost around Dh150.

nearby Hili Fun City (☎ 03-784 5542; admission Dh10-15; ☺ 4-10pm Sun-Wed, 9am-10pm Thu-Fri, Sat closed, Tue-Wed women only) has to be seen to be believed. It's the ultimate antidote to Dubai's brilliant ambition: a dilapidated, dirty, weed-ridden, archaeology-themed 'fun park'. Most of the rides collapsed years ago; parts of the roller-coaster are scattered on the ground below, yet it continues to charge an admission fee and attract the odd glum-looking family. Photographers will have a ball trying to capture its uniquely apocalyptic atmosphere. Astonishingly, it's still described as 'the Disneyland of the Middle East' on some of Al-Ain's tourist literature.

Eating

LUCE Ristorante (03-768 6686; InterContinental Al-Ain; mains Dh55; ☎ 7.30pm-2am) LUCE eschews the staid atmosphere of most Al-Ain restaurants for a smart, colourful and clubby vibe. The menu of pizzas, pastas and salads will please most tastes, but conversationalists be warned: the music gets loud when the DJ comes on at midnight.

Al Diwan Restaurant (☎ 03-764 4445; Khalifa St; mains Dh22; ☎ 11am-2am) A big, bright eatery, with floor-to-ceiling glass windows overlooking the busy street, Al-Diwan is popular with locals, who love the delicious Iranian and Arabic cuisine. Grilled kebabs are its speciality and the juicy, garlicky *shish tawooq* is particularly good.

Grand Café (☎ 03-766 0226; Khalifa St; sandwiches Dh10-16; ☺ 10am-midnight) This brightly painted 1950s-inspired coffee lounge serves excellent coffee (Dh10), popular continental breakfasts (Dh14 to Dh16) and the best toasted cheese-and-tomato sandwiches we've ever tasted. It

also has wireless internet access (Dh10 per hour).

Sleeping

Al-Ain Rotana Hotel (☎ 03-754 5111; alain.hotel@rotana .com; Zayed ibn Sultan St; d Dh450; 🖵 🖭) If you decide to stay the night, the central Al-Ain Rotana is the best choice in town with plush, spacious rooms equipped with all the mod cons and the city's best eateries, including the reliable Trader Vic's.

Hotel Mercure Grand Jebel Hafeet (☎ 03-783 8888; resa@mercure-alain.ae; Jebel Hafeet; d Dh430) The best time to stay at the Mercure is in summer when temperatures at the hotel, located 915m up Jebel Hafeet, are noticeably cooler than those in Dubai. The swimming pool is fantastic, while the rooms are very ordinary and the restaurants disappointing.

THE COASTAL DRIVE

An early start is required if you're going to see the coast in one day and have some time to relax on the beach. If you do this excursion on a Friday, you can catch the bull-butting (opposite) in Fujairah on the way home, although the beaches are likely to be much less crowded during the week.

At first, the road from Dubai to Fujairah is strangely desolate, a dune landscape punctuated only by power poles. But the scenery completely transforms when the grey, jagged Hajar Mountains come into view. The road slices through this dramatic scenery until it reaches the coast, where the Hajars become a stunning backdrop to the glorious blue of the Arabian Sea and pristine stretches of beach, although development is starting to take its toll on this once clear stretch of sand.

About 30km before Fujairah on the road from Al-Dhaid, you'll drive through famous Friday Market (Souq Al-Juma) in Masafi. Contrary to its name, the market is actually open every day from 8am to 10pm. Here you'll find rugs, fruit and vegetables, household goods and some souvenirs, and though the quality of goods isn't high, it's worth 30 minutes of your time.

The charming fishing village of Dibba, also known as Ras Dibba, is enshrined in Islamic history as the site of one of the great battles of the Ridda wars, the reconquest of Arabia by Muslim armies in the generation after the death of the Prophet. Today, Dibba is unique in that it's the only town ruled by two sheikhs

BULLFIGHTING, FUJAIRAH STYLE *Terry Carter & Lara Dunston*

We knew we had arrived at the site of the Fujairah bullfights when we saw what appeared to be a thousand Land Cruisers abandoned at odd angles at the side of the road. It was 4.30pm on a Friday afternoon and the bullring was surrounded by local Emiratis (both men and women) four-deep around the ring, which measured about 100m across. We'd been to bullfights in Mexico, Spain and Portugal, but had never seen anything quite like this, and it felt more than a little surreal. While you could sit happily in the stands and order a *cerveza* (beer) at a Spanish bullfight, with little risk of coming face to face with the sad, snarling bull, here you passed the bull on your way to the ring, praying to any god who'd listen that the knot in the rope securing the bull to the utility truck was secure.

There's no fanfare here, no picadors, no matadors, and no deaths as a metaphor for life. The contest is blunt-horned bull against blunt-horned bull. They push each other around until one exits the ring or loses the will to fight and wanders off. One tradition has it that the Portuguese introduced bullfighting to Fujairah, though other sources say that the bullfights predate the arrival of Islam. A more colourful legend holds that long ago two young men came into conflict over their desire to marry the same woman, so their families decided to let battling bulls settle the matter.

It's kind of ironic that in this version of the bullfight, spectators are at more risk than the bull, as the second fight of the afternoon proved. The two black bulls were tied up on opposite sides of the ring when the MC, a national guy with a megaphone and voice of sandpaper, introduced the next fight. The handlers released the bulls and they were soon in the centre of the ring butting heads, their powerful necks straining. The weaker of the two bulls started going backwards and the more powerful one pushed harder and harder, sending both bulls out of the ring and into a group of national men sitting on a picnic blanket. Dirt, drinks and *dishdashas* flying in all directions, the two bulls made their triumphant exit from the ring. Bulls one, locals nil.

To witness this spectacle, look for an unassuming dirt area on the southern outskirts of town, just before Al-Rughailat Bridge. The butting takes place between 4pm and 7pm on Fridays, and not during Eid al-Fitr, Eid al-Adha or Ramadan (see p185).

and a sultan, because Dibba is actually comprised of the three seaside villages, Dibba Muhallab (Fujairah), Dibba Hisn (Sharjah) and Dibba Bayah (Oman), and you can walk or drive freely across the Omani border. With its palm-fringed beach and low-rise buildings with colourful painted doors, it is a joy to wander around. The town's new mosque, spectacularly sited in front of the mountains, is one of the most impressive on the east coast.

The reefs and waters between Dibba and Khor Fakkan offer some of the best diving and snorkelling in the UAE, with world-class coral and marine life. One of the reasons locals and expats maintain an almost religious devotion to the Sandy Beach Hotel & Resort (p174) is the fact that it is built in front of Snoopy Island (named after its resemblance to the cartoon character), a lovely, safe reef where guests can snorkel. The Sandy Beach Diving Centre (☎ 09-244 5050; www.sandybm .com; Sandy Beach Hotel & Resort; ☼ 8am-5pm) offers a variety of dive trips catering to experienced divers and novices, and knows the coast inside out. Tanks and weights are included in the dive price. If you have your own equipment, a trip to the reef costs Dh75 for the boat trip or Dh50 for beach entry, while a single boat dive including all equipment costs Dh250.

The small fishing village of Badiyah (also spelt Bidyah and Bidiya), 8km north of Khor Fakkan but in the Fujairah emirate, is one of the oldest villages in the Gulf. Archaeological digs show that it has been settled continuously since the 3rd millennium BC. Today, it is known mainly for its mosque (☼ 7am-10pm), a charming earth-coloured structure of stone, mud brick and gypsum built between 1446 and 1668. The building's roof, with its four pointed domes supported by an internal pillar, is particularly distinctive and its simple interior has a lovely contemplative feel. Thought to be the oldest mosque in the UAE, it now functions mainly as a tourist attraction. Non-Muslims may enter if they are appropriately dressed and have taken off their shoes, but women must cover their heads. The mosque is built into a low hillside along the main road just north of the village. On the hillside above and behind it are several ruined watchtowers, from which it's possible to admire what must be the most picture-perfect view in the UAE, featuring the Hajar Mountain range to the west, the gloriously blue ocean speckled with small islands to the east and a small palm plantation with *falaj* directly below.

Heading 8km back south again is Khor Fakkan, home to one of the most attractive harbours and busiest shipping ports in the UAE. With a fabulous white-sand beach and a bustling Corniche with beautiful gardens, which is popular for morning and afternoon strolls, it's only the 'dry' aspect of Khor Fakkan (it's part of the

TRANSPORT: EAST COAST

Distance from Dubai 130km
Direction East
Travel time 90 minutes

Car Take the E11 towards Sharjah and then head in the direction of Al-Dhaid, on the E88. At Masafi you can take the E89 road heading north to Dibba or south to Fujairah. We recommend going north first to Dibba and then driving south along the coast.

Public transport Minibuses leave from the Deira taxi and minibus station (Map pp54–5) every half hour and cost Dh25. It will cost just over Dh200 if you go by taxi. A taxi from Fujairah to Al-Aqah beach costs around Dh75. Unfortunately there's no public transport leaving Fujairah to Dubai.

conservative Sharjah emirate) that makes it less appealing to international tourists.

The town of Fujairah itself is unlikely to delay your journey back to Dubai. But the 16th-century Fujairah Fort, which sits on a small rocky outcrop overlooking Fujairah's old village and date palm oasis, is floodlit at night and looks splendid. The old village is also being restored and reconstructed, and it's possible to walk around the site and take a close look at the architecture of some of the buildings, which really are quite beautiful.

Eating

Taj Khorfakkan Restaurant (☎ 09-237 0040; off Corniche, Khor Fakkan; mains Dh22; ☽ 11am-midnight) Traditionally decorated in a Raj style, Taj serves up home-cooked Indian and Chinese dishes, with the spicy chicken tikka masala (Dh20) and myriad biryanis (Dh15 to Dh28) proving popular. The restaurant is opposite Al-Safeer Centre.

Waves (☎ 09-244 9888; Fujairah Rotana Resort & Spa, Al-Aqah Beach; mains Dh60; ☽ noon-5pm & 7-10.30pm) For an excellent lunch overlooking the beach, the Fujairah Rotana Resort's restaurant is the best bet on the coast. Expect unfussy, perfectly cooked meat and fish dishes and a wide-ranging wine list.

Sleeping

Many people camp on the stretch of beach next to the enormous Le Meridien, providing an incongruous contrast in accommodation choices.

Fujairah Rotana Resort & Spa (☎ 09-244 9888; fujairah.resort@rotana.com; classic room Dh650, ocean front room Dh800) In stark contrast to the enormous Meridien hotel next door, the low-rise Rotana fits congruously into the mountainous landscape. Unsurprisingly, activity centres around the giant-sized swimming pool and the fantastic beach. It's worth spending the extra money on the ocean front rooms – these open straight out onto the beach. Most water sports are free of charge to guests.

Sandy Beach Hotel & Resort (☎ 09-244 5555; www.sandybm.com; d Dh400, ocean view Dh550, 1-/2-bedroom chalet Dh600/800) Located 6km north of Badiyah, near the village of Al-Aqha, this refreshingly old-fashioned beach resort is beloved by European and Arab expats who prefer its laid-back charm to the ritzy Meridien up the road. The high-ceiling rooms in the hotel wing are basic but spacious, if just a tad run-down. The chalets are popular with families, who put the private outdoor barbecues to good use in the evenings. There's a verdant garden and a children's playground, but most people come for the cream-sand beach (beachcombers will love the seashells), the diving, and snorkelling around Snoopy Island.

TRANSPORT

AIR

There are direct flights to Dubai from most European countries and hubs in Africa and Asia. The Americas are increasingly well connected, with Emirates and Etihad (from Abu Dhabi) both flying from New York and Toronto, and Delta flying direct from Atlanta. At research, the only direct flights from South America are from Sao Paulo on Emirates. Dubai's expanding airport is increasingly the major stopover hub between Europe and Asia. For airport information and flight inquiries visit the website at www.dubaiairport.com.

Emirates (www.emirates.com), wholly owned by the Dubai government, remains the major player in the region, flying to more than 90 destinations globally. Secondary carriers include the Bahraini carrier Gulf Air (www.gulfairco.com) and Etihad, the UAE's national airline – by virtue of the fact that it's based in the capital, Abu Dhabi. While Emirates' famed service appears to have wilted (especially in economy class), it has a perfect safety record, which is more than you can say about Gulf Air.

In 2007 Jazeera Airways (www.jazeeraairways.com), a Kuwaiti airline, became the first budget airline to fly to and from Dubai airport. It offers very competitive prices – it's sometimes possible to find return flights to Beirut or Amman for under Dh400 including taxes. The first low-cost airline in the Middle East, Air Arabia (www.airarabia.com) uses Sharjah's airport as its base and covers many destinations in the Middle East and the Indian subcontinent, with return fares typically around Dh1000.

High season for air travel varies between airlines. Generally, it is from late May or early June to the end of August, and from the beginning of December to the end of January. Low season is generally any other time. The tax added to a ticket can also vary wildly depending on the airline, so it pays to shop around.

Airlines

The following is a selection of carriers that fly to and from Dubai.

Air France (Map pp56–7; ☎ 602 5044; www.airfrance co.ae; Al-Shoala Complex, cnr Al-Maktoum Rd & 9 St, Deira)

Air India (Map pp56–7; ☎ 227 6747; www.airindia.com; Sheikh Rashid Building, Al-Maktoum Rd, Deira)

British Airways (Map pp72–3; ☎ 307 5777; www.british airways.com; 21st fl, Al-Attar Business Tower, Sheikh Zayed Rd)

Cathay Pacific Airways (Map pp56–7; ☎ 295 0400; www.cathaypacific.com; Al-Shoala Complex, cnr Al-Maktoum Rd & 9 St, Deira)

Delta Airways (Map pp64–5; ☎ 397 0118; www.delta.com; Sharaf Bldg; Khalid bin al-Waleed Rd, Bur Dubai)

Emirates (www.emirates.com/ae) Deira (Map pp56–7; ☎ 295 1111; DNATA Airline Centre, Al-Maktoum Rd); Sheikh Zayed Rd (Map pp72–3 ☎ 316 7535; Sheikh Zayed Rd, near Interchange No 2)

Gulf Air (Map pp54–5; ☎ 800 2200; www.gulfairco.com; Salahuddin Rd, Deira)

KLM (Map pp64–5; ☎ 800 4744; www.klm.com; 9th fl, Gulf Towers, cnr Oud Metha Rd & 20 St, Oud Metha)

Lufthansa Airlines (Map pp72–3; ☎ 343 2121; www .lufthanza.com; 2nd fl, Lufthansa Bldg, Sheikh Zayed Rd)

Oman Air (Map pp62–3; ☎ 351 8080; www.omanair.aero; mezzanine fl, Al-Rais Centre, Al-Mankhool Rd, Bur Dubai)

Qatar Airways (Map pp54–5; ☎ 229 2229; www.qatarair ways.com; Doha Centre, Al-Maktoum Rd, Deira)

Singapore Airlines (Map pp72–3; ☎ 316 6888; www .singaporeair.com; DNATA Travel Centre, Sheikh Zayed Rd)

Thai Airways International (Map pp56–7; ☎ 268 1702; www.thaiair.com; Al-Muraqqabat Rd, Deira)

Virgin Atlantic (Map pp64–5; ☎ 406 0600; www.virgin -atlantic.com; Sharaf Bldg; Khalid bin al-Waleed Rd, Bur Dubai)

Dubai International Airport

This airport (Map pp56–7) is the busiest in the Middle East, with over 30 million passengers passing through it in 2007. The major international airlines, including Emirates, use Terminal 1, the main terminal. Smaller airlines, mostly en route to East Africa or the countries of the former Soviet Union, use the dismal Terminal 2. The opening of Terminal 3 and three new concourses in 2008 is expected to increase its capacity to 75 million passengers a year, and the Al-Maktoum International Airport in Jebel Ali, which is set to become the largest airport in the world upon its completion, will boost Dubai's ability to receive visitors even further.

CLIMATE CHANGE & TRAVEL

Climate change is a serious threat to the ecosystems that humans rely upon, and air travel is the fastest-growing contributor to the problem. Lonely Planet regards travel, overall, as a global benefit, but believes we all have a responsibility to limit our personal impact on global warming.

Flying & climate change

Pretty much every form of motorised travel generates CO_2 (the main cause of human-induced climate change) but planes are far and away the worst offenders, not just because of the sheer distances they allow us to travel, but because they release greenhouse gases high into the atmosphere. The statistics are frightening: two people taking a return flight between Europe and the US will contribute as much to climate change as an average household's gas and electricity consumption over a whole year.

Carbon offset schemes

Climatecare.org and other websites use 'carbon calculators' that allow travellers to offset the level of greenhouse gases they are responsible for with financial contributions to sustainable travel schemes that reduce global warming – including projects in India, Honduras, Kazakhstan and Uganda.

Lonely Planet, together with Rough Guides and other concerned partners in the travel industry, support the carbon offset scheme run by climatecare.org. Lonely Planet offsets all of its staff and author travel.

For more information check out our website: www.lonelyplanet.com.

For the time being, Dubai airport is a victim of its own success, with its limited facilities being pushed to extremes by large crowds, especially at the beginning and end of the day when the bulk of departures and arrivals are scheduled. At night it's common to find hundreds of transit passengers sleeping on the floor due to a lack of seating.

There are several places to eat in the departures lounge including a small food court, a seafood bar, the Irish Village pub and Starbucks, although finding tables at peak times is problematic. Dubai Duty Free sprawls over an entire floor of the departures terminal, so there's no lack of shopping facilities. Here you can find travel essentials, books and magazines, electronics, perfumes, cigarettes, food and alcohol at competitive, if not worldbeating, prices. There's a hotel at the airport (☎ 216 4289) where rooms are available from Dh150 per hour, as well as credit card–powered internet terminals, banks, several currency exchange outlets, a business centre, a prayer room, a health club and designated quiet lounges.

Ask about airport transfers when you book your accommodation. If you're staying at one of the beach hotels along the Jumeirah strip, a transfer can save you lots of money. All transport leaves outside the arrivals hall, and the areas are well signposted (bus, limo, taxi etc). Unlike other Middle East destinations, getting a taxi isn't at all intimidating in Dubai. The cabs line up patiently, drivers are friendly and honest, and the journey is

metered. There's a Dh20 charge levied on these taxis for the run from the airport. A ride to the Deira souq area will cost around Dh35 while to Bur Dubai it costs around Dh45. A ride to the beginning of the Jumeirah hotel area starts at around Dh65. Going the other way, a taxi ride from the Deira souq area to the airport costs Dh15 to Dh20; from Bur Dubai it's about Dh25; from Jumeirah hotels about Dh45.

To get to Deira from the airport by bus (with fares between Dh2 and Dh4), route 401 goes via Baniyas Rd and Naif Rd. For Bur Dubai, route 402 travels through Deira City Centre and Karama on its way to Mankhool Rd, and the C1 goes to Satwa Bus Station. From here you can take the 93 to Safa Park in Jumeirah, Al-Barsha and The Greens. If you arrive during the night, the C1 bus goes to Jebel Ali Gardens via Ghubaiba Bus Station and Satwa Bus Station.

Compared to many cities, the airport is very conveniently located. If there's no traffic it'll take you 10 minutes to get to Deira, 15 minutes to Bur Dubai, 25 minutes to Sheikh Zayed Rd or Jumeirah, and 45 minutes to reach New Dubai.

Sharjah International Airport

This airport is used mainly by Air Arabia (www .airarabia.com) and cargo flights and has improved considerably in recent years. The opening of a second arrivals hall has sorted out what was a serious overcrowding problem nd it's now a much more viable alternative o Dubai. The main problem, as ever, is the raffic on the roads. Although it's only 15km rom the Dubai–Sharjah border, a journey n the evening when commuters are making heir daily slog home can take up to three ours. If possible, book flights that leave very ate at night, early in the morning, or on a Friday.

To get to/from the airport you have to cake taxis, since there's no public transport. Sharjah taxis are reliable, metered and comfortable. A trip to Dubai's Gold Souq from Sharjah Airport costs approximately Dh65; a trip to Dubai Marina around Dh110.

Abu Dhabi International Airport

With Etihad often offering cheaper fares to the UAE than rival airlines, an increasing number of passengers are using Abu Dhabi's airport as their entry point to Dubai. Landing in the neighbouring emirate might even save you time too. The airport is compact and efficient, meaning that you can sometimes get from the plane to the street in under half an hour. It's situated 22km from Abu Dhabi in the direction of Dubai, which means New Dubai's beach hotels are only an hour's drive away. Travelling to the same hotels from Dubai airport during rush hour traffic can take considerably longer.

A free shuttle bus to the office of Etihad Airways (Map pp72–3; ☎ 343 4443; www.etihadairways.com; Chelsea Tower, Sheikh Zayed Rd) in Dubai is available to Etihad passengers. It's worth booking your seat on the bus at the same time you buy your flights. Business and 1st-class passengers are entitled to limo transfers to Dubai. The taxis that queue up outside Abu Dhabi airport charge between Dh250 and Dh300 for the journey to Dubai. A cheaper, and very reliable alternative is to book a taxi through Al Ghazal (☎ 02-444 7787), which charges a set fee of Dh175 to Dubai. There is no public transport to Dubai from Abu Dhabi airport.

BICYCLE

While you can hire bicycles in Dubai, we can't really recommend cycling as a way to get around the city. With drivers holding a mobile phone in one hand, a cigarette in the other and knee-steering across three lanes in as many metres, you, dear cyclist (and pedestrian for that matter), are way down on the list of driver priorities. It is also illegal to cycle on major roads such as Sheikh Zayed Rd and Jumeirah Rd. However, you will see cyclists around, and if you do want to ride a bike in Dubai, remember to monitor your fluid intake in the heat and humidity. And always yield to cars. To get some practice on the emirate's roads, you can join Dubai Roadsters (www.dubairoadsters.com) on one of their early morning expeditions, and for hire and repairs, contact Wolfi's Bike Shop (Map pp72–3; ☎ 339 4453; Sheikh Zayed Rd).

BOAT
Abras

Around 150 abras (small motorboats) cross the Creek from 5.30am until 11.30pm, taking three routes. The routes link Bur Dubai Abra Station (Map pp62–3; near Bank of Baroda Bldg) with the Deira Old Souq Abra Station (Map pp62–3; cnr Old Baladiya St & Baniyas Rd). The second route connects Al-Seef Station in Bur Dubai to the Baniyas Station (Map pp54–5; Dubai Souq) in Deira, and the third route goes from the Dubai Old Souq Abra Station (Map pp62–3; Dubai Souq) to the Sabkha Abra Station (Map pp62–3; cnr Al-Sabkha & Baniyas Rds). A small number of abras are kept on this third route throughout the night. Like shared taxis, abras leave when full (around 20 passengers), but it never takes more than a few minutes for one of them to fill up. The fare is Dh1 and you pay the driver halfway across the Creek. Note that it can be quite tricky getting on and off the abras – not something to attempt wearing high heels.

It's usually possible to charter your own abra from an entrepreneurial bloke with his own boat. You'll have to haggle for a good deal, but Dh60 for an hour of cruising, or Dh15 for a direct journey to the other side, is a fair price. An alternative is to go with one of the official municipal abras, which cost Dh100 per hour.

Water Buses

For all their charm, abra rides can be a little uncomfortable during the summer months. For air-conditioned, properly seated comfort, you can take a water bus along four Creek-crossing routes from 6am to 11pm daily. Route 1 goes from Sabkha Abra Station (Map pp62–3; cnr Al-Sabkha & Baniyas Rds) to Bur Dubai Abra Station (Map pp62–3; near Bank of Baroda Bldg). Route 2 connects Baniyas Station (Map pp54–5; Dubai Souq) to the Dubai Old Souq Abra Station (Map pp62–3; Dubai Souq). Route 3 starts at Sabkha Abra Station (Map pp62–3; cnr Al-Sabkha

& Baniyas Rds) and ends at Al-Seef Station; and Route 4 goes from Baniyas Station to Al-Seef Station. Tickets are Dh4 – you can pay cash onboard or buy a Dh40 smart card, which gives you a 10 percent discount on journeys.

BUS

The gradual introduction of air-conditioned shelters is making bus travel in the summer months a viable option. While Dubai's long-suffering bus users have welcomed the new shelters, bar some justifiable grumbles that they're far too small, further improvements need to be made. The buses are infrequent and often drive straight past stops; the time-tables are confusing and hard to locate, and the routes are circuitous to say the least. On the plus side, bus travel is very cheap and offers large savings over long distances. A Dh70 taxi journey from Ibn Battuta Mall to Deira's Gold Souq, for example, is reduced to Dh2.50 if you hop on the number 8.

Local buses operate out of the two main stations in Deira and Bur Dubai: the Deira bus station (Map pp54–5; off Al-Khor St, near the Gold Souq) and the Bur Dubai bus station (Map pp62–3; Al-Ghubaiba Rd, next to Carrefour), Dubai's main bus station. In the official timetables the two stations appear as 'Gold Souq Bus Station' and 'Al-Ghubaiba Bus Station', respectively. Numbers and routes are posted on the buses in English as well as Arabic. Fares are Dh1 to Dh3.50, depending on the distance travelled. You pay the driver, so keep some change handy. A free schedule and route map can be picked up from either bus station, or from the tourist office in Baniyas Sq.

Note that most buses start and finish their days a bit later on Friday and there is only a limited service while noon prayers are underway. From Saturday to Thursday, buses run from approximately 5.45am to 11.15pm at intervals of 15 to 20 minutes. There is also a daily night bus that stops at all the major bus stations.

Bus travel between emirates is slowly improving. The Emirates Express leaves the Bur Dubai bus station every 20 minutes at peak times (and every 40 minutes at less busy times) and takes just under two hours to reach Abu Dhabi. It costs Dh15 each way and tickets should be purchased from the Emirates Express ticket office at the bus station. Bus E306 does the journey from Dubai to Sharjah, with Dh5 tickets available on the bus. There is also a bus from Bur Dubai that does the

return journey to Al-Ain (90 minutes one-way) once every half an hour or so. This costs Dh20. Minibuses serve the rest of the country including Ajman, Umm al-Quwain, Ras al-Khaimah and Fujairah. Infuriatingly, these buses will only get you out of Dubai and don't offer return journeys.

For information on public buses, including detailed route maps, check-in with RTA (Roads and Transport Authority; ☎ 800 9090; www.rta.ae).

CAR & MOTORCYCLE

If you are planning on taking a day or overnight excursion from Dubai, hiring a car is the best and cheapest way to do it. If you decide to hire a car to get around the city, don't expect a very relaxing holiday… Traffic congestion in Dubai can be a real problem at peak hours, which occur three times a day (although everyone will say that it's all day): between 7am and 9am, 1pm and 2pm and most of the evening from 6pm onwards. The worst congestion is around the approaches to Al-Maktoum and Al-Garhoud Bridges and along Al-Ittihad Rd towards Sharjah. Accidents are frequent, so it's a good idea to tune into the radio to get traffic updates.

A road toll, known as Salik (meaning 'clear and moving'), was introduced in the summer of 2007 to help combat congestion. Each time you pass one of the two tolling points – at Al-Garhoud Bridge and Sheikh Zayed Rd next to Mall of the Emirates – Dh4 is automatically deducted from the car's prepaid Salik account. If you buy or borrow a car you must make sure there is a Salik tag affixed to the front mirror. These are available from EPPCO, ADNOC and Emarat petrol stations, cost Dh100, and include Dh50 of credit. Citing a dubious Dh1 administrative fee, car hire companies charge Dh5 for each toll point crossing upon the return of the vehicle.

It is compulsory to wear seatbelts in the front, and it is illegal to use a handheld mobile phone while driving, although many motorists seem to ignore this rule. As you would expect, Dubai is not short on petrol stations and gas is cheap compared to the rest of the world. Petrol is sold by the imperial gallon (an imperial gallon is just over 4.5L) and costs around Dh7 per gallon.

It is not possible to hire motorcycles in Dubai – which is probably just as well after you've seen a couple wedged under trucks. Before you drive in Dubai, read the boxed text, p180, for some important safety messages.

ACCIDENT ALERT

If you are unfortunate enough to have an accident, no matter how small, you are required to wait at the scene and report it to the traffic police (☎ 999). Unless your car is causing a major traffic jam, do NOT move it until the traffic police get there. If there has been an injury, or it's not blindingly obvious who was at fault, don't move the vehicles at all. For insurance-claim purposes you must have a police report, and if you move your car, the police may not be able to issue a complete report. Outside Dubai you should leave your car exactly where it is, no matter how bad an obstruction it is causing, and call the police immediately. If you are driving a hire car and you have a crash, your insurance will not cover any damage unless a police report is written.

ire

As in most countries, a credit card is essential for hiring a car at a reputable rental company in Dubai. If you do find a car rental company that will take a cash deposit instead, not only will you probably have to leave your passport with them, but you may not receive full insurance. Some agencies insist on a credit card deposit as well as your passport. Find another agency if this is the case. You do not have to leave your passport with them. A photocopy of it is sufficient.

For tourists, most foreign driving licences are accepted in Dubai so long as you are either a citizen or a resident of the country that issued the licence. However, some companies insist on an international licence, so it's worth getting one of these before you leave home.

At large international agencies, small cars such as a Toyota Yaris start at about Dh145 per day with another Dh40 for collision damage waiver (CDW) insurance. These rates drop to about Dh150 per day including CDW if you pay for a week's hire upfront and around Dh100 per day with insurance if you pay for a month. If you have taken out CDW, the larger agencies do not charge an excess in the case of an accident that is your fault. Always call the police if you are involved in an accident; see above for more details.

At the smaller agencies, you should be able to negotiate a net rate of around Dh135 per day, including CDW insurance. With these agencies, no matter what they tell you, you may still be liable for the first Dh1000 to Dh1500 of damage in the event of an accident that is your fault, even if you have CDW. Sometimes this excess is only Dh250 if you have paid CDW. Ask questions and read the small print on the contract carefully.

The first 100km or 150km per day are usually free with additional kilometres costing 40 or 50 fils each. If you rent a car for more than three days, you should be given unlimited mileage.

Most agencies have free pick-up and delivery within Dubai, either to/from a hotel or the airport. They also offer a chauffeur service, but you'll pay around Dh200 per eight hours for this privilege. If you are just moving around Dubai for the day, it is cheaper to use taxis.

Although smaller agencies are generally cheaper than the larger chain companies, it's worth considering the convenience of being able to contact the local office of a reliable company if you are driving out of Dubai and something goes wrong. It's also worth ensuring complete insurance cover (zero liability).

There are dozens of car rental firms in Dubai, including all the major international chains as well as plenty of local companies. The highest concentrations of local companies are in Deira on Abu Baker al-Siddiq Rd, just north of the Clock Tower Roundabout, and on Omar ibn al-Khattab St. They are also found on the Bur Dubai side of the Creek on Sheikh Khalifa bin Zayed Rd, just north of Al-Adhid Rd; and on Kuwait St in Karama.

Unless you make specific arrangements, your rental car insurance will not cover you when in Oman. This means that if you go to Hatta, which involves passing through about 20km of Omani territory, or visit Buraimi on an excursion to Al-Ain, you will not be covered for any accident while in Omani territory. Ask for this coverage if you intend to head into Oman.

Avis (www.avis.com) Airport (Map pp56–7; ☎ 224 5219; airport arrivals hall; ⏲ 24hr); Deira (Map pp56–7; ☎ 295 7121; Al-Maktoum Rd, Deira)

Budget (www.budget.com) Airport (Map pp56–7; ☎ 224 5192; Airport arrivals hall; ⏲ 24hr); Airport Rd (Map pp56–7; ☎ 282 3030; Airport Rd, just before Cargo Village)

Diamondlease (Map pp72–3; ☎ 343 4330; www.diamondlease.com; Sahara Towers, Sheikh Zayed Rd)

Europcar (Map pp56–7; ☎ 224 5240; www.europcar-dubai.com; Airport arrivals hall; ⏲ 24hr)

Hertz (www.hertz-uae.com) Airport (Map pp56–7; ☎ 224 5222; Airport arrivals hall; ⏰ 24hr); Airport Rd (Map pp56–7; ☎ 282 4422; Airport Rd, just before Cargo Village)

Thrifty (☎ 355 6732; www.thrifty.com) Airport (Map pp56–7; ☎ 224 5404; Airport arrivals hall; ⏰ 24hr) Plus various locations around Dubai.

Road Rules

Most people drive on the right in Dubai, which is the side you're supposed to drive on. The speed limit is 60km/h on city streets and 80km/h on major city roads – if you actually reach these speeds, send us a postcard. On Sheikh Zayed Rd and on other dual-lane highways around the UAE the official speed limit is 100km/h on some sections, but otherwise it's 120km/h. If you are caught speeding, you will be fined, but in some cases you will simply be sent a bill by the police. For this reason, most car rental companies require customers to sign a statement acknowledging that they are aware of this and authorising the rental company to charge their credit card for any tickets that turn up after they have left town. So if you see a flash of light while powering down Sheikh Zayed Rd, check your credit card statements when you get home. There are also speed cameras on the major highways.

Increasingly, the busier city streets have a strictly enforced four-hour limit on parking. Tickets must be purchased from one of the many orange machines and displayed on your dashboard. Rates start at Dh2 for an hour. Parking rates apply from 8am to 1pm and from 4pm to 9pm Saturday to Thursday. Compliment the parking inspectors on their groovy safari suits all you like, but good luck getting out of a fine – they are ruthless and scarily efficient. Parking in the centre of Dubai is free on Friday and holidays. Fines for not buying a ticket start at Dh100, and you can't re-register your car until you've paid up.

TAXI

Dubai has a 5000-strong, modern fleet of metered taxis. During the day the starting fare is Dh3 plus Dh1.68 per kilometre, and at night (10pm–6am) the starting fare is Dh4. If you book a taxi in advance, the starting fare is Dh6, or Dh7 at night. Dh4 is added to your fare every time you pass a *Salik* toll point. We've heard complaints that a small number of drivers are taking advantage of tourists by charging more than Dh4 at the toll points or charging for a toll when no toll point has been crossed. Such misbehaviour is rare and most drivers are honest, speak good English know all the major hotels and landmarks, and drive safely. Tips are not expected, but drivers work a 72-hour week (and sometimes over 100 hours) for a low wage and appreciate the acknowledgement of their hard work.

It's usually fairly easy to catch a taxi, especially during the night or from major malls and hotels, but there are a few trouble spots where hour-long waits are not unusual. Due to the road toll, it's particularly hard to hail taxis on the streets in the area near Al-Garhoud Bridge, especially in Oud Metha. There's also

MOTORING MAYHEM

Driving in Dubai is not for the faint of heart. Although it's not as chaotic as in other parts of the Middle East, drivers tend to cut in front of you, turn without indicating and view roundabouts as a lane-less free for all. Out on the freeway, driving in the lane closest to the centre of the road at speeds of less than 160km/h will invoke some serious headlight flashing from the latest model Mercedes trying to break the Dubai–Abu Dhabi land-speed record. It's no wonder that Sheikh Zayed Rd is the deadliest road in Dubai.

So it's no surprise that UAE has one of the world's highest rates of road deaths per capita. Inappropriate speed and reckless driving are the major causes as well as pedestrians crossing against the lights or not at crossings. In 2007 an average of 23 people a month died on Dubai's roads. The worst aspect of this is that there doesn't seem to be sufficient incentive not to drive badly. Although speeding fines are meted out, many people view speed cameras as toll booths you don't have to stop at. Causing a death through an accident requires the payment of blood money (*dhiyya*) to the victim's family. Although this is a large sum (up to Dh200,000), nationals are insured against it. This often means that the only punishment for causing death or injury through reckless driving is an increased insurance premium.

If you're used to counting drinks down at the local to see whether you're over the alcohol limit or not, we'll make it easy for you – if you've had one, or even half of one, you've had one too many. Dubai has a zero-tolerance policy on drink-driving, and if your vehicle is stopped and you're found to have been driving under the influence of alcohol, you'll be a guest of Dubai Police for at least one night. If you have been involved in an accident and have been drinking, your insurance will be voided whether you were responsible for the accident or not.

SLOW TRAIN COMING

Dubai's driverless light-rail system is scheduled to partially open in September 2009 and be fully completed by 2012. The Dubai Metro will consist of at least four lines. The red line will run from the airport past BurJuman, the Emirates Towers and Burj Dubai to the Jebel Ali Port Station. To travel the entire length of the line will take an hour and trains will run daily from 5.30am to 12.30am. The green line, expected to be fully operational by March 2010, will loop through the city centre, starting at Festival City and ending at Rashidiya. The purple line will connect the current airport to the new airport in Jebel Ali, and the blue line will run along Emirates Rd. At the time of writing, unspecified fifth and sixth lines are expected to be announced, but these won't link Dubai to Sharjah or Abu Dhabi. This being Dubai, the trains will have a VIP class with leather seating, along with a separate area for women and children, and economy class.

a chronic taxi shortage in the area near the *abra* stations in Deira, by the shopping district of Karama, and in Bur Dubai by the bus station. You can also expect lengthy queues at the shopping malls on weekday evenings and Friday afternoons. At City Centre and Mall of the Emirates, two of the worst offenders, you can often bypass the queues by catching taxis from in front of the Sofitel Hotel and the Kempinski Hotel respectively.

A serious problem is that it's extremely difficult to find a free taxi between 4pm and 5.30pm in all parts of the city. This is when most drivers end their shifts and have to deliver their cars to their partners (usually two drivers share a car, working 12 hours each). Few drivers are willing to risk picking up customers who might extend their shift and delay their partner's start time. The thought of staggering shift times, it seems, hasn't occurred to the taxi companies. You can book taxis in advance by calling the numbers below, although sometimes it's hard to get through and you can expect up to a 30-minute wait at peak hours.

An army of unlicensed drivers in unmarked cars seek to take advantage of the shortages. These are usually men trying to earn some money on top of their normal jobs. Often four of five people will club together to buy a car, take turns working as drivers and share the profits. Bear in mind that it's illegal to pay for a ride in an unlicensed taxi, and if you're involved in an accident, you could face a fine.

Several private taxi companies (also known as 'luxury taxi' companies) serve the major hotels and shopping malls. It's common to hear drivers of these taxis reply 'same, same' when you ask if their ride will be more expensive than normal taxis. Ignore them – these taxis will charge at least 30 percent more for the same journey and can hit your pockets hard if you're stuck in traffic.

Most taxi drivers know the city well and are good at their jobs, but some really don't have a clue. New drivers are expected to learn on the job, which means you'll occasionally get somebody in his first week who doesn't know the city at all. To avoid an expensive and frustrating journey, ask the driver to radio his office or flag down a colleague to get directions as soon as it's clear he's inexperienced.

Dubai Transport Corporation has women taxi drivers (in pink taxis, no less) and if you book in advance, it can provide eight-seater vehicles or wheelchair-accessible taxis at no additional cost.

Taxi companies include the following:

Cars Taxis (☎ 269 3344)

Dubai Transport Company (☎ 208 0808)

Metro Taxis (☎ 267 3222)

National Taxis (☎ 339 0002)

BUSINESS HOURS

Most people work a five-day week from Sunday to Thursday, although the six-day week is still fairly common and many work on Saturdays. Private companies usually work a 9am to 6pm day and government departments generally work between 7am and 2pm, although government offices that deal with the public often have extended business hours and are sometimes open on Saturdays. Banks are generally open from 8am to 2pm Saturday to Thursday, while most shops are open from 10am to 10pm Sunday to Wednesday and 10am to midnight Thursday to Saturday.

CHILDREN

Families are well catered for in Dubai. There are plenty of beaches, parks and activity centres to keep kids amused, and the shopping malls and hotels usually have play areas for young children. Many restaurants have children's menus, especially in shopping malls. We have highlighted Dubai's best family restaurants by using the child-friendly icon in the Eating chapter. All the major parks have playgrounds too. There is very little crime in Dubai, but driving standards are poor, so parents should take extra care when crossing roads with kids. For the best children's activities, check out our Top 10 For Kids (see the boxed text, p71). Lonely Planet's *Travel with Children* by Cathy Lanigan is a good book that prepares you for the joys and pitfalls of travelling with the little ones, while the website Dubai Kidz (www.dubaikidz.biz) contains detailed and up-to-date listings specific to children.

Babysitting

Most of the large hotels offer babysitting services at around Dh75 for three hours. These tend to be reliable as hotels are very used to large numbers of children visiting. Locals and expats with children generally have maids, and those who don't often 'borrow' a maid from a neighbour for the night if they want to go out – the maids are usually more than happy to earn the extra money.

CLIMATE

We can't stress strongly enough that Dubai turns into a sauna in the summer months (May to September). In July and August average daytime temperatures are around 43°C with 85% humidity. Sometimes the heat reaches 48°C and the humidity 95% – and rumours always swirl around in the heat that it has reached 50°C somewhere in the UAE. The sea temperature in the height of summer (July and August) is about 37°C, which provides no relief, and hotel swimming pools have to be cooled during this time so the guests don't assume they're being parboiled for dinner. Don't expect to do any sightseeing beyond shopping malls and hotel lobbies during these months. See p15 for more information on the best times to visit Dubai.

In March and April, and October and November, the weather is very pleasant, with temperatures in the low 30s. In winter (December to February), the weather is usually perfect, although there are the occasional cold patches around New Year. Unlike the desert area inland, Dubai doesn't get too cold on winter nights, with the lowest temperature hovering around 15°C, but bring a warm jacket if you're visiting at this time of year.

It doesn't rain often, or heavily, although when it does (usually in December or January), getting around can suddenly become difficult as streets turn into rivers and traffic becomes chaotic, with accidents everywhere. Drivers are not used to wet road conditions, and the city planners decided Dubai didn't need a drainage system, so there are no gutter or storm-water drains. The average annual rainfall is about 6.5cm per year (and it rains only five days a year on average), but rainfall

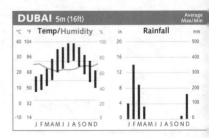

varies widely from one year to the next. Sandstorms can occur during March and April, although Dubai is protected from the swirling dust and sand to some degree by its ever-increasing number of tall buildings.

COURSES

Most language courses on offer are for English. There are only a few places where English speakers can study Arabic. This is because of the great demand by UAE national students and expats from the Subcontinent who want to improve their employment opportunities in the world of business, which is dominated by the English language. The following centres offer Arabic courses:

Arabic Language Centre (Map pp72–3; ☎ 308 6036; alc@dwtc.com; Dubai World Trade Centre, Sheikh Zayed Rd) Runs five courses a year in Arabic from beginner to advanced levels. Private tuition starts at Dh185 per hour and group classes cost around Dh1800 for 30 hours.

Berlitz Language School (Map pp76–7; ☎ 344 0034; Jumeirah Beach Rd) Offers courses in a number of languages, including Arabic and Urdu. The latter is useful to know to some extent, as this is the language of many of the Pakistani expats in the UAE.

Polyglot Language Institute (Map pp54–5; ☎ 222 3429; www.polyglot.co.ae; Al-Masaeed Bldg, Al-Maktoum Rd, Deira) Beginner courses and conversation classes in Arabic, French, German and English. A 10-week Arabic course with three classes per week costs Dh2050 including materials. Private tuition costs around Dh8000 for 25 90-minute lessons.

Sahary Gate (Map pp62–3; ☎ 353 5660; www.sahary gate.com; Bastakia House no 14, Bur Dubai) Offers courses in spoken Arabic from beginner to advanced levels. A four-week course costs around Dh1000.

Cultural

Dubai International Art Centre (Map pp76–7; ☎ 344 4398; www.artdubai.com; Villa 27, Street 75B, near Town Centre, Jumeirah Rd) Offers a plethora of art-related courses, but it's the Arabic calligraphy lessons that are most appealing. DIAC is expected to relocate to more spacious premises in the future, so visit its website for up-to-date info.

CUSTOMS REGULATIONS

The duty-free allowances for tobacco are 400 cigarettes, 50 cigars or 500g of loose tobacco. Non-Muslims are allowed to import 4L of alcohol or two cartons of beer, each consisting of up to 24 355ml cans. You are generally not allowed to bring in alcohol if you cross into the UAE by land. No customs duties are applied to personal belongings. The following goods cannot be brought into the country: controlled substances (see boxed text, p186), materials that insult Islam (this includes books such as Salman Rushdie's *The Satanic Verses*), firearms, pork, raw seafood and pornography. For a full list see www.dubaicustoms.gov.ae.

ELECTRICITY

The electric voltage is 220V AC. British-style three-pin wall sockets are standard, although most appliances are sold with two-pin plugs. Adaptors are inexpensive and available in small grocery stores and supermarkets. The two-pin plugs will go into the three-pin sockets, but this does involve a technique that won't be seen in a workplace safety video anytime soon.

EMBASSIES

Generally speaking, the embassy will not be much help in emergencies if the trouble you're in is your own fault. Remember that you are bound by the laws of the UAE. Your embassy will not be very sympathetic if you end up in jail after committing a crime locally, even if such actions happen to be legal in your own country.

In genuine emergencies you might get some assistance, but only if other channels have been exhausted. For example, if you need to get home urgently, a free flight is exceedingly unlikely – the embassy would expect you to have insurance. If you have all your money and documents stolen, it might assist with getting a new passport, but a loan for onward travel is out of the question.

Embassies & Consulates in Dubai

Most countries have diplomatic representation in the UAE. Dubai is home to several consulates and one embassy, the British embassy; other embassies are in Abu Dhabi and are listed in the front pages of the Dubai phonebook. The telephone area code for Dubai is ☎ 04.

Australia (Map pp62–3; ☎ 508 7100; www.uae.embassy .gov.au; 25th fl, BurJuman Centre, Bur Dubai; ☾ 8am-3.30pm Sun-Wed, 8am-2.45pm Thu)

Canada (Map pp62–3; ☎ 352 1717; dubai@international .gc.ca; 7th fl, United Bank Bldg, Khalid bin al-Waleed Rd, Bur Dubai; ☾ 8am-4pm Sun-Thu)

Egypt (Map pp64–5; ☎ 397 1122; 11 St, Bur Dubai; ☾ 9am-noon Sat-Wed)

France (Map pp72–3; ☎ 332 9040; www.consulfrance -dubai.org.ae/; 18th fl, API World Tower, Sheikh Zayed Rd; ☾ 8.30am-1pm Sat-Thu)

Germany (Map pp64–5; ☎ 397 2333; www.dubai .diplo.de; 1st fl, Sharaf Bldg, Khalid bin al-Waleed Rd, near BurJuman Centre, Bur Dubai; ☾ 8-11am Sun-Thu)

India (Map pp64–5; ☎ 397 1222; www.cgidubai.com; 7B St, Bur Dubai; ☾ 8am-4.30pm Sun-Thu)

Iran (Map pp76–7; ☎ 344 4717; www.iranconsul.org.ae; cnr Al-Wasl Rd & 33 St, Jumeirah; ☾ 8am-1pm Sat-Wed)

Italy (Map pp72–3; ☎ 331 4167; www.ambabudhabi .esteri.it; 17th fl, Dubai World Trade Centre, Sheikh Zayed Rd, Za'abeel; ☾ 9am-noon Sun & Tue-Thu)

Netherlands (Map pp64–5; ☎ 352 8700; www .netherlands.ae; 5th fl, ABN-Amro Bank Bldg, Khalid bin al-Waleed Rd, Bur Dubai; ☾ 9am-noon Sat-Thu)

Oman (Map pp64–5; ☎ 397 1000; general@ocodubai .com; 11 St, Bur Dubai; ☾ 7.30am-2.30pm Sat-Wed)

Qatar (Map pp62–3; ☎ 398 2888; qatar98@emirates.net .ae; cnr Al-Adhid Rd & 52 St, Al-Jafiliya; ☾ 9-11.30am Sun-Thu)

South Africa (Map pp64–5; ☎ 397 5222; www.southaf rica.ae; 3rd fl, Sharaf Bldg, Khalid bin al-Waleed Rd, near Bur Juman Centre, Bur Dubai; ☾ 8.30am-12.30pm Sun-Thu)

Syria (Map p52; ☎ 266 3354; cnr 15 & 10C Sts, Al-Wuheida Street, Deira; ☾ 8.30am-2.30pm Sat-Wed)

Turkey (Map pp72–3; ☎ 331 4788; tcdubkon@emirates .net.ae; 11th fl, Dubai World Trade Centre, Sheikh Zayed Rd; ☾ 10am-noon Sun-Mon, Wed & Thu)

UK (Map pp62–3; ☎ 309 4444; www.britishembassy.gov .uk/uae; Al-Seef Rd, Bur Dubai; ☾ 7.30am-2.30pm Sun-Thu)

USA (Map pp72–3; ☎ 311 6000; www.dubai.usconsulate .gov; 21st fl, Dubai World Trade Centre, Sheikh Zayed Rd, Za'abeel; ☾ 7.30am-4pm Sat-Wed)

EMERGENCY

Ambulance (☎ 998/999)

Fire department (☎ 997)

Police (☎ 999)

GAY & LESBIAN TRAVELLERS

Homosexual acts are illegal under UAE law and can incur a jail term. You will see men walking hand in hand, but that's most likely a sign of friendship and is no indication of sexual orientation. Although no bars, clubs or cafés would dare identify themselves as gay-friendly for fear of being raided and shut down, there are venues in the city that attract a sizeable gay and lesbian crowd. It is sometimes possible to get info on these venues from websites, but you can't access gay and lesbian interest websites from inside the UAE.

We don't recommend Dubai as a holiday destination for same-sex couples. Booking a hotel room can be awkward and potentially risky, and open displays of affection are likely to land you in trouble.

HOLIDAYS

See the Islamic Holidays table (opposite) for the approximate dates of the religious holidays observed in Dubai. Lailat al-Mi'raj is the celebration of the Ascension of Prophet Mohammed. Eid al-Fitr is a three-day celebration that occurs after Ramadan, and Eid al-Adha is a four-day celebration that occurs after the main pilgrimage to Mecca, or *haj*.

Secular holidays are New Year's Day (1 January) and National Day (2 December). The death of a minister, a member of the royal family or the head of state of another Arab country is usually marked by a three-day holiday. Newspaper websites (p37) are the quickest way to find details when this occurs. If a public holiday falls on a weekend (ie Friday or Saturday), the holiday is usually taken at the beginning of the next working week.

The Islamic calendar starts at the year AD 622, when Prophet Mohammed fled Mecca for the city of Medina. It is called the Hejira calendar (hejira means 'flight'). As it is a lunar calendar, it's roughly 11 days shorter than the Gregorian (Western) calendar, which means that Islamic holidays fall 11 days earlier each year. However, this is not a fixed rule, as the exact dates of Islamic holidays depend upon the sighting of the moon at a particular stage in its cycle. This can be as informal as a group of elderly imams being taken on a night-time drive into the desert to confer on whether or not the new moon is visible. This is why Islamic holidays are not announced until a day or two before they occur, and why they differ from country to country.

Ramadan

This is the month during which Muslims fast during the daylight hours. They must also refrain from sex, swearing, smoking or any

ISLAMIC HOLIDAYS

Hejira	New Year	Prophet's Birthday	Ramadan	Eid al-Fitr	Eid al-Adha
1430	29 Dec 08	09 Mar 09	21 Aug 09	21 Sep 09	28 Nov 09
1431	18 Dec 09	26 Feb 10	11 Aug 10	09 Sep 10	16 Nov 10
1432	07 Dec 10	15 Feb 11	01 Aug 11	30 Aug 11	06 Nov 11
1433	27 Nov 11	05 Feb 12	21 Jul 12	19 Sep 12	26 Oct 12

ther indulgence. This is to clean the mind nd body to better focus on their relationship vith Allah.

During Ramadan, government offices ease ack to about six hours' work (well, attendnce) a day. Bars and pubs are closed until 7pm each night, live music is prohibited and lance clubs are closed throughout the month. Camel racing ceases too. Some restaurants do not serve alcohol during this month. Everyone, regardless of their religion, is required to observe the fast in public (see p106)

For visitors interested in Islam or religion n general, this is a fascinating time to visit Dubai. If you walk the backstreets of areas uch as Satwa at Iftar, you'll see mosques with mats and carpets laid out with food ready or mosque attendees, and witness the streets come to life – well into the wee hours.

NTERNET ACCESS

Dubai is the most wired city in the Middle East and you should have no trouble getting online. In the UAE the internet is accessed hrough a proxy server, which blocks pornogaphy, gay interest sites, websites considered critical of Islam or the UAE's leaders, dating nd gambling sites, drug-related material and he entire Israeli domain. To the irritation of he country's huge foreign workforce, peero-peer and Voice over Internet Protocol VoIP) software such as Skype is banned in he UAE.

Every major hotel offers in-room internet access, either broadband or wireless. Hotels usually charge extortionate rates for an hour of access (Dh40 to Dh60 is not uncommon) and more reasonable rates if you pay for 24 nours up front (around Dh80 to Dh100).

Hotels aren't the cheapest source of wi-fi access. Etisalat's Hotspots service is available at all branches of Starbucks, Barista and Coffee Bean & Tea Leaf, as well as the major shopping malls and various other restaurants and cafés (see www.etisalat.ae for the full list). The easiest way to gain access is by buying a prepaid card from the venue itself, or by

using your credit card. You enter your card number and mobile phone number in the fields provided, and you'll be sent an access code by text message. It costs Dh15 for one hour, Dh30 for three hours and Dh70 for 24 hours. If you have a UAE mobile phone and subscribe to Etisalat's Wasel service, you can use Hotspots for Dh10 an hour. In addition to Hotspots venues, many other malls, hotels, restaurants and cafés offer their own wireless services, which are often free if you make a purchase.

Visitors without wi-fi on their machines can access Etisalat's Dial 'n' Surf service at ☎ 500 5555; all you need is a modem and a phone line. No account number or password is needed. It is charged at 12 fils per minute directly to the telephone you are connected to. If you're staying at a hotel, you should check whether the hotel will charge you an additional fee for using their phone line.

If you don't own a computer, nearly all hotels have business centres although your best bet is likely to be an internet café, which may charge as little as Dh2 an hour for access. The following are pleasant and reliable:

Al-Jalssa Internet Café (Map pp62–3; ☎ 351 4617; Al-Ain Shopping Centre, Al-Mankhool Rd; ✆ 8am-1am) Wireless internet at Dh10 per hour.

F1 Net Café (Map pp76–7; ☎ 345 1232; Palm Strip Shopping Centre, Jumeirah Rd; ✆ 10am-10pm)

LEGAL MATTERS

Dubai maintains the death penalty for drug importation, although the penalty usually ends up being a very long jail term (see boxed text, p186). Jail sentences for being involved in drugs by association are also fairly common. That means that even if you are in a room where there are drugs, but are not partaking, you could be in as much trouble as those who are. The UAE has a small but growing drug problem, and the authorities are cracking down hard on it. The secret police are pervasive, and they include officers of many nationalities. Theft and writing bad cheques

DRUGS: ZERO TOLERANCE

We can't shout the following words loudly enough: do not attempt to carry illegal drugs into Dubai. In fact, even if you're not attempting to import drugs, you should double-check that there isn't the faintest speck of anything illegal anywhere in your baggage or on your person. You must also ensure that medicines and drugs legal in your country are legal in Dubai before travelling with them. If you have illegal substances in your bloodstream, this still counts as possession too, and a urine test could see you found guilty. Several drugs available over the supermarket counter in other countries are banned substances in the United Arab Emirates. Fair Trials International (www.fairtrials.net) publishes a list of banned substances on their website.

There are a number of tourists in Dubai prisons or detention centres still waiting to discover what they're being charged for. Some recent cases reveal just how unforgiving Dubai's drug laws are:

- A British tourist was arrested at Dubai airport after 0.03g of cannabis, an amount smaller than a grain of sugar and invisible to the human eye, was detected on the stub of a cigarette stuck to the sole of his shoe. He was sentenced to four years in prison.
- A British TV producer was arrested and held for possessing the health supplement melatonin, which is taken to cure jet lag and is legal in the UK and Dubai. After being cleared of importing an illegal substance, he was held for over a month without charges in a Dubai prison while they tested the rest of his possessions. See www.freediz .com for more information on this case.
- A Saudi man was sentenced to four years in prison after a tiny and dried up leaf of Qat (a mild stimulant, which is legal in Yemen) was found on his clothing.
- A Swiss man was reportedly imprisoned after customs officials found three poppy seeds on his clothes. These had fallen off a bread roll he ate at Heathrow.
- A British woman was held in custody for two months before UAE customs officers accepted that the codeine she was using for her back problem had been prescribed by a doctor.

are also taken pretty seriously and usually involve jail and deportation.

If you are arrested, you have the right to a phone call, which you should make as soon as possible (ie before you are detained in a police cell or prison pending investigation, where making contact with anyone could be difficult). Call your embassy or consulate first. If there is an accident, it's a case of being guilty until proven innocent. This means that if you are in a road traffic accident, you may be held under police guard until an investigation reveals whose fault the accident was. Note that drinking alcohol in a public place that is not a licensed venue is illegal. The penalties vary from a warning to a fine. If police approach you when you're camping, put away any alcohol.

Dubai Police has established a Department of Tourist Security (☎ 800 4438) to help visitors with any legal complications they may face on their trip.

MAPS

Maps of Dubai are available from the bigger bookshops (see the Shopping chapter, p86). All the maps mentioned here should also be available in the bookshops at five star hotels. The *Dubai Mini Map* (Dh15), published by Explorer, provides a large fold-out overview map with detailed maps of key areas. Explorer also publishes a more detailed *Dubai Map* (Dh45) and an *Off-Road Map* (Dh30), which is very useful if you plan to drive in the desert.

MEDICAL SERVICES

There are pharmacies on just about every street in Dubai. See the daily newspapers for a list of pharmacies that are open 24 hours on that particular day. If you need to get to a pharmacy urgently, call ☎ 223 2323, a hotline that will tell you where the nearest open pharmacy is. As a visitor you will receive medical care, but you will be charged for it. It's important to have health cover for your trip as a lengthy stay in a hospital in Dubai will be expensive. Generally the standard of medical services is good.

The following government hospitals have emergency departments:

Al-Maktoum Hospital (Map pp54–5; ☎ 222 1211; Al-Maktoum Hospital Rd, near cnr Omar ibn al-Khattab Rd, Rigga)

Al-Wasl Hospital (Map pp64–5; ☎ 324 1111; Oud Metha Rd, south of Al-Qataiyat Rd, Za'abeel)

New Dubai Hospital (Map pp54–5; ☎ 271 4444; Abu Baker al-Siddiq Rd, near cnr Al-Khaleej Rd, Hor al-Anz)

Rashid Hospital (Map pp64–5; ☎ 337 4000; off Oud Metha Rd, near Al-Maktoum Bridge, Bur Dubai)

If you need nonurgent care, ask your consulate for the latest list of recommended doctors and dentists. Some are listed here in case you need to find one and your consulate is closed:

Al-Zahra Private Medical Centre (Map pp72–3; ☎ 331 5000; Za'abeel Tower, Sheikh Zayed Rd)

Dubai London Clinic (Map pp76–7; ☎ 344 6663; Al-Wasl Rd, Jumeirah) The clinic also has an emergency section and dental services.

Manchester Clinic (Map pp76–7; ☎ 344 0300; Jumeirah Rd, just north of McDonald's)

MONEY

The UAE dirham (Dh) is divided into 100 fils. Notes come in denominations of five, 10, 20, 50, 100, 200, 500 and 1000. There are Dh1, 50 fils, 25 fils, 10 fils and 5 fils coins. The coins only show the denomination in Arabic, so it's a great way to learn. At the time of writing, the UAE dirham is pegged to the US dollar, but rising inflation has fuelled speculation that this will soon change.

ATMs & Credit Cards

There are globally linked ATMs all over Dubai, at banks, shopping malls and at the upmarket hotels. Visa, MasterCard and American Express are widely accepted at shops, hotels and restaurants throughout Dubai and debit cards are accepted at bigger retail outlets.

Changing Money

You'll probably get a better deal at Dubai airport than you will at your home country, but the best rates are to be found in the city itself. In central Deira, especially along Sikkat al-Khail St, and around Baniyas Sq, every other building seems to contain a bank or a moneychanger. In Bur Dubai there are plenty of moneychangers (though most of them only take cash and not travellers cheques) around the abra dock. Thomas Cook Al-Rostamani has a number of branches around the city, including one on Sheik Zayed Rd (Map pp72–3), south of the Crowne Plaza Hotel; on Kuwait St (Map pp64–5) in Bur Dubai; and on Rd 14 (Map pp54–5) in Deira, near Al-Khaleej Hotel.

If you are changing more than US$250 it might pay to do a little shopping around. Moneychangers sometimes have better rates than banks, and some don't charge a commission. The problem with moneychangers is that some of them either will not take travellers cheques or will take one type only. Some places will only exchange travellers cheques if you can produce your original purchase receipt. If you don't have the receipt, try asking for the manager.

Currencies of neighbouring countries are all recognised and easily changed with the exception of the Yemeni rial. American Express (Amex) is represented in Dubai by Kanoo Travel (Map pp64–5; ☎ 336 5000; Sheikh Khalifa bin Zayed Rd, Karama; ⏰ 8.30am-5pm Sat-Thu). The office is on the 1st floor of the Hermitage Building, next to the main post office.

NEWSPAPERS & MAGAZINES

English-language newspapers in Dubai include the free *7 Days* (www.7days.ae – amusingly published six days a week), the government-owned and infuriatingly obsequious *Emirates Business 24/7* (www.business24-7.ae), the high-design weekly tabloid *Xpress* (www.xpress4me.com), and the long-established dailies (*Gulf News, Khaleej Times* and *Gulf Today*). At the time of writing, the Abu Dhabi government was preparing to launch *The Nation,* the region's most ambitious English-language daily newspaper to date, with a staff of around 180 journalists. For more on the local media, see p37.

International newspapers and news magazines such as the *International Herald Tribune* and *The Economist* are fairly easy to find, though expensive and sometimes several days or a week out of date. *The Times* is the first UK newspaper to print a daily Dubai edition and the *Financial Times* publishes a Middle East edition.

Many shops also sell Indian newspapers such as *Malayalam Manorama* and the *Times of India.* The Arabic dailies are *Al-Bayan* (published in Dubai), *Al-Khaleej* and *Al-Ittihad* (both published in Abu Dhabi). Foreign newspapers are available in larger bookshops and hotels as well as Spinneys and Choithrams supermarkets. *Time Out Dubai* is produced weekly and has detailed listings and stories on upcoming events. It costs Dh5, although you'll find it free in Dubai's better hotel rooms. *What's On* is the other listings monthly and costs Dh10, although it's a lot tamer than the competition.

ORGANISED TOURS
Creek Cruises

Bateaux Dubai Cruises (Map pp64–5; ☎ 399 4994; Al-Seef Rd, opposite British Embassy, Bur Dubai Creek;

GETTING YOUR GOAT *Matthew Lee*

While researching this book, I was almost arrested for taking a photograph of a goat. It was Eid-al-Adha, a festival traditionally marked in Pakistan by the sacrificing of a goat, and the butcher's shop on Al-Musallah Rd was heaving. There were at least 10 goats in the tiny shop, and another five animals and their owners were queuing outside. Even in Bur Dubai this wasn't an everyday sight, so I instinctively pulled my mobile phone out my pocket to take a snapshot. Within seconds a policeman was threatening to arrest me. After demanding to know my nationality, the purpose of my visit to Dubai and the reason why I was taking a photograph of a goat, he announced that he would be taking me to the station for taking an 'illegal photo'. But it was my lucky day. After talking to one of his colleagues, he suddenly changed his mind; he'd let me go free if I deleted the photo from my phone, apologised to the goat concerned (he didn't seem too concerned about an apology for the goat-owner), and promised never to take a photograph of a goat ever again. Chances are this won't happen to you. But it's worth bearing in mind that people in Dubai can be very sensitive about tourists taking photographs.

dinner cruise with 4-course set menu Dh175) Dinner cruises on an elegant boat with a stylish contemporary design and floor-to-ceiling glass windows.

Danat Dubai Cruises (Map pp64–5; ☎ 351 1117; opposite British Embassy, Bur Dubai Creek; dinner cruise Dh175) Boarding at 8pm, the licensed two-hour dinner cruise sails by the historical waterfront.

Tour Dubai (Map pp54–5; ☎ 336 8407; www.tour-dubai .com; tour Dh45, dinner cruise Dh200; ◷ tours 11.30am, 1.30pm, 3.30pm, 5.30pm, dinner cruise 8.30-10.30pm) Departs in front of Radisson SAS, Deira. Succinct one-hour guided *dhow* tours of Dubai Creek. Plenty of scheduled cruise times mean you get a good intro to sights at your convenience. The licensed dinner cruise with belly dancer is popular.

Bus Tours

Big Bus Company (Map pp64–5; ☎ 340 7709; www .bigbus.co.uk; Wafi City Mall, Bur Dubai; adult/child/ family Dh175/100/450, discounts on online bookings) One of Dubai's most surreal sights is that of the Big Bus Company's open-topped London double-decker buses plying a red city route (every 20 minutes) and blue beach route (every half hour) from 9am to 5pm every day. The 24-hour ticket allows you to get off and back on at any one of 23 well-positioned stops (maps and stops online) and includes free entry to the Dubai Museum (p61), Sheikh Saeed al-Maktoum House (p66) and a Wafi City discount card. There's a running commentary in English.

Wonder Bus Tours (Map pp62–3; ☎ 359 5656; www .wonderbusdubai.com; BurJuman Centre, cnr Khalid bin al-Waleed (Bank St) & Trade Centre Rds, Bur Dubai; adult/ child/family Dh115/75/350) Twice a day (11am and 3pm) this amphibious bus drives down to the Creek, plunges into the water, cruises for an hour, and then drives back onto land and returns to the BurJuman Centre.

City Tours

Arabian Adventures (Map p52; ☎ 303 4888; www.ara bian-adventures.com; Emirates Holidays Bldg, Interchange No 2, Sheikh Zayed Rd; city tours adult/child 2-12 yrs Dh135/70) Arabian Adventures operates daily half-day city tours. From Tuesday to Thursday and on Sundays, it also runs a fascinating Al-Jadeedah tour (Dhs425), which covers the sites of Dubai's most audacious future megaprojects, before high tea at the Burj Al Arab.

Lama Tours (Map pp64–5; ☎ 334 4330; www.lama .ae; Al-Sayegh Building, Suite No 202/203, Oud Metha Rd; adult/child Dh120/70) As well as the usual city tours, Lama arranges shopping tours, although whether you really need a guide to show you round Deira City Centre and BurJuman is another matter entirely.

PHOTOGRAPHY

Dubai loves technology, so memory cards, batteries and other accessories for digital cameras are available everywhere. The best range and prices are usually found at Carrefour (p92) or Plug-Ins (p94). The UAE uses the PAL video system and all imaginable accessories are available from Carrefour and Plug-Ins.

If you take photographs of government offices and military areas, you will arouse suspicion and could get into trouble. You should also be wary of photographing people without their permission (see boxed text, above), especially covered women.

The best spots for photography tend to be near the Creek, where you can capture *dhows*, *abras*, historical buildings and Dubai's most colourful city scenes. Lonely Planet's *Urban Travel Photography* by Richard I'Anson will help you get the best results.

POST

Emirates Post is the UAE's official postal service. There are post boxes at most of the major shopping centres. There are also a number of fax and postal agencies dotted along the small streets in Bur Dubai and Deira. Prices are similar to those in Western countries; a small letter to Europe, for example, costs Dh3.50, while a postcard costs Dh2.50 and a 500g parcel costs Dh31.50. Expect the price to double if you send by registered post.

Major post offices:

Al-Musallah Post Office (Map pp62–3; ☺ 8am-2pm Sat-Thu, 5-9pm Fri) At Al-Fahidi Roundabout in Bur Dubai.

Al-Rigga Post Office (Map pp56–7; ☺ 8am-8pm Sat-Thu, 5-9pm Fri) Near the Clock Tower Roundabout.

Main Post Office (Map pp64–5; Za'abeel Rd; ☺ 8am-8pm Sat-Thu, 5-9pm Fri) On Bur Dubai side of the Creek in Karama.

Satwa Post Office (Map pp76–7; Al-Satwa Rd; ☺ 8am-8pm Sat-Thu, 5-9pm Fri)

Mail generally takes about a week to 10 days to Europe or the USA and eight to 15 days to Australia. If you need to send something in a hurry, it's best to use one of the following courier agencies:

Aramex (☎ 600 544 000)

DHL (☎ 800 4004)

FedEx (☎ 800 4050)

RADIO

The quality of radio programming is improving in Dubai (especially talk radio), but it's generally a cringe-worthy and ad-saturated affair wherever you point the dial.

Channel 4 FM (104.8) Contemporary Top 40.

Dubai Eye FM (103.8) News, talk and sport.

Dubai FM (92) Classic hits from the '80s, '90s etc, as well as dance and lounge on weekends.

Emirates 1 FM (100.5 and 104.1) Popular music.

Emirates 2 FM (90.5 and 98.5) Eclectic programming.

It's worth searching through the dial, as there are stations playing Hindi, Arabic and Indian regional music, and stations where you can hear recitations of the Quran – very soothing when you're stuck in Dubai's horrific traffic.

RELOCATING

If you like Dubai so much you don't want to leave, you may not have to. In most cases, relocating to Dubai is easy. To secure a three-year residency permit, you need either an employer to sponsor you (see Work, p192), a spouse with a job who can sponsor you, or ownership of freehold property, which comes with a renewable residency permit.

It seems almost inconceivable that 20 years ago foreign workers in Dubai were eligible for a 'hardship allowance' – financial compensation for having to live in a boring, conservative and unbearably hot place. Back then, working hours were short and salaries were high. Today some people will accept a drop in salary to experience the much-feted 'Dubai dream', despite the fact that inflation is on the rise, rents are higher than they've ever been and wages haven't increased in years (and are now on a par with salaries in the West). For many, these conditions are offset by the fact that the salary is tax free, and that myriad perks are still considered standard in many expat packages, such as a relocation allowance, annual plane tickets home, housing, health insurance, kids' education allowance, long paid holidays, and generous gratuity payments for when you decide you've had enough. Still, veteran expats are often heard grumbling that things ain't like they used to be.

These days many people are moving to Dubai for reasons that are less to do with financial reward, and more to do with job satisfaction and being part of the exciting developments that are taking place in the region. The opportunities for career progression are fantastic. Competition exists, but it's nowhere near as tough as it is back home. Whereas the expat of the oil-boom days was in his or her 40s or 50s, white, middle class, and more than likely worked in oil, gas, petroleum, construction, nursing, teaching or foreign relations, times have changed. The new expats come in all ages, races, nationalities and classes, and the work itself is more glamorous, with the most coveted opportunities being in tourism, hospitality, marketing, PR and advertising, real-estate development, project management, architecture, interior design, fashion and entertainment. While the opportunities are fantastic, the work culture can be intense. Late nights and weekends in the office are commonplace and it can be tricky achieving the right life balance.

While Dubai may not be as culturally active as many other cities (there's very little theatre, live music and quality cinema), it's easier to get noticed if you are a budding playwright, actor, musician or film director. The opportunities to travel from Dubai are fantastic, with the Indian subcontinent, Eastern Europe, East Africa and all of the Middle East accessible within a few hours' flying time. And then there's the affordable fine dining, the beaches, the desert trips at weekends, the inspiring multiculturalism and the chance to learn about the Arab World and Islam.

For a detailed guide to relocating to the Gulf, see Lonely Planet's *Oman, UAE & Arabian Peninsula* guide. For information on long-term rentals, see p150.

SAFETY

On the whole, Dubai is a very safe city, but you should exercise the same sort of caution with your personal safety as you would anywhere. Due to Dubai's location at the heart of the Gulf, the US Department of State and British Foreign Office both warn travellers of a general threat from terrorism.

One very real danger in Dubai is bad driving. We also don't recommend that you swim, water-ski or jet-ski in the Creek. The tides in the Gulf are not strong enough to flush the Creek out on a regular basis, so it is not a clean waterway, despite what the tourist authorities might tell you. Also, be careful when swimming in the open sea. Despite the small surf, currents can be very strong and drownings are not uncommon.

SMOKING

At the start of 2008, Dubai Municipality extended its smoking ban to cover most public places, with the exception of nightclubs and bars. Most shopping malls, hotels, restaurants and cafés have designated smoking areas, and most hotels have designated smoking rooms. The fine for lighting up in a nonsmoking area is typically between Dh500 and Dh1000.

While smoking is not particularly prevalent among UAE nationals, the large expat communities from India, Pakistan, Lebanon and Egypt tend to be fond of their cigarettes. The relatively low cost of cigarettes (around Dh7 for a packet of 20) often entices European smokers to stock up before heading home. Although smoking – of cigarettes and *sheesha* – is still seen as a male activity in some quarters, women smokers should have no qualms about lighting up.

Many people who don't smoke cigarettes do smoke *sheesha* (water pipes filled with scented or fruit-flavoured tobacco). There are *sheesha* cafes all over Dubai and these are great places in which to strike up a conversation with local people.

TELEPHONE

The UAE has an efficient and modern telecommunications system. Until 2007, Etisalat (Map pp54–5; cnr Baniyas & Omar ibn al-Khattab Rds; 24hr) had monopolised the industry. The much-heralded advent of a competitor, Du (Map pp76–7; Jumeirah Centre, Jumeirah Rd; 10am-10pm), turned out to be an anticlimax. The government owns the majority stake in both companies and their tariffs are almost identical.

Coin phones have almost been completely taken over by cardphones. Phonecards are available in various denominations from grocery stores, supermarkets and petrol stations – do not buy them from street vendors. Note that there are two phonecards, one for cardphones and one for mobile phones operating on the Wasel GSM service.

To phone another country from the UAE, dial 00 followed by the country code. If you want to call the UAE, the country code is 971. The area code for Dubai is 04, though if you are calling from outside the UAE you drop the zero.

Directory enquiries (181)

International directory assistance (151)

Faxes

Most typing and photocopying shops also have fax machines you can use. You'll find the highest concentration of these just north of the Clock Tower Roundabout on Abu Baker al-Siddiq Rd in Deira (North).

Mobile Phone

Mobile numbers begin with either 050 (Etisalat) or 055 (Du). If you don't have a worldwide roaming service and want to use your mobile phone in Dubai, you can buy a prepaid SIM card from Etisalat, Dubai Duty Free or one of Dubai's myriad mobile phone shops. This excellent-value Ahlan Visitor's Mobile Package lasts 90 days, costs Dh90 and includes Dh35 of credit. Domestic calls cost Dh0.50 a minute and international calls are priced at Dh2.50 a minute. Recharge cards are available for purchase from grocery stores, supermarkets and petrol stations – once again, do not buy them from street vendors.

TIME

Dubai is four hours ahead of GMT. The time does not change during the summer. Not taking daylight saving into account, when it's noon in Dubai, the time elsewhere is as follows:

City	Time
Auckland	8pm
London	8am
Los Angeles	midnight
New York	3am
Paris & Rome	9am
Perth & Hong Kong	4pm
Sydney	6pm

TIPPING

Service charges are often included in restaurant bills. If not, 10% is usually sufficient. However, tips in Dubai don't always reach the pockets of the person who served you. See p105 for more information.

TOILETS

The best advice is to go when you can. The very few public toilets on the streets are usually only for men. Public toilets in shopping centres, museums, restaurants and hotels are Western style and are generally well maintained. On an excursion outside Dubai you might have to contend with 'hole in the ground' loos at the back of restaurants or petrol stations.

TOURIST INFORMATION
Local Tourist Offices

The Department of Tourism & Commerce Marketing (DTCM; ☎ 223 0000; www.dubaitourism.ae) is the official tourism board of the Dubai government. It is also the sole regulating, planning and licensing authority for the tourist industry in Dubai. It has three main welcome bureaus you can call for information or for help in booking hotels, tours and car hire: the airport arrivals area (just after customs, on your left), Baniyas Sq and way down Sheikh Zayed Rd on the way to Abu Dhabi (around 40km out of Dubai). There are also smaller information desks at all the major shopping malls.

Airport (Map pp56–7; ☎ 224 5252/224 4098; ⊙ 24hr)

Baniyas Sq (Map pp54–5; ☎ 228 5000; Baniyas Sq; ⊙ 9am-9pm Sat-Thu, 3-9pm Fri)

Sheikh Zayed Rd (☎ 883 3397; Sheikh Zayed Rd; ⊙ 9am-9pm Sat-Thu, 3-9pm Fri)

Dubai National Travel & Tourist Authority (DNATA), part of the Emirates Group, is the quasi-official travel agency in Dubai; it has a monopoly on travel services at a wholesale level. The DNATA head office (Map pp56–7; ☎ 295 1111; Al-Maktoum Rd, Deira) is at the DNATA Airline Centre. There are other branches opening around the city.

TRAVELLERS WITH DISABILITIES

Dubai has made a big effort in recent years to improve its services for physically challenged people. Most major hotels can cater to the needs of wheelchair users and the Department of Tourism & Commerce Marketing (DTCM; ☎ 223 0000; www.dubaitourism.co.ae) has a highly detailed list of facilities for disabled people at dozens of hotels, which it will fax to you on request. The DTCM website includes a Special Needs section, which contains information on wheelchair-accessible parks, heritage sites, cinemas and malls. All the major shopping centres have wheelchair access, but ramps in car parks and into most buildings in the city are few and far between. The airport is particularly well equipped, with a quick check-in and porters, and most parking areas in town contain spaces for disabled drivers.

You can order taxis that are equipped to carry wheelchairs from Dubai Transport (☎ 208 0808). The airport has facilities for the disabled, including low check-in counters, lounges and carts, but things get more difficult once you are out of the airport even though many hotels in Dubai now claim that they are disabled-friendly. Dubai Museum has ramps; however, other tourist attractions are difficult places for disabled visitors to get around on their own.

VISAS

To visit Dubai your passport must have at least six months validity from your date of arrival. Visit visas valid for 60 days are available on arrival in the UAE at approved ports of entry, including all airports and ports, for citizens of most developed countries. These include all Western European countries (except Malta and Cyprus), Australia, Brunei, Canada, Hong Kong, Japan, Malaysia, New Zealand, Singapore, South Korea and the USA. Tourist visas are valid for 60 days despite the fact that the stamp on your passport, which is in Arabic, says it is valid for 30 days. No fee is charged for tourist visas. If you overstay on your visa, you will be fined Dh100 for each day over.

VIS-À-VIS OMAN

Coming from Dubai, many nationalities can enter Oman without visa charges if they have tourist visas or entry stamps issued by Dubai authorities. They are also free to depart for, or return from, a third destination through land or air facilities in either country.

If you are visiting Oman on a tourist visa, these same nationalities can enter the UAE by land, air or sea without visa charges.

It is not possible to enter with an Israeli passport, although following a change in policy you can now enter Dubai with an Israeli stamp in a non-Israeli passport. Don't worry if you have a Jewish-sounding name. This is not an issue at all.

Citizens of the other Gulf Cooperative Council (GCC) countries do not need visas to enter the UAE, and can stay pretty much as long as they want. For citizens of other countries, a transit or tourist visa must be arranged through a sponsor. This can be a hotel, a company or a resident of the UAE. Most hotels charge a fee of around Dh200 for arranging a visa.

Visa Extensions

Visit visas can be extended once for 30 days by the Department of Immigration and Naturalisation (Map pp62–3; ☎ 398 1010; Sheikh Khalifa bin Zayed Rd), near the Za'abeel Roundabout, for Dh500 and a fair amount of paperwork. You may be asked to provide proof of funds. It's much easier, and usually cheaper, to leave the country for a few hours and head back for a new stamp. People have been known to stay in Dubai for a year or more simply by flying out to Bahrain, Doha, Muscat or Kish (an island off the Iranian coast) every two months and picking up a new visa on their return at a total cost of about Dh400 per trip.

Visas can only be extended in the city or emirate you arrived in, so if you landed in Sharjah, you can't get your visa extended in Dubai.

WOMEN TRAVELLERS
Attitudes Towards Women

In general, Dubai is one of the best Middle East destinations for women travellers. Checking into hotels is not usually a problem, but unaccompanied women might want to think twice about taking a room in some of the budget hotels in Deira and Bur Dubai.

Although things might be better in Dubai than other parts of the Gulf, it does not mean that some of the problems that accompany travel in the Middle East will not arise here as well, such as unwanted male attention and long, lewd stares, especially on public beaches. Try not to be intimidated; it helps to retain a sense of humour.

Safety Precautions

Dubai is a relatively liberal place and people here are used to Western women. While it is liberal, do yourself a favour and wear more than a skimpy tank top to places like shopping malls where Emiratis will be present. While they're too good a host to actually say anything, most Emiratis find this disrespectful. When it comes to beach parties and nightclubs almost anything goes, but take a taxi there and back. Keep in mind also that many of Dubai's bars and clubs (even some five-star hotels) have 'working women' operating in them.

If you travel outside Dubai, keep in mind that everywhere else in the UAE is far more conservative. Apply common sense – don't wear tight and revealing clothes that are just going to make your life difficult. It's sensible to sit in the back seat of taxis. You'll find that you'll often be asked to take the front seat in buses or be asked to sit next to other women. This is so you can avoid the embarrassment of men's stares.

In banks, Etisalat offices, post offices and libraries there are usually separate sections or windows for women – great when there's a queue – so take advantage of it. In small Arab and Indo-Pakistani restaurants you will often be ushered into the 'family room'. You don't have to sit here, but the room is there to save you from being stared at by men.

WORK

You can pre-arrange work in the UAE, but if you enter the country on a visit visa and then find work, you will have to leave the country for one day and re-enter under your employer's sponsorship.

If you have arranged to work in Dubai you will enter the country on a visit visa sponsored by your employer while your residence visa is processed. This process involves a blood test for HIV/AIDS and lots of paperwork. Those on a residence visa who are sponsored by a spouse who is in turn sponsored by an employer are not officially permitted to work. This rule is often broken, and it is possible to find work in the public or private sector. If you are in this situation, remember that your spouse, and not the company you work for, is your sponsor. One effect of this is that you may only be able to apply for a tourist visa to another Gulf Arab country with a consent letter from your spouse. In some cases you will need to be accompanied by your spouse, who has company sponsorship. Similarly, if you want to apply for a driving licence, you will also need a consent letter from your spouse.

If you obtain your residence visa through an employer and then quit because you've found something better, you may find yourself under a six-month ban from working in the UAE. This rule is designed to stop people from job hopping.

If you are employed in Dubai and have any work-related problems, you can call the Ministry of Labour Helpline (☎ 800 665) for advice.

Finding Work

While plenty of people turn up in Dubai on a visit visa, decide they like the look of the place and then scout around for a job, this isn't really the most effective way to go about it. Firstly, most employees are on a contract that's generally for three years. Secondly, there are a lot of sums to be done before you can really figure out whether the amount you're offered is going to make financial sense. Things such as a housing allowance, medical coverage, holidays and schooling (for those with kids) have to be taken into account before you can decide.

Target who you want to work with and try to set up meetings before you arrive. Email and follow up with a phone call or two. Employers in Dubai are very fond of people with qualifications. However, it's of little consequence which higher learning establishment you attended – it's of lesser importance than the paper it's written on. Teachers, nurses and those in engineering are highly valued in Dubai and are well paid.

The *Khaleej Times* and the *Gulf News* publish employment supplements several times a week. When you find a job, you will be offered an employment contract in Arabic and English. Get the one in Arabic translated before you sign it.

Business Aid Centre (☎ 337 5747; www.bacdubai.com; PO Box 8743, Dubai)

SOS Recruitment Consultants (☎ 396 5600; www.sos .co.ae; PO Box 6948, Dubai)

LANGUAGE

Arabic is the official language of the UAE, but English is also widely understood. Despite the prevalence of English, you'll find that locals appreciate travellers trying to speak Arabic, no matter how muddled you may think you sound. Learn a few key Arabic phrases before you go. Write them down on pieces of paper and stick them on the fridge, by the bed or even on the computer – anywhere that you'll see them often. A good way to start learning is through Lonely Planet's compact but comprehensive *Middle East Phrasebook*. It covers the predominant languages and Arabic dialects of the region and includes script throughout.

LANGUAGE SOCIAL

SOCIAL
Meeting People
Hello/Welcome.
marhaba
Peace be upon you.
al-salaam alaykum
Peace be upon you. (response)
wa alaykum e-salaam
How are you?
kay fahlak?
Good, thanks.
zein, shukran
Goodbye.
ff'man ullah or ma'al salaama
Goodbye. (response)
(to a man) alla ysalmak
(to a woman) alla ysalmich
Goodbye.
(to a man) hayyaakallah
(to a woman) hayyachallah
Goodbye. (response)
(to a man) alla yhai'eek
(to a woman) alla yhai'eech
Please.
(to a man) min fadhlak
(to a woman) min fadhlich
Thank you (very much).
shukran (jazeelan)
You're welcome.
al-afu
Excuse me.
(to a man) lau tismah
(to a woman) lau tismahin
Yes.
na'am
No.
la'
If God is willing.
insha'allah
Do you speak English?
titkallam ingleezi?

Do you understand (me)?
hal bitifhaam (alay)?
I understand.
(by a man) ana fahim
(by a woman) ana fahma
I don't understand.
(by a man) ana mu fahim
(by a woman) ana mu fahma

Could you please ...?
mumkin min fadhlak ...?
  repeat that   a'id hatha
  speak more slowly   takalam shwai shwai
  write it down   iktbha lee

Going Out
What's on ...?
maza yahdos ...?
  locally   mahaleeyan
  this weekend   fee nihayet hatha
                           alesboo'a
  today   al-yom
  tonight   al-layla

Where are the places to eat?
wayn el mahalat al-aakl?

PRACTICAL
Question Words
Who?   mnu?
What?   shu?
When?   mata?
Where?   wayn?
How?   chayf?
How many?   cham?

Numbers & Amounts
0   sifr
1   wahid
2   ithneen

3	thalatha
4	arba'a
5	khamsa
6	sitta
7	sab'a
8	thimania
9	tis'a
10	ashra
11	hda'ash
12	thna'ash
13	thalathta'ash
14	arba'ata'ash
15	khamista'ash
16	sitta'ash
17	sabi'ta'ash
18	thimanta'ash
19	tisi'ta'ash
20	'ishreen
21	wahid wa 'ishreen
22	ithneen wa 'ishreen
23	thalatha wa 'ishreen
30	thalatheen
40	arbi'een
50	khamseen
60	sitteen
70	saba'een
80	thimaneen
90	tis'een
100	imia
101	imia wahid
102	imia wa-ithneen
103	imia wa-thalatha
200	imiatain
300	thalatha imia
1000	alf
2000	alfayn
3000	thalath-alaf

Days

Monday	yom al-ithneen
Tuesday	yom al-thalath
Wednesday	yom al-arbaa'
Thursday	yom al-khamis
Friday	yom al-jama'a
Saturday	yom as-sabt
Sunday	yom al-had

Banking

I want to ...
ana areed an ...
  cash a cheque
  asref el-chek
  change money
  asref beezat
  change some travellers cheques
  asref chekat siyaheeya

Where's the nearest ...?
wayn aghrab ...?
  automatic teller machine (ATM)
  alet saref/sarraf alee
  foreign exchange office
  maktab al-serafa

Post

Where is the post office?
wayn maktab el-bareed?

I want to send a ...
ana areed an arsell an ...

fax	faks
parcel	barsell/ta'rd
postcard	beetaga bareediya/kart

I want to buy ...
ana areed an ashtaree ...

an aerogram	reesala jaweeya
an envelope	zaref
a stamp	tab'eh bareed

Phones & Mobiles

I want to buy a (phone card).
ana areed ashtaree (beetaget hatef/ kart telefon)
I want to make a call (to ...)
ana areed an atsell (bee ...)
I want to make a reverse-charge/collect call.
ana areed tahweel kulfet al-mukalama ila al-mutagee

Where can I find a/an ...?
wayn mumkin an ajed ...?
I'd like a/an ...
ana areed ...
  adaptor plug
  maakhaz tawseel
  charger for my phone
  shahen leel hatef
  mobile/cell phone for hire
  mobail ('mobile') leel ajar
  prepaid mobile/cell phone
  mobail moos baq aldaf'
  SIM card for your network
  seem kart lee shabaket al-itsalaat

Internet

Where's the local internet café?
wayn magha al-internet?

I'd like to ...
ana abga an ...

check my email	chayk al-emayl malee
get online	ahsaal ala khat internet

Transport

When does the ... leave?
mata yamshi ...
When does the ... arrive?
mata yusal ... (m)
  boat   il-markab
  train   il-qittar
mata tusal ... (f)
  bus   il-bas
  plane   il-tayara

What time's the ... bus?
mata ... bas?
  first   awal
  last   akhar

What time's the next bus?
mata il-bas al-thani?
Are you free? (taxi)
anta fathee?
Please put the meter on.
lau samaht shagal al-addad
How much is it to ...?
bcham la ...?
Please take me to (this address).
lau samaht wasalni la (hadha elonwan)

FOOD

Can you recommend a ...
mumkin an tansahanee ala ...?
  bar/pub   baar
  café   magha
  restaurant   mata'am

Is service/cover charge included in the bill?
hal al-fattoora tashmole al-khadma aidan?

breakfast   futtoor
lunch   ghadha
dinner   asha
snack   akal khafif
eat   kol
drink   ishrab

For more detailed information on eating and dining out, see p104.

EMERGENCIES

It's an emergency!
halet isa'af!
Could you please help me/us?
mumkin an toosaadnee min fadhlak?
Call the (police/a doctor/an ambulance)!
etasell bil (shurta/tabeeb/sayyaret al-isa'af)!
Where's the police station?
wayn marekaz al-shurta?

HEALTH

Where's the nearest ...?
wayn aghrab ...?
  chemist (night)   saydalee (laylee)
  dentist   tabeeb asnan
  doctor   tabeeb
  hospital   mustashfa

I have (a) ...
ana andee ...
  diarrhoea   is-haal
  fever   sukhoona
  headache   suda or waja' ras
  pain   alam/waja'

GLOSSARY

This glossary contains a list of terms you may hear on your travels through Dubai. For food terms you'll commonly find in the city, check out the Lebanese Food Lingo 101 (p111) and Farsi Food (p108) boxed texts.

abaya – woman's full-length black robe
abra – small, flat-decked boat; water taxi
adhan – call to prayer
agal – headropes used to hold a *gutra* in place
al-housh – courtyard
areesh – palm fronds used to construct houses
asr – mid-afternoon
attar – perfume
ayyalah – Bedouin dance
azan – call to prayer

baiti – romantic Arabic poetry style
barasti – traditional Gulf method of building palm-leaf houses; house built with palm leaves
barjeel – wind-tower; architectural feature of *masayf* houses designed to keep the house cool
bateel – young shoot of date-palm plant
burj – tower
burqa – head scarf

dabar – cheap eatery
dosa – flat grilled bread
dhuhr – noon
dhow – traditional sailing vessel of the Gulf
dishdasha – man's shirt-dress

fajr – dawn
falaj – traditional irrigation channel

ghatic – large tree like a weeping willow
gurdwara – Sikh place of worship
gutra – white headcloth

habban – Arabian bagpipes
haj – Muslim pilgrimage to Mecca
halal – meat from animals killed according to Islamic law
hammam – bathhouse
hammour – common species of fish in Gulf waters
haram – forbidden by Islamic law
hawala – written order of payment
Hejira – meaning 'flight' the Islamic calendar is called the Hejira calendar

imam – prayer leader, Muslim cleric
isha'a – twilight

jasr – drum covered with goatskin, which is slung around the neck and hit with sticks
jebel – hill, mountain

kandoura – casual shirt-dress worn by men and women
khaleeji – traditional Gulf-style music
khanjar – traditional curved dagger

khor – inlet or creek

liwa – traditional dance performed to a rapid tempo and loud drumbeat; it is usually sung in Swahili and most likely brought to the Gulf by East African slaves
luban – frankincense

maghrib – sunset
majlis – formal meeting room or reception area
Majlis, The – parliament
mandir – temple
manior – percussion instrument of a belt decorated with dried goat hooves
masayf – traditional summer house incorporating a *barjeel*
masgouf – fish dish
mashait – traditional winter house incorporating a courtyard
masjid – mosque
mathaf – museum
mihrab – niche in a mosque indicating the direction of Mecca
mimzar – oboe-like instrument
mina – port
muezzin – mosque official who sings the *azan*
mullah – Muslim scholar, teacher or religious leader

nabati – Arabic vernacular poetry

oud – wooden Arabian lute; also the wood used to burn with frankincense

qibla – the direction of Mecca, indicated in a mosque by the *mihrab*

Ramadan – Muslim month of fasting

sabkha – salt-crusted coastal plain
saruj – clay and manure building material mix
shayla – black veil
sheesha – tall, glass-bottomed smoking implement; also called a water pipe or hubbly-bubbly
sheikh – venerated religious scholar, tribal chief, ruler or elderly man worthy of respect
sheikha – daughter of a *sheikh*

tafila – prose-style Arabic poetry
talli – ancient Nubian art
tamboura – harplike instrument with five horse-gut strings that are plucked with sheep horns
tolah – a measure of perfume; 12mL or 12g
Trucial States – former name of the United Arab Emirates; also called Trucial Coast and Trucial sheikdoms

umrah – little pilgrimage

wasta – influence gained by connections in high places
wind-tower – *barjeel*; architectural feature of *masayf* houses designed to keep the house cool
wudu – practice of ritual washing before daily prayer

BEHIND THE SCENES

THIS BOOK

This 5th edition of *Dubai* was coordinated by Matthew Lee, who researched and wrote Getting Started, Background, Neighbourhoods, Desert Safaris & Day Trips, Transport and Directory.

Matthew's co-author, John A Vlahides, researched and wrote all the other chapters: Shopping, Eating, Entertainment, Sports & Activities and Sleeping. The previous (4th) edition of this guide was written by Terry Carter and Lara Dunston.

Commissioning Editor Kerryn Burgess

Coordinating Editors Jocelyn Harewood, Simon Williamson

Coordinating Cartographer Erin McManus

Coordinating Layout Designer Jacqui Saunders

Senior Editor Katie Lynch

Managing Cartographer Shahara Ahmed

Managing Layout Designers Adam McCrow, Celia Wood

Assisting Cartographers Hunor Csutoros, Andy Rojas

Cover Designers Marika Mercer, Amy Stephens

Project Managers Sarah Sloane, Glenn van der Knijff

Language Content Coordinator Quentin Frayne

Thanks to Helen Christinis, Ryan Evans, Jennifer Garrett, Mark Germanchis, Lisa Knights, John Mazzocchi, Naomi Parker

Cover photographs Man walking past a Dubai building, Phil Weymouth/Lonely Planet Images (top); City skyline and sand dunes, Greg Newington/Photolibrary (bottom)

Internal photographs by Lonely Planet Images, and by Terry Carter except p2 Phil Weymouth; p6 (#2), p11 (#2) Brent Winebrenner; p7 (#5) Izzet Keribar; p10 (#1) Mark Daffey; p11 (#1), p12 (#1) Holger Leue; p12 (#2) Christine Osborne; p12 (#3) Chris Mellor.

All images are copyright of the photographer unless otherwise indicated. Many of the images in this guide are available for licensing from Lonely Planet Images: www.lonelyplanetimages.com.

THANKS
MATTHEW LEE

A big thanks to Kerryn Burgess for her guidance and support, Shahara Ahmed for her help on the maps, Cath Lanigan for giving me the opportunity to write for Lonely Planet in the first place, and John A Vlahides for sharing his experience, expertise and great company. I'd also like to express my gratitude to Lara Dunston and Terry Carter, whose work on *Dubai 4* provided the basis of many of these chapters. *Shukran* Arsalan Mohammad for letting me camp on his living room floor after the lease on my apartment expired, my sister Eli for her helpful input, and the rest of my family for putting up with my habitual pre-deadline grumpiness.

JOHN A VLAHIDES

The in-house staffers at Lonely Planet never get proper credit for all they do to produce such kick-ass books. I'm particularly grateful to Kerryn Burgess for her painstaking prep, gracious support and marvellous sense of humour.

THE LONELY PLANET STORY

Fresh from an epic journey across Europe, Asia and Australia in 1972, Tony and Maureen Wheeler sat at their kitchen table stapling together notes. The first Lonely Planet guidebook, *Across Asia on the Cheap*, was born.

Travellers snapped up the guides. Inspired by their success, the Wheelers began publishing books to Southeast Asia, India and beyond. Demand was prodigious, and the Wheelers expanded the business rapidly to keep up. Over the years, Lonely Planet extended its coverage to every country and into the virtual world via lonelyplanet.com and the Thorn Tree message board.

As Lonely Planet became a globally loved brand, Tony and Maureen received several offers for the company. But it wasn't until 2007 that they found a partner whom they trusted to remain true to the company's principles of travelling widely, treading lightly and giving sustainably. In October of that year, BBC Worldwide acquired a 75% share in the company, pledging to uphold Lonely Planet's commitment to independent travel, trustworthy advice and editorial independence.

Today, Lonely Planet has offices in Melbourne, London and Oakland, with over 500 staff members and 300 authors. Tony and Maureen are still actively involved with Lonely Planet. They're travelling more often than ever, and they're devoting their spare time to charitable projects. And the company is still driven by the philosophy of *Across Asia on the Cheap*: 'All you've got to do is decide to go and the hardest part is over. So go!'

Charming Shahara Ahmed made drafting the maps a breeze. My stellar co-author and restaurant expert, Matthew Lee, guided my way; I couldn't have written this book without him. Nor could I have penetrated Dubai's underbelly without my new best friends, Mark Smith and Helen Spearman. *Shukran* to Hamad M bin Mejren, who graciously opened many doors for me in Dubai, as did Mary Rachelle Cherpak and Sharon Harper.

OUR READERS

Many thanks to the travellers who used the last edition and wrote to us with helpful hints, useful advice and interesting anecdotes:

Nathan Anand, Karen Boothe, Susan Collins, Zoe Cuming, Brendan Duggan, Angela Halse, Trevor Hay, Tim Holliday, Rosalind Labow, Michelle Lau, Heydon Letcher, Sam Lowden, Larry Mcgrath, Claire O'Connor, Benjamin Childs Pendleton, Martine Reurings, Nick Sitzler, Bohdan Zuk

SEND US YOUR FEEDBACK

We love to hear from travellers – your comments keep us on our toes and help make our books better. Our well-travelled team reads every word on what you loved or loathed about this book. Although we cannot reply individually to postal submissions, we always guarantee that your feedback goes straight to the appropriate authors, in time for the next edition. Each person who sends us information is thanked in the next edition – and the most useful submissions are rewarded with a free book.

To send us your updates – and find out about Lonely Planet events, newsletters and travel news – visit our award-winning website: www.lonelyplanet.com/contact.

Note: We may edit, reproduce and incorporate your comments in Lonely Planet products such as guidebooks, websites and digital products, so let us know if you don't want your comments reproduced or your name acknowledged. For a copy of our privacy policy visit www.lonelyplanet.com/privacy.

BEHIND THE SCENES OUR READERS

Notes

Notes

INDEX

55° Time Dubai 81

A

abras 68, 177, **7**
Abu Dhabi 25, 28
accommodation 150-64,
 see also Sleeping *subindex*
 Bur Dubai 155-7
 check-in & check-out
  times 150
 costs 150, 151
 Deira 151-5
 Jumeirah 159-62
 New Dubai 162-3
 rentals 150
 reservations 151
 Sheikh Zayed Rd 157-9
activities 138-48, 166-9,
 *see also individual
 activities*, Sports &
 Activities *subindex*
air travel 175-7
 Abu Dhabi International
  Airport 177
 airlines 175
 Dubai International
  Airport 175-6
 Dubai World Central Inter-
  national Airport 81
 Sharjah International
  Airport 176-7
Al-Ahmadiya School 58,
 59-60, **7**
Al-Ain 170-2
alcohol 117, 124, 126, 180,
 183, 186
Alliance Française 135

000 map pages
000 photographs

Al-Musallah 79
Al-Qusais 61
ambulance 184
animals 33-4, *see also
 individual animals*
Arabian Gulf 34
Arabian oryxes 34, 166
architecture 39-42, **2**
 ecoconscious 35
 modern 42
 traditional 39-42
area codes 190, *see also
 inside front cover*
Art Dubai 16, 43
art galleries 43, *see
 also* Sights *subindex*
arts 42-6, *see also
 individual arts*
ATMs 187
azan 155

B

babysitting 182
Badiyah 173
Bani Yas tribe 20
barasti 41
bargaining 87
barjeel, see wind-towers
bars 124-30, *see also*
 Entertainment *subindex*
 Bur Dubai 126-7
 Deira 126
 Jumeirah 128-30
 New Dubai 130
 Sheikh Zayed Rd 127-8
Bastakia Quarter 33, 39,
 61, 66, **7**
bathrooms 191
Bawadi 81
beaches 78
Bedouin people 166
bicycle travel 177
bin Butti, Maktoum 20
bin Rashid, Mani 23
birds 34, *see also individual
 species*
black-crowned finch
 larks 34
boat tours 187-8
boat travel 177-8, *see also
 abras*
books, *see also* literature,
 Shopping *subindex*

carpets 88
children, travel with 182
 history 21, 22
 off-road driving 168
British colonisation 21
broad-billed sandpipers 34
bullfighting 173
Bur Dubai 61-70, *62-5*
 accommodation 155-7
 bars 126-7
 clubbing 126-7
 food 110-14
 itineraries 125
 shopping 95-8
 walking tour 68-70, **69**
Bur Dubai Souq 66
Burj Al Alam 81
Burj Al Arab 36, 40, 75,
 144, 159, 161, **4**
bus tours 188
bus travel 178
business hours 182, *see also
 inside front cover*
 restaurants 104
 shops 87

C

cafés, *see also* Eating
 subindex
 sheesha cafés 133-5
call to prayer 155
camels 146, 169, **12**
 racing 146
 riding 169, **12**
 souvenirs 100
camping 166, 168
car travel 178-80
 hire 179-80
 insurance 179
 off-road driving 168-9
carpets 90, *see also*
 Shopping *subindex*
 books 88
cell phones 190
censorship 34, 38, 185
chemists 186
children, travel with 182
 child-friendly restaurants
  105
 Children's City 67
 Wild Wadi Waterpark
  143, **9**

Christianity 19
cinema 16-17, 43-4, 135
climate 15, 182-3
 change 176
clothing, *see also* Shopping
 subindex
 sizing chart 89
clubbing 124-32, *see also*
 Entertainment *subindex*
 Bur Dubai 126-7
 dance clubs 130-2
 Deira 126
 Jumeirah 128-30
 New Dubai 130
 Sheikh Zayed Rd 127-8
conservation, *see*
 environment
consulates 183-4
cormorants 34
cosmetic surgery 140
cosmetics 89-90, *see also*
 Shopping *subindex*
costs 17-18, 104
 accommodation 150, 151
 alcohol 126
 food 104
courses
 cultural 183
 language 183
courtyard houses 40-1
crab plovers 34
credit cards 187
cricket 146, 147
cruises 187-8
culture 3, 29-32
 courses 183
Culture Village 81
customs regulations 183
cycling 177

D

dance 44-5
Darwish, Mahmood 45
dates 96
Deira 53-60, *54-7*
 accommodation 151-5
 bars 126
 clubbing 126
 food 106-10
 itineraries 125
 shopping 91-4
 walking tour 59-60, **59**

INDEX

000 map pages
000 photographs

INDEX

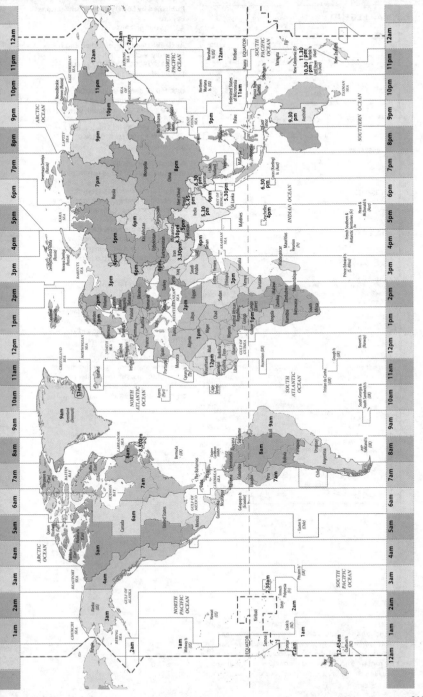

211

MAP LEGEND
ROUTES

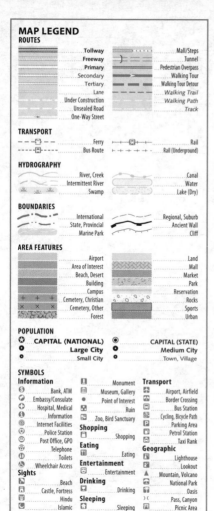

Tollway
Freeway
Primary
Secondary
Tertiary
Lane
Under Construction
Unsealed Road
One-Way Street

Mall/Steps
Tunnel
Pedestrian Overpass
Walking Tour
Walking Tour Detour
Walking Trail
Walking Path
Track

TRANSPORT

Ferry
Bus Route

Rail
Rail (Underground)

HYDROGRAPHY

River, Creek
Intermittent River
Swamp

Canal
Water
Lake (Dry)

BOUNDARIES

International
State, Provincial
Marine Park

Regional, Suburb
Ancient Wall
Cliff

AREA FEATURES

Airport
Area of Interest
Beach, Desert
Building
Campus
Cemetery, Christian
Cemetery, Other
Forest

Land
Mall
Market
Park
Reservation
Rocks
Sports
Urban

POPULATION

CAPITAL (NATIONAL)
Large City
Small City

CAPITAL (STATE)
Medium City
Town, Village

SYMBOLS

Information
Bank, ATM
Embassy/Consulate
Hospital, Medical
Information
Internet Facilities
Police Station
Post Office, GPO
Telephone
Toilets
Wheelchair Access

Sights
Beach
Castle, Fortress
Hindu
Islamic

Monument
Museum, Gallery
Point of Interest
Ruin
Zoo, Bird Sanctuary

Shopping
Shopping

Eating
Eating

Entertainment
Entertainment

Drinking
Drinking

Sleeping
Sleeping

Transport
Airport, Airfield
Border Crossing
Bus Station
Cycling, Bicycle Path
Parking Area
Petrol Station
Taxi Rank

Geographic
Lighthouse
Lookout
Mountain, Volcano
National Park
Oasis
Pass, Canyon
Picnic Area

Published by Lonely Planet Publications Pty Ltd
ABN 36 005 607 983

Australia Head Office, Locked Bag 1, Footscray, Victoria 3011,
☎ 03 8379 8000, fax 03 8379 8111,
talk2us@lonelyplanet.com.au

USA 150 Linden St, Oakland, CA 94607,
☎ 510 250 6400, toll free 800 275 8555,
fax 510 893 8572, info@lonelyplanet.com

UK 2nd fl, 186 City Rd, London, EC1V 2NT,
☎ 020 7106 2100, fax 020 7106 2101,
go@lonelyplanet.co.uk

© Lonely Planet 2008
Photographs © as listed (p198) 2008